Kirtley Library
Columbia College
8th and Rogers
Columbia, MO. 65201

WITHDRAWN

THE COMMONWEALTH AND INTERNATIONAL LIBRARY
Joint Chairmen of the Honorary Editorial Advisory Board
SIR ROBERT ROBINSON, O.M., F.R.S., LONDON
DEAN ATHELSTAN SPILHAUS, MINNESOTA

PROBLEMS AND PROGRESS IN DEVELOPMENT
General Editor : DR. J. H. KAHN

LEGAL ABORTION: THE ENGLISH EXPERIENCE

LEGAL ABORTION: THE ENGLISH EXPERIENCE

ANTHONY HORDERN, MD, FRCP Ed, MRCP, DPM
Consultant Psychiatrist, King's College Hospital, London, England
Formerly Chief of Research, Department of Mental Hygiene,
State of California, USA

with a Foreword by
MICHAEL BRUDENELL, FRCS, MRCOG
Consultant Gynaecologist, King's College Hospital, London, England

PERGAMON PRESS
Oxford · *New York* · *Toronto*
Sydney · *Braunschweig*

Pergamon Press Ltd., Headington Hill Hall, Oxford
Pergamon Press Inc., Maxwell House, Fairview Park, Elmsford,
New York 10523
Pergamon of Canada Ltd., 207 Queen's Quay West, Toronto 1
Pergamon Press (Aust.) Pty. Ltd., 19a Boundary Street,
Rushcutters Bay, N.S.W. 2011, Australia
Vieweg & Sohn GmbH, Burgplatz 1, Braunschweig

Copyright © 1971 A. Hordern

All Rights Reserved. No part of this publication may be reproduced, stored in a retrieval system, or transmitted, in any form or by any means, electronic, mechanical, photocopying, recording or otherwise, without the prior permission of Pergamon Press Ltd.

First edition 1971

Library of Congress Catalog Card No. 71-141567

Printed in Great Britain by The European Printing Co., Bletchley

This book is sold subject to the condition
that it shall not, by way of trade, be lent,
resold, hired out, or otherwise disposed
of without the publisher's consent,
in any form of binding or cover
other than that in which
it is published.

08 016567 2

"Problems and Progress in Development"
An Editorial Note

EVERY book in this series will take up a topic that in the past has been dealt with by a variety of professions, each working independently of the other professions which have a contribution to make. The aim of the series is to find a common language in which workers of different professions can communicate.

The topics that have been selected will come under three headings: disorders of function; critical stages of development; and special situations.

"Disorders of function" refers to difficulties in the acquisition of skills and performance such as speech, reading, bladder and bowel control, and also the various educational and occupational performances. The nature of the difficulties or defects in any of these activities will be affected by constitutional and organic factors, environmental and educational influences, and, amongst the psychological processes, there will be those within the individual as well as the interaction between the individual, his family, and others in the world outside.

"Critical stages of development" will include the landmarks in biological growth and maturation, and cultural adaptation. From infancy onwards through childhood, each stage carries with it new satisfactions but involves difficulties in transition from a previous stage. Each stage has its separate characteristics concerned with rearing, schooling, and adjustment to cultural expectations. The adult stage has its crises of physical, domestic, and occupational life as have the stages of the climacteric with its anticipation of a somewhat postponed old age in a lengthening span of life.

"Special situations" will refer to family reactions to illness or defect in one member, to changing material circumstances, and to events which tend to break up the family unity.

It is not intended that any of the books will provide a definitive or exhaustive study of the chosen topic. Each book is, however, intended to appeal to the growing number of workers in all professions who are called upon to deal with the personal and interpersonal aspects of human needs.

Contents

Foreword		ix
Preface		xiii
Acknowledgements		xv
Chapter 1	Abortion in Britain Before 1968	1
2	Attitudes Towards Abortion	13
3	Sexuality and Contraception	34
4	Unwanted Pregnancies and Therapeutic Abortions	55
5	The Abortion Act	69
6	Psychiatric Considerations	80
7	Techniques of Termination	91
8	The First Year of the Act	102
9	Aftermaths: The Spring of 1969	128
10	Summer and Autumn	152
11	Winter: The End of the Beginning	183
12	Abortion Problems in Other Countries	219
Appendix I	The Abortion Act—Form of Notification	275
II	Patient's Follow-up Questionnaire	279
III	Illustrative Cases	280
References		291
Index		307

Foreword

PHYSICIANS have traditionally regarded induced abortion as wrong on many counts. It represents the destruction rather than the preservation of life, and it endangers the life and health of the woman concerned. The doctor is left with a feeling that he has frustrated the "natural" outcome of the sexual act, contravening the moral code which lays down that marriage is for the procreation of children and that premarital or extramarital sexual relationships are a sin. If this attitude be characteristic of the doctor in general, how much more is it true of the modern gynaecologist whose life is devoted so largely to the treatment of infertility, the management of the complications of early pregnancy, and, especially, the promotion of maternal and foetal well-being in the later stages of pregnancy with the ultimate achievement of a healthy mother and new-born baby. The irony of calling upon such an individual to perform a deliberately destructive operation on a normal foetus in early pregnancy is inescapable, and it is hardly surprising that over the years the gynaecologist has turned his back on the problem of therapeutic abortion as being altogether too much at variance with the principles upon which his other professional work is based. Whilst this attitude was understandable in earlier days, it cannot be maintained in modern times, for, of all the medical specialities, none have been quicker to appreciate the importance of social, psychological, and economic factors in relation to the health of their patients. Maternal and perinatal mortality, to use the crudest measure of obstetric success, relate directly to social class, nutrition, and parity, especially high parity, whilst the effect which wanting or not wanting the baby has upon the course of a woman's pregnancy—though less easily measured—is apparent to the discerning. In this context the gynaecologist has found his efforts increasingly frustrated by the growing numbers of unplanned and unwanted pregnancies, occurring, as they often do, in the least favourable sections of the obstetric population. He could not fail to be concerned, also, by the admission to his gynaecological wards of women suffering and sometimes dying from the effect of abortion induced by the woman herself or some other individual variously qualified but almost always motivated by financial reward. The recurring nature of this tragedy forces the abortion problem to the attention of the gynaecologist—particularly, perhaps, the younger gynaecologist whose training has been directed towards the preventive aspects of his speciality. In such circumstances it is surprising and regrettable that gynaecological efforts in support of family planning have until recently been relatively small. It is hard to find a sensible explanation for this gap in preventive gynaecology, but perhaps an unconscious identification between contraception and induced abortion with its many difficult implications has led the gynaecologist to overlook the obvious and concentrate on the large volume of work to be done in other gynaecological fields—fields which none the less contain the problems of women suffering from the early and late complications of induced abortion!

The passing of the Abortion Act 1967 was a recognition by the community that the occurrence of "illegal" abortion had reached such a level that it posed a serious social problem. The contribution made by the illegal abortionist to maternal mortality and morbidity, and the growing publicity given to the abortion racket with its implication of one law for the rich and another for the poor, were the main weapons used by powerful pressure groups to influence Parliament to try to improve matters by defining the conditions under which an abortion might legally be performed. Medical reaction to the proposed law before it was passed was very mixed, but among gynaecologists there was a general feeling that the law would easily be interpreted as abortion on demand and that there would be a great upswing in numbers of women seeking abortions in gynaecological departments, many of which were already overworked. In the event, both these fears have been justified, and the abortion "racket", now legalized but in many ways still a racket, remains. Nevertheless, the new legal situation has given the opportunity for the thinking gynaecologist to explore the possible value of induced abortion in its widest therapeutic terms. Furthermore, it has focused gynaecological attention on the other important aspects of unplanned pregnancy, contraception and sterilization, and, as a result, on the wider issue of population control. Whether or not legalized abortion makes much contribution to population control in the long run is debatable. Abortion goes on in spite of the law, and the incidence in Western countries probably does not much differ ultimately whatever the law says, although the initial changes in birth rates are often dramatic following a change in the law. The "combined" approach to population control—abortion plus contraception and the free use of sterilization, male and female—has not yet really been given a proper trial, but it is to be hoped that it will, and that it will provide the answer to the world population problem which by most estimates looks like engulfing mankind in the foreseeable future unless it can be overcome. Countries contemplating a change in their abortion laws would do well to consider the whole question of unplanned pregnancy and not to legislate on the basis of abortion alone. Free abortion and contraception that has to be paid for is not a combination best designed to keep abortion rates down, and, as easier methods of achieving abortion are developed—and the abortion "pill" that is effective and safe cannot be long delayed—there will be a temptation to concentrate on this treatment of unplanned pregnancy. To do so will be to ignore the fact that widespread use of contraception and sterilization and an educational approach to introduce the idea of planned pregnancy to the young could do much to render abortion unnecessary.

The individual doctor does not have to solve demographic problems in his consulting room, but he may well be faced by a patient demanding an abortion. Sooner or later such a patient will be seen by a gynaecologist who, because he must accept the responsibility for carrying out the operation, has the onerous task of deciding whether or not he will do so. By those who stand between the invariable "yes men" and the invariable "no men" an evaluation of the benefits and evils of an abortion in a particular woman has to be made. In such an emotion-charged situation, the advice of psychiatric colleagues is frequently sought—less often now perhaps by those gynaecologists who interpret the law liberally and are prepared to be advised by the patient's family doctor but often enough to make the psychiatrist a vital member of the "team". Especially is this so where abortion seems likely to cause a severe psychological reaction or where the unplanned pregnancy and demand for abortion are parts of a wider emotional disturbance requiring help long after the need for gynaecological treatment has passed. Dr. Anthony Hordern, as a practising psychiatrist, has had considerable experience in dealing with this situation and, for this reason, his account of legal abortion is of particular value, covering as it does every facet of the situation. The ideal world where every pregnancy is planned, and every country's population level is optimal, remains a dream for the present, but in the realization of the dream lies mankind's hope for the future. The following pages do not offer a final solution but give, at least, a clear understanding of one important part of the problem.

MICHAEL BRUDENELL

Preface

THE second anniversary of the Abortion Act, which became law on 27 April 1968, provided a convenient opportunity to review the history of induced abortion in Great Britain. The Act, whilst in some respects breaking new ground, evolved naturally from existing case law and represented an attempt to deal with a significant social problem in a realistic and humane way. Though it is too early to assess its effect on the incidence of criminal abortion, the birth rate, and other statistics, the problems created for hospital services, gynaecologists, psychiatrists, and general practitioners have already begun to emerge.

This book examines the position regarding abortion in Britain prior to the Act and studies the attitudes that became apparent during its passage through Parliament. Sexuality and contraception are considered, and the sequelae of unwanted pregnancies are described and compared with the results of therapeutic termination. The Abortion Act is outlined as a precursor to a scrutiny of the psychiatric indications for termination of pregnancy. Twelve relevant practical criteria are listed on the basis of which a psychiatrist—or any other medical practitioner—can reach an appropriate decision. The techniques employed to terminate pregnancy are outlined, and the consequences of the first year of the Act are considered in detail. Aftermaths of the Act during its second year are described, and in a final chapter the English experience is afforded perspective by a consideration of abortion problems in other countries. The case histories of six women whose unwanted pregnancies were terminated on psychiatric grounds are appended as an illustration of acceptable criteria.

Most British gynaecologists were initially opposed to the Abortion Act, which was forced upon them by Parliament with the approval of public opinion, a few of their colleagues, the majority of psychiatrists, and a large proportion of general practitioners. The Government was ambivalent about the measure, following the Royal College of Obstetricians and Gynaecologists in underestimating the need, and refusing to make the necessary additional

National Health Service facilities available, whilst some of its supporters castigated the private clinics for filling the vacuum the new legislation had created. Once in practice, the Act revealed the enormous latent demand for legal abortion, the size of which had previously been underestimated by the majority of observers, but which created difficult problems for gynaecologists. The Act was of assistance to numerous women with unwanted pregnancies but proved unavailable to a few; it accelerated the development of safer, more rapid, techniques of termination, and it revealed the widespread ignorance and irresponsibility of the public towards family planning, as well as the lack of educational programmes and contraceptive facilities.

This book is in part scientific, in part anecdotal; it is a patchwork of "hard" and "soft" data derived from medical and lay articles, clinical experience, and inference. Such a treatment has been forced on the author by the nature of the subject, which is partly medical, partly religio-philosophical, partly eugenic, partly psychiatric, and partly socio-economic. The views expressed, except where otherwise indicated, are the author's own and cannot be taken as applying generally to psychiatrists in Britain; yet as reference to the literature, by now voluminous, will show, they are not entirely unrepresentative.

Acknowledgements

THE author owes an especial debt of gratitude to Mr. Michael Brudenell, Dr. P. K. Bridges and Dr. J. L. Taylor for their constructive criticism and invaluable advice. Thanks are also due to Mr. R. W. Beard, Professor S. G. Clayton, Mr. R. M. Feroze, Professor P. J. Huntingford, and Dr. M. H. Symes, all of whom provided comments and helpful suggestions. The libary staff of King's College Medical School assisted in locating many of the references; Mr. T. Harlow kindly xeroxed much of the relevant material. Many secretaries typed and retyped successive drafts of the manuscript, much of which was xeroxed by King's College Hospital. Finally, thanks go to my wife for support and help at every stage of the book's preparation.

CHAPTER 1

Abortion in Britain Before 1968

IN BRITAIN prior to 1967, abortion—as in many other countries—was an issue that the majority of the public, most of the medical profession, and the Government chose to ignore. Some believed the problem to be considerable, but others played it down; apart from religious opposition this was, perhaps, the principal reason why efforts to change English law prior to the Abortion Act 1967 were unsuccessful.

Strictly speaking, "abortion" signifies expulsion of the products of gestation before the 28th week of pregnancy, i.e. before the foetus is viable, but, like its synonym "miscarriage", the term is sometimes given a different meaning. Thus in some clinics abortion is used to denote expulsion of the uterine contents before the 16th week of pregnancy, whilst miscarriage signifies the same process occurring between the 16th and the 28th week. The matter is further complicated by the fact that in speaking and writing to the general public many doctors use miscarriage rather than abortion, since to the lay mind the latter term carries overtones of criminality.

Size of the Problem

Abortion in the lay sense has probably always been carried out on an extensive scale in Britain, though its actual incidence has long been in dispute. Paul Ferris,[1] a journalist commissioned by an English Sunday newspaper to make an inquiry into abortion, estimated that in 1967, before the Abortion Act became law, between 100,000 and 200,000 women had abortions performed, the vast majority of which were criminal. Despite the widespread tendency to condemn it, Ferris observed "the one certain thing about abortion is that there's no stopping it". He pointed out that, though a true figure for the number of abortions carried out every year in Britain was hard to obtain, a reasoned estimate could nevertheless be made.

The rate of spontaneous abortion has been estimated by M. C. Macnaughton[2] to be of the order of 20 per cent of pregnancies. In such cases abnormalities of the embryo or foetus are common, and abortion seems to be Nature's way of dealing with abnormal pregnancies. These patients contribute to the substantial number of women with serious miscarriages (abortions) who have to receive in-patient hospital treatment. In 1961, 69,410 women were discharged from National Health Service hospitals in England and Wales as a consequence of abortion, and by 1966 the number had risen to 78,500. Since in the latter year legal abortions numbered only 6380—less than 10 per cent—most of the cases consisted of spontaneous and induced abortions. How many were due to interference? Albert Davis,[3] reporting on a consecutive series of 2665 women with abortion, 2350 of them married, whom he had treated in two hospitals in south London in "respectable" neighbourhoods, estimated that 90 per cent of their abortions had been induced, the majority by the patients themselves. Peter Diggory,[2] reporting on 379 cases of abortion admitted to two hospitals on the periphery of London, thought that about two-thirds had probably been criminally induced, though patients often denied it, whilst David Bateman,[4] in a more recent study of 1746 women hospitalized in Lambeth between 1960 and 1967, thought that at least 20 per cent of cases had resulted from interference. If it is assumed that about one-half of all cases of abortion that are hospitalized are the result of interference, this provides a figure of 35,000 women with criminal abortions treated in National Health Service hospitals annually; and if, as seems possible, three or four uncomplicated abortions were performed for every woman admitted to hospital, this gives a figure of 120,000–175,000 abortions every year. One hundred thousand cases annually is probably therefore a conservative estimate of the annual number of criminal abortions that were being performed.

Ways of Obtaining an Abortion

Before having recourse to an abortionist, many women with unwanted pregnancies attempted to end them by utilizing a series of time-honoured measures of dubious efficacy. Skipping, jumping from heights, and falling downstairs were tried, but such manoeuvres were more likely to harm the woman than the foetus. Hot baths and self-medication with a variety of substances were next resorted to, and, whilst it is illegal to advertise or supply abortifacients in England and Wales, it is possible to purchase at chemists or rubber-goods shops "female pills" for "irregularity". Apart from iron salts, the constituents of these pills are mainly purgatives or emmenagogues and, since none would be likely to induce an abortion even if the stated dose was considerably exceeded, their reputation, as Martin Cole[2] has pointed out, is probably based on the occurrence of fortuitous spontaneous abortion after they have been taken. Peter Tarnesby[5] has classified the drugs commonly used in illegal abortions as follows:

(i) purgatives and emetics such as castor oil, aloes and colocynth;
(ii) substances causing uterine contraction—ergot, oxytocin, oestrogen, and quinine;
(iii) herbal oils producing pelvic congestion—the essential oils of bergamot, juniper (gin), rue, savin, tansy, saffron, laburnum, nutmeg and pennyroyal;
(iv) local applications to the vagina—mercury salts, copper sulphate, lead preparations (diachylon), and potassium permanganate; and
(v) specific drugs, such as folic acid, which deprive the foetus of essential vitamins.

To be effective, these substances have to be used in near-fatal doses, and in producing abortion they may severely poison or even kill the mother. If such measures failed or were not tried, douching under pressure was frequently employed. Hot soapy water with varying quantities of lysol added was the commonest agent, though on occasion formaldehyde, mustard, or turpentine solutions were injected through an enema syringe or a "whirling spray".[3] Occasionally, desperate women would attempt local interference with knitting needles, crochet hooks, scissors, hat pins, bicycle spokes, pencils, or other household objects; these were pushed into the vagina or cervix, often with dangerous results. Sometimes strips of slippery elm bark were inserted into the cervix, the bark swelling as it absorbed moisture and dilating the cervix gradually.

If these measures were ineffective, or if the woman was too enlightened or too ignorant to use them, prior to April 1968 she would probably have tried to have her pregnancy terminated through (i) a "backstreet" abortion, (ii) an "illegal medical" operation, (iii) a legal medical abortion performed privately, (iv) via the National Health Service.[1]

Backstreet abortionists, most of whom were women, might or might not have had a nursing training. Many were sufficiently wise not to interfere with women whose pregnancies were of longer duration than 12 weeks, and since most women did not seek their aid until they had missed two periods their clientele frequently required emergency action and there was little time for delay. Moya Woodside,[2] a psychiatric social worker, interviewed forty-four women abortionists sentenced to Holloway Prison in the early 1960s, and found that most were lower-middle-class women aged between 50 and 70. They did not perceive abortion as a crime, but asserted that they had wanted to help women in difficulties with unwanted pregnancies out of sympathy for their plight. They denied that financial gain was their chief consideration, but Weir[2] and others are more sceptical, feeling that money was usually their main objective. Fees, nevertheless, were lower than for "illegal medical" abortions, and the abortionist commonly used a Higginson's syringe or an enema with soapy water. Catheters were sometimes employed, but the most dangerous method, the introduction of objects into the uterus, was seldom used. Albert Davis[3] mentions that in his series of 2665 cases, some of the abortionists had "stirred up" the uterine contents with a long sound, but Professor Rhodes[2] has reported that in his own series of 5000 cases of abortion, unequivocal evidence of the use of instruments was non-existent. The number of abortions performed by backstreet abortionists is uncertain but is probably very large.

Illegal medical abortions procured for money—and also perhaps out of sympathy—were much rarer than the backstreet variety, and were usually carried out in a practitioner's surgery (office) or in premises obtained for this purpose. Abortifacient paste was sometimes used—a bad method since it was not always successful and since it left evidence that an illegal operation had been performed; alternatively, glucose or saline solutions might be injected; or, lastly, a standard dilatation and curettage could be carried out with or without a general anaesthetic. If in the latter case the practitioner was accused of performing an illegal operation, he could perhaps claim that he was intervening surgically to treat the consequences of a spontaneous abortion.

Legal medical abortions performed privately, mainly in the West End of London, have long been carried out by liberal gynaecologists prepared to use the precedent of the Bourne case (see page 8). Supported by the opinion, given in good faith, by a psychiatrist that a continuation of the pregnancy would be deleterious to the mental health of the pregnant woman, a few gynaecologists were prepared to terminate an unwanted pregnancy in its early stages, though they were much more reluctant to do so after the first trimester had passed. Ten thousand or more unwanted pregnancies were probably being terminated annually in this way prior to April 1968.[1] Money was involved, but the additional independent medical opinion made the procedure respectable, and relatively little risk was attached.

National Health Service abortions prior to 1968 were only gradually increasing in numbers, no fee being involved. Again the gynaecologist was able to take advantage of an opinion by a psychiatrist, or in some cases a small committee, to the effect that termination was advisable on psychiatric grounds. Between 1961 and 1966 the number of these cases performed annually rose from 2280 to 6380. The additional resources of a hospital *vis-à-vis* a nursing home made the operation, in skilled hands, slightly less risky than its private counterpart.

Risks and Complications

The most serious risk of abortion is death, which can result from a variety of causes; since, like suicide, some cases are probably never notified, its true incidence is hard to determine, but at approximately fifty women per annum the reported death rate in England and Wales has been "remarkably low" over the last decade, Mant[6] observes, if it be accepted that 44,000-60,000 abortions have been carried out annually. In the 3 years 1964-6, there were 2,600,367 births in England and Wales, and of the 755 maternal deaths 133 were due to abortion. Most of the latter died from haemorrhage and sepsis, two factors which should be susceptible of better control.[7] According to Professor Rhodes,[2] the chance of dying from an abortion is about twice as high as that of dying from childbirth after the 28th week of pregnancy.

The complications of abortion can be divided into physical and psychological, immediate and remote. They are appreciably greater in illegal abortions, in which the operator may be inexperienced, the setting adverse, the equipment dirty, and blood and antibiotics not available. Operations after the first trimester substantially increase the risks.

When abortifacients are taken, death from poisoning or renal damage may ensue, specific toxic effects being produced by some agents, such as gangrene after the ingestion of ergot. Because the practice is so common, syringing is the commonest cause of death from criminal abortion. Air embolism can occur, as little as 10 cc being sufficient to produce a fatal air lock in the lungs or in the brain within a few minutes of the procedure being carried out. Fat embolism may be produced from soapy particles used in solution, and infected embolisms can also occur as a result of dirty instruments. A *Clostridium welchi* infection, with death from septicaemia, endocarditis, and peritonitis, is a possibility, and renal failure may develop. Cardiac arrest from shock can occur when the cervix is dilated, and may be fatal. Household objects used clumsily or unskilfully can cause anatomical damage, and laceration of the vagina and cervix with perforation of the uterus and lesions of the peritoneum and the intestines may be produced, with haemorrhage, infection and pelvic thrombosis. Tissue necrosis, infection, and thrombosis may also be produced by the local application of potassium permanganate. More remote physical effects incluse amenorrhoea, sterility, and chronic pelvic infection, which develops in perhaps 1–2 per cent of cases. The dilatation necessary before a curettage can be performed may split the internal cervical os, leading to subsequent miscarriages and a tendency to enter subsequent labours prematurely; on the other hand, widening of the cervical canal may make the woman more fertile than was hitherto the case. [5]

From the psychological aspect, relief at having escaped an intolerable situation may be the immediate prevailing sentiment; subsequently guilt and self-reproach may develop, and may usher in a lasting aversion to sexuality and the opposite sex.

Despite the misgivings voiced at an early stage by the Royal College of Obstetricians and Gynaecologists,[8] it seems likely that therapeutic abortions performed in good conditions by competent gynaecologists have few risks and that serious complications are relatively uncommon. Of the ten deaths due to therapeutic abortions in England and Wales in 1964–6, five were associated with abdominal hysterotomy, two with injections of paste into the uterus, and two with injections of hypertonic saline into the amniotic cavity; no deaths occurred from vaginal termination of pregnancy.[7] The effect of implementing the Abortion Act on a widespread scale should in the course of time permit an accurate assessment of the complications of therapeutic termination at different stages of pregnancy.

Abortion and the English Law

Prior to 1803 English common law permitted abortion provided it was carried out before "quickening", the point reached at about 20 weeks (sometimes as early as 20, sometimes as late as 24, when it was believed that the soul entered the body). After 1803, however, abortion became an offence from the time of conception. In 1861 Parliament passed the Offences Against the Person Act which laid down that an abortion, whenever induced, was a felony punishable by life imprisonment. Whether the woman herself or a second person performed the act, the crime and punishment in each case were theoretically the same, and the crime lay in the attempt to procure an abortion and not in the successful outcome of the act. Part of the Act read: "every woman being with child who, with intent to procure her own miscarriage, shall unlawfully administer to herself poison or other noxious thing, or shall unlawfully use any instrument or other means whatsoever with the like intent. . . . "

No further legal change occurred in England until 1929, when the Infant Life (Preservation) Act amended the law in regard to "the destruction of children at or before birth" to provide that this would no longer be regarded as a felony if carried out in good faith for the sole purpose of preserving the life of the mother. Following the passage of this legislation relatively few cases continued to be brought under the Offences Against the Person Act, the woman procuring the abortion rather than the pregnant woman being prosecuted. In 1934, however, following the economic depression, there were 100 inquests in Britain on women who had died after criminal abortions. The following year there were 70 prosecutions, a figure which has remained more or less constant ever since; for example, in 1961, 59 were prosecuted, 40 men and 19 women; in 1962, 82 were prosecuted; in 1963, 65; and in 1964, 80. Usually three-quarters of those prosecuted were convicted. In recent years the advent of antibiotics has made abortion of all types much safer, and since its incidence is customarily ascertained through death or serious illness in the women who undergo it, it does not follow that, though the numbers prosecuted have remained constant, the number of abortions procured have not in fact risen.

The unsatisfactory nature of the law *vis-à-vis* the problem of abortion led to the formation of the Abortion Law Reform Association in 1936. The following year an Interdepartmental Committee on Abortion was established with Norman Birkett (later Lord Birkett) as chairman, but despite its recommendation that the law should be amended to make it clear that abortion was legal when it was performed by a medical practitioner who was satisfied that the continuance of a pregnancy "was likely to endanger the mother's life or seriously to impair her health", it remained unaltered for many years.

The Bourne Case

In 1938, Mr. Aleck Bourne, a London gynaecologist, openly performed an abortion at St. Mary's Hospital, Paddington, on a 14-year-old girl pregnant as a result of having been raped by two soldiers in the Guards' Barracks.

> The patient was referred by Dr. Joan Malleson, who, like Mr. Bourne, was a member of the medico-legal council of the Abortion Law Reform Association and who correctly judged him sufficiently courageous to risk a *cause célèbre* in order to get the laws liberalized. Mr. Bourne took the girl into hospital for eight days, confirmed that she was pregnant and free from venereal infection and, seeing in her a "God-given opportunity", emptied her uterus on 14 June. He told the Chief Inspector who called that afternoon that he wanted to be arrested, and on 1 July he was charged at Marylebone Police Court whence after a brief hearing he was released on £100 bail. On 18 and 19 July Mr. Bourne was put on trial at the Central Criminal Court; he was prosecuted under the 1861 Offences Against the Person Act and pleaded Not Guilty. The facts were not disputed; when the prosecution's evidence had been given, Mr. Bourne's Counsel asked the judge, Mr. Justice Macnaghten, to direct the jury on the relevant law. After this had been done Mr. Bourne testified on his own behalf; later three eminent medical men—Dr. J. R. Rees, a psychiatrist, Mr. William Gilliatt, a gynaecologist, and Lord Horder, a physician—independently gave evidence approving Mr. Bourne's action since each held that a continuance of the pregnancy would have adversely affected the girl's health.

In summing up Judge Macnaghten very liberally interpreted the words of the exceptions clause of the 1929 Infant Life (Preservation) Act so as to cover the circumstances of the case.[9] He held that since it was a crime unlawfully to attempt to procure an abortion there must be instances when to procure an abortion was lawful, and he suggested that these might occur when the act was done in good faith to save the life of the mother. He instructed the jury to take a broad view of what was meant by preserving the woman's life and to couple with it the broader, more comprehensive concept of preserving her health: "if the doctor is of the opinion on reasonable grounds and with adequate knowledge that the probable consequences of the continuance of pregnancy will be to make the woman a physical wreck or a mental wreck, then he operates in that honest belief 'for the purpose only of preserving the life of the mother'." The Judge stated that the attitude that abortion was wrong in any circumstances was not the law. On the contrary, a person holding such a belief should not be an obstetric surgeon, for if a woman whose life could have been saved by performing the operation died, and the doctor had refused to carry it out on religious grounds, he would be in peril of being brought before the court on a charge of manslaughter by negligence.[10] The Judge thus indicated that in certain circumstances a doctor had not only the right but the duty to terminate pregnancy, and he pointed out that a husband who denied his wife such medical assistance would stand in the same jeopardy as a doctor in that situation. Further, apart from criminal liability, the Judge observed that a civil action might lie against an obstetrician who unreasonably refused to terminate pregnancy with the result that death or serious harm to the patient supervened.

Mr. Bourne was acquitted and the judgement passed into English case law. Later it was supported by two further cases (*Rex* v. *Bergmann and Ferguson,* 1948, and *Rex* v. *Newton and Stungo,* 1958) in both of which it was established that what mattered was not whether the doctor's opinion on the necessity for abortion was correct, but whether it was honest and had been given in good faith. Unfortunately, though these decisions were never subsequently challenged, and unequivocally endorsed abortion where adequate medical grounds existed, they were generally believed to give physicians "only a tenuous and ill-defined right to induce abortion".[11] As a result many medical men were inhibited in advocating or performing therapeutic abortions because of fear of legal consequences or of damage to their professional reputations. The legal situation, though flexible and reasonable, fell short of the desirable.

Attempts at Reform

In 1938, the same year as the Bourne case, Sweden passed a relatively liberal Abortion Law which 8 years later was extended still further by permitting abortion on medico-social grounds. In 1948 Japan passed its Eugenic Protection Law which in effect permitted abortion on demand. In 1952, despite this international climate of abortion law reform, a Labour Member, Mr. Joseph Reeves, was unsuccessful in introducing a Private Member's Bill into Parliament, and 2 years later a further Bill presented by Lord Amulree also met with failure. Between 1955 and 1957 Russia and many countries in eastern Europe legalized abortion prior to the 12th week of pregnancy, but in 1961 a Private Member's Bill introduced by Mr. Kenneth Robinson, a Labour Member who later became Minister of Health, was again rejected, even though its proposals were purely permissive. [12] The following year the aftermath of the thalidomide tragedy re-awakened interest in reform of the law, especially in regard to abortion for deformed foetuses, but no further attempt was made for 3 years. Lord Silkin then tried on three separate occasions to introduce a Bill into the House of Lords. His Bill was far-reaching: it would have justified abortion on several grounds: serious risk or grave injury to the health of the pregnant woman; the possibility that the child, if born, would suffer from such physical and mental abnormalities as to deprive it of any prospect of reasonable enjoyment of life; the fact that the pregnant woman was physically or mentally inadequate to be the mother of a child; or when the pregnancy had occurred as a result of rape or under the age of 16. Lord Silkin's Bill did not succeed, and a further Bill which a Labour Member, Mrs. Renee Short, tried to introduce into the Commons during the same year was similarly unsuccessful.

The Medical Termination of Pregnancy Bill

By 1966, however, the time at last was ripe and public opinion was in favour of reform; Ferris [1] has described the events that occurred. On 8 July the Abortion Law Reform Association inserted a full-page advertisement in the *New Statesman* asking readers to write to their Members of Parliament in favour of a Bill to be presented in the Commons on 13 July by David Steel, the young Scottish Liberal Member for Roxburgh, Selkirk and Peebles. The new measure, introduced as a Private Member's Bill, had as its object "to amend and clarify the law relating to the termination of pregnancy by registered medical practitioners". It provided that pregnancy could be terminated only on the agreement of two doctors under the following conditions: (1) that continued pregnancy would involve serious risk to the life and health, physical and mental, of the woman; (2) that a substantial risk existed that the child would be born suffering from physical or mental abnormalities that would be a severe handicap; (3) that the pregnant woman's capacity as a mother would be severely overstrained by the care of a child or another child – the "social" clause; and (4) that the pregnant woman was defective, under 16, or had become pregnant as a result of rape. In the latter case medical evidence of sexual assault would be required.

The debate on the second reading of David Steel's Bill was fixed for 22 July; a few days earlier letters went out to the *New Statesman*, the *Observer*, *The Times*, and the *Sunday Telegraph* signed by such well-known abortion law reformers as Mrs. Vera Houghton (the chairman of the Abortion Law Reform Association), Professor A. J. Ayer, Sir Dugald Baird, the Bishop of Woolwich, Sir Robert Platt, Professor Glanville Williams, Lord Silkin, and four other peers. The opponents of the measure in the meantime sought to prevent it being passed. A Lancashire lawyer wrote a leaflet *To Be or Not to Be* which became popular in the Catholic north-west of England, and which announced "if the Abortion Bill goes through Herod will laugh in Hell". The Catholic Doctors' Guild issued a memorandum opposing the Bill, and the *Catholic Herald* revealed that Judge Macnaghten, who had presided in the Aleck Bourne case, was an "Irish Protestant". The (Labour) Government for its part adopted an attitude of benevolent neutrality; the then Home Secretary, Roy Jenkins, however, made a speech during which he personally supported the Bill, and the second reading was passed by 223 votes to 29.

After the vote the supporters and the antagonists of abortion law reform increased their activities. The Abortion Law Reform Association stated in its newsletters that those opposing the Bill consisted mainly of "Roman Catholics, elderly and extreme Anglicans, and the moral rearmers", but in this it oversimplified the issue, for many members of the Royal College of Obstetricians and Gynaecologists, as well as other medical practitioners, were opposed to the measure on medical or ethical, as apart from religious, grounds. In October 1966 the Guild of Catholic Doctors expressed their concern regarding the new Bill, affirming that the embryo was a human organism from the time of fertilization, and as such was entitled to the full protection of the law. Perceiving abortion as murder, they took strong exception to the "social" clause. Since the clause was widely objected to and was opposed by the Royal College of Obstetricians and Gynaecologists, David Steel took it out before the Committee stage of the Bill was reached, though a phrase referring to the appropriateness of taking into account the pregnant woman's "actual or reasonably foreseeable environment" survived. The gynaecologists wanted two further restrictions to be inserted into the Bill—that every abortion should be performed by a consultant gynaecologist and that the procedure should only be carried out in either a National Health Service hospital or in another place approved by the Minister of Health. The first request was defeated, but the second was eventually adopted. In the twelve meetings that were held once or twice weekly between January and April 1967 in the Committee stage of the Bill every aspect and nuance of the subject was debated and discussed. The report stage of the Bill, reached in June 1967, was, Ferris remarks, a narrower version of the original draft. The lengthy debate had made the public aware of the problem and the majority appeared to favour the main principles of the Bill. After a second all-night sitting on 15 July which ended a 27-hour continuous debate, the longest for 30 years, the Bill was passed by 167 votes to 83.

All was not over, however, for the Bill then went to the House of Lords, where in the Committee stage it was discussed by Lord Silkin and several amendments were passed. Two were especially significant. The first required that one of the two doctors giving an opinion on lawful termination should be a National Health Service consultant or a doctor approved by the Minister of Health (this was in accord with the wishes of the British Medical Association, though the Royal College of Obstetricians and Gynaecologists had wanted one of the doctors to be a consultant gynaecologist). The second amendment, carried by 87 votes to 86, excluded the "social" clause which had justified abortion for "non-medical" reasons. In addition, the Lords redrafted the "conscience clause" to ensure that with certain safeguards those who had a conscientious objection to abortion were not legally obliged to participate in it. They also amended the title of the Bill to "The Abortion Bill". Realizing, however, that if they insisted on the first two amendments their own status, as well as the passage of the Bill, would be seriously jeopardized, they decided to withdraw them and finally returned the Bill to the Commons in a virtually unaltered form. On 27 October 1967 it received the Royal Assent, and on 27 April 1968 it became law.

CHAPTER 2

Attitudes Towards Abortion

ABORTION is a topic which still arouses deep feelings based on underlying attitudes towards an area generally regarded as taboo. These attitudes can conveniently be considered in terms of the general public and the medical profession, especially gynaecologists, psychiatrists, and general practitioners.

The General Public

As far as the public is concerned, attitudes appear to have changed a great deal since the Second World War. Prior to 1939 society in England was relatively conformist, religion played a prominent role, and the danger and unpleasantness of an abortion were regarded by many as a talion punishment for indulgence in illicit sexual intercourse. The various churches held dissimilar views on abortion, an anomaly that becomes more comprehensible when considered in historical perspective.

Whilst Greek philosophers such as Aristotle and Plato were in favour of abortion, Cicero and Galen condemned it, as did the early Christians, who called it infanticide.[5] In AD 314 the Christian (Roman Catholic) Church prescribed 10 years' penance for abortion, and in the tenth century those who practised it could be excommunicated from the Church, for it was held that the animated soul of the foetus was murdered. In the twelfth century, exemption was granted when abortion was performed within 80 days of conception in the case of a female foetus and 40 days in the case of a male foetus. However, in 1869 Pope Pius IX decreed that the foetus had a soul from the time of conception, and the Roman Catholic Church reverted to its pre-twelfth-century position. In 1930, the year after the British Parliament had passed the Infant Life (Preservation) Act—which exempted a physician from prosecution for child destruction if this had occurred as a result of an abortion performed to save the life of a pregnant woman—Pope Pius XI declared that abortion was sinful even if it was done to save the mother's life, because of the equal sanctity of the life of the foetus. Twenty-one years later his successor, Pope Pius XII,[13] reiterated the same view:

> "Any direct abortion whatsoever, even if it is performed in the presence of a manifest therapeutic indication to save the mother by its means, when otherwise she together with the child would perish, is immoral and forbidden by divine law."

In April 1968, before the Abortion Act became law, the Catholic Church advised Roman Catholic doctors and nurses that they "should not participate in any capacity" in an abortion operation.

The Protestant Church has traditionally differed from the Roman Catholic position in laying greater stress on the right of the individual to make up his or her own mind in the light of what he or she believes to be right. It did not follow the 1930 Roman Catholic lead in condemning abortion for any reason whatsoever, and a committee of the Church Assembly Board for Social Responsibility published its views on the matter in 1965.[14] The committee stated that it favoured permitting interruption of pregnancy where adequate justification existed—for instance, a grave threat to the life or health of the mother—but in general it felt that abortion should be forbidden for three reasons: (i) the right to life of the foetus, (ii) the interest of society in its own survival, and (iii) the possibility that there could be weakening of reverence in and trivialization of the sexual act.

In discussing these views Professor Glanville Williams[2] pointed to the difficulty of deciding whether a foetus was a human being and if so whether it had a soul: because of this, the Church's first point was hard to assess; its second appeared odd in view of the problem of overpopulation; and its third point militated against contraception as well as abortion. He pointed out that the committee did, however, strongly reject the opinion that a woman with an extramarital pregnancy should be compelled to bear and rear the child as a punishment for her wickedness.

The Methodist Church also approved the general provisions of Mr. Steel's Bill.

In the early 1960s the Abortion Law Reform Association, founded in 1936 with the comparatively limited aims of permitting termination of pregnancy when this was felt necessary to preserve the mother's physical and mental health, or when there was a serious risk of a defective child being born, or after rape, was revived. The Association believed that the experience of centuries had shown that there was no way of curing the immense social evil of illegal abortions with all the suffering and morbidity they entailed other than by legalizing the operation for the medical profession.[15] In 1963 the Association's president, Professor Glanville Williams, advocated abortion as late as the 17th week of pregnancy, and the campaign was energetically continued during the ensuing years, spurred on by the Bills that were introduced into Parliament. Later Madeleine Simms,[16] the Association's general secretary, herself a wife and mother, campaigned for the Abortion Act—in a sense the culmination of the endeavours of the Association—until its final stages. Disputing the view that their maternal instincts would dissuade women from seeking abortions, Simms pointed out that whilst most women had a maternal instinct, at the same time they wished to have not more than two or three children, and they were appalled if they found they were having more children than they believed they could adequately care for. Should they accidentally become pregnant, they would then seek an abortion because of their feelings of responsibility to their husband and family, and because of their maternal instinct towards their existing children. Feckless, irresponsible women were happy to continue to produce children irrespective of their capacity to care for them and irrespective of the fact that the children might end up in the care of local authorities; such women were, Simms felt, hardly the ones whom women wished to emulate. Taking issue with Professor McLaren, a prominent gynaecologist who opposed liberalization of the law on abortion, she drew attention to the cruelty of rejecting a pregnant woman's urgent plea for termination, pointing out that not only were such women in Professor McLaren's words "emotional and their judgement unsound" in regard to their attitudes to pregnancy and abortion, but also that doctors themselves were "so riddled with emotion and religious prejudice about this subject that they are unable to approach it scientifically".[17]

In connection with the activities of the Association, it is significant that in the last 5 or 6 years British social attitudes have become increasingly permissive—films, books, plays, and television programmes dealing with hitherto-forbidden subjects in a frank way have been passed by the censor, who himself has been almost eliminated, and legislation regarding mental illness, suicide, and homosexuality, for example, has become less oppressive—thus in Britain today homosexual acts between consenting adult males in private are no longer illegal. But aside from this it is likely that, on an individual level, many British people had long realized that much personal tragedy could result from the birth of an illegitimate baby, that "forced" marriages often ran into grave difficulties, and that in families of the lower socio-economic strata the addition of an unwanted child could impose additional financial hardship and adversely affect the health of the mother and the existing children. Whatever was said publicly, people knew that in practice there was one law for the rich and another for the poor: the former could obtain an abortion in hygienic surroundings whilst the latter were debarred from such opportunities.

And yet, despite the anomalies of the situation, ambivalent feelings towards abortion were widely held. John Peel[2] has suggested that this may have stemmed in part from the propaganda of birth control clinics, which, in emphasizing the advantages of contraception, simultaneously stressed the evils and perils of criminal abortion. But, as Diane Munday[2] has pointed out, the law against abortion had been broken every day in every country in every age; legislation against attitudes and practices as basic as this has always been doomed to failure. Moya Woodside[2] found that the women abortionists she interviewed did not perceive abortion as a crime. They did not regard syringing in early pregnancy as taking a life, but rather as an attempt to re-start a period, or as a belated birth-control measure. They felt that the law, drafted and administered by men, was unfair and out of touch with the realities of life; abortion should, they believed, be available to every woman as a right, for they held that society would benefit from a reduction of unwanted and illegitimate children. These attitudes were so widespread that it is not surprising that the majority of the British public were in favour of Mr. Steel's Bill. Only a minority feared that it might lead to the destruction of unwanted children and be used as a form of social eugenics; opinion polls showed that the public had become "abortion minded".[8]

Medical Attitudes: The Hippocratic Tradition

Although it is usually taken for granted that the oath on which Western medical ethics is based was composed by Hippocrates, the Father of Medicine (?460–359 BC), there is disagreement regarding its origin, its true form and the date it was written. A modern translation of the oath is as follows:

> I swear by Apollo the healer, by Aesculapius, by Health and all the powers of healing, and call to witness all the gods and goddesses that I may keep this Oath and Promise to the best of my ability and judgement.
>
> I will pay the same respect to my master in the Science as to my parents and share my life with him and pay all my debts to him. I will regard his sons as my brothers and teach them the Science, if they desire to learn it, without fee or contract. I will hand on precepts, lectures and all other learning to my sons, to those of my master and to those pupils duly apprenticed and sworn, and to none other.

I will use my power to help the sick to the best of my ability and judgement; I will abstain from harming or wronging any man by it.

I will not give a fatal draught to anyone if I am asked, nor will I suggest any such thing. Neither will I give a woman means to procure an abortion.

I will be chaste and religious in my life and in my practice.

I will not cut, even for the stone, but I will leave such procedures to the practitioners of that craft.

Whenever I go into a house, I will go to help the sick and never with the intention of doing harm or injury. I will not abuse my position to indulge in sexual contacts with the bodies of women or of men, whether they be freemen or slaves.

Whatever I see or hear, professionally or privately, which ought not to be divulged, I will keep secret and tell no one.

If, therefore, I observe this Oath and do not violate it, may I prosper both in my life and in my profession, earning good repute among all men for all time. If I transgress and forswear this Oath, may my lot be otherwise.

The proscription of remedies to produce abortion, like some of the other ethical statements in the oath, do not reflect general Greek thought and practice throughout antiquity, even amongst the followers of Hippocrates. Ludwig Edelstein,[18] as a result of a detailed analysis of the oath, has suggested that it probably had its origins in the doctrines attributed to the followers of Pythagoras by Plato and Aristotle in the fourth century BC. The Pythagoreans, who represented only a small segment of Greek opinion, unlike other Greeks, saw the physician as ministering to the soul as well as to the body, and considered that his actions should reflect the asceticism they advocated. Believing that he should be guided by holiness, purity, justice, and forbearance, they bridged the gap between heathendom and Christianity and, at the end of the period of antiquity, medical practice began to conform to the philosophy embodied in the oath.

Gynaecologists

Prior to the passage of the Abortion Act, except on rare occasions, the majority of gynaecologists were opposed to terminating pregnancies, especially on psychiatric grounds, since the operation ran counter to their training and philosophy, contravened accepted medical ethics, and was of uncertain legality. Roman Catholic gynaecologists were opposed to abortion because of their religious beliefs, but the majority of gynaecologists entertained grave reservations concerning the probity of termination of pregnancy. The average gynaecologist had grown up with the threat of being struck off the Medical Register if he performed an "illegal" abortion: small wonder that his approach was conservative. As Professor Norman Morris [19] points out, most gynaecologists found terminating a pregnancy very disturbing, since technically it was a "bloody, miserable and thoroughly unpleasant procedure". Operators could not escape the obvious conclusion that they were destroying life, albeit in an early form of development; and as they became older they found that destruction of life became progressively more repulsive. Receiving little assistance from his colleagues, the gynaecologist frequently found himself in the invidious position of being both judge and executioner. This was especially repugnant, Professor Morris [2] later observed, since most gynaecologists functioned also as obstetricians, and in this role had usually spent years studying and discussing ways of improving the environment of the foetus *in utero*. They were dedicated to the progressive reduction of perinatal death and, like most doctors, had an obsessive desire to prolong and preserve life. Deliberate abortion, a "haemorrhagic exercise in destruction", was thus especially odious and was not even technically satisfying since, though the operation had some hazards, it demanded only limited manual dexterity and was the most unpleasant and unsatisfactory procedure they were called on to perform. If they did carry out therapeutic abortions—and Professor Morris, [2] despite his feelings, was in favour of them in suitable cases— they were faced, as Professor Rhodes [2] pointed out, not only with overcoming their own distaste but with altering hospital attitudes which in many cases were much opposed to the operation.

In view of these considerations, it is understandable that Albert Davis, [20] a gynaecologist to whose work reference has been made earlier [2] could not agree with the views expressed by Eustace Chesser. [21] The latter, a phychiatrist, made a plea for a wider use of therapeutic abortion, observing that it had been performed in only 1 per cent of the 2665 cases of abortion listed by Davis, even though Davis had concluded that in over 90 per cent of cases the abortion had been improperly induced. "Surely of these 2400 cases there must have been a number of individual instances where there were in fact legal grounds for termination?" Chesser wondered. Davis responded merely that if Chesser considered that the number treated in this way was too small and that his interpretation of the law was too narrow, "I can only reply that I believe it to be the correct one and his arguments do not convince me to the contrary." In this connection White, [22] an American author, observed that the feeling engendered in the gynaecologist by the demand for an abortion could sometimes lead him to impose a "package deal" on the woman, abortion not being sanctioned without sterilization, not always a desirable procedure.

Taking all these considerations into account, it is not surprising that the report adopted unanimously by the Council of the Royal College of Obstetricians and Gynaecologists in March 1966 took a conservative line.[9] It observed that the legal position then extant was adequate for the majority of cases and commended itself to most gynaecologists. It then went on to consider the possibility that existing practices might be encouraging criminal abortion with its attendant hazards. The Council pointed out that various estimates that 50,000, 100,000 or 250,000 criminal abortions were induced in the United Kingdom every year were without secure factual foundation, and it stated that, in its view, of the 72,400 abortion cases treated in National Health Service hospitals in 1962, not more than one in five, i.e. 14,600, were procured by patients themselves or by other persons; the rest it believed occurred spontaneously. The report observed that widening the indications for legal abortion rather than reducing criminal abortion might actually (as in Japan) produce the reverse effect, and might lead (as it had in Japan, Sweden, and Czechoslovakia) to recurrent demands for the operation. The report went on to emphasize the difficulties and dangers of inducing an abortion, stressing the danger of immediate physical complications and the hazard to subsequent pregnancies. It also pointed out that, whilst the continuation of pregnancy could have psychological ill effects, abortion also could have adverse effects and might leave a lasting sense of guilt. Clearly, therefore, the report stated, the person performing the operation had to satisfy himself that the risk of allowing pregnancy to continue was for that particular woman greater than the risk of terminating it; termination of pregnancy could never be regarded lightly in the individual case, and liberalization of the indications required knowledge of many facts which were not available.

The Council did, however, accept the case for amending the law to make it "positively rather than negatively clear" that there were circumstances when abortion was justified—namely when it was in the interests of the physical and mental health of the woman—and it went on to lay down some principles to be observed in framing a new Bill. These included (i) abortion not carried out in the circumstances stated in the Bill should remain a legal offence; (ii) the indications for legal abortion should not be too precisely defined, e.g. the patient's age, the circumstances of conception, or the extent of the risk of deformation or disease in the child that would be born; (iii) gynaecologists and others concerned should be left with freedom of action, and the gynaecologist undertaking the operation should be one of those certifying the need for it; the other signatory should be a senior member of the hospital staff and never of less than consultant status; (iv) care should be taken that the new Bill did not merely regularize criminal abortions, and that the operation was notifiable wherever it was performed; and, (v) radical alterations in the indications for abortion should be deferred until more information had become available.

More specifically, the Council recommended that abortion should only be legal if it were performed (a) by a National Health Service consultant obstetrician and gynaecologist or by another person also employed in the National Health Service to whom he had specifically designated the task in a particular case; (b) in a National Health Service Hospital or an institution (hospital or nursing home) specially licensed for the particular purpose by the Minister of Health; and (c) when two registered medical practitioners, both National Health Service consultants and one the consultant gynaecologist responsible for the operation, were of the opinion that continuance of pregnancy beyond the time when the child was viable would (i) involve serious risk to the life or grave injury to the physical and mental health of the pregnant woman, either before or after the birth of the child, or (ii) involve substantial risk that the child, if born, would suffer from such physical or mental abnormalities as to deprive it of any prospect of reasonable enjoyment of life. The Council also made other recommendations, and ended its report by discussing contraception and sterilization, the two principal means of making abortion unnecessary. It strongly emphasized the important role of these two procedures, and pointed out that the law on sterilization should be clarified at the same time as a new Abortion Bill was introduced.

Following this report, it became possible to assign gynaecologists to positions on a spectrum between those like Professor McLaren of Birmingham who were opposed to therapeutic abortion and those like Professor Baird of Aberdeen who favoured it in appropriate cases. Whilst most gynaecologists were midway in the spectrum, a consideration of the two extremes is of interest in illustrating differences in attitude.

Amongst those who deplored the Act was Richard de Soldenhoff who, writing from Ayrshire, Scotland, commented: "As a senior obstetrician who has been in charge of an obstetrical service in a large provincial district for 20 years, I think to bring in legalised abortion would be a terrible mistake...."
He added, however: "It has been our policy to carry out an abortion when

necessary in any case deserving it on therapeutic, social, economic or moral reasons."[23] Professor Ian Donald of Glasgow, speaking at a public meeting of the recently formed Society for the Protection of Unborn Children,[24] said that he recognized that abortion was sometimes desirable but pointed out that under the new law many healthy babies would be destroyed. He thought that the only way to get rid of the backstreet abortionist was to make abortion generally available under the National Health Service. In Romania, where some women had 20–30 abortions, Professor Donald said, the birth rate was falling, the population structure was changing, and there were 300 cases of renal failure annually. He feared that in Britain the long-term effects of the Bill would be to increase pressure and perhaps the threat of legal action if anything went wrong in a continued pregnancy. Medical standards would be lowered, social services would be discouraged, those with large families would be criticized, and social responsibility would be reduced. Later at the same meeting, Professor Scott of Leeds reported that of Fellows of the Royal College of Obstetricians and Gynaecologists, 192 had recorded opposition to social abortion and only five supported it. Although the prospective mother did not want the child, both mother and child were the gynaecologist's responsibility. He thought that mothers were "filled with joy at the child's birth" and that, even if the baby had to be adopted, it usually went on to have a happy life. Professor McLaren of Birmingham, who also spoke, declared that his attitude was "to support the woman through her pregnancy until her courage returned". He amplified his views in subsequent letters to journals: thus he remarked that at the second reading of the Bill he had hoped it would be stillborn because "I have strong objections to emptying the womb for social reasons and in this I am probably amongst 95 per cent of my colleagues in gynaecology who practise in the National Health Service".[25]

Eighteen months later, in the same vein, Professor McLaren wrote: "In 20 years I have never had a request from my colleagues in the Department of Psychiatry to carry out an abortion to cure 'social stigma' or 'lack of emotional support' ";[26] on another occasion he expressed concern that the act might lead to loss of candidates for gynaecological posts.[27] A. L. Deacon,[28] one of McLaren's colleagues in Birmingham, where Myre Sim (see page 24) also practised, later pointed out that McLaren saw the problem of the psychiatric indications for termination "too clearly in black and white", and aptly remarked: "To ask for an opinion only of one whom one knows to believe that there is no psychiatric indication for termination would be to prejudge the issue." Deacon went on to observe: "Surely much of the controversy over termination is due to the involvement of the medical profession, and particularly the gynaecologists and psychiatrists, who are being asked to recommend and carry out destruction of new life which, however desirable it may be or seem to be to the patient, is nevertheless contrary to the instinctive feeling that is nurtured through our medical training and in all other aspects of our medical practice." Nevertheless, Professor McLaren's views prevailed in one region in Bedfordshire where three consultant gynaecologists sent a "rather curt" communication to the general practitioners in the area declaring that they did not recognize either social or psychiatric reasons for termination of pregnancy. This provoked a protest from one family doctor. [29]

These attitudes were in direct contrast with the views and activities of Sir Dugald Baird, Emeritus Professor of Obstetrics and Gynaecology in Aberdeen. [30] Sir Dugald studied intelligence, personality, and family size in a group of women in that city over a 10-year period, and found that 30 per cent had had more children than they had wanted; moreover, the size of the family was inversely related to its socio-economic status, the poorest families having the most children. Helped by the fact that the law in Scotland at that time was more liberal than the law in England, he then embarked on a programme of abortion and sterilization in carefully selected cases. To the time-honoured indications for termination on medical or surgical grounds and debility from excessive child-bearing, he added such other considerations as the personality of the patient, her capability as a mother, the number of previous pregnancies, their outcome, the family living conditions, the presence of prolonged or serious illness in the family, the mother's fear of giving birth to a defective child, her education, and her socio-economic status.

In regard to the latter two points, Professor Baird found that the problem was often greatly affected by the social status of the woman. Upper-class women usually were in good physical health and had few medical indications for termination; often they were doing a professional job, running a house at a high level of efficiency, and trying to make themselves available for their children as needed. Working at this pitch they were vulnerable to extra strain, and an unwanted pregnancy could impose more stress than they ought to be asked to bear. Abdominal hysterotomy combined with tubal ligation was often the answer, Sir Dugald felt, especially if they were in their middle thirties and definitely did not want further children. Women from the lower socio-economic classes, in contrast, were often less accustomed to long-term planning; having had little education they had usually held an unskilled or semi-skilled job prior to a marriage which rapidly produced more children than they were able physically and financially to manage. Whilst some desired an unwanted pregnancy to be terminated, many were prepared to go through with it provided they knew it would be the last; tubal ligation in the puerperium was the answer to their problem. For both classes of women, removal of the constant threat of pregnancy enabled them to be better wives and mothers. In emergency situations, e.g. in an unmarried woman or in a married woman who wanted a pregnancy later, perhaps when her psychological condition had improved, curettage was employed unless the pregnancy was of greater duration than 12 weeks, when hysterotomy might be performed. Termination *per se* was more commonly practised in the upper classes in which the illegitimacy rate was lower, unwanted pregnancies were less well accepted, their effects were more disruptive, and more patients were referred by family doctors.

In conformity with this liberal policy, between 1960 and 1963, 210 women in Aberdeen had therapeutic abortions and 412 women were sterilized by *post-partum* tubal ligation. Indications for sterilization included (i) medical condition—severe heart, chest and kidney diseases; (ii) psychiatric illnesses—severe disturbances necessitating treatment and making further childbearing dangerous to health; (iii) obstetric disorders; (iv) debility and multiparity; and (v) other—eugenic, social circumstances, and so forth. Later, a follow-up of 186 women 2–9 years after sterilization showed that 161 (86%) were satisfied afterwards and that the vast majority, including twenty-one women who reported reduced satisfaction in coitus and forty-four who mentioned gynaecological complaints, were enthusiastic advocates of the procedure. [31]

Psychiatrists

Unlike the gynaecologist, the psychiatrist seldom takes part in the actual physical process of terminating an unwanted pregnancy, and, as he does not himself have to destroy life, his involvement in termination is less charged with emotion and less disturbing personally. His distance from the procedure makes it possible for him to have less compunction about recommending termination, so that in some ways it is easy for him to be more objective than the gynaecologist. Before the Abortion Act became law, it was wise for the psychiatrist, as Brian Ackner[32] pointed out, to remember that the gynaecologist had the responsibility of making the final decision, and that his own role was normally to confine himself to offering an opinion to the gynaecologist, and not to prejudge the situation by prematurely informing the patient or her general practitioner of his views. The psychiatrist spends longer than his professional colleagues with the patient, and so is better able to ascertain her strengths and vulnerabilities; accustomed to empathy with patients and assessing the significance of environmental factors, he is usually, like Chesser,[21] moved by their pleas for help in a situation in which in any case, as Franklin[33] has observed, pity tends to dominate medical attitudes. From his everyday work, the psychiatrist, considering the possible outcome from the standpoint of the unwanted child, probably gains a clearer idea of the overwhelming handicap of being born unwelcome into a hostile and rejecting environment. These factors made the average psychiatrist favour therapeutic termination of unwanted pregnancies and made him eager to reform the law to this end.

In contrast, a few psychiatrists have always opposed termination of pregnancy on psychiatric grounds, the best-known exponent of this point of view being Myre Sim of Birmingham. Seventeen years ago Sim[34] observed that the main issue for the psychiatrist to decide in considering whether to recommend termination of pregnancy was whether the woman was likely to develop a puerperal psychosis and, if so, the effect of such a psychosis on her subsequent health. The question of suicide during pregnancy was also relevant. He reported the findings of a 12-year study of 213 women with puerperal psychoses, all of whom were married, and he concluded: (i) that puerperal psychoses carried a good prognosis and was virtually unpredictable; (ii) that instability in pregnancy did not contribute materially to the incidence of a puerperal psychosis; (iii) that married women were relatively immune to puerperal psychosis; (iv) that abortion, even if therapeutic, could itself produce a psychosis; and (v) that there were no psychiatric grounds for termination of pregnancy.

In 1957 James Arkle[35] commented on the tendency for psychiatrists "to condone the operation of abortion for reasons which appear to deviate from both the ethic of medicine and the law of the land". He outlined the historical reasons for what he termed "the Christian opposition to therapeutic abortion", and discussed the legal position in England before describing twenty-two patients in which he said his experience had supported the view that therapeutic abortion was "hardly ever justified on psychiatric grounds". Arkle arrived at this conclusion by insisting on a strict interpretation of Mr. Justice Macnaghten's verdict in the Bourne case, i.e. that continuation of pregnancy would make the woman a mental wreck, and he stated that "lesser degrees of emotional upset are not enough, nor are social disturbances of any magnitude nor eugenic forebodings of any kind". Arkle believed that psychiatric indications for terminating pregnancy were present only if deterioration in the mental state of the patients would occur if abortion was not performed, even though he admitted that in over half his patients the social aspect of the situation could not be regarded as even moderately satisfactory, and in several cases the mother was incapable of looking after the child.

Similarly, as recently as 1967 David Stafford-Clarke,[36] another well-known psychiatrist, wrote in his textbook: "In this writer's view termination of pregnancy on psychiatric grounds can only be justified when continuation of the pregnancy would certainly carry a risk to the mother's life, or permanent destruction of her health. It can never be justified on purely sociological or personal grounds. Severe depression, with the open threat of suicide if the pregnancy is not terminated, cannot in itself constitute an indication for termination." A fourth psychiatrist, R. E. Hemphill,[37] remarked the change that had occurred over the years in patients referred for consideration of termination of pregnancy on psychiatric grounds; he foresaw practical problems in implementing the provisions of the Abortion Act, and feared the consequences of an unrestrained demand which might, he felt, endanger the stability of social relations and the family in later generations. Elizabeth Tylden[38] also sounded a note of caution. The stringency of past laws against abortion, whilst in part ethical, had also been due, she pointed out, to the hazards of the procedure; in Western society, marriage was the only acceptable and generally practicable way in which a woman could have and bring up a child, and the only way in which a child could readily obtain the continuity of emotional support and care it required in early life. Efficient contraception, Tylden observed, was far preferable to abortion, which usually necessitated the use of a much-needed hospital bed and, by flouting the medical ethic of the preservation of life, mobilized feelings of resentment and hostility in medical attendants and nurses, and fear, ambivalence, and guilt in patients.

The views expressed by Sim in 1953 were immediately attacked in a number of letters to the editor of the *British Medical Journal*. Amongst other things, he was accused of unfamiliarity with the law, of misinterpreting the reports of psychiatrists from the Continent, of ignoring socio-economic factors, of unwarrantably generalizing from an unrepresentative sample of patients, and of over-simplifying the problem. He had been wrong, it was said, to ignore the problem of neurotic ill health and unhappiness and to focus solely on the psychotic disorders produced by unwanted pregnancies. William Sargant, the Registrar of the Royal Medico-Psychological Association, pointed out that only a small minority of its over 2000 members held similar views. In 1964 an objective, relatively dispassionate, assessment of many of the attitudes surrounding termination and the psychiatric problems which arise from recommending this operation was provided by R. F. Tredgold.[39] Neither he nor Professor Anderson[40] was inclined to agree with Sim, and Professor Anderson in particular made the relevant and often-repeated plea that each case be judged on its own merits, taking account of the woman in her total life situation. "Whether formally or legally recognized or not," Anderson commented, "the social indication will always enter into the decision, and it is idle to suppose the final decision will be made on the pure medical indication alone, abstracted from all other considerations."

To many psychiatrists who considered the problem it was becoming clear, as Neustatter[2] pointed out, that a change of outlook was needed. Termination should not be regarded as a crime but as an operation. The law needed to be made more positive, and it was desirable to get away from the phrase "mental wreck", a residue from the Bourne case. Neustatter thought that as matters stood there was insufficient concern for the welfare of the child, as well as for the sociological effect of bringing unwanted children into the world in bad physical circumstances—an action that was illogical in view of the acknowledged contribution of bad homes to delinquency. He favoured reform of the law to permit termination when a pregnancy was likely adversely to affect the family's well-being.

In 1966 the first authoritative general statement of British psychiatric opinion appeared when the Royal Medico-Psychological Association published its "Memorandum on Therapeutic Abortion".[11] This stated the Association's belief that certain courses of action in relation to therapeutic termination should be made permissible by law since the best available knowledge suggested that they contributed to the promotion of health and the prevention of disease. Leaving members who disagreed with its own pragmatic view of medical ethics free to differ, it opposed legislation which might bring pressure on an individual doctor to act contrary to his conscience. The Association stated that it approached therapeutic abortion "with the firm view that, in addition to traditionally accepted medical and psychiatric criteria, all social circumstances should be taken into account. If, after considering all these factors, a psychiatrist should form the opinion that the mental health of the mother and the whole family would be promoted by termination, then it should be lawful for him to recommend it." The Memorandum observed that it was desirable that children should be born as a result of being wanted and planned, and it noted that in regard to therapeutic termination, existing case law (the Bourne decision with its later additions) was not really satisfactory. This was due to confusion in the minds of doctors concerning their legal position, which meant that many had become inhibited in advising on or performing termination of pregnancy—they feared prosecution or damage to their professional reputations. A clear statement of the law regarding therapeutic termination was therefore desirable, the Association felt. The Memorandum noted that in considering the possible deleterious effects of pregnancy a psychiatrist had to assess not only the direct but also the remote effects on the health of the mother; decisions involving the social environment were, the Memorandum observed, part of the everyday practice of psychiatrists who brought to them expert knowledge and a responsible professional attitude. The Association was opposed to the establishment of Statutory Boards to make decisions on termination, and also to the notification of cases to the Ministry of Health or to a Medical Officer of Health; both these procedures were considered unnecessary and likely to constitute additional strains for patients. It thought that the inclusion of a clause to permit termination when there was a substantial risk that the child that was born would be handicapped was advantageous, provided that it was purely permissive and that no pressure was brought to bear on the parents. The Memorandum gave three types of case to illustrate its views, and ended by emphasizing that, except in cases of severe mental illness or subnormality, therapeutic termination of pregnancy should always be voluntary and at the request of the pregnant woman herself.

Professor Ferguson Rodger[10] has described some of the thinking that lay behind the Memorandum. From the first the Association favoured as justifications for therapeutic termination the inclusion of social grounds which might affect the future mental health of the mother or the other children of the family, but it was determined that these grounds should not be too closely defined as it felt this might create imperative demands for abortion and force doctors to act without being prompted by their own judgement. Professor Rodger stated that he himself thought that since the majority of patients referred to psychiatrists came because of failure of contraception, the need for abortions would diminish as effective contraceptive measures became more widespread; accordingly he felt that the Abortion Act should be regarded "as a measure introduced during a transitional phase in the reproductive history of our society which may cease to be useful when contraception is perfected." He went on to consider the interests of the child, and in particular whether it could ever be to its advantage to be destroyed before birth. Whilst this ran counter to the conventional religious views on the "gift of life," Professor Rodger pointed out that as a result of an abortion not having been carried out, the child might not be able to enjoy the health and happiness to which it was entitled. Further, though illegitimacy *per se* was probably an insufficient basis for the child to sue for "wrongful life", the Professor observed that one case had been successful when the child had sued on the grounds that his father knew that he, the father, had syphilis at the time of the child's conception, and another had succeeded when a child in North America brought an action against the state authority for negligence in the supervision of patients in a state hospital because he had been conceived as a result of the rape of his mother by another patient. Professor Rodger was of the opinion that to bring a physically or mentally handicapped child into the world, or even to risk doing so, might be an injustice to an individual who might have the right to question the decision and to sue the doctor for its consequences.

The Memorandum's comments regarding the inadequacy of the law struck a receptive chord. As one psychiatrist, F. P. Haldane,[41] pertinently put it, prior to the Abortion Act he had "often been faced with an unhappy patient in whom compassion and humanity cried out for termination of her pregnancy which was clearly in the best interest of herself and her family, yet being unable conscientiously to affirm that there really was a serious threat of mental illness, such as the law then required, I had either to reject termination or take part in procuring a criminal abortion". Many had the same problem. Three hundred senior psychiatrists in Britain were circulated with questions regarding the Abortion Bill. Of the first 100 replies, 24 thought termination should be freely available to all women, 56 felt the indications for termination should be based on evaluation, including the social situation, and only 16 felt that existing case law (i.e. the Bourne case) should be made into statute law.[42] Further consideration of this topic was given by Professor Pond[43] and by Joyston-Bechal.[44] An endorsement of termination on appropriate psychiatric grounds was implied in a report from

University College Hospital, London, where of 426 women referred to the Department of Psychological Medicine between 1961 and 1967, 257 were recommended for this operation.[45]

Myre Sim,[46] however, continued to oppose the Abortion Act, even interpreting the "conscience" clause as the "medical" conscience rather than in the accepted religious sense. In a letter to the editor of the *British Medical Journal* he appeared to imply that some "permissive" psychiatrists and "permissive" gynaecologists who recommended and performed abortions were deficient in "medical conscience" and were primarily motivated by financial considerations. Alan Sanderson,[47] another psychiatrist, objected to this, pointing out that many highly conscientious doctors favoured abortion on psychiatric grounds. Whether the addition of an unwanted child would endanger the health of other children in the family was not known, Sanderson said, but there was strong evidence of an association between criminality and psychiatric disorder on the one hand and emotional and maternal deprivation in childhood on the other. Far-sighted action was often necessary if advances were to be made, and such action had often to be taken before incontestable evidence of its value was available: doctors tended to shrink from performing abortions, and some rationalized their inertia on the grounds of their "medical conscience".

In passing the Abortion Act, Parliament made it legal for doctors to terminate pregnancy on wider indications than the British Medical Association thought ethically permissible; the Association nevertheless decided that their opinion should not be changed and a leading article[48] observed that "the essence of professional freedom for a doctor is his right to act in professional matters uninfluenced by any consideration other than the judgement of his fellows". This soon produced remonstrances from two well-known psychiatrists, who pointed out in no uncertain terms that a doctor's first duty was to his patient regardless of the interests of any third party.[49, 50]

J. G. Howells, speaking at a combined meeting of the American Psychiatric Association and the Royal Medico-Psychological Association in Boston, Massachusetts, in June 1968, made it clear that he thought that termination early in pregnancy could be regarded as "extended birth control". Developing a theme he had expressed earlier,[51] Howells said he felt that many women did not want their bodies to be used to bear unwanted children; a woman, he thought, wanted a child born of love and gaiety and affection, not from chance, alcoholic intoxication, or a casual sexual contact. Howells believed that women do not regard the foetus *in utero* as an entity prior to quickening (at 8 weeks the crown-rump length of the foetus is only 30 mm, but thereafter it grows rapidly), and he advocated termination in suitable cases until the 15th or 16th week. Heinz Wolff, speaking at the same meeting, pointed out that psychiatrists could be (i) illness-orientated, (ii) patient-orientated, or (iii) society-orientated. Thus whilst no psychiatric illness constituted an absolute indication for therapeutic termination, the psychiatrist had to realize that the woman was often in distress and had come for help. One had to listen for conscious and unconscious motives since conflict over the situation was quite common. The psychiatrist had to become aware of his own biases—for instance, rationalizing his own beliefs by citing the sanctity of life. The society-orientated psychiatrist might have a broader attitude still, feeling that society would suffer deleterious consequences from the birth of unwanted children who did not have parents who loved them and who would care for them in after-life.

In summary it is clear that the vast majority of British psychiatrists, unlike their gynaecologist colleagues, were very much in favour of therapeutic termination in suitable cases, and wanted liberalization of the law to this end.

General Practitioners

The attitude of the general practitioner to therapeutic termination was for the most part closer to that of the psychiatrist than to that of the gynaecologist. Family doctors seldom participate in the operative procedure of termination but have unique opportunities to see at first hand the problems imposed by unwanted pregnancies, and female practitioners are often especially sympathetic. One such family doctor, Evelyn Fisher,[52] replying to a consultant surgeon who had opposed liberalization of the law on abortion, wrote that he was "much less likely to see at first hand, as do general practitioners, the day to day struggles of the ill-housed, impoverished mother of a young family, whose husband may be sick or unemployed or 'ne'er do well'. Has [he] really never", she asked, "read of a desperate, distraught mother driven to suicide, usually by gas poisoning—because she could not face another pregnancy?

"Often the mother who seeks an abortion", Fisher went on, "has a truer conception of the dignity and sanctity of human life than those who preach the doctrine to her while rating the quality of her mental and physical life and her value to her family below that of a foetus less than 13 weeks old." In

ATTITUDES TOWARDS ABORTION

a survey carried out among doctors in the London area in 1964, Fisher observed that of 750 who replied, 70 per cent approved the liberalization of the abortion law and only 10 per cent were flatly opposed to it.

Unfortunately, even though the general practitioner might favour termination of pregnancy, as Stuart Carne[2] has pointed out, he was left with the problem of finding a gynaecologist who would concur and would be prepared to do the operation. The difficulty did not end there, for the gynaecologist usually sought the opinion of another specialist—that of a psychiatrist or whoever was relevant. How did the patient herself feel, Carne wondered, when she believed she might be an expectant mother and did not want to expect? He surmised, "No doubt she asks herself, 'How will my doctor respond when I tell him? By showing me the door? By laughing? By fobbing me off with a useless pill? Or by asking me if I have got 150 guineas to get it done privately?' " Carne thought that this was the predicament of the ordinary doctor and the ordinary patient: neither knew how to proceed correctly. Yet if a woman was really determined to get a termination, in Carne's experience she usually succeeded somehow or another.

In Rowena Woolf's[2] experience, more and more general practitioners were becoming prepared to take an active part and to help the woman, though a much larger group refused to be involved. In hospitals, sisters and social workers sometimes sat in judgement on the patient before she had been seen by the consultant, and the state of affairs described by Professor Baird in Aberdeen seldom prevailed. Woolf wanted to see this "official" attitude of condemnation and withdrawal change to one of understanding and helpfulness; and she wanted to see the rights of the mother take precedence over the rights of the foetus.

Writing in a similar vein, a senior physician, Duncan Leys,[53] observed that women did not desire abortions—they either wanted a child or wished to avoid a pregnancy. He thought that most women who sought an abortion were married, perhaps because they had the greatest difficulty in avoiding pregnancies. They feared that they could not provide a new child with the love and care it needed and were afraid that it would impose too great a strain on themselves and their families and might even endanger their marriages. Prior to the Abortion Act, unless they were able to afford high fees they were unable to obtain a safe and hygienic abortion and were driven to backstreet practitioners. Leys thought the physical hazards of termination had been much exaggerated, especially when the operation was performed by good surgeons on healthy women in good condition. Similarly, the psychological hazards of the operation had been magnified without any evidence to support the contention that the operation had a high incidence of psychiatric sequelae. Leys could not see why a fertilized ovum had more claim to respect than its unfertilized counterpart, and he concluded: "It is a pity that the process of development initiated by fertilization should be deliberately arrested, but I do not understand how anyone with experience of the lives of deprived children can believe it to be better that an unwanted pregnancy should survive. Those who condemn the continued denial of the right of hospital abortion must accept responsibility for the lives of unwanted children and also for the social injustice of a system which provides hygienic abortions for only those who can afford to pay heavily for it."

A special committee of the British Medical Association, in a sense the official body most accurately representing the views of family doctors, published its report on therapeutic abortion in July 1966.[9] After reviewing the historical and legal aspects of the problem, it recommended that therapeutic abortion should be made lawful provided that it was carried out by a registered medical practitioner of the requisite skill and experience after consultation with and with the approval of a professional colleague who had examined the patient. Subject to these conditions, the special committee advocated that termination performed in good faith, either in the interests of the health of the mother or because of the risk of serious abnormality of the foetus, should be made legal. Later the same year, a sub-committee of the Medical Women's Federation[54] agreed in their report that the law then extant required revision, that the phrase "termination of pregnancy" was preferable to "abortion", and that a new law should aim at eliminating the performance of abortion by unskilled persons. They considered that Mr. Steel's Bill (then in the Committee stage) needed revision along lines they indicated, that outside such legal limits abortion should be regarded as criminal (except accidental termination from live-saving emergency procedures) and that no doctor or patient should be required to act against their consciences in the matter of termination of pregnancy. The committee recommended wider teaching of medical students and nurses on contraception and on the social, psychological, and medical problems involved in marriage guidance and psychosexual counselling. It advocated health education for children, young people, and parents, and suggested a fact-finding prospective study of the effects of termination or non-termination of pregnancy on a national basis. In hospitals, termination should be followed by after care and suitable advice, contraceptive clinics should be established, and funds should be provided to expand services. Family doctors also, the committee felt, had an important role to play.

In January 1968 the British Medical Association Committee on Therapeutic Abortion issued a report on the indications for termination of pregnancy of less than 28 weeks' duration.[55] The report, avoiding discussion of social factors, set out the maternal indications system by system, including the psychiatric indications, and ended with a section on conditions causing foetal abnormality. As a leading article[56] commented, it "provides a framework of general guidance to the practitioner faced with what may be one of the most complex and onerous decisions in medicine". The indispensable role of the family doctor in relation to the therapeutic termination of pregnancy was described by a psychiatrist in 1968 who wrote: ". . . psychiatrists do not have a monopoly of ordinary understanding of humanity. And if any individual gynaecologist feels that he is alien from appreciation of the human predicament he can surely rely on the family doctor for this . . . the law now allows abortion to be carried out to prevent a general deterioration of the patient's mental health standards, the likelihood of which can be assessed more reliably by the family doctor, with first hand knowledge of the family and its social and economic setting, than by the psychiatric specialist in his clinic. . . ."[41]

CHAPTER 3

Sexuality and Contraception

UNWANTED pregnancies result from sexual activity and inadequate contraception. Consideration of these two topics is vital in any comprehensive survey of the issues involved in termination of pregnancy.

Sexual Behaviour in Britain

In recent years sexual behaviour in the United Kingdom has changed in two ways: it is less clandestine and it is more freely indulged in by adolescents and young adults. Both within and outside marriage, sexual activities have become more open and less furtive. Hypocrisy in sexual matters has steadily declined as the recognition has grown that lifelong monogamy preceded by absolute chastity is no longer the practice of most people: sex is now regarded by the majority as a normal component of adult life and as one of the prerequisites of a secure relationship between the sexes. The long engagement, much of it chaperoned, has disappeared; in its place has come earlier marriage, usually with postponement of a family because the wife for economic reasons has to work, because no suitable accommodation is available, because most families are neither unduly poor nor abnormally wealthy, and because, as a rule, there are too few relatives able to help with child-rearing. In 1921 there were 48,000 brides under the age of 21 in England and Wales; by 1965 the number had risen to 152,000. Two out of three girls marrying under the age of 20 in 1964 were pregnant, and in that year 22 per cent of all births to mothers under 20 were illegitimate.

The major change that has occurred has been the new-found independence and sexual freedom of the adolescent. As Gordon Stewart Prince[57] has pointed out, a "new race of teenagers" probably does not exist, but today's adolescents differ in several respects from their predecessors. Adolescence now often begins at 10, and puberty follows soon afterwards. Girls in Britain begin to menstruate at 13 and, like boys, are more mature physically and sexually than their parents were at the same age. The influences of the family and of religion have declined, whilst the power of the teenage group has grown as a result of its larger numbers and its increased spending capacity. There are almost a million more teenagers now than there were 10 years ago, an increase of 20 per cent, and $3\frac{1}{2}$ million young people are aged between 15 and 19. From a monetary standpoint, school-leavers are capable of earning as much as their fathers who have many more demands on their incomes, and teenage expenditure, whilst amounting to only 5 per cent of total consumer spending, is especially noticeable in that it involves highly audible and visual articles. Adolescents purchase 42 per cent of records and record players, 37 per cent of bicycles and motor-cycles, and 29 per cent of cosmetics and toilet preparations; they contribute 30 per cent of the money spent on entertainment. Because of their numbers and spending power, the press and other media have created a teenage mythology, and a teenage subculture with pressures towards conformity has developed with an attendant image of how a teenager should look, feel, and behave. The old pattern of adolescent subservience compelled in part by economic bondage has given way to an insistence on participation in decision-making processes of which one of the more obvious manifestations has been student demand for self-government. The zone of demarcation between adolescence and adulthood has become blurred, and in a highly literate society in which television, magazines, films, and radio programmes reach every age group, it has no longer been possible to preserve two sets of behavioural norms—one for adolescents and the other for adults.

The fame and wealth gained so rapidly and with so little apparent effort by members of "pop" groups thrust into prominence by the mass media have disproportionately impressed some young people who are no longer willing to settle down to years of study and thrift as a precursor to secure but undramatic advancement. The television screen, across which flit the faces of persons in vastly different walks of life, can mislead teenagers by providing spurious implications of equality and accessibility, though it appears that the commonality of interests now shared by adolescents often transcends the barriers raised by education, class, and nationality. In "swinging Britain", as in other countries, young people share interests in dress, music, and fast vehicles, and many cast the old in the role of scapegoat, regarding them as prejudiced, hidebound, lacking in understanding, and corrupted by life. Some of the young, Professor A. J. Ayer[58] has observed, consider they have been failed by the old because they feel that the latter have created a world that is not worth inheriting. Cut off from their seniors in this way by feelings of scorn and resentment, the young are denied "corrective feedback" and function almost as a separate race setting itself up in opposition to the old and determined not to adhere to their values and mores. This "generation gap" or "alienation of youth", Iago Galdston[59] has suggested, is a definitive break resulting from the decline of the patriarchal family structure, "the homestead", and with it its patriarchal or "Protestant" ethos, brought about by the continuing and increasingly disruptive effects of the advances in machine technology which began in the Industrial Revolution.

Teenage Sexuality

In Britain, as in other Western countries, schools now have the unenviable task of redressing the excesses of the permissive society without being Victorian about it; it is easier and less dangerous to compromise on alcohol and nicotine than on sexuality, and the problems arising out of the latter are increasingly formidable. Whereas most of the available information formerly relied on guesswork and conjecture, Michael Schofield's[60] study, in which 1873 boys and girls between 15 and 19 were interviewed in London and in the south and in the north of England, provides baseline data on adolescent sexual education, sexual behaviour, and contraceptive practices. From the standpoint of sexual education, at the age of 13 two-thirds of the girls and three-quarters of the boys in his investigation knew or believed they knew about "the facts of life", but as most had obtained the information from their friends, much of it was inaccurate and obscene. Half the boys and 14 per cent of the girls had had no sexual education at school; strangely, teachers often believed they had provided it, but the pupils did not perceive it as such, and 47 per cent of the boys and 43 per cent of the girls felt they should have been given more instruction. From the standpoint of sexual behaviour, the girls in Schofield's investigation started younger than the boys, but by the age of 17 the boys had caught up, and by the age of 18, 34 per cent of the boys and 17 per cent of the girls were sexually experienced. The boys, wanting to prove their masculinity to their friends and themselves, were in search of sexual adventure, whilst the girls were seeking romance. By the age of 20, about 350,000 boys and girls—10 per cent of the number of adolescents in Britain between 15 and 19 years old—had had sexual intercourse.

Despite their sexual activities, less than half the boys in Schofield's sample used contraceptive techniques (most commonly withdrawal or a sheath, the latter sometimes being regarded as a status symbol), and a quarter never used them. The girls for the most part left contraception to their sexual partners, though most feared pregnancy. Forty per cent of the boys were unconcerned about it, though many said that they would be prepared to marry the girl if she became pregnant and the girl expected or hoped for this. Since the teenage girls in Schofield's sample, who were interviewed before the Abortion Act was in prospect, did not favour abortion or adoption, pregnancies were likely to lead to hasty marriages or to illegitimate births. The risk of pregnancy was therefore quite high, especially as sexual intercourse was frequently an impulsive, unpremeditated act.

How do British girls regard contraception? Whilst contraceptive advice and materials have always been difficult for them to obtain, the results of a recent survey suggest that the attitudes middle-class girls entertain towards contraception have changed quite markedly in the last few years. R. W. Kind,[61] who investigated the attitudes of a carefully constructed sample of 400 18-year-olds by questionnaire at an interval of 5 years, found that in the middle-class subjects in 1963, 67 per cent of the boys and 43 per cent of the girls said that they would take the risk of sexual intercourse without contraceptives, whereas in 1968 the figures were 33 and 68 per cent respectively: the boys had grown more cautious and the girls less so. In the working-class members of the sample, there was no marked discrepancy between the sexes: 77 per cent of the boys and 66 per cent of the girls thought that the risk was worth taking. The results suggested that in 1968 about 90 per cent of the boys and 60 per cent of the girls were sexually experienced compared with 20–25 per cent of the boys and 10–15 per cent of the girls in 1963. But, whilst taking oral contraceptives had made some girls more emancipated, in Kind's sample for the most part they still believed that it was the man's job to take precautions, and many were quite reckless about the risks. Simms[62] has suggested that this could be because birth control had acquired a drab image, whilst the unmarried mother had more glamorous connotations. In some girls the drama of pregnancy was probably a temporary compensation for other forms of failure and dissatisfaction.

Education is not the complete answer to problems of contraception. In 1968, according to S. E. Finlay,[2] between 2 and 3 per cent of female undergraduates in British universities—admittedly a much more heterogenous group than formerly and mostly grant supported—were becoming pregnant each year. Two-thirds of the pregnancies went to term, and one-third ended in abortion, which was "illegal" in the majority of cases. Compared with other women students, those who became pregnant showed more evidence of previous instability, but sexual promiscuity in students as a whole is probably on the increase.[63] The larger incidence of illegitimate pregnancies occurring in female students could, however, merely reflect what was going on in the population generally. The desire of the young to expand experience and the old to turn their backs on it has been dramatically expressed in the tendency of some of the former to experiment with amphetamines and cannabis, whilst the latter continue to have recourse to alcohol and barbiturates.

Illegitimate Births

In 1968 James Weir, the medical officer of health for the London Borough of Kensington and Chelsea, reported that the borough had the highest illegitimacy rate in Britain—211 per 1000 live births.[64] This was associated with large numbers of girls living in bed-sitters or in flats away from home, a high percentage in the "at risk" years between 15 and 29, abundant temptation, numerous temporary residents, and many individuals seeking anonymity. In addition, the "permissive society", pressures towards promiscuity, and lack of parental supervision played their parts. The rise of illegitimacy which began in 1954 in London spread steadily northwards, reaching Scotland in 1958 and reversing the traditional rural : urban ratio. For England and Wales in 1967 illegitimate births totalled 69,928—8.4 per cent of all live births for the year; this contrasted with 31,145 illegitimate births in 1955—4.7 per cent of the total births for that year. In Scotland in 1967, 9.4 per cent of all city births were illegitimate.[65]

The trend towards more illegitimate babies has been on the increase in all age groups under 35, and about a third are now born to mothers below 20. But whilst at first sight the illegitimacy rate in teenagers is abnormally high, this is fallacious because the proportion of illegitimate to total births in that group is unduly large; this is because the total number of births to girls under the age of 20 (72,000) is much lower than the number born to women aged 25–29 (263,000).[60] However, whereas illegitimate births in adolescents and young women were in the past associated with lack of education and adverse home conditions, these factors no longer obtain, for, as Professor Baird[66] has observed, the illegitimacy rate has risen in all social classes and is linked with affluence. It has occurred in a society which has become permissive towards extramarital sexuality, but has been unwilling to make contraception available to the unmarried.

In conformity with the earlier age of puberty, in England and Wales between 1956 and 1966 the number of pregnancies in girls aged 13–15 increased from 269 to 1288 per year, and, apart from immediate obstetric problems, Professor Russell[67] has pointed out, these pregnancies have caused serious family difficulties and long-term physical and psychological sequelae for the girls themselves. In 1964 teenagers accounted for 27 per cent of all live births compared with 13 per cent in 1951. As a leading article[68] observes: "We seem to be in a transition between the older sexual-marital pattern and a new code based on premarital sexual experience, experimentation with effective contraception and abortion as the last resort."

Venereal Disease

Venereal disease, traditionally one of the major deterrents to sexual promiscuity, has also been on the increase. With the discovery of penicillin during the Second World War and the effectiveness of this and other drugs, venereal diseases for a time seemed destined to disappear. This did not occur, and the number of patients seeking advice at venereal disease centres rose from 69,393 males and 25,303 females in 1955 to 119,545 males and 56,729 females in 1967. Whilst infectious syphilis has remained at a low level in England and Wales (4.56 per 100,000 men and 0.99 per 100,000 women), the incidence of gonorrhoea has risen in a disquieting fashion; in 1967 there were 41,829 cases, an increase of 11.6 per cent over 1966, and 15 per cent of those who acquired gonorrhoea in sexual intercourse were under the age of 20.[69] In 1968 the total number of cases of gonorrhoea—up again at 44,962— was nearing the level of the post-war epidemic (47,300 cases seen in 1946). Possibly the widespread use of oral contraceptives has been a factor in increasing the incidence of the sexually transmitted diseases, not only by making women more promiscuous, but also by making it easier for the disease to establish itself. Modern methods of transportation—air travel in particular —have helped to make gonorrhoea the second commonest notifiable infectious disease in the world.[70]

Attitudes Towards Contraception

Attitudes to contraception, like those regarding abortion, have only latterly begun to change. For many years it was customary for a large segment of British public opinion to equate ignorance with innocence and to believe that sexual behaviour should be confined to the marital relationship. Accordingly it was thought immoral and unnecessary for single persons, especially unmarried women, to be knowledgeable about contraception. Public opinion was more liberal towards men, and "solved" the problem by turning a blind eye to its existence. Contraceptive issues are still conveniently omitted from films, television programmes, and so forth—even the most detailed descriptions of sexual behaviour contained in contemporary novels usually leave it out—so that some members of the public, especially adolescents, may be led to conclude that such problems do not exist. The enjoyment of sexual pleasure without consideration of its after-effects is now regarded as a right by many adolescents and young adults, who lack the maturity and foresight to envisage the consequences of their behaviour.

RELIGIOUS PROBLEMS

Whilst the Church of England—to which the majority of the population of the British Isles belongs—was not directly opposed to birth control, for the 6 million Roman Catholics in Britain the advent of the oral contraception created a moral dilemma. The Church of Rome has always condemned "artificial" methods of contraception, though an encyclical letter published by Pope Pius IX in 1930 held that it was none the less lawful to regulate family size "for grave reasons" by using the rhythm technique described by Ogino and Knaus in 1929. Reliance on the calendar was later replaced by the temperature method, which is more accurate, and the prohibition of artificial contraception was restated by Pope Pius XII in 1951. The biological end of sexual intercourse was considered to be the initiation of new life, but the Roman Catholic Church held that the interposition of the dimension of time between the sperm and the ovum did not have the same disruptive effect on the act as space, occasioned by a sheath, cap, or diaphragm. [71] Thus when the contraceptive pill became available, its use was deemed unlawful except in case of gynaecological disease, since it rendered the woman temporarily sterile. In 1963 Pope John XXIII set up a commission consisting of theologians, physicians, and other experts, which was charged with the study of population, the family, and reproduction. The following year this body was enlarged by Pope Paul VI. Although after investigating the problem the majority of members of the commission were in favour of changing the position of the Roman Catholic Church in regard to birth control, its views were not accepted by Pope Paul VI, whose encyclical *Humanae Vitae* published in 1968 reaffirmed the traditional ban on artificial contraception. In Britain, with the advent of the Abortion Act in 1968, a number of priests who publicly opposed the Papal encyclical were disciplined and some were suspended, though the majority were later reinstated.

The encyclical produced fresh problems for some Roman Catholic doctors who had hoped that the ban on contraception might be relaxed. It was difficult to apply "safe period" contraception to the socially and medically unfortunate, to the unintelligent, and to those with limited education. The "safe period" has recently been shown to be more of a misnomer than ever, for studies of the menstrual cycles of 2300 American and Canadian women by F. T. Brayer of Georgetown University, Washington, D.C., have demonstrated that only 3 out of 10 women who menstruate can expect to use the rhythm method dependably as a technique of birth control.[72]

One way round the problem is for an oral contraceptive to be prescribed for some female disorder, such as irregular menstruation. This is permissible under the 1968 encyclical:

"The Church does not consider illicit the use of those therapeutic means truly necessary to cure disease of the organism, even if an impediment to procreation, which may be foreseen, should result therefrom, provided such impediment is not, for whatever motive, directly willed."

In Italy, the centre of the Roman Catholic Church, the birth rate has been unobtrusively declining; contraceptive methods are widely practised and it has been alleged that in many areas chemists (pharmacists), rather than cardinals, govern sexual morality.

The Popular Explosion

Despite the Papal encyclical it is becoming increasingly apparent that the principal danger the world now faces is over-population—"Noah's new flood" in the telling phrase employed in an article published in 1966 by (now Sir) Theodore Fox.[73] The problem was formally recognized by the United Nations 2 years later when, at an eighty-four-nation international conference convened to mark the twentieth anniversary of the Universal Declaration of Human Rights, a resolution drawing attention to the link between population growth and human rights was passed without a single dissenting vote. The resolution stated that it considered that couples had "a basic right to decide freely and responsibly on the number and spacing of their children and a right to adequate information and education in this respect". [74] Its success had been presaged by a Declaration on Population Growth and Human Dignity and Welfare which, on Human Rights Day 1967, had been communicated to the Secretary-General by the heads of states or prime ministers of thirty countries. The Declaration read as follows:

> The peace of the world is of paramount importance to the community of nations, and our governments are devoting their best efforts to improving the prospects for peace in this and succeeding generations. But another great problem threatens the world—a problem less visible but no less immediate. That is the problem of unplanned population growth.
>
> It took mankind all of recorded time until the middle of the last century to achieve a population of one billion. Yet it took less than a hundred years to add the second billion, and only thirty years to add the third. At today's rate of increase there will be four billion people by 1975 and nearly seven billion by the year 2000. This unprecedented increase presents us with a situation unique in human affairs and a problem that grows more urgent with each passing day.
>
> The numbers themselves are striking, but their implications are of far greater significance. Too rapid population growth seriously hampers efforts to raise living standards, to further education, to improve health and sanitation, to provide better housing and transportation, to forward cultural and recreational opportunities—and even in some countries to assure sufficient food. In short, the human aspiration, common to men everywhere, to live a better life is being frustrated and jeopardized.
>
> As heads of governments actively concerned with the population problem, we share these convictions:
>
> We believe that the population problem must be recognized as a principal element in long-range national planning if governments are to achieve their economic goals and fulfil the aspirations of their people.
>
> We believe that the great majority of parents desire to have the knowledge and the means to plan their families; that the opportunity to decide the number and spacing of children is a basic human right.
>
> We believe that lasting and meaningful peace will depend to a considerable measure upon how the challenge of population growth is met.
>
> We believe that the objective of family planning is the enrichment of human life, not its restriction; that family planning, by assuring greater opportunity to each person, frees man to attain his individual dignity and reach his full potential.
>
> Recognizing that family planning is in the vital interest of both the nation and the family, we, the undersigned, earnestly hope that leaders around the world will share our views and join with us in this great challenge for the well being and happiness of people everywhere.

Contraception and the Medical Profession

Sir Theodore,[74] speaking as the first director of the new Family Planning Association at a conference held at the Royal College of Physicians in London in 1968, told leading educators from the United Kingdom and the United States that there were three reasons why the medical profession should be concerned with contraception. Firstly, the techniques most generally effective and acceptable required a doctor's assistance; secondly, since almost all infants now survived, contraception was an indispensable part of preventive medicine; and, thirdly, any good doctor should be profoundly concerned by a population explosion inside the family of which he was in medical charge. In regard to Sir Theodore's third point, the investigation carried out by Professor Baird[30] in the early 1960s showed that many families were larger than the parents desired or felt they could adequately care for, and an inquiry made by John Loudon[75] in 1968 indicated that the situation has not altered for the better. Of 82 pregnant women attending a Booking Ante-natal Clinic in Edinburgh over a 3-week period, only 42 had planned their pregnancies and only 47 had used contraception.

The medical profession's current awareness of the problems of birth control is, however, a comparatively recent development. John Peel and Malcolm Potts[76] have shown that prior to the First World War the profession had been opposed to contraception for upwards of 40 years. In 1798 the Reverend Thomas Malthus, in his famous essay on population, had set out the reasons for his belief that whilst the population was increasing geometrically—doubling in size every 25 years—supplies of food were only increasing arithmetically. As a result, Malthus thought, the excess of population was bound to outstrip the food supply unless its growth was curtailed. This was normally achieved, he believed, by "positive" checks—war, famine, and disease—but he also accepted that it could be affected by "preventive" methods—abstinence and the postponement of marriage. His ideas were neglected until 1877 when the extensive newspaper coverage of the Bradlaugh–Besant trial, which led to the reformation of the recently founded Malthusian League, made the British public aware of and interested in birth control, and began the era of commercial traffic in contraceptives. The medical profession, which had vigorously denounced contraception in 1869, continued to oppose it, though in 1880 a Medical and Scientific Branch of the Malthusian League was founded by two physicians, G. Drysdale and H. A. Albutt. The branch organized the first international conference on birth control in 1881, but it never managed to attract more than a small number of British physicians. In 1887 the cause of contraception was damaged when Albutt's name was erased from the Medical Register after he had been found guilty of publishing and offering for sale an "indecent" work, *The Wife's Handbook*, actually an innocuous manual of domestic hygiene, costing sixpence. In consequence, birth control did not become respectable to British physicians until 1913 and for years thereafter gained only lukewarm acceptance.

It is hardly surprising that the long-standing disinclination of the medical profession to involve itself in problems of sexuality and contraception was carried over into the teaching curricula of British medical schools, even though the recent unprecedented accumulation of knowledge in these areas could and should have been imparted to medical students. Thus the results of a survey of 1167 undergraduates with more than 20 months of clinical experience showed that whilst all but 3 per cent had had teaching in infertility, only between one-fifth and three-fifths had had teaching on normal psychosexual development, marital adjustment, and sexual difficulties, and less than three-fifths felt that their knowledge was adequate in any of these fields. One student commented, "The only teaching we have here on sex, marital adjustment, etc., is one lecture on the mating habits of cats", whilst another remarked, "It is ridiculous that the study of venereal disease is compulsory when the study of sexual relations is ignored."[77]

It seems likely that medical schools will now rectify this defect in their teaching programmes and that the medical profession as a whole will become more aware of the importance of sexuality and contraception. John Loudon,[75] discussing the training of family-planning workers, has considered the problems involved in educating doctors, nurses, and lay personnel, and in regard to the former has shown that the subject impinges on almost every speciality of medicine—oral contraceptives and thrombosis, which involves the physician; discontinuation of the pill prior to the surgeon's activities; oral contraceptives affecting the prescription of contact lenses by the ophthalmologist; the intra-uterine device presenting the radiologist with an unsuspected pelvic opacity; and contraceptive techniques proving important to the psychiatrist considering the aftermaths of termination of pregnancy.

Within the last 4 years, reports from several official medical bodies have called attention to the need for better family-planning facilities. In 1966 the report on Legalized Abortion by the Council of the Royal College of Obstetricians and Gynaecologists[8] observed that fewer than 10 per cent of users of contraceptives in Britain had had professional advice, and suggested that many potential users were unaware of the methods and facilities available. The Council strongly advocated that advice on and materials for contraception should be made available to all who sought them by means of hospital, general practitioner, and local authority services; and it thought that sterilization, in either sex, was of value in certain cases. The Royal Medico-Psychological Association's Memorandum on Therapeutic Abortion,[11] also published in 1966, was of the opinion that educational measures should be directed to ensure better family planning so that the requisite balance between young and old was preserved, and so that every child that was conceived was wanted. The sub-committee of the Medical Women's Federation on Abortion Law Reform,[54] which also published its memorandum in 1966, observed that many men and women had had no expert medical advice on sexual matters, including contraception and family planning. The committee thought that the tragedies of undesired and undesirable pregnancies could and should be reduced. Amongst the factors responsible for these, it deemed, were ignorance and prejudice about sex and sexual relationships, lack of responsible appreciation of the results of the sex act, inadequate contraceptive advice, and the limitations of contraceptive techniques. In 1968 the Chief Medical Officer of the Ministry of Health,[69] reporting on the state of the public health in 1967, pointed out that planned parenthood strengthened family life, whereas lack of planning, due to ignorance, led to marital disharmony, ill health, social breakdown, criminal abortion, and (occasionally) unnecessary death.

Family-planning Clinics

The history of family planning in Britain, as that of population control in general, has been well reviewed by Elizabeth Draper.[78] The first birth-control clinic in Britain—designed mainly for the guidance of the "working classes"—was founded in London by Marie Stopes and her husband in 1921. Six years later the Report of the Medical Committee of the National Birth Rate Commission, by emphasizing the lack of scientific knowledge of the efficiency of contraceptives and the need for accurate data, led to the establishment of the Birth Control Investigation Committee (BCIC). This analysed the work of the predominantly lay-inspired voluntary clinic movement, the most significant of which were the nine clinics affiliated to the Society for the Provision of Birth Control Clinics (SPBCC). In 1938 all the societies engaged in the movement, except that of Marie Stopes, amalgamated into one organization which was named the Family Planning Association. The Second World War imposed a temporary check on its activities, but by 1954 it had 400 clinics, and the following year it achieved "respectability" when it was visited by the Minister of Health. The Association, though employing doctors and nurses, remained largely voluntary, and ran most of its clinics with help from local authorities. To assist in the task, in June 1967 the National Health Service (Family Planning) Act, which secured the provision by local health authorities of services in connection with contraception, came into operation. A year later, Edwin Brooks, the then Member of Parliament who had sponsored the Act, castigated local authorities for their timorousness in implementing it. He reported that of 204 local authorities in England and Wales only 49 (about 25%) were providing a full service and 117 (more than 50%) were restricting the services they provided to married women, to those too poor to pay, and to those in whom contraception was necessary for health reasons.[79] None the less, by July 1968, 810 clinics had been opened, and 77,595 new patients were examined in 1967-8. The work of the second-oldest local authority family-planning service in Britain—that of Aberdeen—has been well described by MacQueen.[80]

In Britain generally, staffing the family-planning clinics has sometimes been difficult, for medical practitioners—because of their inadequate training in sexual problems and contraception and because of the traditional orientation to which reference has earlier been made—have seldom been enthusiastic about the work. The Committee of the London Society of Family Planning Doctors pointed out in 1967 that specialized postgraduate teaching was necessary for doctors advising on contraception, particularly for those working with young unmarried people.

Despite these problems, family doctors have long been employed in the clinics and have found the work rewarding. In an interesting article Mary Peberdy[81] has pointed out that different approaches are required by the different persons catered for by a family-planning clinic. For example, the sophisticated young unmarried girl from professional parents, after weighing the risks, often takes an oral contraceptive, whereas her less-sophisticated teenage factory counterpart, scared by reading the Sunday newspapers, will not do so. Again, after childbirth, the wife of a skilled worker usually takes contraceptive precautions, whilst the unskilled labourer's wife fails to observe them and often rapidly becomes reimpregnated with an unwanted child. The unsophisticated mother with three or four children frequently wants to be sterilized, but in the more sophisticated marriage the husband will sometimes

SEXUALITY AND CONTRACEPTION 47

elect to undergo vasectomy. Understanding, tact, and competence are necessary to cater for such disparate needs, especially with the variety of newer contraceptive techniques now available—the pill, intra-uterine devices, and vasectomy. Another family-planning doctor, Alexandra Tobert,[82] has pertinently emphasized that in every *post-partum* patient, in every country, a discussion on contraception is necessary. This has long been recognized by some gynaecologists who have advocated family-planning advice after abortion as well as after pregnancy.[83] Because of the wide range of contraceptive techniques now available, hospital-based contraceptive clinics, starting perhaps with a nucleus of post-abortion and *post-partum* cases, have much to recommend them.[84]

Contraceptive Methods

As so many methods of birth control are currently available it is necessary to be able to compare them in terms of efficiency as well as by other criteria. The "use-effectiveness" of a contraceptive method is defined in terms of its capacity to prevent unwanted pregnancies, the latter being expressed as the failure rate per hundred women years of exposure, abbreviated to HWY.[76] Apart from continence and the safe period, the most widely used method of contraception, especially amongst social classes IV and V, is coitus interruptus. This, like the safe period when assessed by the temperature method, has a failure rate of about eight per HWY, and so is not as ineffective as is generally believed; in a proportion of families, coitus interruptus is said to be regarded as the normal mode of sexual intercourse.[76] Next in frequency of use is the male contraceptive sheath or condom, first described by Fallopio in 1564, and originally devised to protect the wearer from venereal infection; early condoms were made from the caeca of sheep and other animals, but the modern latex sheath, which has a failure rate of about three per HWY, dates from the early 1930s. Chemical contraceptives, which act as spermicides and as physical barriers to impregnation, are also widely employed; with a failure rate of five or more per HWY they are much more effective when used in conjunction with a sheath or with female occlusive devices. The commonest of these is the vaginal diaphragm or "Dutch cap", which initially has to be fitted by a doctor or a trained nurse; cervical caps are now seldom used. In recent years three further methods of contraception have become popular— oral contraceptives, intra-uterine devices (IUDs), and sterilization. Only the first, which is virtually 100 per cent effective if "combined" contraceptive "pills" are taken, is really "new". The rate of failure with most IUDs is two to three per HWY, and whilst sterilization is virtually 100 per cent effective, it differs from other methods in being usually irreversible.

ORAL CONTRACEPTIVES: THE PILL

Many women who attend family-planning clinics—and many who do not—prefer oral contraceptives because of their aesthetic acceptability and efficacy. Forty-four per cent of the 77,595 new patients who attended British family-planning clinics in 1967-8 chose or were prescribed the pill. In all, over a million of the 11 million women of child-bearing age in Britain were ingesting oral contraceptives in 1968, and probably half a million more were taking them in 1965. The pill, as Sir Dugald Baird[66] has pointed out, has "released women from the tyranny of excessive fertility".

The history of the development of oral contraceptives has been outlined by Peel and Potts.[76] Oestrogen and progesterone, the two female sex hormones, were isolated in the 1930s, and later in the same decade Russel Marker synthesized progesterone from plants. In 1956 the Syntex Corporation patented norethisterone (norethindrone in the United States), a potent oral progestational agent. Early trials demonstrated that it was an effective contraceptive, but the occurrence of "break-through" bleeding due to shedding of the endometrium at irregular times during the menstrual cycle necessitated the addition of an oestrogen. In 1957 another progestogen, norethynodrel, was combined with mestranol, and was marketed by Searle as an oral contraceptive, Enovid. Two years later, Enovid was in widespread use in the United States, and in 1960 it was approved by the Family Planning Association of Great Britain. In 1963 Goldzieher and his associates introduced the sequential or "second generation" oral contraceptive, in which oestrogen is given alone for the first 14-16 days of the cycle, followed by a combination of oestrogen and progestogen, terminated by a final period without tablets or on placebo. Finally, in 1967, Martin-Manautau and his colleagues reported success with chlormadinone acetate, another Syntex product, the so-called "third generation" progestogen-only oral contraceptive, which was given in low daily doses throughout the cycle (the mini-pill).

Oral contraceptives act by inhibiting ovulation (probably by depressing pituitary gonadotropins), by altering the character of the cervical mucus, by interfering with the tubal transport of the ovum, and by rendering the endometrium less able to accept implantation. When taken conscientiously, the failure rate—especially in non-sequential preparations—is infinitesimal (0.028 per HWY among 14,840 women over 116,000 cycles). Useful side-effects include relief of dysmenorrhoea, reduction of premenstrual tension, regularization of menstruation, relief of acne, reduction of hirsuties, alleviation of mid-cycle pain, alteration of libido, and an enhanced sense of well-being. Troublesome side-effects include weight gain, breast discomfort, headache, migraine, alopecia, hypertrophic gingivitis, corneal oedema, and vaginal discharge. Choosing the pill with the most appropriate proportions of oestrogen and progestogen for the individual patient is important for, in addition to the side-effects listed above, quite severe depression can be produced, especially by long-term use of pills with a high progestogen content; this may be related to their capacity to produce a functional deficiency of pyridoxine and so a derangement of tryptophan metabolism.[85] The most serious side-effects, however, are thromboembolic phenomena (deep vein thrombosis, pulmonary embolism, and cerebral thrombosis), jaundice, and hypertension. The incidence of thromboembolic phenomena at 0.5 per 1000 for married women using oral contraceptives, according to Vessey and Doll,[86] is appreciably higher than the 0.06 per 1000 incidence in those who are not taking them, but in the women included in their study, after allowing for age and height, the pill-takers were on average 10 lb. heavier than the controls. Fears that using the pill might lead to carcinoma of the cervix aroused by the study performed by Melamed et al.[87]—which showed that in New York the prevalence rates of cervical carcinoma *in situ* were slightly higher in pill-takers than in diaphragm-users—have not been substantiated, and the study and its conclusions have been extensively criticized.[88] Further, although misgivings have recently been expressed by gynaecologists and others, there is no evidence that fertility is adversely affected by taking oral contraceptives.[76] Finally, despite widely and incautiously reported fears of the harmful effects of the pill, Peel and Potts insist that it is currently the safest and most effective birth-control agent available. A woman who decides to take the pill is likelier to be alive at the end of the year than her sister who chose to have a baby or who selected an alternative method of contraception; or—to put the risk another way—one cigarette is three times as dangerous to life as one contraceptive pill.[76]

INTRA-UTERINE DEVICES (IUDs)

The medical precursor of the contemporary intra-uterine device was probably the stem pessary, introduced for the management of retroversion of the uterus and described in the *Lancet* as long ago as 1868.[76] In bygone years some women apparently used stem pessaries for contraception, but the first IUDs to come into general use for contraception were the 18 mm diameter coiled silver rings advocated in the 1920s by Grafenberg in Germany and Haire in the United Kingdom. Inserted through the dilated cervix without anaesthesia, the Grafenberg ring frequently led to infection, with pelvic inflammation, endometritis, septicaemia, and peritonitis; by the mid-1930s this type of complication had led to its general abandonment in Europe. In Japan after the Second World War the population explosion, which was only in part controlled by legalizing abortion, led to research on contraception and to the development of IUDs made of nylon and polythene. The results attracted American attention in the late 1950s, and between 1959 and 1962 the American Population Council provided $1½ million to support the work. In 1967, 14 per cent of women attending British family-planning clinics were provided with IUDs.

The mode of action of these devices is unknown, for ovulation and fertilization still apparently occur with IUDs *in situ*; it may be that in some way they render the uterine environment hostile to the fertilized ovum. Three types of IUD are commonly used in Britain: the Lippes loop, the Margulies spiral, and the Birnberg bow.[89] The large loops have a low failure rate (2.5 per HWY) and acceptable expulsion and removal rates (21.9% and 13.6% in one year), whilst the large spirals, which have still lower failure rates (1.6 per HWY), have higher expulsion and removal rates (25.2% and 26.6% in one year). The large bows have higher failure rates (5.3 per HWY) but extremely low expulsion rates (2.4%) combined with higher removal rates (16.5% in one year).[76]

Because of the difficulty of inserting these devices they are contra-indicated in nulliparous women, in unmarried mothers, and in patients with salpingitis and menorrhagia, but they are useful in grand multipara, in cases of oral contraceptive failure, and in women with social problems. Shock at the time of insertion sometimes occurs, as also, especially if the device is inserted during the puerperium, perforation of the uterus. Death is very occasionally associated with IUDs: the results of a questionnaire circulated to over 8000 Fellows of the American College of Obstetricians and Gynaecologists suggested that 8 out of 10 deaths reported in women who were wearing IUDs were associated with the devices over a total woman-year usage of, perhaps, 1–2 million. Much commoner complications include menorrhagia, especially in the first few months after insertion, dysmenorrhoea, between-period pains, expulsion, infection, and perforation. Though at first sight numerous, these complications are not severe or significantly disabling in the vast majority of IUD-users followed up throughout the world.[90] It is advisable for women with IUDs to be examined one month after insertion and yearly thereafter; the devices should probably be changed every 2 or 3 years or when the need arises.[89] Following removal of an IUD, fertility is high—1 in 3 women became pregnant in the next cycle, three-quarters are pregnant in 6 months, and 9 out of 10 in the first year.[76]

STERILIZATION

Sterilization is the final and most irrevocable method of contraception, and though it has been carried out most frequently in women, it is now being increasingly employed in men. As late as 1960 it was widely believed that it was illegal to sterilize a person of either sex in Britain unless there was a clear indication that failure to do so would seriously endanger physical or mental health.[91] Opinion has now changed, and with the passage into law of the Abortion Act, sterilization is being performed more liberally, though it is still possible for patients to sue successfully if they are sterilized against their wishes—one 40-year-old woman who was sterilized without her consent after having her third child by Caesarean section was recently awarded £750.[92]

The first surgical sterilization was carried out in 1897 in the United States, but initially the operation was performed for eugenic reasons. Similar considerations—prevention of transmission of hereditary disease—were expressed in the Report of the 1934 British Departmental Committee on Sterilization. During the Second World War the widespread practice of sterilization in Nazi Germany brought it into disrepute, but in the last decade voluntary sterilization has gained in popularity. In Great Britain today some 20,000 tubal ligations are performed annually, and it is estimated that by 1968 some 4000 vasectomies had been carried out. The latter figure is still far below the 50,000 or more vasectomies that are performed each year in the United States.[76]

Grounds for sterilization include: (a) eugenic—in mental defectives, some mentally ill individuals, and those with hereditary disorders; (b) therapeutic—predominantly in women whose health would suffer from further pregnancies; (c) socio-economic—where contraception is impractical or unreliable, so that unwanted children would otherwise be born which would adversely affect the health of the mother or the other members of the family; and (d) convenience—all reasons other than the first three, vasectomy being quite frequently employed. [91]

In women the commonest methods of sterilization comprise tubal ligation, tubal excision, and total salpingectomy, all of which usually involve an intra-abdominal operation under general anaesthesia. Performed by the Pomeroy or Madelener technique, tubal ligation is the commonest method used but lacks some of the advantages of the more complex and sophisticated operations. The procedure can readily be carried out after a Caesarean section—many surgeons offer it at the third or subsequent Caesarean operation—or after hysterotomy; it can also readily be performed after a delivery. Other methods include laparoscopic sterilization, hysterectomy, and irradiation. Laparoscopic sterilization, developed by H. Fragenheim in Germany and R. Palmer in France, was introduced into England by P. C. Steptoe, who in 1969 reported that it could be combined with aspiration termination, required only a short time in hospital, and could be done on day patients. [6] Hysterectomy produces sterility but some Roman Catholic gynaecologists may possibly perform it more frequently in Catholic patients then is strictly justifiable since they feel that the removal of a "diseased" organ is ethically more acceptable than unequivocal sterilization by simpler methods. Irradiation with X-Rays or radio-active substances also produce sterility but has many adverse effects and carries the risk of malignancy; it has no place in contraception. [76]

After tubal ligations and excisions, death, like infection, is extremely rare, and the ovarian cycle, menstruation, and the incidence of gynaecological disease are unaffected. The good results that followed the sterilization of female patients in Aberdeen by Professor Baird and his colleagues have already been mentioned. [30] More recently, ascertaining gynaecological attitudes and practices, Blacker and Peel[93] sent questionnaires to 1401 Fellows and Members of the Royal College of Obstetricians and Gynaecologists resident in the United Kingdom. The replies they received showed that very few gynaecologists were deterred from sterilizing women by legal fears or moral scruples when they felt the operation was indicated. In conjunction with this investigation a questionnaire was sent to fifty-nine hospitals; this showed that practices varied throughout Great Britain and revealed that the commonest indications for sterilization were domestic and family problems (48.7%), repeated Caesarean sections or termination of pregnancy (27.7%), physical disease or defect (16%), and psychiatric disabilities (7%). These last can be increased by sterilization, especially in predisposed women, and it is generally accepted that no patient—female or male—should be coerced or cajoled into sterilization by spouse or by doctor. Whilst after the operation some women state that their sex life is better, others are dissatisfied and express regret, sometimes tending to attribute all subsequent setbacks to sterilization. In some women a tendency to overprotect their children becomes manifest, accompanied by backache, dysmenorrhoea, and other gynaecological discomforts. The failure rate of tubal ligation by the Pomeroy and Madelener techniques is 0.4 per cent and 1.4 per cent respectively. In the small number of women who regret having been sterilized and want more babies, Williams [94] and others have shown that reversal is possible by reconstruction of the ovarian tube involving either tubo-ovarian implantation or end-to-end anastamosis.

In the male, vasectomy, a quick, simple, permanent operation which can be carried out under local anaesthesia as an out-patient, has many advantages and fewer drawbacks than most other forms of contraception.[95, 96] The medical defence organizations were advised in 1960 that male sterilization was not illegal and soon afterwards its use in suitable cases began to be advocated by the Simon Population Trust.[91] H. G. Hanley[97] has outlined the technique, morbidity, and long-term results of vasectomy, and has stressed the importance of discussing the operation with patients beforehand; he advocates the operation be restricted to those who are happily married and already have a family. Husband and wife should sign a prior written consent form, witnessed in each other's presence, and should be warned that the male may not be sterile until several months after the operation. In Philip Alderman's[98] series of 2000 vasectomies there was a failure rate of 0.68 per cent, and 20 per cent of men had a positive sperm count at 3 months: a more radical resection of the vas under general anaesthesia can, in Paul Hickinbotham's[99] experience, reduce the failure rate, which is probably due to leakage of sperms across too small a gap. Most authorities agree that vasectomy has a negligible effect on the testes, has no endocrine side-effects, and is free from complications other than occasional psychiatric sequelae.[76, 95, 96] The majority of men operated on are pleased they have had it done.[95, 96] Should they change their minds and desire to regain their fertility the divided vas can be reconstructed even after as long a period as 16 years,[95] so that the fantasied castration the operation represents to some is symbolic rather than real.

Reviewing the present status of sterilization, Peel and Potts [76] have pointed out that for most people it comes too late in reproductive life. They feel that in the female the risks of sterilization (unless the abdomen is opened for another purpose) and of taking oral contraceptives are approximately evenly balanced. If a couple considered its family complete they might, Peel and Potts believe, consider oral contraceptives for 1 or 2 years as a precursor to sterilization. Since a high proportion of babies die within the first 24 hours after birth, *post-partum* sterilization should not be performed for a day or so; infants become much more secure members of the family after the first few months. Male sterilization, whilst not immediately effective, is simple and safe; in some cases it can if necessary be reversed.

The Future of Contraception

Newer forms of contraception that will circumvent the risks and disadvantages of existing methods are constantly being sought. In Hungary the use of C-film, a thin water-soluble film 4 cm square which contains a highly active non-toxic spermicide, has started, and is reported to have been successfully employed by over 100,000 couples. The film is sold in folders of 10 and can be inexpensively mass-produced. In use, a square is placed over the wetted glans penis or into the vagina immediately prior to intercourse or up to 3 hours before it. The film dissolves rapidly and by rendering the cervical mucus impenetrable to spermatozoa, affords time for the contained spermicide to be effective; further, the jelly-like solution does not run out of the vagina, so that women can stand and walk about after inserting it.[100] In the United States a different approach has led on a smaller scale to experiments with vaginal rings impregnated with progesterone, or alternatively to the use of IUDs with capsules containing this hormone attached to them.[101] Such methods, though promising, are but limited advances, and the investigations continue.

Future research on contraceptive methods, Peel and Potts[76] observe, have, for the female, centred on hormones and drugs which affect the hypothalamus and pituitary, agents which block the action of pituitary gonadotropins at "target organ" level, post-coital pills, and abortifacients. In the male, chemical methods of reducing sperm production and maturation are being sought, and the possibility of employing immunizing techniques has become apparent. However, much remains to be done, and as the two authors have observed, whatever success is achieved, sociological issues will probably crucially affect its application.

CHAPTER 4

Unwanted Pregnancies and Therapeutic Abortions

THE consequences of an unwanted pregnancy can be conveniently considered in terms of its effect on the mother and on the child. The effects are in the main adverse to both. They contrast strikingly with the results of therapeutic abortion, which are usually excellent, especially when the abortion is performed early in pregnancy.

Maternal Consequences of Unwanted Pregnancies

Whilst single women with unwanted pregnancies have always had a difficult time in Western society, an increasing proportion today are teenagers pregnant as a result of deficient chaperonage, loosened restraints, lack of foresight, inability to obtain contraceptive advice, and a mistaken idea that pregnancy will strenthen their relationship with their sexual partner. The much-prized but precarious independence of the working girl is based partly on her capacity to support herself, and partly on the emotional support she receives from the man involved, both of which may be imperilled by pregnancy. Once she has become pregnant the man, to her consternation, frequently "doesn't want to know", so that she may be compelled to turn for help to parents or other relatives whose sympathies her behaviour has alienated. Being betrayed and rejected by the man responsible for her condition is a bitter blow at an especially difficult time.

For the majority of women, a recent study has shown, much depends on the attitude of the father of the child and on her experience in previous pregnancies.[102] Rejection by the father, or by society as a whole, creates great difficulty, especially if the woman is single, deserted, widowed, or bearing a child her husband or sexual partner does not want. Again, the experience of having had a previous child who is defective or severely disturbed is a factor preventing the acceptance of pregnancy by some women. The woman's age, maturity, socio-economic position, marital status, and psychic constitution are of great importance. The additional burden that an unwanted pregnancy can constitute in a "worn-out" housewife has long been recognized: the pregnancy may be the "final straw" leading to decompensation in the mother's health, with a resultant inability to provide adequate love and care for her husband and other children. For a single woman especially, to the hazards normally accompanying pregnancy may be added financial stress, through loss of her own earnings or loss of financial support, which may result in lack of shelter or food; in addition, guilt and distress through rejection by relatives frequently develop, coupled with concern about her future. Undecided whether or not to complete the pregnancy, the woman may be torn by conflict between her emotional needs which urge her to continue it, on the one hand, and a desire to escape from an intolerable situation, on the other.

Once the pregnancy has begun, its inexorable advance affords little time to solve these problems. Frequently, there is no one in whom a single woman feels it possible to confide. Her sexual partner may be immature, ill-informed, antagonistic, or absent; guilt, fear of rejection, loss of face, and a wish to spare her parents the embarrassment of her plight may prevent her from talking to them; and she may be afraid to consult her family doctor for fear that he will inform her mother and father. It is paradoxical that at this late stage the girl's mother's inhibitions, which may have earlier prevented her from giving adequate sexual instruction to her daughter, can still debar her from being asked for help in a situation to which they have critically contributed. Isolated and distressed, hoping vainly she is not pregnant after all, the woman may handle the situation by mechanisms of denial and non-realization, losing valuable time in seeking the professional help for which, in any case, she may not know where to look. But despite the distress and obloquy suffered by single women who become pregnant, some are probably impelled to pregnancy by a deep biological urge, an unconscious need, to occupy the pregnant role. This is evident in the "carelessness" of some intelligent women towards contraception: asserting that they wish to avoid pregnancy, they nevertheless behave in such a manner as to make the contingency extremely likely—a phenomenon which, as Leontine Young has pointed out, may be due to unconscious self-prescribing of a pregnancy as a solution to emotional problems.[33]

A depressive state with anxiety is much the commonest response to an unwanted pregnancy; the symptoms may be severe and, as in all depressive illnesses, there is a risk of suicide. Sim[34] asserted that suicide was less of a risk in pregnant women than in non-pregnant women, implying that pregnancy tended to "protect" women from committing self-destructive acts. Whether or not this is so is of considerable practical importance, for the danger of suicide should an unwanted pregnancy not be interrupted has been remarked by general practitioners[52] as well as by psychiatrists,[39, 40] who formerly frequently justified their recommendations for therapeutic abortion by citing this danger. Despite the views expressed by Sim, experience teaches that suicide in pregnancy does occur; the relevant issue is not to question its existence but to ascertain its frequency and the gravity of the risk to which the woman with an unwanted pregnancy is exposed. In this connection Burke[103] has reported that 7 (12%) of 58 females in the reproductive age range admitted to a group of northern English hospitals in a 4-week period following the ingestion of poison in suicidal attempts were pregnant; most were young, unmarried, and in the first 4 months of pregnancy. Whitlock and Edwards[104] in an Australian study, compared 30 women who made suicidal attempts during pregnancy with 453 women who were not pregnant at the time of their suicidal attempts. Pointing out that at any time about 7 per cent of the female population were pregnant, and that approximately 7 per cent of women who attempt suicide were pregnant, the two authors concluded that pregnancy afforded little "protection" against suicide, and since it did not appear to be the sole, or even the most important, cause of suicide, therapeutic termination would not necessarily deter the patient from making a suicidal attempt. Clearly, therefore, with regard to the possibility of suicide, every woman with an unwanted pregnancy has to be assessed on her individual merits.

The dangers and complications of a criminal abortion have been outlined in Chapter 1. The experience, which has been described in detail by many writers, is clearly unpleasant and anxiety provoking.[1, 2, 105] Should an abortion be impossible to obtain, the continuance of her pregnancy is likely to become increasingly difficult for the woman, especially if she is single, abandoned, separated from her sexual partner, or lacking in financial and emotional support. For the adolescent, continuation of pregnancy may mean leaving school or losing a university career; for women who earn their living, e.g. in the nursing or teaching professions, their condition may lead to dismissal, loss of face, and rejection by relatives, colleagues, and friends. But despite all this, before the birth of her baby, a woman with an unwanted pregnancy can fare marginally better than an unmarried mother with a child, for in England and Wales there are 172 mother and baby homes catering for the weeks round confinement, three-quarters of which are provided by religious organizations. In addition, the National Council for the Unmarried Mother and her Child, founded in 1918 but still pitifully underbudgeted with £5000 per annum from the Government, has some 700 families on its books with whom women can reside during their pregnancies. However, the prospective mother's stay in hospital may be embarrassing and humiliating, and after her baby is born she may be in conflict between the desire not to see or keep it (as a precursor to its adoption) and the wish to bring it up herself.

Official recognition of the problem of unmarried mothers and their children in Britain began in 1918 when the Child Welfare Act became law. At that time, the death rate in illegitimate infants was double that in their legitimate counterparts, but the position has now improved markedly. The size of the problem of illegitimacy is hard to assess, for some conceptions end in abortion, and, whilst others go to term, the parents marry. In England and Wales the number of illegitimate maternities has steadily increased: 31,649 in 1955; 55,376 in 1962; 63,340 in 1964 and 67,056 in 1966. *Pari passu* the number of illegitimate live births has also increased: 31,145 in 1955; 55,376 in 1962; 63,340 in 1964 and 67,056 in 1966. Since 1955 the proportion of illegitimate live births to total live births has risen by just over one-half.[69] In 1967, of the 832,164 live babies born in England and Wales, 69,928 were illegitimate.[65] Some 3167 were put into institutions and 18,313 were adopted, leaving the remainder—more than two-thirds—to be brought up fatherless by their unmarried mothers.[106]

In the latter case, life can be extremely difficult for both mother and child despite the activities of the National Council, which believes that the single woman is the "worst fed, the worst housed, and the worst off financially" of all unsupported mothers. As Joanna Slaughter[107] has pointed out, pressures on the mother to have the baby adopted soon became enormous. Poverty is the greatest single problem; next is accommodation.[108] Without money it is hard to find somewhere to live, and because of the shortage of day nurseries—there were 448 in 1966 in England and Wales with less than 22,000 places, in contrast to 1431 day nurseries in 1945 with accommodation for 70,000 children[109]—it may be impossible for the mother to leave her baby so as to go to work. Even with money, accommodation can be hard to secure: most advertisements state "no pets, no children", and until the woman has a permanent address no (governmental) supplementary financial benefits are payable. Even the term "unmarried mother" implies that the new mother is singled out for unfriendliness and rejection, if not actual hostility from others. Officials tend to regard her as "a statistic", and by being made to feel foolish, she frequently becomes bitter and socially isolated. The need, single-handed, to give her baby the love that two adults would normally provide, and the lack of a husband in whom to confide and with whom to discuss and share her problems, make her position particularly difficult, especially if she has no secure home in which to rear the child, whom she may fear will resent her in later life because of the circumstances of the birth. At the present time there are about 70,000 unmarried mothers in England and Wales who, Joanna Slaughter observes, "are coping with the problems of not enough money, not enough accommodation, and a society, if not overtly punitive, ill prepared to afford them public tolerance and insufficiently appreciative of the enormous difficulties they face".

REFUSED TERMINATIONS

What happens to those women who seek termination of pregnancy and who are refused or fail to secure it? In a Swedish study made possible by the liberalization of the Swedish law on abortion, Aren and Amark[110] followed up 195 women who 3 years earlier had been approved for legal abortion but did not have it performed (only 21% had been approved on psychiatric grounds). Twenty-one per cent of these women were in a worse psychiatric state after delivery, but only 11 per cent were thought to be worse because they had not been aborted. In another Swedish investigation, Kerstin Hook[111] studied 294 women 7 years after they had been refused abortions; 70 per cent had intended to have illegal abortions, and whilst 18 per cent had been unsuccessful, 11 per cent had succeeded in this. The 40 per cent who had sought abortions for psychiatric reasons had four times as many psychiatric complications as the others. In all, 29 per cent of Hook's cases showed significant psychiatric sequelae; 16 per cent needed therapeutic abortions in their next pregnancy; and 13 per cent required sterilization. Thirty-one per cent of those who completed their pregnancies were felt to be providing a poor environment for their child.

In London, Pare[112] followed up 118 patients 1–5 years after he had seen them to consider termination of pregnancy on psychiatric grounds. Of the 61 patients whom he had refused—22 of whom were single—23 (38%) had had an abortion in one way or another or, in 3 cases, had had a premature delivery and/or a stillbirth. Of the ones who continued the pregnancy, nine (16%) had had the baby fostered or adopted. Two-thirds of the patients who were married had accepted their babies and had been glad to have them; but amongst the patients who were single or were estranged from their husbands, only one-quarter had continued the pregnancy and had kept the baby. Furthermore, two patients (one married and one single) who had kept their babies developed serious and disabling neurotic symptoms as a result of the stress of looking after the child; and two others had died, one from suicide following a depression which relapsed after an illegal abortion, and one from status asthmaticus after a similar procedure. More recently, Clark et al.[45] in a second British study followed up 109 women referred for consideration of termination in whom the operation had not been advised. Although psychiatric help and support were made available, only half of these women went to full term, and of the 55 babies born only 39 were accepted. Thirty-eight of the women secured an abortion in one way or another, and the authors concluded "it seems that a determined, desperate woman will somehow abort".

Effects on the Child

Illegitimate children born as a result of an unwanted pregnancy have a higher infant mortality rate than legitimate babies (19 versus 15 per 1000) and begin life at a legal, social, and psychological disadvantage; it is likely that the unwanted children of married mothers are also handicapped to some extent. The gift of life is regarded by some religious authorities as outweighing any physical or mental disadvantage: yet, as John Bowlby[113] has shown, emotional deprivation in early life—lack of affection and emotional security—can have the most deleterious psychological consequences. Better, perhaps, not to be born than to come unwanted into a world where there is no assurance of affection.

INSTITUTIONALIZATION

Of the 70,000 illegitimate children born annually, those most likely to suffer severe emotional deprivation are the 3200 placed in institutions. Despite the devoted efforts of those working in them, lack of affectionate responsive parents or parent-figures is a great shortcoming. Frank Norman,[114] in his autobiography *Banana Boy*, provides a moving account of the hardships with which institutionalized children have to contend. Of course, a much larger number of children are in the care of the local authorities at any one

UNWANTED PREGNANCIES AND THERAPEUTIC ABORTIONS 61

time, but for the most part their situation is temporary. On 31 March 1968, 69,358 children were being cared for in this way in England and Wales, and whilst, as McGregor [115] observes, 59 per cent of children in care come from broken homes, between March 1967 and March 1968 26,495 of the 50,938 children taken into care were there as a result of the illnesses of their parents or guardians. [116] Studying the wide variation in the numbers of children in care in different regions, Jean Packman [117] found that in areas of maximum need (such as Tower Hamlets, London, which had 26.1 per 1000 children in care, in contrast to 1.8 per 1000 in Harrow) there was a rapid inflow of population, heavy pressure on housing, and a high illegitimacy rate; many families had no relatives nearby, and psychiatric illness and marital breakdown were major problems. Preventive services provided by local authorities, such as home helps, day nurseries, and accommodation for homeless families, could, however, offset the pattern.

ADOPTION

In 1967 some 18,313 illegitimate children were adopted, slightly more than a quarter of the total number that were born; the need for adoptors is still far from being met, especially for babies of mixed race and those which appear to be physically handicapped.[106, 118] In 1966, 40 per cent of the adoption applications to the courts in England and Wales were arranged by adoption societies, 17 per cent were made by local authorities, and 5 per cent by third parties. In 8 per cent of cases the adoptions were direct placements by a parent, and in the remaining 30 per cent one of the adoptors or the sole adoptor was a parent. In practice, under the 1958 Adoption Act, the child has to stay with its adoptive parents for a probationary period of at least 3 months before the final order is made. During this period, which starts after the child is 6 weeks old, the natural parents—even after signing consent to adoption—can demand the return of the child; but once the order is made they lose their parental rights.

In England, many children do not go directly from their natural mother to their adoptive parents: about 60 per cent of babies adopted through societies are briefly fostered out before being placed with adoptive parents. Two separations within a short period are thus their lot, and the insecurity that may be engendered can lead to problems later in life. Good foster-parents are hard to recruit and the supply is very limited; one obstacle that could be removed is the pitifully small financial allowance they secure for caring for what can be very difficult children. [119] Adoptive parents, who ultimately reap the emotional rewards of bringing up another's child as their own, also have to face a series of far from easy problems. Initially, they have to contend with the probationary period, during which the biological parents may demand the return of the child; then comes the problem of adjusting to their feelings for the child's natural parents and in some cases to their feelings in regard to their own childlessness; finally, there are doubts regarding their capacities as parents and anxiety regarding telling the child the circumstances of its birth. With suitable adoptive or foster-parents a child stands a good chance; but early insecurity, as already mentioned, may leave a lasting scar.

STAYING WITH MOTHER

For the many children who stay with their unmarried mothers, lack of a father and the difficulties which the mother may experience in regard to money and accommodation have already been mentioned.[108] Mother love is more vital still.[113] Whilst it is frequently taken for granted—sometimes the very difficulties that overshadowed the mother's pregnancy and pervade her current life seem to bring her closer to her child—it is by no means universal. A child conceived as a result of rape, an unhappy relationship, or a lapse from marital fidelity may never come to be loved and valued by its mother. If she lacks an example to follow—perhaps because her own mother was antagonistic or absent—if she is very immature, if the child thwarts her ambitions—for instance, in regard to a career—if it reactivates sibling rivalry problems, or if she is too unintelligent or too inadequate to cope with the situation, the mother may be unable or unwilling to give the child the love and security it needs.

Those children who are born unwanted into too-large families share in the financial deprivation and the generally reduced quality of life that often ensues. As McGregor[115] has pointed out, 70 per cent of delinquents come from families of five or more; in these circumstances the survival of an unwanted child may be contingent on its ability to be anti-social and to get away with it. Rejected by its environment, such a child may be isolated and insecure at school: neurotic symptoms or delinquency commonly develop. Research has borne this out: thus in Sweden, Forsmann and Thuwe[120] performed a 21-year follow-up study on 120 children born after abortion had been refused to their mothers and compared them with a group of controls. In the former group, a significantly higher incidence of anti-social behaviour was found, together with a higher incidence of delinquency, drunken misconduct, and subsistence on state-provided welfare. Michael Power, analysing the high delinquency rate in boys between 10 and 16 years of age from Tower Hamlets,

London—double that for England and Wales in general—found that for first offenders who reappeared in court, three-quarters of the boys came from disrupted families, and the family was as important as his other four factors—clinical assessment, school, delinquency, and group and neighbourhood—put together.[121] Again, W. R. Lyster has demonstrated that a year-by-year comparison of the annual illegitimacy rate in England and Wales with the total annual number of all indictable offences reported to the police reveals a correlation of the highest possible mathematical significance.[122] He surmised that an illegitimate birth created feelings of resentment in the father of the child which during the Second World War were vented on the enemy but which in present times can lead to crime. The teenage borthers of pregnant girls, disturbed by the general atmosphere of criticism, may also get rid of their resentment by delinquency and anti-social activities. Illegitimate and unwanted pregnancies, as well as causing unhappiness for mother and child, can thus produce diverse adverse social effects.

The Results of Therapeutic Termination

In contrast to the picture just portrayed, the results of therapeutic termination of pregnancy have in general been extremely encouraging. The topic has excited much interest in recent years, and Simon and Senturia,[123] White,[22] Kay and Schapira,[124] and others have reviewed the situation. It is unnecessary to repeat the substance of their reviews, but a few highlights merit consideration.

Studies in Scandinavia and North America

In Sweden the passage of the Abortion Act in 1938 enabled therapeutic termination of pregnancy to be performed on medical, medico-social, humanitarian, and eugenic grounds. The new law made it possible $2-4\frac{1}{2}$ years later for Martin Eckblad[125] to follow-up 479 women whose pregnancies were terminated in 1949 and 1950. His findings appeared in 1965; 65 per cent of the women he had studied were married and 27 per cent were single, the rest being divorced or widowed. Forty-two per cent had normal personalities, whilst those of the remaining 58 per cent were abnormal, being psychaesthenic, neurotic, dysphoric, sensitive, schizoid, or emotionally immature. Most of the women were aged between 26 and 30, and belonged to the middle class; 80 per cent had had only an elementary schooling. The three principal reasons for granting therapeutic abortions were: (i) the woman had had previous chronic psychiatric trouble and was felt to be living "at the limit of her resources"; (ii) she had been abandoned by her male partner; or (iii) the male partner was alcoholic or otherwise abnormal. The risk of illegal abortion or suicide, Eckblad thought, was greatest in the women who were in conflict with convention—especially those who had been deserted by their sexual partners. At follow-up, 25 per cent expressed self-reproach or regret over the operation, but these feelings were severe only in 11 per cent (6% of normal personalities and 15% of abnormal personalities), and of these few had consulted the doctor and only 5 (1%) of the 479 were unable to work. Four of the five had manifested severe neurotic symptoms long prior to the operation, and Eckblad felt that their symptoms were attributable to abandonment by the male partner rather than to the operation itself.

The generally favourable picture afforded by Eckblad's study has kept emerging in other series. In 1963 Kummer,[126] surveying the opinions of American and other psychiatrists from a study of the literature and from personal contact, concluded that post-abortion psychiatric illness was "a myth". Peck and Marcus,[127] who reported their findings in 1966, obtained excellent results at follow-up in fifty Jewish women aged between 17 and 41 whose pregnancies had been terminated 6 months earlier. White,[22] also writing in 1966, stated that he believed that the answers to two questions were crucial in regard to psychiatric complications. (i) What was the woman's motive in seeking an abortion, i.e. was she having it for valid reasons or was it being forced on her by emotional pressures? (ii) Was she able to obtain help from a sympathetic legitimate physician? In White's experience, psychiatric complications were rare; he listed them as follows: immediate guilt, which was not uncommon; delayed guilt, for which there was no evidence; impaired development of an adult personality with frigidity and sterility—he thought this seldom occurred; and the development of hatred towards the spouse or lover.

In 1967 Niswander and Patterson[128] reported the results of a questionnaire follow-up on 161 of 170 women over the age of 16 years whose pregnancies had been terminated in or near Buffalo, New York, in the years 1963, 1964, and 1965. One hundred and sixteen (87.9%) had returned the questionnaire completed, the shortest interval between operation and follow-up being 8 months. Ninety-five per cent of those responding were certain that termination had been the best answer; single girls aborted for psychiatric reasons had had the least doubts, and when pregnancy had been socially untenable, abortion had not been regretted. The few women who had had regrets were almost all married women aborted for medical reasons or those who had been pregnant in a socially acceptable milieu. Niswander and Patterson concluded: "... when the decision to abort is made ... the treatment is usually therapeutic in the best sense of the word. ...." Simon et al.[129] also published relevant findings in 1967; they found little new psychiatric illness related to the abortion in forty-six women aborted at the Jewish Hospital of St. Louis in the 10 years 1955–64. Sorrel,[130] who discussed the psychodynamic effects of abortion the same year, drew attention to the ambivalent attitudes many women have towards pregnancy, and the irrationality of American cultural attitudes which encouraged permissive dating, on the one hand, and deplored its consequences, on the other. With pregnancy, Sorrel pointed out, a woman became more emotionally dependent; and, since the child within her could represent her inclusion in her lover as well as an entity in itself, an abortion could signify the deterioration of a wanted love relationship. Psychically normal women appeared better able to tolerate the stress of an abortion; and, whilst an undesired pregnancy could precipitate a severe depression, post-operative depression and guilt might sometimes follow an abortion, the patient mistakenly believing that the operation had been responsible for her condition.

In one of the most recent American studies, reported in 1969, Patt et al.[131] commented on the marked differences of opinion that exist between psychiatrists and gynaecologists on many aspects of therapeutic abortion, not least of which are its after-effects. These three investigators followed up 35 of 48 patients who had had therapeutic abortions for psychiatric reasons at Michael Reese Hospital in Chicago between 1964 and 1968. By present-day standards the criteria employed had been extremely strict: a high possibility of suicide or of psychotic decompensation if abortion was not performed. Patt and his colleagues found that short-term results had been entirely favourable in twenty patients and that long-term results had also, on the whole, been quite favourable, three-quarters of the patients reporting subjective improvement. The investigation concluded that, with rare exceptions, abortion was "genuinely therapeutic".

Findings in the United Kingdom

British findings have been descirbed by Sir Dugald Baird, C. M. B. Pare, M. Clark *et al.*, and D. R. McCoy. Sir Dugald [30] reported in 1967 that in his experience as Professor of Gynaecology in Aberdeen a decline in the woman's emotional health after therapeutic termination was practically non-existent. He cited a student survey which showed that when guilt feelings were present they had usually been produced by the reception accorded the patient by cruel and unsympathetic doctors, or by the malicious gossip of neighbours. The same year, Pare,[112] a London psychiatrist, described uniformly good results in a follow-up of fifty-three patients terminated on his recommendation. Two Newcastle psychiatrists, Kay and Schapira,[124] who reviewed the literature in 1967, concluded: (i) the outcome after legal abortion is very good (considering the adverse circumstances that often exist) in 85 per cent of cases; (ii) some 10–15 per cent of women experience for a time rather severe self-reproaches or regrets, but with little actual disability; (iii) about 1–2 per cent suffer definite psychiatric illness not necessarily connected with the abortion; and (iv) when abortion is refused, the personality disorders and other unfavourable factors present in many cases render the outlook for future adjustment precarious both for the mother and for the child.

In 1968 Clark *et al.*,[45] writing from the Department of Psychological Medicine of University College Hospital, London, noted that they had advised termination of pregnancy on psychiatric grounds in 257 of the 426 women referred during 1961–7. Of the 120 women terminated who were followed-up, 108 by their own testimony were "wholeheartedly satisfied" and only 3 were dissatisfied; by the testimony of their general practitioners, 70 were improved, 39 were ultimately unchanged, and only 1 was worse. McCoy,[132] however, a gynaecologist who in 1968 also published the results of a follow-up study, struck a discordant note. He reported on 68 patients whose pregnancies had been terminated at the Grosvenor Hospital, London, in 1965 and 1966, 42 of whom (62%) had been sterilized. He sought "to identify those patients who, on their own analysis of the situation, regretted the operation". Indications for termination in ascending order of frequency were medical, social, social and psychiatric, and psychiatric. Termination was performed vaginally in nineteen cases, by amniotic saline injection in one case, and by abdominal hysterotomy in forty-eight patients (thirty-nine of whom were sterilized). Thirteen women tried to procure an abortion during the course of their assessment for termination, and twenty-nine (42%) threatened to commit suicide. Subsequently, 73 per cent of patients were satisfied with the results of the operation, but 27 per cent expressed long-term regrets and these were "bitter" in nine. When pregnancy was socially untenable, however, abortion was seldom regretted. Whilst clear cut, McCoy's findings are not representative of the majority of legal abortions carried out today. Unlike the patients in his sample, most women now undergoing terminations have them performed on psychiatric gounds, are operated on in the first trimester of their pregnancy, do not undergo hysterotomy, and are not sterilized. Accordingly, McCoy's results should, the author feels, be interpreted with considerable reserve.

Effect on Criminal Abortion Rates

Finally, what effect does the availability of legal termination of pregnancy have on the incidence of criminal abortion? It is still too early to answer this question as far as the United Kingdom is concerned, but figures from other countries in Europe are of interest. In eastern Europe abortion has been legalized for over a decade—the operation was made legal in Russia in 1955; in Bulgaria, Hungary, Poland, and Romania in 1956; in Czechoslovakia in 1957; and in Yugoslavia in 1960. In all these countries, Professor Mehland[133] has observed, the significant increases that have occurred in legal abortions have been associated with a considerable reduction in criminal abortions and a decline in the birth rate. There has also been a clear decline in deaths due to abortion—the rate is of the order of 6 per 100,000 cases— and the risk of the operation has been shown to be less than that of a normal birth and of other operations regarded as harmless. Secondary sterility has not exceeded 5 per cent. In Czechoslovakia in particular, where a widely permissive law on abortion, coupled with severe penalties for clandestine surgery, has been in effect for 11 years, illegal termination is claimed to have been eliminated. Between 1958 and 1967, 723,833 legal abortions were performed there in comparison with some 2 million live births in the same period—a pregnancy interruption rate of the order of about one-third. Unfortunately, the new law, according to Havranek, has become "a drastic impediment to contraception", and few Czechoslovakian women take oral contraceptives or use intra-uterine devices.[134]

A recent study of the outcome of all pregnancies between 1950 and 1965, in the City and County of Stockholm, Sweden, carried out by Huldt[135] indicated, according to this author, that, despite the advent of legal abortion, the rate of criminal abortion had not decreased to any real extent. This conclusion was disputed by Rushton,[136] who criticized Huldt's method of lumping together criminal and spontaneous abortions, and suggested that Huldt's findings of a 2.8 per cent fall in the combined group rate might, in fact, represent a rather more high and significant decline in the rate of criminal abortions. Harrison,[137] on the other hand, believed that liberalization of the abortion laws simply increased the total number of abortions, and merely determined how many were to be called legal. Taking a rather different approach, Frederiksen and Brackett[138] have pointed out that Huldt's use of proportional pregnancy rates is inappropriate for this purpose, and they suggest that evidence to establish the nature and magnitude of the relationship between abortion and births should be based on incidence rates. Data from countries in which a substantial amount of contraception was already practised indicated, the two authors stated, that legalization of abortion reduced the effective practice of contraception rather than the birth rate. They concluded "substantial and simultaneous prevention of unwanted births as well as unwanted abortions await the prevention of unwanted pregnancies by couples attempting to regulate tempo and size of family formation".

The state of the law in regard to abortion has been reviewed for the world generally by Roemer,[139] for Europe by Tietze,[140] and for the United States by Schwartz.[141] In the latter country, many state legal codes on abortion have recently been changed or are under scrutiny: the position at the time of writing is dealt with in Chapter 12 (p. 219). Unfortunately, it seems evident that a proportion of women will continue to seek illegal abortion because of shame, reticence, or ignorance of their rights in the matter. Though education and better contraceptive methods superficially seem to be the answer, in view of the ambivalent attitudes towards pregnancy to which reference has earlier been made, these measures will probably never be entirely successful in preventing unwanted pregnancies.

CHAPTER 5

The Abortion Act

THIS Act became law in England, Wales, and Scotland on 27 April 1968. It is permissive only, creating exceptions to sections 58 and 59 of the Offences Against the Person Act 1861, to provide that no offence will be deemed to have occurred when a pregnancy is terminated in certain circumstances by a registered medical practitioner. Termination of pregnancy other than under the provisions of the Act is unlawful in England, Wales, and Scotland, and constitutes a criminal offence.

The wording of the Act, the regulations that became law when the Act became operative, and schedule 1—comprising certificate A, which must be completed before an abortion is performed under section 1(i) of the Act, and certificate B, which is completed when abortion is carried out as an emergency—are set out below. A copy of schedule 2—the form used to notify the Chief Medical Officer that abortion under section 1 of the Act has been performed—is shown in Appendix I (p. 275).

ABORTION ACT 1967

An Act to amend and clarify the law relating to termination of pregnancy by registered medical practitioners. [27th October 1967]

Medical termination of pregnancy

1.—(1) Subject to the provisions of this section, a person shall not be guilty of an offence under the law relating to abortion when a pregnancy is terminated by a registered medical practitioner if two registered medical practitioners are of the opinion, formed in good faith—

(a) that the continuance of the pregnancy would involve risk to the life of the pregnant woman, or of injury to the physical or mental health of the pregnant woman or any existing children of her family, greater than if the pregnancy were terminated; or

(b) that there is a substantial risk that if the child were born it would suffer from such physical or mental abnormalities as to be seriously handicapped.

(2) In determining whether the continuance of a pregnancy would involve such risk of injury to health as is mentioned in paragraph (a) of subsection (1) of this section, account may be taken of the pregnant woman's actual or reasonably foreseeable environment.

(3) Except as provided by subsection (4) of this section any treatment for the termination of pregnancy must be carried out in a hospital vested in the Minister of Health or the Secretary of State under the National Health Service Acts, or in a place for the time being approved for the purposes of this section by the said Minister or the Secretary of State.

(4) Subsection (3) of this section, and so much of subsection (1) as relates to the opinion of two registered medical practitioners, shall not apply to the termination of a pregnancy by a registered medical practitioner in a case where he is of the opinion, formed in good faith, that the termination is immediately necessary to save the life of or to prevent grave permanent injury to the physical or mental health of the pregnant woman.

Notification

2.—(1) The Minister of Health in respect of England and Wales, and the Secretary of State in respect of Scotland, shall by statutory instrument make regulations to provide—
- (a) for requiring any such opinion as is referred to in section 1 of this Act to be certified by the practitioners or practitioner concerned in such form and at such time as may be prescribed by the regulations, and for requiring the preservation and disposal of certificates made for the purposes of the regulations;
- (b) for requiring any registered medical practitioner who terminates a pregnancy to give notice of the termination and such other information relating to the termination as may be so prescribed;
- (c) for prohibiting the disclosure, except to such persons or for such purposes as may be so prescribed, of notices given or information furnished pursuant to the regulations.

(2) The information furnished in pursuance of regulations made by virtue of paragraph (b) in subsection (1) of this section shall be notified solely to the Chief Medical Officers of the Ministry of Health and the Scottish Home and Health Department respectively.

(3) Any person who wilfully contravenes or wilfully fails to comply with the requirements of regulations under subsection (1) of this section shall be liable on summary conviction to a fine not exceeding one hundred pounds.

(4) Any statutory instrument made by virtue of this section shall be subject to annulment in pursuance of a resolution of either House of Parliament.

Application of Act to visiting forces, etc.

3.—(1) In relation to the termination of a pregnancy in a case where the following conditions are satisfied, that is to say—
- (a) the treatment for termination of the pregnancy was carried out in a hospital controlled by the proper authorities of a body to which this section applies; and
- (b) the pregnant woman had at the time of the treatment a relevant association with that body; and

(c) the treatment was carried out by a registered medical practitioner or a person who at the time of the treatment was a member of that body appointed as a medical practitioner for that body by the proper authorities of that body, this Act shall have effect as if any reference in section 1 to a registered medical practitioner and to a hospital vested in a Minister under the National Health Service Acts included respectively a reference to such a person as is mentioned in paragraph (c) of this subsection and to a hospital controlled as aforesaid, and as if section 2 were omitted.

(2) The bodies to which this section applies are any force which is a visiting force within the meaning of any of the provisions of Part I of the Visiting Forces Act 1952 and any headquarters within the meaning of the Schedule to the International Headquarters and Defence Organisations Act 1964; and for the purposes of this section—

(a) a woman shall be treated as having a relevant association at any time with a body to which this section applies if at that time—
  (i) in the case of such a force as aforesaid, she had a relevant association within the meaning of the said Part I with the force; and
  (ii) in the case of such a headquarters as aforesaid, she was a member of the headquarters or a dependant within the meaning of the Schedule aforesaid of such a member; and

(b) any reference to a member of a body to which this section applies shall be construed—
  (i) in the case of such a force as aforesaid, as a reference to a member of or of a civilian component of that force within the meaning of the said Part I; and
  (ii) in the case of such a headquarters as aforesaid, as a reference to a member of that headquarters within the meaning of the Schedule aforesaid.

Conscientious objection to participation in treatment

4.—(1) Subject to subsection (2) of this section, no person shall be under any duty, whether by contract or by any statutory or other legal requirement, to participate in any treatment authorised by this Act to which he has a conscientious objection:

Provided that in any legal proceedings the burden of proof of conscientious objection shall rest on the person claiming to rely on it.

(2) Nothing in subsection (1) of this section shall affect any duty to participate in treatment which is necessary to save the life or to prevent grave permanent injury to the physical or mental health of a pregnant woman.

(3) In any proceedings before a court in Scotland, a statement on oath by any person to the effect that he has a conscientious objection to participating in any treatment authorised by this Act shall be sufficient evidence for the purpose of discharging the burden of proof imposed upon him by subsection (1) of this section.

Supplementary provisions 1929 c. 34

5.—(1) Nothing in this Act shall affect the provisions of the Infant Life (Preservation) Act 1929 (protecting the life of the viable foetus).

(2) For the purposes of the law relating to abortion, anything done with intent to procure the miscarriage of a woman is unlawfully done unless authorised by section 1 of this Act.

Interpretation

6. In this Act, the following expressions have meanings hereby assigned to them—

1861 c. 100

"the law relating to abortion" means sections 58 and 59 of the Offences against the Person Act 1861, and any rule of law relating to the procurement of abortion;

"The National Health Service Acts" means the National Health Service Acts 1946 to 1966 or the National Health Service (Scotland) Acts 1947 to 1966.

Short title, commencement and extent

7.—(1) This Act may be cited as the Abortion Act 1967.

(2) This Act shall come into force on the expiration of the period of six months beginning with the date on which it is passed.

(3) This Act does not extend to Northern Ireland.

THE ABORTION REGULATIONS 1968

Citation and commencement

1. These regulations may be cited as the Abortion Regulations 1968, and shall come into operation on 27th April 1968.

Interpretation

2.—(1) In these regulations "the Act" means the Abortion Act 1967 and "practitioner" means a registered medical practitioner.

(2) The Interpretation Act 1889 shall apply to the interpretation of these regulations as it applies to the interpretation of an Act of Parliament.

Certificate of opinion

3.—(1) Any opinion to which section 1 of the Act refers shall be certified in the appropriate form set out in Schedule 1 to these regulations.

(2) Any certificate of an opinion referred to in section 1(1) of the Act shall be given before the commencement of the treatment for the termination of the pregnancy to which it relates.

(3) Any certificate of an opinion referred to in section 1(4) of the Act shall be given before the commencement of the treatment for the termination of the pregnancy to which it relates or, if that is not reasonably practicable, not later than 24 hours after such termination.

(4) Any such certificate as is referred to in paragraphs (2) and (3) of this regulation shall be preserved by the practitioner who terminated the pregnancy to which it relates for a period of three years beginning with the date of such termination and may then be destroyed.

Notice of termination of pregnancy and information relating thereto

4.—(1) Any practitioner who terminates a pregnancy shall within 7 days of the termination give to the Chief Medical Officer of the Ministry of Health notice thereof and the other information relating to the termination in the form set out in Schedule 2 to these regulations.

(2) Any such notice and information shall be sent in a sealed envelope to the Chief Medical Officer, Ministry of Health, Alexander Fleming House, Elephant and Castle, London, S.E.1.

Restriction on disclosure of information

5. A notice given or any information furnished to the Chief Medical Officer in pursuance of these regulations shall not be disclosed except that disclosure may be made—
  (a) for the purposes of carrying out their duties,
     (i) to an officer of the Ministry of Health authorised by the Chief Medical Officer of that Ministry, or
     (ii) to the Registrar General or a member of his staff authorised by him; or
  (b) for the purposes of carrying out his duties in relation to offences against the Act or the law relating to abortion, to the Director of Public Prosecutions or a member of his staff authorised by him; or
  (c) for the purposes of investigating whether an offence has been committed against the Act or the law relating to abortion, to a police officer not below the rank of superintendent or a person authorised by him; or
  (d) for the purposes of criminal proceedings which have begun; or
  (e) for the purposes of bona fide scientific research; or
  (f) to the practitioner who terminated the pregnancy; or
  (g) to a practitioner, with the consent in writing of the woman whose pregnancy was terminated.

SCHEDULE 1

IN CONFIDENCE

Certificate A

Not to be destroyed within three years of the date of operation

ABORTION ACT 1967

CERTIFICATE TO BE COMPLETED BEFORE AN ABORTION IS PERFORMED UNDER SECTION 1(1) OF THE ACT

I, ...

(Name and qualifications of practitioner in block capitals)

of ....

....

(Full address of practitioner)

and I, ...

(Name and qualifications of practitioner in block capitals)

of ....

....

(Full address of practitioner)

hereby certify that we are of the opinion, formed in good faith, that in the case of

....

(Full name of pregnant woman in block capitals)

of ....

....

(Usual place of residence of pregnant woman in block capitals)

(Ring appropriate number)

    1. the continuance of the pregnancy would involve risk to the life of the pregnant woman greater than if the pregnancy were terminated;
    2. the continuance of the pregnancy would involve risk of injury to the physical or mental health of the pregnant woman greater than if the pregnancy were terminated;
    3. the continuance of the pregnancy would involve risk of injury to the physical or mental health of the existing child(ren) of the family of the pregnant woman greater than if the pregnancy were terminated;
    4. there is a substantial risk that if the child were born it would suffer from such physical or mental abnormalities as to be seriously handicapped.

This certificate of opinion is given before the commencement of the treatment for the termination of pregnancy to which it refers.

Signed ....

Date ....

Signed ....

Date ....

THE ABORTION ACT

SCHEDULE 1

IN CONFIDENCE   Certificate B

Not to be destroyed within three years of the date of operation

ABORTION ACT 1967

CERTIFICATE TO BE COMPLETED IN RELATION TO ABORTION PERFORMED
IN EMERGENCY UNDER SECTION 1(4) OF THE ACT

I, ...
(Name and qualifications of practitioner in block capitals)

of ....

....
(Full address of practitioner)

hereby certify that I *am/was of the opinion formed in good faith that it *is/was necessary immediately to terminate the pregnancy of

....
(Full name of pregnant woman in block capitals)

of ....

....
(Usual place of residence of pregnant woman in block capitals)

(Ring appropriate number)
in order   1. to save the life of the pregnant woman; or
           2. to prevent grave permanent injury to the physical or mental health of the pregnant woman.

This certificate of opinion is given—
(Ring appropriate letter)
   A. before the commencement of the treatment for the termination of the pregnancy to which it relates; or,
      if that is not reasonably practicable, then
   B. not later than 24 hours after such termination.

Signed ....

            Date ....

*Delete as appropriate

Interpretation of the Abortion Act

A memorandum from the Medical Defence Union,[142] an article by D. F. Robb[143] of the same organization, and the Proceedings of a Symposium held by the Medical Protection Society in collaboration with the Royal College of General Practitioners, London, on 7 February 1969[144] provide guides to the interpretation of the Act.

The consensus of opinion is set out below.

MEDICAL TERMINATION OF PREGNANCY

Under the Abortion Act, a person is not guilty of an offence under the law relating to abortion when a pregnancy is terminated by a registered medical practitioner if two registered medical practitioners are of the opinion, formed in good faith, that one of the four criteria set out in certificate A (see p. 74) are satisfied.

In determining whether the continuance of the pregnancy would involve risk to the health of the pregnant woman or her existing child(ren), the Act provides that account may be taken of both her actual and reasonably foreseeable environment.

INVESTIGATION OF THE PATIENT

Before completing certificate A, the practitioner must consider all the relevant circumstances of the case. This may necessitate the obtaining of a complete psychiatric history as well as investigation of the medical and social background of the patient. It may be necessary to obtain data from other doctors, social workers, probation officers, relatives, and so forth. Should a practitioner have a conscientious objection to recommending termination, it is advisable for him to refer the patient to a colleague.

MEANING OF THE TERMS IN THE ACT

The term "children" includes a single child and might in exceptional circumstances also include an individual over the age of 21 years (now 18 years) who was dependent on the pregnant woman because of mental or physical handicap. "Existing children of the pregnant woman's family" connotes not only the legitimate children to which the woman has given birth, but also the adopted and illegitimate children of herself or her husband. On rare occasions other children, such as the brothers and sisters of an unmarried woman who live with her, might be included. The test is the dependency of the child(ren) on the pregnant woman. "Substantial risk" of being "seriously handicapped" must be more than a mere possibility; it must be a risk of a degree which merits consideration and which the doctor is not justified in ignoring. A child is "seriously handicapped" if it is unable to live an independent life when of an age to do so.

"Treatment" authorized under the Act must be carried out at a National Health Service Hospital, or in a place approved for the purpose by the Minister of Health in respect of England and Wales, and by the Secretary of State in respect of Scotland. Examination by the certifying practitioner is not "treatment" as defined under the Act, and so need not be performed in any particular place. If immediate treatment to save the life or to prevent grave permanent injury to the physical or mental health of the pregnant woman is required, it may be carried out elsewhere than in a NHS hospital or an approved place; in such circumstances a second opinion is not necessary.

DUTIES OF THE PRACTITIONER PERFORMING TERMINATION

Whilst the practitioner who terminates the pregnancy will frequently be one of the two certifying practitioners, this is not mandatory. It may be that, though two practitioners have certified that circumstances justify termination of the pregnancy under the Abortion Act, the gynaecologist (or other practitioner) does not consider termination clinically indicated. If this is the case, he should advise the patient to obtain a further opinion through her family doctor. On the other hand, he may have a conscientious objection to performing termination. The Act states that no person shall be under any duty, whether by contract or by any statutory or other legal requirement, to participate in treatment authorized by the Act to which he has a conscientious objection. However, in the event of legal proceedings, the burden of proof of conscientious objection rests on the person claiming to rely on it. A plea of conscientious objection cannot be advanced if treatment under the Act was necessary to save the life or to prevent grave permanent injury to the physical or mental health of the pregnant woman.

Documentation

The Act imposed duties on practitioners in regard to documentation. Schedules 1 (pp. 74, 75) and 2 (Appendix I, p. 275) have to be completed. Scrupulous care in respect of these matters is enjoined, and failure to comply with them is an offence for which the practitioner can be fined up to £100.

Consent to Termination of Pregnancy

The written consent of the woman whose pregnancy is to be terminated should always be obtained, and where relevant the views of her husband should be taken into account. The latter's views, however, cannot prevent an operation necessary to "save the life or to prevent grave permanent injury" to the mother. The consent of a common law husband or the man believed to be responsible for the pregnancy is not necessary in law. Should the indications for abortion concern the "health of the pregnant woman or any existing children of her family", the husband's views are but one aspect to be considered when assessing "the pregnant woman's actual or reasonably foreseeable environment".

In girls aged between 16 and 18 years, a parent's consent is no longer necessary, under the provisions of the Family Law Reform Act which came into operation on 1 January, 1970. Such a patient is entitled to professional secrecy and may expressly not wish her parents to know that she is to undergo an operation for termination of pregnancy.

In girls aged below 16, written consent from a parent or guardian should be secured whenever possible, the girl's agreement to this being done being if possible obtained. Refusal of the parent or guardian to give consent should not be allowed to prevent a lawful termination to which the girl herself consents and which is clinically indicated; conversely, her pregnancy should not be terminated against her wishes.

In no case should an emergency wait on consent.

Immediate Problems the Act Created

The passage of the Act into law created a number of immediate problems, some minor, others more serious. The British Medical Association had difficulty in integrating the legal position with their code of ethics, the Royal

College of Obstetricians and Gynaecologists were disappointed that one of the two practitioners certifying the desirability of termination was not a consultant gynaecologist, and the medical profession in general objected to the fact that the abortions notified to the Chief Medical Officer under the Act could be disclosed on request to senior police officials. The size of the demand the Act would make on gynaecological beds at the expense of routine cases was unknown, and, as many gynaecologists were psychologically and professionally unprepared for the flood of women demanding termination, efficient techniques had not been fully worked out. Withal, it was clear that the Act was generally wanted and was a genuine expression of the feelings of the majority of Members of Parliament on a free vote.

The Act made abortion legal on certain grounds, but did not provide it on demand, and no practitioner is required to certify a patient for abortion or to perform an abortion if, in his clinical judgement, he believes the operation is not in the best interests of the patient and her children. Independently of the conscience clause, a gynaecologist is not compelled to perform an abortion on a patient on whom certificates under the Act have been completed by two practitioners if, in his clinical judgement, the operation is not indicated. Conversely, he commits no offence if he operates on the basis of these certificates unless he has reason to believe that one or both of the supporting opinions were not given in good faith. Confronted with a woman seeking an abortion, a practitioner must (i) ascertain whether or not an abortion would be permitted on the specified grounds and, if so, (ii) decide whether it would be in the best interests of herself and her family for the operation to be carried out. In this dilemma, the family doctor and the gynaecologist may seek psychiatric help.

CHAPTER 6

Psychiatric Considerations

WITH the general advances in therapeutics that have taken place in the last three decades, the number of pregnancies terminated in the United Kingdom for medical, i.e. non-psychiatric reasons, has dwindled steadily, and according to one gynaecologist, Peter Diggory,[2] the proportion performed on psychiatric grounds just prior to the passage of the Abortion Act had reached 90 per cent. *Pari passu* with this, most psychiatrists had developed a flexible attitude towards termination of pregnancy.

The Psychiatrist's Task

Three decades ago the psychiatric indications for interrupting a pregnancy were generally restricted to the possibility of a severe or irreversible psychosis developing should the pregnancy continue, and perhaps an imminent danger of suicide. Even in the latter cases, supervision in hospital, if necessary under certification, was advocated, the unfortunate woman being literally forced against her will to complete her unwanted pregnancy. In the United States as recently as 1964, Professor Simon[145] points out, abortion was a statutory crime in all fifty-one US jurisdictions, though in forty-five states therapeutic abortion was legal to preserve the mother's life, and in a few to safeguard her life or health or the life of the child. The risk to maternal life and health inherent in depression, the risk of suicide, and the danger of precipitating or exacerbating a psychosis or a severe neurosis were the chief psychiatric indications, and for their evaluation it was necessary to assess the patient's age, her number of children, her wishes regarding abortion, her family situation, her interpersonal relations, her socio-economic situation, and the foetal indications if any; the psychiatrist's own ethics, social values, and socio-economic status had also to be taken into account.

In Great Britain, Tredgold[39] observed, there were in practice two main questions: (i) Would the patient's health break down irretrievably? (ii) Would she commit suicide if the pregnancy continued? Judgement was difficult and was, he thought, especially complicated if either sterilization or the payment of fees was involved. Information from the family doctor was helpful but was not always available. From North America, White[22] furnished four practical criteria—a suicidal attempt, a recurrent psychotic reaction to previous pregnancies, an impending psychosis reasonably linked to the pregnancy, and perhaps the exacerbation of a severe neurosis. Professor Anderson,[40] a leading English psychiatrist, concluded that therapeutic abortion was practically never indicated in affective illness unless it was associated with a personality disorder likely to be intensified by the arrival of a child; he thought that termination was of doubtful value in schizophrenia. In obsessional states and anankastic personalities, termination was usually inadvisable, since there was a danger of severe guilt reactions; but termination was often indicated in asthenic women with a poor reaction to stress, the so-called "worn-out mothers". He emphasized the value of social support in the latter patients and the necessity for each case for termination to be judged on its own merits.

Joyston-Bechal[44] has pointed out the practical problems of the psychiatrist faced with referrals for termination: agree, and there is risk of a deluge which displaces other clinical work; refuse, and referrals may cease. He noted the genuine risk of suicide in some cases. In women who were reactively depressed as a result of the unwanted pregnancy there might be, he observed, a number of contributory factors: eugenic when the patient was preoccupied with the risk of having a deformed foetus; when she had too large an existing family; and when social stress was produced by a psychopathic, psychotic, or unsympathetic husband or sexual partner, or by an absent male partner. Endogenous depressions might sometimes necessitate termination, as might severe neurosis and psychopathy complicated by the considerations listed. Subjective factors also could influence the psychiatrist in *recommending* termination: age under 17, pregnancy from rape or against the patient's will, pregnancy in a patient from his own social background, or pressure from professional colleagues. Joyston-Bechal mentioned some considerations militating *against recommending* termination: an hysterical, demanding patient; "blackmail" through threats of suicide or recourse to "backstreet" abortion; an unmarried state; religious, philosophical, or legalistic scruples in the doctor; and a history suggesting that termination would recur as an annual event. Finally, to assess cases for termination, he recommended the establishment of abortion panels consisting of psychiatrists, social workers, almoners, and obstetricians.

Professor Pond[43] has emphasized the problems that can arise when a "professional", i.e. a physician, is asked or expected to perform a procedure such as a termination with "no questions asked". The professional's task was, he believed, "to look behind the demands of his client for the right course of action, not only to see whether this action is in the client's best interests, but also to try to understand what the client is really demanding". Thus in regard to termination the physician, he thought, should ask, "Why did this woman get pregnant in the first place, and why does she not want the baby now?" Abortion on demand, he felt, did not necessarily represent an irresponsible attitude, but might denote a sane adult appreciation of the best course of action for the family and the existing children. In some pregnant unmarried girls, he thought, "unconscious" motivations for pregnancy existed—for example, stemming from a deprived upbringing and incapable of making satisfactory human relationships, they might identify with the baby inside them, wanting it, like them, to be wanted and loved. Here the psychiatrist's role was important in deciding which terminations could be harmful as apart from helpful.

Aarons[146] has discussed some of the problems encountered by American psychiatrists in relation to therapeutic abortion. He observed that often the psychiatrist was hard put to show that for reason of some emotional disturbance a continuation of pregnancy would endanger a woman's life. Apart from psychiatric considerations, biological, social, and psychological factors had to be considered. Overpopulation, a cause for concern in poor countries, could not be regarded as a pressing danger in countries with expanding, prosperous economies. Economic considerations entered into the problem: there should be adequate material means of rearing the children that were born, and perhaps children for whom these resources did not exist should not be born. The interests of the individual, e.g. continuing a programme of education, had sometimes to be subordinated to those concerned with preserving the species, i.e. preserving a marriage and rearing children. Aarons pointed to the conscious and unconscious wishes that might surround a pregnancy, and he emphasized the difficulty of evaluating the true situation in one interview; in his view, the psychiatrist usually had to evaluate the woman's emotional fitness for motherhood by determining her neurotic conflicts, her ability to form object relationships, and her appreciation for reality conditions. In his opinion the pregnant woman should have a free choice whether or not to have her child; this would, he felt, make the task of psychiatrists much easier: when consulted, he would then be able to explore the woman's motives and the reality of the situation. He questioned whether pregnancy or termination had any crucial effect in altering a basic emotional condition or in affecting a chronic emotional illness—a conclusion in agreement with the Scandinavian findings mentioned in Chapter 4.

In January 1968 the Committee on Therapeutic Abortion of the British Medical Association published a general guide to the state of current medical opinion. [55] It stressed that there were few medical conditions which comprised automatic indications for termination of pregnancy, and emphasized that the decision as to whether or not to terminate had to be made in the light of the circumstances of the particular case. Account had to be taken of the mother's total environment, actual and reasonably foreseeable. As well as alimentary, cardio-vascular, respiratory, renal, neurological, skeletal, dermatological, endocrine, malignant, gynaecological and obstetric conditions *(sic)*, it cited psychiatric illnesses and conditions causing foetal abnormality. Amongst the psychiatric illnesses mentioned were reactive depressions, anxiety states, endogenous depressions, obsessional states, hysteria, schizophrenia, and mental defect. Reactive depressions were the commonest conditions for which termination was sought and, when severe, sometimes constituted adequate grounds for termination. The Committee felt that the psychiatrist's task was difficult because of the brief time he frequently had in which to examine the patient, because she might exaggerate or minimize her symptoms, and because she might exert moral pressure by threatening or committing suicide. An account from the patient's general practitioner was helpful, and the support available to the patient from relatives, social services, and doctors had to be assessed.

Kenyon [147] has recently provided a study of sixty-one patients sent to him in 1967 for consideration of termination of pregnancy whom he compared with sixty-eight routine referrals matched for age. He recommended termination in twenty-eight patients (46%) and found that, in comparison with the control group, more were separated or divorced, more were foreign born, the menarche had occurred earlier, and their sexual life had started sooner. More of the termination patients had lost their mothers by death, and more of the married termination patients admitted infidelity, were unhappily married, and had a poor sexual adjustment. The mean duration of pregnancy on referral was 11 weeks; in over 70 per cent of single patients it was their first. In 21 per cent of cases, pregnancy had resulted from contraceptive failure. Almost 60 per cent had a previous psychiatric history. The predominant diagnosis (57%) was a neurotic (reactive) depression with a risk of suicide in 33 per cent.

Role of the Family Doctor

In the United Kingdom at the time the Abortion Act became law, the first professional individual to whom the average woman with an unwanted pregnancy turned for help was probably the family doctor. She might not have consulted him if she were single, adolescent, living in a rural area, or if she knew her doctor was opposed to therapeutic abortion; but barring these contingencies she could well have discussed her difficulties with her doctor, and if he agreed that reasonable grounds existed—and because of his role he was in a unique position to evaluate the situation in the light of his knowledge of her personality and background—he might have referred her on for a therapeutic abortion. The woman who for some reason could not consult her family doctor might have travelled to London or to some other large city in order to chance her luck with a general practitioner picked at random or, if she were better informed, with a general practitioner known to be liberal in his attitudes. Alternatively, she might have attempted to consult a gynaecologist or a psychiatrist direct, a procedure unlikely to be successful since in the United Kingdom it contravenes professional etiquette for a specialist to see a patient who has not been referred by another physician.

Was it better for the family doctor to refer a patient in whom he felt termination of pregnancy was desirable to a gynaecologist or to a psychiatrist first? If he knew a liberal gynaecologist who was prepared to accept his recommendation, the problem was simple—though, as Stuart Carne[2] has pointed out, such gynaecologists were hard to find and even then often wanted a further opinion from a second specialist—but if he did not, he could have reflected that a gynaecologist might reject the patient, unless additional support was provided; and he might judge it best for a psychiatric opinion to be obtained to justify the proposed termination. This could have led the general practitioner to refer the patient to a psychiatrist before a gynaecologist, in the author's view the more undesirable form of arrangement to make in many cases.

Why should the patient see the gynaecologist before the psychiatrist? The gynaecologist can answer six questions which are directly relevant to the situation in which the woman finds herself. These are: (i) Is she definitely pregnant? (ii) If so, how far advanced is the pregnancy? (iii) How feasible would interruption of pregnancy be? (iv) Are there non-psychiatric grounds for termination? (v) Would the gynaecologist be prepared to terminate on psychiatric grounds if termination were advised? (vi) What are his views on subsequent contraception and the question of sterilization? Clearly, if the patient sees the psychiatrist first, the latter is ill equipped to answer any of these questions. He may well spend an appreciable time assessing the socio-psychological position only to find, for example, that he is attempting to persuade a gynaecologist into an operation which is not necessary because the woman is not pregnant at all, or which is unduly hazardous because the pregnancy is too far advanced. In general, therefore, it is best for the psychiatrist mainly to see cases which a liberal gynaecologist has screened and which the latter regards as suitable for termination if psychiatric grounds justify it.

PREGNANCY TESTING

Early pregnancy has become very much easier to diagnose since 1960, when immunological techniques for laboratory use were first described.[148] These were based on the observation that sheep red cells sensitized with human chorionic gonadotrophin (HCG) were not agglutinated by antiserum to HCG in the presence of urine from a pregnant woman. In practice, the urine was mixed with the antiserum and the sheep cells were added later; however, the test was time-consuming for, before the result could be ascertained, the urine–antiserum system had to be given time to react and the cells had to be allowed to settle. To reduce delay, speedier tests employing sensitized latex particles rather than sheep-cells were devised, and have gradually replaced the older, slower, more complicated, and expensive biological tests on animal systems. Accuracy levels of 98 per cent have been reported with some latex tests, though the claim that they can be performed by individuals with little training[148] has been disputed.[149, 150] False-positive and false-negative reactions occur, and the wide range of HCG concentrations in the urine has been the principal obstacle in devising a reliable test. For this reason the development of techniques based on the levels of HCG in the serum and the plasma—where they are much steadier than in the urine—was a great step forward. The test, which employs anti-HCG serum-coated latex particles that agglutinate when fluids are added containing 1 or more IU of HCG per ml, is simple and cheap, and can detect the presence of HCG in the blood as early as 4 days after a missed period; its accuracy and reliability have not as yet been fully evaluated. Meanwhile, Leit Wide [151] has described an even earlier method of detecting pregnancy—8–10 days after the day of ovulation and so 4–6 days before anticipated menstrual bleeding— by differentiating plasma and urine HCG and luteinizing hormone with two radioimmunoassays in parallel.

Practical Criteria for Reaching Decisions on Termination

Since no absolute criteria exist, the psychiatrist usually has to make a decision regarding the advisability of termination on the patient's state at interview, the history she provides, and the statements of others—the referring doctor, the husband or sexual partner, or perhaps the parents. In most cases a systematic interview will provide adequate information, the decision being reached in the light of the total picture that emerges. Though some patients clearly warrant termination on psychiatric grounds, in others few such grounds exist; there is a continuum of indications, and the "level" at which termination is recommended is a matter for the individual gynaecologist and psychiatrist to decide. As mentioned earlier, it is advisable, if possible, for the patient to be seen by the gynaecologist before she sees the psychiatrist; it is helpful to the latter to know, for example, that the pregnancy is only 6–8 weeks advanced, so that termination should be a safe, straightforward procedure which the gynaecologist will be prepared to carry out should he so advise.

The following considerations are especially relevant and can be covered consecutively at an interview designed to elicit them:

(1) *Age.* A chronological age below 17 years would be viewed by many as an indication for recommending termination, since a girl younger than this (rather arbitrary) limit would lack maturity and life experience, and would be unlikely to be able to "mother" and to support a child. Over the age of 40, on the other hand, many modern women have problems in undergoing pregnancy; they may already have had all the children they desire, and they may be reluctant to give up a newly established career to revert to a role they contentedly played earlier in life.

(2) *Intelligence.* A woman who is markedly mentally defective is frequently incapable of displaying the foresight necessary to ensure that she does not become pregnant, and after her child is born she may be unable to bring it up with adequate care. Conversely, a woman of unusually high intelligence may have problems with an unwanted pregnancy, finding it catastrophic to her

career if she is unmarried and an unwelcome handicap if she is older and is established in a responsible position.

(3) *Occupation, socio-economic status, and religion.* A woman of low socio-economic status in an unskilled or semi-skilled job may tolerate an unwanted pregnancy better than her counterpart in a responsible professional job; the latter, being higher in the social scale, has farther to fall. The birth of an illegitimate baby can spell disaster to the career of a nurse, a teacher, or many types of professional worker. Termination can cause conflicts in Roman Catholics with unwanted pregnancies, but many welcome the operation if it is made available.

(4) *Previous pregnancies and their outcome.* A history of difficulty in earlier pregnancies and of complications during the labour and in the puerperium is not infrequently found in women who present with unwanted pregnancies. If such a woman has had traumatic experiences in this regard, and has already borne the number of children she and her husband want, this will be a consideration in recommending termination.

(5) *Mental state at interview.* The extent to which the patient is distressed at interview is a partial guide to the amount of mental turmoil the situation has produced. It should be noted, however, that the most overtly disturbed patients are not necessarily the most distressed, for some women put a good face on things, hiding their true feelings beneath a mask of flippancy or spurious cheerfulness; others, through denial and non-realization, present with a mien of misleading calm. As the history unfolds, however, sensitive areas may be uncovered which may be manifested in the patient's behaviour.

(6) *Type of reaction.* The extent, severity, and progression of the reaction which the patient has developed as a response to the unwanted pregnancy must be evaluated. A depressive reaction with tearfulness, gloom, preoccupation with the problem, impaired concentration, forgetfulness, reduced work efficiency, and social withdrawal is common. Ruminations regarding the possibility of inducing an abortion are frequent and attempts may have been made to perform this. Self-reproach, tension, irritability, anergia, insomnia, dyspepsia, anorexia, nausea, vomiting, and constipation may occur, and there may be loss of weight. Suicidal ruminations are not unusual, and serious suicidal attempts—though not very common—sometimes occur. The severity of the reaction is related to the desperateness of the situation (as the woman perceives it) and the extent of her vulnerability, i.e. her predisposition to psychiatric illness.

(7) *Circumstances of conception*. Termination would be more likely to be recommended, other things being equal, if the woman in question had been raped or forced into intercourse against her will; or if she was young and/or ignorant and so unaware of contraception; if contraceptive failure had occurred despite stringent precautions; or if the situation had resulted from a chance encounter with a stranger—perhaps under the influence of alcohol. Conversely, a pregnancy in an intelligent adult woman which had resulted from a continuing sexual liaison in which inadequate or no contraceptive precautions had been taken would be a less adequate indication for termination, for it might imply that in some degree the woman unconsciously desired the pregnancy she consciously wished to reject.

(8) *Relationship to and status of sexual partner*. A pregnancy resulting from a brief encounter with a psychopathic, psychotic, or mentally defective man would be more suitable for termination than one in which the husband was responsible. When deserted by the man in question, or when determined not to marry him—a resolve that unfortunately often develops only after the damage is done, as it were—many single girls will go to almost any lengths to avoid having the baby, and their determination in this regard brings them into danger in regard to an illegal abortion. Again, in married women who have been deserted by their husbands or who have become pregnant by other men, the advent of an unwanted baby may interfere with a desired divorce, or may bring lasting unhappiness to the spouse, the children, or the relatives of the patient.

(9) *Existing supports*. The patient's situation is important in regard both to her physical (shelter, food, clothes, money) and her emotional (love, understanding, sympathy) supports. Clearly, the weaker these are—as, for example, in an impoverished unmarried girl far from home—the less well will she be able to tolerate the stress of an unwanted pregnancy and its aftermaths.

(10) *Psychiatric vulnerability*. This can be assessed from the account the patient gives of her habitual personality, her family history, and her personal history. An anxious, apprehensive, insecure, dependent, ultra-sensitive individual is clearly more liable to decompensate under the stress of an unwanted pregnancy than one who is more robust. Again, a family history of emotional disturbance or mental illness, together with difficulties and deprivation in early life, presupposes a reduced resistance to stress, as does evidence in the personal history of lack of affection, neurotic traits, inability

to adjust to school or to work, and the development of emotional symptoms at times of stress.

(11) *Effects of continuation.* These must be carefully considered in the light of the information that has already been obtained. Has the woman the capacity to adjust to an unwanted pregnancy? Will the continuation of the pregnancy significantly disrupt her education or her earning capacity? Will continuation lead to rejection by family members, ostracism, and lasting unhappiness? Will adequate support remain available, or is there a possibility of penury, hardship, and physical or psychiatric illness? Such problems are likely to be less severe in the case of a married woman pregnant by her husband unless he has deserted her or unless he is psychopathic or psychotic. However, a child conceived through an extramarital relationship may lastingly disrupt marital harmony, and a child born to a "worn-out mother" may, perforce, divert needed attention and affection from existing children. Will the continuation of the pregnancy make it impossible for the woman to accord care to an ailing husband or to sick parents or to other relatives? Such contingencies would favour termination.

(12) *Patient's true wishes.* Although this consideration is primary—for termination should never be performed against the woman's wishes—it should be elicited last because consideration of this point at the outset of an interview can befog the issue and lead to difficulty in obtaining vital data. Many women with unwanted pregnancies are ambivalent towards the situation—unconsciously wanting and welcoming the pregnant role yet overtly rejecting it. It is particularly important to ensure that a pregnancy is not terminated against the woman's wishes through pressure by husband, man friend, parents, guardians, or others. If a woman in such circumstances is coerced into agreeing to termination, guilt and subsequent depression are a common aftermath.

Finally the question of termination can be examined in the light of the considerations just enumerated, together with any special features which pertain to the individual case. In some patients, clear psychiatric grounds for termination can readily be found; in others no such direct indications exist; and in a large intermediate group the decision is difficult and has to be made in the light of the available information from the standpoint of the subsequent health of the woman, mental and physical, and the welfare of her family. The more vulnerable and the more psychiatrically handicapped the woman, the more readily can grounds for termination be found; but, as Hook[111] observes, the less likely is the operation to solve her problems, e.g. those of a chronically inadequate individual in a stressful situation. Yet to many women freedom of choice is a great boon, and given this, a proportion of patients (especially married women) decide to continue the pregnancy and to keep the baby. The psychiatrist should resist the temptation of trying to persuade an unwilling patient (especially a single, separated, divorced or widowed woman) to continue with an unwanted pregnancy if she asks for an abortion and adequate grounds for termination exist, especially in the first trimester when the procedure is safe and simple. To furnish continuing psychiatric support throughout an unwanted pregnancy can be very difficult, and as Pare[112] has shown, problems do not end at the puerperium for the stress of caring, or arranging care, for the baby can precipitate a psychiatric illness in those who are so predisposed. Requests for termination in "repeat" pregnancies—second, third or even further pregnancies in a patient who has already undergone one or more induced abortions—are hard to assess; the safest rule is to evaluate each patient on her merits at the time of referral.

Should termination of pregnancy be decided upon, many women find comfort in realizing that it is a considered decision, taken by two independent medical practitioners in the light of the total situation, and that it is not being performed merely because they (the patients) are worried or are evading their responsibilities. This should be clearly pointed out, for the knowledge helps to reduce the guilt and self-recrimination that a few women feel after a therapeutic abortion. Subsequently, whatever the patient's age, advice on contraception should be given and, where necessary, psychiatric care and support should be provided. This will reduce the chances of further unwanted pregnancies occurring as a result of ignorance, but such "repeat" pregnancies are not uncommon in the impulsive, the psychopathic and the unintelligent. In married women in their thirties—or even younger—who have a stable marital relationship and a "completed" family, sterilization should be considered in addition to termination of the unwanted pregnancy. Alternatively, sterilization of the husband by vasectomy is a possibility.[95]

CHAPTER 7

Techniques of Termination

IT IS one thing to be in favour of therapeutic termination of pregnancy, but it is quite another to do it. Whilst the psychiatrist and the family doctor are seldom called upon to participate in termination procedures, it is advisable for them to be fully acquainted with the techniques that are now employed.

Methods of Terminating Pregnancy

Once termination is decided upon, a technique is selected which is primarily influenced by the duration of the pregnancy.[152] In the first trimester, since medical measures are unsatisfactory, surgical techniques—dilatation and curettage, and vacuum aspiration—are usually employed. In the second trimester, since surgical methods—hysterotomy, abortifacient paste and mechanical stimulation of the uterus—have drawbacks, medical measures—intra-amniotic injections and prostaglandin therapy—are gradually being introduced to replace them.

The First Trimester

DILATATION AND CURETTAGE

Formerly, during the first 14 weeks of pregnancy, the commonest method of therapeutic termination was by a one-stage vaginal operation—the "classic technique" of dilatation of the cervix and curettage of the internal uterine wall. In this operation, which is usually performed under general anaesthesia (though a combination of a local anaesthetic and a tranquillizer can be used), slow, careful cervical dilatation with a series of graduated Hegar dilators is first carried out. Each of the dilators, which start with a diameter of 2 mm, is 1 mm larger than the previous one, and for a 12-week pregnancy a 14-mm Hegar is usually required. Before withdrawal, each dilator is transiently left *in situ* in order to minimize the danger of longitudinally splitting the cervix and to promote uterine contraction. Care has to be taken not to perforate the anterior wall of the soft, pregnant uterus if retroversion is present but has not been recognized, or its posterior wall if the uterus has been mistakenly thought to be retroverted. At 14 weeks, the usual upper limit for this procedure, a 16-mm or even an 18-mm dilator may be needed, but it is considered unwise to use larger dilators than these, since cervical tears and incompetence can result. Alternatively, after 12 weeks, if the vaginal route is favoured and there is no urgency, one or more laminaria tents can be inserted into the cervix the day before uterine evacuation is planned. The small cylinders of desiccated seaweed absorb moisture and swell steadily, dilating the cervix to a point at which evacuation of the uterine contents occurs, or at which further enlargement with metal dilators becomes possible.

Once adequate dilatation of the cervix is achieved, the wall of the uterus is scraped with a curette, care being taken not to perforate it. Ovum forceps are used when necessary to complete the removal of the uterine contents, and an intravenous injection of ergometrine is given to assist the natural contraction of the uterus and to reduce bleeding. Bi-manual compression may be employed, and some surgeons flush out the uterus with saline at a temperature of 48°C through a blunt curette.

Despite careful operative technique, haemorrhage can be alarming, perforation of the uterine wall occasionally occurs and shock can be produced. Perforation may not be recognized, but if it seems likely that the bowel or the omentum has been damaged, an immediate laporatomy may be necessary. Haemorrhage may call for blood transfusion, though blood loss does not normally exceed 100 ml. Shock may call for resuscitative measures. An idea of the frequency of these complications can be gained from the figures provided by Jurukovski,[6] who in 1969 reported on their incidence in 7833 legal terminations carried out by the classic technique in a university department in Yugoslavia during the years 1965-8. Operative complications occurred in 74 women (0.94% of those operated on). They comprised: prolonged haemorrhage, 44 (0.56%); perforated uterus, 23 (0.25%); severe haemorrhage, 19 (0.24%); shock, 17 (0.21%); peritonitis, 3 (0.03%); and an unknown number developed colpitis and cervicitis.

Following a dilatation and curettage, several hours in bed may be all that is required, but it is advisable, nevertheless, for the woman to stay under observation in the hospital or nursing home for at least one night so as to minimize the danger of complications. A few days' rest are desirable after return home.

TECHNIQUES OF TERMINATION

VACUUM ASPIRATION (SUCTION CURETTAGE)

This method of emptying the uterus in early pregnancy is said to have first been described by Wu and Wu in China in 1958.[76] Dorothea Kerslake,[2] who introduced it to Britain, notes that, though she had heard of the method some years previously, she did not meet anyone who had actually used it until the summer of 1964. This was at the London Conference of the International Planned Parenthood Federation where she encountered a Polish gynaecologist who spoke highly of vacuum aspiration and showed her a photograph of the curette used in his native land. He explained that the technique had been employed in Soviet Russia, and he said that it was being used in several countries east of the Iron Curtain.

Kerslake's original apparatus for terminating pregnancies at 6, 8, 10, and 12 weeks consisted of four straight, transparent, perspex tubes, each 2 mm greater in diameter than the number of weeks of the pregnancy. Just below the tip, each tube had a large hole, and at the proximal end there was a small hole for thumb control of pressure. The tubes could be attached by pressure tubing to a Kliner-Woulfe bottle and thence to an ordinary operating theatre suction apparatus, capable of producing negative pressures of up to 30 lb/in^2. The patient was given 1 mg of ergometrine intravenously before light general anaesthesia was induced with intravenous thiopentone. After the bladder had been emptied by catheter, 6 ml of 2 per cent lignocaine was injected into the paracervical tissue on either side to relax the internal cervical os and to provide local "block" analgesia. Prior to the 9th week, dilatation of the cervix was often unnecessary, Kerslake found, but thereafter dilatation had to be performed prior to the insertion of the suction curette, which was moved gently yet thoroughly up and down, facing all directions inside the uterus. Within 3–5 minutes, the products of conception were broken up and aspirated into the suction bottle; the size of the perspex tube imposed a limit of about 12 weeks on this method of termination, for in more advanced pregnancies the parts of the foetus were too large and too well formed to be macerated and to pass through the tube. Subsequently, gentle scraping of the uterine wall with a blunt curette was sometimes necessary, but the entire procedure was speedier and safer than dilatation and curettage.

Kerslake and Casey,[153] reporting on a large series of terminations carried out by this method, observed that, in contrast to the standard dilatation and curettage, vacuum aspiration could, when necessary, be performed under local anaesthesia, and, as the wall of the uterus was less damaged, there was a negligible risk of perforation (none in their 14,000 cases). The time taken to evacuate the uterus by the suction method was only a third of that necessary for a dilatation and curettage, pain was less severe, and blood loss was half that of the standard operation. Jurukovski,[6] reporting in 1969 on 10,586 suction terminations carried out in a university department in Yugoslavia, noted that its total morbidity was 3.90 per cent compared with a corresponding rate of 4.82 per cent associated with the classic technique. Operative complications occurred in 28 women (0.26% of those operated on). They comprised: severe haemorrhage, 12 (0.11%); shock, 9 (0.08%); cervical tears, 4 (0.03%); and perforations, 3 (0.03%). There were no deaths. Early post-operative complications occurred in 385 women. They included: retained products, 192 (1.82%); genital organ inflammation, 120 (1.13%); prolonged haemorrhage, 73 (0.67%); and an unknown number developed colpitis and cervicitis. With the suction method, therefore, complications are fewer than with the classic technique, but skill is needed to avoid leaving behind small segments of the placenta which can give rise to secondary haemorrhage, and there is also a danger of air embolism. The technical competence required to perform vacuum aspiration is not less than that needed for a dilatation and curettage.

As time has passed, the technique of vacuum aspiration has been refined and improved in a number of ways. Various types of curette are now available and they can be made of either plastic or metal. Plastic (perspex) curettes are less traumatizing to the uterus and enable the aspirated contents to be continuously inspected, but they are more difficult to sterilize than their metal counterparts, they occasionally fracture, and, having thicker walls than metal curettes, cannot be used as late on in pregnancy (the larger metal curettes can be used as late as the 16th week). Whatever type of curette is employed, however, it is vital before use to ensure that air cannot be blown out through it and that it is aspirating satisfactorily.

Early in pregnancy—up to about the 8th week—vacuum aspiration can be carried out in the morning and the patient allowed home after a few hours' rest in bed. Later in pregnancy, an overnight stay in the hospital or nursing home is desirable. In general, however, termination by this method is a safe, rapid, uncomplicated procedure.

The Second Trimester

ABDOMINAL HYSTEROTOMY AND OTHER TECHNIQUES

When the uterus is palpable abdominally and is enlarged to greater than the size of a 14-week pregnancy, an abdominal hysterotomy is often carried out. A general anaesthetic is administered and access to the uterus is gained through either a "classical" midline incision between the umbilicus and the symphysis pubis or via a Pfannensteil incision, which runs horizontally below the line of the pubic hair. The former incision allows better access to the uterus and the abdominal contents, but the latter is more frequently employed since, though it increases the technical problems of the operation, it leaves a better cosmetic result. Once through the abdominal wall, the bladder peritoneum is reflected downwards and 5 units of oxytocin are given into the uterine wall or parenterally. If the hysterotomy is to be combined with sterilization, a short longitudinal incision is made into the anterior wall of the uterus below the fundus, but if further pregnancies are envisaged and the uterus is sufficiently large to have a differentiated lower segment, a transverse incision is made into it and a "miniature Caesarean section" is performed. The ovum protrudes through the scar and can often be delivered intact; parenteral ergometrine is given, and the thick decidua of early pregnancy is removed with a curette before the cervix is dilated from above. Finally, the uterine wall is sutured in two layers with interrupted or herringbone chromic catgut sutures, and the peritoneum is closed separately.

Abdominal hysterotomy carries the risk of any intra-abdominal operation, and may be complicated by haemorrhage, shock, sepsis, and weakening of the wall of the uterus. In addition, there is an appreciable risk of implanting decidual cells elsewhere and causing endometriosis. A rate of up to 20 per cent in patients 1–4 years after the operation has been reported and the bladder is affected in about 1 per cent of cases. [76] The lesions, however, are usually symptomless.

Vaginal hysterotomy is now seldom performed since the operation can only be used in multiparae under 16 weeks pregnant, offers poor access to the uterus, and is not well adapted for dealing with emergencies. Tubal ligation combined with vaginal hysterotomy has an appreciable failure rate, and endometriosis under the bladder following this operation is especially troublesome.

In general, patients who have had abdominal hysterotomies require 10–20 days in hospital and a subsequent period of convalescence. It is a more formidable procedure than vacuum aspiration and its disadvantages—an intra-abdominal operation, the necessity of general anaesthesia, the risks of endometriosis, and blocking a hospital bed—have stimulated the development of other methods of inducing a therapeutic abortion.

ABORTIFACIENT PASTE

This method of terminating pregnancy was introduced in Germany in the 1930s, and for a time enjoyed a vogue in Russia as well as in other countries. In Britain, Utus paste is employed; this is a soap medicated with iodine, potassium iodide, thymol, and astringents which, when injected into the uterus, acts as an irritant and causes contraction of the uterine wall with expulsion of its contents.

Lachelin and Burgess[154] have reported successfully using Utus paste to terminate the pregnancies of 182 women in Carshalton Hospital, Surrey, between January 1964 and May 1968. Half their cases were given a general anaesthetic, but the remainder required only premedication. The paste was injected via a catheter introduced 2 in. into the uterus through the undilated cervix. If no contractions occurred in 24 hours, the patient was given an enema and encouraged to get up; if she still failed to abort, she was given buccal or intravenous oxytocin. The pregnancies terminated in this way varied in duration from 9 to 20 weeks; there was no relationship between the duration of the pregnancy, on the one hand, and the time between the injection of Utus and the expulsion of the uterine contents, on the other. In 121 cases the uterus was explored: initially, curettage was always performed, but later it was restricted to abortions which were incomplete after 24–48 hours or in which excessive bleeding had occurred. The patients' stay in hospital varied between 3 and 16 days; Lachelin and Burgess never found hysterotomy necessary as an alternative.

More recently, Walker[6] has described his experience with Utus paste in terminating the pregnancies of 112 women in Manchester. All were over 12 weeks pregnant and, whilst of his first group of 58 patients who received a general anaesthetic (usually halothane, which relaxes the uterus) 57 (98%) aborted, 41 (71.9%) subsequently required the removal of retained products. This high rate contrasted with the much lower proportion (33%) requiring removal of retained products in a second group of 58 women who received the paste after premedication only (as in the anaesthetized group, 57 aborted). The first group required 98 general anaesthetics (57 for insertion and 41 for evacuation), whilst the second required only 19. On average, the women in the anaesthetized group took 32 hours to abort, whilst those in the other group were 2 hours quicker; the induction–abortion interval was shortened in the two groups by $8\frac{1}{2}$ and 12 hours, respectively, when an oxytocin drip was given before the paste was inserted. Complications included haemorrhage and infection (5.5% when the abortion was complete, 31.6% when it was incomplete), but there were no deaths. Walker notes that it was possible to treat bleeding by speeding up the oxytocin drip, and he advocated antibiotics and pre-operative investigation of the vaginal flora as methods of controlling infection.

Whilst Lachelin and Burgess state that the employment of Utus paste to terminate pregnancy has been ". . . the method of choice . . . for the past 20 years", others have been less enthusiastic. The abortion that results after its injection may be more painful than a confinement at full term, and a dilatation and curettage is not infrequently also needed. Sudden death from embolism or vagal inhibition has been reported, and infection and/or necrosis of the uterine wall can be produced. Twenty-five deaths were reported in the literature in the 1930s, and the method is now hardly ever used in Russia, where it was popular two or three decades ago.

INTRA-AMNIOTIC INJECTIONS

As Schiffer[155] and others have pointed out, Professor Aburel of Bucharest, who described the termination of pregnancy by the intra-amniotic injection of 33 per cent saline in 1934, is credited with being the first to use this method. Three other independent groups later studied the technique, great impetus coming from the legal abortion policy in Scandinavia where after 1938 the increasing number of terminations necessitated the development of simple, safe methods of inducing abortion in the second trimester. The occurrence of endometriosis after abdominal hysterotomy was a further spur, as was the development of methods for investigating the mechanisms of the initiation of labour. Finally, Schiffer notes, at approximately the same time that the injection of hypertonic solutions was gaining in popularity, amniocentesis for spectrophotometric analysis of amniotic fluid in the management of the Rh-isoimmunized pregnancy came into prominence, and, as a result of greater familiarity with amniotic fluid aspiration, it became easier to proceed with injection techniques.

After abortion was legalized in Japan in 1948, intra-amniotic infusions of hypertonic saline were increasingly used in that country to terminate pregnancy. The method had been introduced to Japan in 1946, and 2 years later the first death was reported. T. Wagatsuma[156] estimated that between 1946 and 1950 a total of twenty-five deaths occurred after intra-amniotic saline terminations, and he classified the causes into four groups: (i) technical failure—infection or direct injection into the bloodstream or the myometrium; (ii) aggravation of complications of pre-existing, carelessly evaluated illness;

(iii) *post-partum* haemorrhage, cervical lacerations, and uterine rupture; and (iv) deaths from unknown causes, including two sudden fatalities following shock-like symptoms or vascular collapse. Nevertheless, as Reiss [6] has recently pointed out, the deaths reported by Wagatsuma ". . . occurred in a population of unselected patients, many suffering from malnutrition or other systemic disease, operated on by inexperienced operators under poor conditions with no antibiotic or transfusion facilities". Reiss thought that they bore no relation to modern conditions. Intra-amniotic injections were abandoned after 1950 in Japan, but they continued to be employed in other countries for the "dead foetus" syndrome as well as for therapeutic termination. In 1966, Cameron and Dayan [157] reported three deaths in the United Kingdom in which, after amniotic fluid replacement with hypertonic saline, acute haemorrhagic infarction of the cerebral centres had occurred. Death in these cases was probably due to faulty technique, Reiss observes, leading almost certainly to excessive absorption of saline into the maternal circulation.

Evidence that when carefully employed the intra-amniotic injection method of terminating pregnancy is safe and effective is provided by the experience of H. de Watteville, [6] who, in 1969, reported on 942 mid-trimester terminations carried out successfully in the years 1951–68 in the University Clinic at Geneva, Switzerland. Three deaths occurred (total mortality 0.3%), two being due to infection and one to accidental intravascular injection of the hypertonic saline. The amniotic fluid was tapped in a closed circuit and was replaced with 1 litre of 10 per cent saline; finally, 2 million units of penicillin and 1 g of streptomycin were injected into the amniotic cavity. Curettage was performed routinely after spontaneous expulsion of the foetus and the placenta. This usually occurred within 36 hours of the injection of the hypertonic saline, but if it was delayed an intravenous oxytocin drip infusion was administered. Seventy per cent of de Watteville's patients left hospital within 3 days after expulsion and two-thirds had left within 7 days of admission.

There is disagreement on the nature and strength of the fluids to be injected, but all agree that general anaesthesia should be avoided since it would conceal the characteristic reactions produced by the accidental intravascular injection of hypertonic solution. Most gynaecologists restrict the operation to pregnancies of over 16 weeks' duration because intravascular injections are commoner with a smaller uterus. The bladder is emptied and, with careful sterile precautions, local anaesthesia is induced in a small area of the abdominal wall. A Tuohy epidural needle and stylet is inserted below the umbilicus through the midline, care being taken to avoid the bladder. The amniotic sac is punctured and 200 ml of liquor is aspirated and replaced with an equal volume of 20 per cent saline or 50 per cent glucose containing 0.5 g of oxytetracycline. Great care must be taken to ensure that the needle is not in a blood vessel or in an intervillous space; frequent aspirations and slow injections are important safeguards. If a clear, blood-free tap is not obtained in two attempts, the injection is not administered and amniocentesis is either carried out through the vagina or postponed for 2 weeks. The patient is closely observed throughout the procedure, which is immediately abandoned if pain occurs or untoward reactions develop. Subsequently, the patient is encouraged to walk about the ward, and labour generally commences within about 36 hours; the process can, if necessary, be speeded with an oxytocin drip. As a rule, the uterine products are expelled cleanly, but curettage is sometimes necessary. Pethedine or other analgesics can be given for pain.

The mode of action of intra-amniotic hypertonic injections is not fully understood. The solution damages the placenta and may locally affect the wall of the uterus; the foetus is unequivocally dead. Because of the rise of sodium concentration produced, intra-amniotic hypertonic saline is contraindicated in cardiac disease, renal disorder, and pre-eclampsia. Some gynaecologists, mainly in Scandinavia, have advocated the extra-amniotic transcervical injection of hypertonic solutions, especially early in pregnancy when trans-abdominal puncture of the amniotic sac is still hazardous.

MECHANICAL STIMULATION OF THE UTERUS

After the intra-amniotic injection of hypertonic saline was abandoned as too dangerous in Japan, Yukio Manabe[158] observes, alternative methods of terminating pregnancy in the second trimester were devised. Since Japan had learnt modern medicine largely from Germany, techniques originating in the latter country were tried and modified as seemed necessary. These included the insertion of a rubber bougie between the membranes and the wall of the uterus—which had first been described by Krause in 1855—and the introduction, through the cervix, of an inflatable bag—the colpeurynter described by Carl Braun in 1851 and the metreurynter described by Champetier de Ribes in 1888. Extra-ovular instillation of 0.1 per cent rivanol solution through a catheter was also employed. All these methods were based on mechanical stimulation of the uterus, and, as a result of the efficient sterilization of instruments and the use of antibiotics, had proved extremely safe, Manabe claimed. They were simple and effective, he noted, and were more "physiological" than other techniques in that the foetus was delivered alive. In

Britain, however, the danger of infection, together with the availability of acceptable alternative methods, has prevented their use.

PROSTAGLANDIN THERAPY

U. S. von Euler in 1936 bestowed the name prostaglandin on a substance found in human seminal fluid which stimulates smooth muscle and lowers blood pressure; it is now known to be a mixture of at least thirteen related compounds. The prostaglandins are currently conceptualized as a group of chemically related 20-carbon long chain fatty acids which are widely distributed in mammalian tissues and have a variety of pharmacological actions. Amongst these is the property of stimulating and causing contraction in the pregnant and the non-pregnant human uterus.

Clinical studies of the abortion-inducing potential of prostaglandins have been carried out by three groups of investigators led by Professor S. M. M. Karim at Makerere in Uganda, M. P. Embrey at Oxford and M. Bygdman and M. Wiqvist at Stockholm, Sweden.[159] Professor Karim was encouraged to use prostaglandins F2α and E2 early in pregnancy by his success in inducing labour with these compounds given at or near term. Working with G. M. Filshie,[160] he studied two series of patients, one in Mulago Hospital, Uganda, and the other in King's College Hospital, London. The prostaglandins were administered in intravenous drips of saline or 5 per cent dextrose: with F2α given to 15 women at 50μg/min, 14 pregnancies were terminated; with E2 given to 52 women at 5μg/min, 50 pregnancies were terminated, but in 7 patients surgical evacuation of retained products was necessary. With both prostaglandins uterine activity habitually commenced within a few minutes and delivery occurred some hours (usually about 15) later. Blood loss was minimal (usually about 50 ml) and ergometrine 0.5 mg was given to each patient after her abortion. Diarrhoea and vomiting were common with F2α but were rare with E2, which was given in only one-tenth the dose. M. P. Embrey working in Oxford has reported similar results. Clearly prostaglandins of both the E (E1 and E2) and the F (F2α) series, given by intravenous infusion, will produce abortion in over 90 per cent of women with pregnancies of between 9 and 28 weeks' gestation.

M. Bygdman and M. Wiqvist in Stockholm have also studied the effect of prostaglandins E1 and F2α in inducing abortion, giving the two compounds by intravenous infusion and by subcutaneous injection. They early found that intravenous infusion was the more successful method, and did best in pregnancies of less than 8 weeks' duration. Later in pregnancy the dose that was necessary to induce abortion was increased, and the proportion of side-effects (dysmenorrhoeic pain, nausea and diarrhoea) steadily mounted. The investigators conjectured that direct administration into the genital tract offered the best possibility of producing a high local concentration in the myometrium and so of reducing side-effects. Accordingly they gave prostaglandins F2α and E2 by intermittent injection through a catheter positioned between the foetal membranes and the wall of the uterus. Efficacy was high—in one of their early studies 11 out of 12 pregnancies were terminated even though the dose was one-tenth that of the intravenous dose—and side-effects were minimal. Compared with intravenous infusion, intra-uterine administration produced a less dramatic uterine response, but resulted in more sustained and effective uterine contractions; in addition, local administration required less supervision of the patient. Recently Professor Karim has described a simpler method still, the administration of prostaglandin E2 (20 mg) or prostaglandin F2α (50 mg)—in a pessary inserted into the vagina every $2\frac{1}{2}$ hours; in 45 women in which this method was employed, abortion occurred within 15 hours in every case.[159] It seems too that prostaglandins can act as uterine cathartics and can be administered in vaginal pessaries a few days after a missed period to produce "menstruation" without adverse side-effects.[159]

It is too early fully to assess the role of the prostaglandins in terminating pregnancy, but preliminary experience suggests that the compounds have great promise. Therapeutic possibilities have improved because these substances, formerly only obtainable by expensive animal extraction procedures, were chemically synthesized in 1969. The intravenous administration of prostaglandin is a safe, simple, rapid technique which does not require a skilled practitioner (as does intra-amniotic injection and the techniques used in Japan) or the use of an operating theatre (as does an abdominal hysterotomy or the injection of abortifacient paste). The risk of infection is minimal and, as in intra-amniotic injections, the patient experiences the labour in clear consciousness. In prostaglandin terminations, the foetus is extracted alive, and though it does not breathe, movements may be felt in its limbs; curettage for retained products is seldom needed. The local use of prostaglandin in the genital tract opens the possibility of self-administration. When this becomes a reality abortion may be controlled entirely by the woman herself, who will use a prostaglandin pessary whenever, against her wishes, a period is delayed. In practice, such a procedure may only be required three or four times a year; the physician of the future may be called in only to check for side-effects and to prevent damage to the health of the mother.

CHAPTER 8

The First Year of the Act

THE immediate consequences of the Abortion Act were, firstly, that a greatly increased number of women were referred to gynaecologists for consideration of termination of pregnancy and a greatly increased number of terminations were performed; and, secondly, that pressure was exerted on existing facilities, especially within the National Health Service, with the result that initially some became overstrained. In the difficult situation that developed, advisory services were established to help women to obtain legal terminations.

By the time the Act had been in operation for a year, issues regarding the working of the necessary but ambivalently regarded supporting role of the private clinics were beginning to arise, and the need for better contraception had become very evident. Because of the Abortion Act, the roles of the gynaecologist, the psychiatrist, the general practitioner, and the nurse had changed; and as a result their attitudes had begun to alter.

Increased Demand

The size of the demand once the Act became law surprised those who had been inclined to doubt the estimate that some 100,000 criminal abortions were being performed annually in Britain prior to April 1968. As Marks [161] observes, the increased number of women referred to gynaecologists was due, on the one hand, to their new awareness of their rights under the Act—the parliamentary debates during its passage and the publicity it had attracted had made them better informed and more clamant regarding therapeutic abortion—and, on the other, to the larger number of general practitioners who, long in favour of termination of unwanted pregnancy when adequate justification existed, now felt it at last appropriate to refer them. The result was increased pressure on gynaecological facilities, especially in the National

Health Service, which was ill prepared to meet such a demand. The figures for legal abortions performed during the first year of the Act give an idea of its size.

Between 27 April 1968 and 30 April 1969—during the first calendar year of the Act—37,736 abortions were notified as having been performed in England and Wales, 22,509 (60%) in National Health Service hospitals, 15,140 (40%) in approved premises, and 87 in other places.[162] From the time the Act became law, the number of women with unwanted pregnancies referred for termination and the number of terminations performed rose steadily: 4412 in the second quarter (2 months) of 1968; 7939 in the third; 9905 in the fourth; and 9957 in the first quarter of 1969.[163]

From the time the Act became law, a small number of foreign women began to come to Britain to take advantage of its provisions—it had no statutory residence requirement. Initially, about seventy women a week were thought to be arriving in the country for this purpose, but as the majority went to private clinics they did not increase the pressure on National Health Service facilities. By the end of the first year of the Act, 2265 women from abroad had had pregnancies terminated (7% of the total legal abortions performed). Of these, 1076 came from West Germany, 481 came from the United States, 236 from Canada, 138 from France, 86 from Holland, and 248 from unspecified countries.[164] The figure of 7 per cent, as Diggory et al.[165] have observed, presumably includes nurses and *au pairs* working in Britain. Yet their tendency to inflate it is probably counterbalanced by under-recording due to the fact that, as Goodhart[166] points out, the form of notification (see Appendix I) gives only the woman's usual place of residence and not her nationality (if she wished she could give her address in Britain; and there is no reason to suppose that physicians or clinics would trouble to check on the veracity of her statement). Overall, however, it seems likely that the number of foreign women that came to Britain for termination operations was quite small, and was not a serious burden on national resources.

For the 37,736 abortions carried out in the first year, the grounds were as follows: risk of injury to the physical or mental health of the woman, 27,293 (72%); risk of injury to physical or mental health of existing child(ren) combined with other reason(s), 5442 (14%); risk to life of woman, 1696 (5%); risk of injury to physical or mental health of existing child(ren), 1490 (4%); substantial risk of child being born abnormal, 1134 (3%); risk of injury to physical or mental health of woman combined with substantial risk of child being born abnormal, 616 (2%); emergency, to prevent grave permanent injury to physical or mental health of woman, 48; and emergency, to save life of woman, 17. Abortions performed on girls under 16 years of age numbered 862 (2%); on girls aged 16–19, 5637 (15%); on women aged 20–34, 23,310 (61%); on those aged 35–44, 6794 (18%); and on those over 45, 247 (1%); in 883 cases (2%) the age was not stated. Of the 37,736 women who underwent therapeutic termination of pregnancy, 17,924 (47%) were single, 16,615 (44%) were married, 3064 (8%) were widowed, divorced, or separated, and the status of 133 was not reported. Clearly, the most frequently cited reason for performing therapeutic termination was risk of injury to the physical or mental health of the woman (72% of cases); the majority of women operated upon (61%) were aged between 20 and 34; and the operation was only slightly more commonly performed on single than on married women (47% versus 44%).

During the first 8 months of the Act, the period most commonly spent in hospital was 3 days in National Health Service hospitals and 1 day in approved places: a larger number remained in NHS hospitals for 7 days or longer than occurred in alternative facilities. About 13 per cent of patients were operated on before the 9th week of pregnancy, 50 per cent were operated on when between 9 and 13 weeks pregnant, and 37 per cent had their pregnancies terminated at over 13 weeks of gestation. Patients whose pregnancies were terminated in the 25th, 26th and 27th weeks of gestation numbered 53, 34, and 21 in England and Wales.[167] The type of termination procedure employed was: dilatation and curettage, 42 per cent (most commonly used in the North West Metropolitan Region—64% of 9417 cases); abdominal hysterotomy, 26 per cent (Sheffield, with 56% of 659 cases, had the highest proportion of all hospital regions); vacuum aspiration, 25 per cent (the London teaching hospitals employed this in 43% of 1638 cases); and other methods, 7 per cent.[168]

Deaths associated with abortion in the 12 months that preceded the Act numbered 36 (medical and other legal, 3; criminal, self-induced, 18; spontaneous, 4; and non-specified, other, 11). The figures during the Act's first year were very similar; total deaths 41 (medical and other legal, 4; criminal, self-induced, 18; spontaneous, 9; non-specified, other, 10).[169] Deaths from legal abortion in the first year of the Act numbered 8, of which 6 took place in NHS hospitals; in 5 of these cases termination was carried out later than the 13th week of pregnancy. The danger of death as a consequence of legal abortion (21 per 100,000 cases) in the first year of the Act was slightly lower than that of dying in childbirth (24 per 100,000 cases).[170]

Pressure on Facilities

The strain caused by the increasing number of patients referred for termination, and the necessity for operation in a substantial proportion, was accentuated by the urgency of their situation. Often the woman was uncertain that she was pregnant until her condition was 7 or 8 weeks advanced, and if she waited a week before obtaining help, only 3 or 4 weeks were left for termination by the vaginal route. Initially, referrals were made more or less evenly to the 662 consultant gynaecologists practising in the NHS throughout the country—had each NHS gynaecologist performed only one therapeutic abortion weekly, the 34,000 pregnancies terminated in this way would have almost equalled the number of terminations performed in the first year of the Act—but doctors and patients soon learned to avoid gynaecologists who, on ethical or religious grounds, objected to performing terminations. Centres such as Birmingham, where conservative gynaecology (and psychiatry) prevailed, were avoided, and recourse was had to others, such as Newcastle and London, where more liberal policies were practised. The pressure on "liberal" hospitals soon began to overstrain their facilities for routine gynaecological services: 82,787 of the 500,217 patients awaiting non-urgent NHS operations on 31 December 1968 were gynaecological cases,[171] and the "full-time" equivalent of the 555 consultant gynaecologists practising in England and Wales in 1968 amounted to only 436.[170] Middle-aged and elderly patients waiting for the removal of painful fibroids, for pelvic floor repairs, and for other operations, as well as younger women awaiting investigation for infertility, for example, had to wait longer still because of the inrush of adolescents and young women whose need for rapid termination prevented them from joining the customary queue. To safeguard routine gynaecological services for patients resident in the zone for which they were responsible, many "liberal" hospitals had to set up catchment areas, from outside which they would not accept patients for NHS terminations. This intensified the problem.

One of the main reasons why NHS facilities for termination varied so markedly was the "conscience clause" that had been built into the Act. This made it possible for doctors and nurses who had conscientious objections to refrain from involving themselves in therapeutic abortion, and those gynaecologists who were opposed to the Act virtually refused to carry out terminations short of an acute threat to the mother's life. Many felt that hypocrisy had been built into the Act: what were, in fact, social criteria were, they believed, masquerading as medical criteria. Unhappily for the women who required legal terminations, the result was that the two opposing ideologies that had warred during the passage of the Act through Parliament continued to fight with each other in the context of the NHS after it had become law—a circumstance which perpetuated the social iniquities the Act had been brought in to remedy. [161]

Despite the time the Act took to become law, little provision was made for the new situation, and the Government appeared to expect the Act to be translated into action without expansion of existing facilities, which, in the NHS, came under the Regional Hospital Boards over which the (then) Ministry of Health exercised a supervisory function. Believing that demand might slacken off and reluctant to separate legal abortion from other gynaecological procedures, the Government resisted the idea of establishing specialized NHS abortion units staffed on a rota basis by willing nurses and gynaecologists. The inevitable consequence was development of the private sector. [172, 173] The provision of the Act made private abortions less difficult legally, and clinics licensed under the Act rapidly expanded their termination activities. To the indignation of many physicians, they began to advertise in medical journals. Fees, which averaged £150 per termination, ranged between £50 and £250, and it soon became evident that, as had been even more the case before the Act, there was one law for the rich and another for the poor. The rich could rapidly have their unwanted pregnancies terminated in private clinics, whilst the less affluent, dependent on NHS facilities, were often unable to obtain abortions, or could be forced into a delay that could necessitate an abdominal hysterotomy instead of a simple vaginal termination. Providing their customary alternative to expensive private clinics and inadequate NHS facilities, and kept going in part, perhaps, by patients' fears that abortions performed in these settings might become known to parents, spouses, fiancés, or employers, the private abortionists continued to flourish, and, as Professor Stallworthy [144] observed, were driven from the backstreets not into obscurity but "in a Rolls-Royce to more fashionable accommodation in the High Street or on Ascension Square".

The Act had a beneficial effect, however, in reducing the number of women admitted to hospital with the complications of an illegal abortion, and so liberating hospital facilities. In the first quarter of 1966, the London Emergency Bed Service admitted 1363 abortion cases; in the first quarter of 1969, the corresponding figure was 870. [170] Further, whilst in March 1966 abortions constituted 8.8 per cent of all emergency admissions, by March 1969 the proportion had fallen to 5.4 per cent. [174]

Advisory Services

In the unsatisfactory situation that prevailed, the Abortion Law Reform Association, long the champion of women with unwanted pregnancies denied needed terminations, stepped up its activities. Whilst it could take no part in performing terminations, it strengthened its advisory services. It did this, generally, by means of a booklet—*Guide to the Abortion Act 1967*—which it distributed in September 1968 to the 22,000 general practitioners in the United Kingdom, and, specifically, by advising individual clients on facilities available to them and on appropriate action to take when they were deficient— such as for doctors and patients to write to the Minister of Health complaining of the situation. The Abortion Law Reform Association, like Diggory [175] and others, advocated the establishment of specialized abortion units, and it strongly supported the Pregnancy Advisory Service (PAS).

PAS started its activities in Birmingham the day the Abortion Act became law. Founded by a group of professional men and women under the lead of Dr. Martin Cole, a geneticist, PAS was formed to provide sympathetic advice to women distressed as a result of pregnancy; 6 months later a similar service which, like its predecessor, was accorded charitable status, was established in London. [176] Describing the work of PAS, Madeleine Simms [62] observed that in an ideal world it would have had no reason to exist. It was necessitated by the uneven availability of NHS termination facilities throughout the country; indeed, the statistics during the first 6 months of the Abortion Act showed that a woman in Birmingham had one-third to one-half the chance of obtaining an abortion that she had in East Anglia, Newcastle, Wales, and other regions. Responding to disapproval from Professor McLaren [177] and Myre Sim, [173] Simms [179] pointed out that it had been no accident that PAS had started in the city where they worked, for it had come into being as a direct response to a situation which had made it virtually impossible for patients who had legitimate grounds under the Abortion Act to obtain terminations. Continuing her castigation, she sharply observed: "It is hypocritical to create a situation in which abortion is virtually unobtainable under the National Health Service and then condemn as 'unethical' the selfless endeavours of those humanitarian individuals who are left to cope with the consequences."

In Birmingham, 32 per cent of the clients of PAS were referred by general practitioners who, having recommended termination, found that a local gynaecologist would not accept the case or that the waiting list was too long for the patient to wait; 24 per cent were referred by social agencies, often the Citizens' Advice Bureau; and the remaining 44 per cent came to PAS direct. In the first 8 months of its existence, the Birmingham PAS interviewed 786 women of whom 609 (77%) later obtained an abortion. A lay counsellor or a social worker saw the patients and a small fee was charged to cover expenses; later, if necessary, a PAS doctor saw them, too, and usually had to refer them to London for termination because of inadequate local facilities. Most of the clients, rather disturbingly, were young, 63 per cent being aged between 15 and 25 years; only 30 per cent were married. By April 1969 the London PAS in its shorter life had seen about 600 women, of whom 90 per cent succeeded in obtaining terminations. It was receiving 40–50 inquiries each day, mostly from women whose general practitioners had recommended termination but knew it was useless to send them to local gynaecologists.

Private Facilities for Abortion

As mentioned earlier, the effect of pressure on NHS gynaecological facilities and their failure in some areas of the country to meet the need stimulated the activities of the private hospitals and clinics which had been licensed under the Abortion Act. There were fifty-nine of these, half of them situated in the home counties and fifteen actually in London. A year after the Act had become law, statistics showed that for every six abortions carried out under the NHS, four were being performed privately, the vast majority in the West End of London. Thus of 15,140 abortions notified as having been performed in approved places, 14,104 (92%) had been carried out in the North West Metropolitan Area. A further 502 (3%) had been performed in the South East Metropolitan Area, and whilst the North East and South West Metropolitan Areas between them contributed another 30 cases, the remaining 504 cases had been terminated in the eleven non-metropolitan hospital regions covering the rest of England and Wales.

Swelling the number of women with unwanted pregnancies who were resident in the North West Metropolitan Area were women from the provinces who had been unable to obtain a NHS abortion locally and had come to London to get one privately and a number of women from abroad who had come to England for a similar purpose. The latter constituted, perhaps, 7 per cent of the total number of terminations performed. [164] Some of the private terminations were carried out by orthodox gynaecologists with part-time

NHS contracts who could not perform NHS terminations on all the women they saw and found suitable, since the latter's admission to NHS beds would have prevented gynaecological treatment being provided for women residing in their hospital's catchment area. Others were "professionals": individuals who did little obstetrics and who had had a paucity of gynaecological training and experience apart from practical knowledge gained in performing abortions. The Act in a sense "legitimatized" their activities, and whilst they provided a service—and apparently a speedy and reasonably safe one—many deplored their existence, regarding them as unscrupulous individuals, exploiting the anxiety of patients and the lack of NHS facilities for greed and personal gain.

Two charges often levelled at the private abortion clinics and the medical practitioners who spent their time working in them were, a *Medical Tribune* leading article [180] observes, that the lives of patients were being endangered and that profiteering was rife. In regard to the first charge, the article stated, the death rate for legal abortions—4-6 women per year—had remained remarkably constant for a decade; the death rate for illegal abortions—20-30 annually—had also been constant over the preceding 10 years. In regard to profiteering, abortion has always, Ferris [173] notes, attracted "peculiar characters", involving as it does sex, guilt, and money. One doctor he met, the principal owner of a nursing home where abortions were carried out, was probably grossing £10,000 a year in that home alone, and he was part owner of six others, in one of which private abortions were being performed. Nevertheless, to put the matter into perspective, the *Medical Tribune* article pointed out, profiteering had occurred in only a small number of the private institutions performing abortions, and overcharging for surgical operations was by no means confined to the private abortionists.

On 17 January 1969 a 35-year-old mother of six children died after a £50 abortion carried out at a nursing home at New Cross, London.

> At the inquest which was held on 4 February, the consultant gynaecologist who had performed the operation said that during it, he feared that he might have perforated the patient's uterus. He told the coroner, "I made particular examinations and probings to see whether this had happened. In view of what had occurred to me, I asked for a special watch to be kept on the patient." At about 6.00 p.m. the matron of the nursing home checked the woman's condition and found her complaining of backache. She telephoned the gynaecologist and called for an ambulance to take her to West Hill Hospital, Dartford, where the gynaecologist said he would meet the patient. The ambulance arrived 25 minutes later, but the ambulance men refused to take the patient to Dartford because it was too far. They took her instead to a hospital at Greenwich where she was given 2 pints of blood and 2 pints of plasma; more blood was sent for, but she died at 8.15 p.m.

When the coroner was informed that the nursing home involved was carrying out 400 legal abortions annually, he commented: "In this matter there is a state of affairs whereby a danger to the public arises. Looking at the nursing home in the terms of the Abortion Act it is self-evident that two necessary criteria are missing—that of having blood and being able to administer it. Such places should cease to exist."[181]

This tragedy gave rise to serious concern, and shortly afterwards Richard Crossman, the then Secretary of State for Social Services, seized the opportunity to tighten the regulations in premises approved under the Abortion Act, using requests for reapproval after one year as a justification for new safeguards. He was determined to do everything possible to minimize the risk to a woman's life and health, and, in a statement issued on 9 April 1969 he called for information about arrangements for medical supervision of patients, methods of moving women from operating theatres to wards, and facilities for blood transfusion and resuscitation. Since all the premises approved under the Abortion Act were also registered with local authorities under the Public Health Act 1936, and as such were subject to the Conduct of Nursing Homes Regulations 1963, which imposed specific requirements relating to patient care, the Minister was in a position to request local authorities to inspect the premises they registered in order to check the facts contained in applications for approval under the Abortion Act. In addition, during the following year, medical officers from the Department of Health and Social Security were to make special inspections of all premises.[182] Before a centre could be registered to carry out abortions under the Act after 26 April 1969, satisfactory answers to two new questions had to be obtained: (i) What facilities exist in the event of a power failure? and (ii) What arrangements are made for the sterilization of dressings?"[183] But desirable though these additional safeguards were, as a *British Medical Journal* leading article commented: "Inspection alone can never do more than detect the occasional abuse or deficiency. The real safeguard must be the vigilance of the medical attendants."[184]

On 28 April 1969, Richard Crossman, speaking in Parliament, stated that 55 out of the 59 private homes licensed in the first year under the Abortion Act had sought reapproval, and 47 had been granted it for a further year. Approval was withheld from one home and was given for 2 months only because of "apparent deficiencies in their facilities" to seven others—all in the London area and in all responsible for terminating 4522 pregnancies in the first quarter of 1969.[185] Since, numerically, these were the only private centres that counted, what seemed to be going on, Ferris [186] commented, was not an assault on the minority of abortion clinics but an attack on the whole private sector which in the first year of the Abortion Act was responsible for two-fifths of the terminations performed under it. In taking the unusual step of publicizing the names of the clinics and the numbers of terminations that had been carried out in them, the Government appeared to be making a show of opposition to the Act that it had sanctioned. Unable to do this on moral grounds, it had had to fall back on technical requirements. A consultant gynaecologist who performed operations in both NHS and private clinics told Ferris: "The hypocrisy of the situation is that there are dozens and dozens of NHS hospitals, including ones that I use and have used, that wouldn't stand up to this kind of inspection but no one says a thing about them. The fact is that the authorities have it in for the private clinics."

The Need for Contraception

The huge number of women of all ages referred to gynaecologists with unwanted pregnancies emphasized in no uncertain terms the need for better contraception. In August 1968, 3 months after the Abortion Act became law, it became clear a few days after the Pope's encyclical proscribing artificial forms of birth control that many Catholic priests disagreed with the Holy Father's ruling. [187] In the community generally, the 204 local authorities had been authorized to provide family-planning facilities, but though many had established these, only a handful had provided them on the scale needed. Apart from inevitable financial arguments, "no sex on the rates", little more than half supplied a service to the unmarried, and sixty flatly refused to do so; in this they were blindly refusing to face facts, the Family Planning Association felt. The cost of an abortion was far less than the cost to the community of providing for an unwanted child, but the cost of contraception was much lower than either; and those who feared that the provision of contraceptive service would be promoting a permissive society had failed to note that only 10 per cent of women seeking abortions did so after a casual relationship. [188] The Association preferred councils to provide an unrestricted family-planning service entirely free of charge in all cases, since it felt that charges tended to discourage women from seeking help.

One stimulus to the Family Planning Association's new stand on contraception was the finding that lack of advice was often present in women who sought termination of their unwanted pregnancies. Diggory,[175] a gynaecologist who described a personal series of 1000 abortions, amongst whom were 18 doctors, 99 nurses, 29 teachers, 84 students, and 42 schoolgirls, questioned the last 249 patients and found that many were "sadly lacking in knowledge about contraception". Forty-eight per cent of his patients had employed no contraceptive techniques during the sexual act that had led to their impregnation and 30.5 per cent habitually used none. His findings were in rough alignment with those obtained by the Birmingham Pregnancy Advisory Service between 27 April and 31 December 1968; in Birmingham, 73.5 per cent of women had employed no contraceptive technique on the critical occasion, whilst 45.8 per cent habitually did not use any. In the London Pregnancy Advisory Service, S. R. Abels[189] reported, analysis of the first 500 patients showed that 70 per cent of women were unprotected at the time of conception and 42 per cent normally used no contraceptive technique.

Speaking at the National Conference of the Family Planning Association in June 1969, Richard Crossman, the then Secretary of State for Social Services, told the conference that he did not want Britain to be known as the "capital of abortion" but as a place where contraception was so much a part of the way of life that abortion was unnecessary. Nothing compensated for the fact that a child was unwanted, but abortion was always a sign of failure. There were too many cases where large families caused mothers an unsupportable physical and emotional strain, Crossman said, not to mention the burden on local authorities. The latter should provide family-planning services free of charge and be persuaded to do so by the Family Planning Association. To assist the Association in this task, the Government was making a grant of £20,000 which was to be renewed annually for 5 years. In the Press Conference earlier Edwin Brooks, the sponsor of the Family Planning Act, said he would welcome a change in the law entitling a doctor to give contraceptives to a girl below the age of 16 years, though when pressed Brooks said he could not ask an FPA doctor to risk prosecution "for aiding and abetting a child in committing sexual intercourse" by prescribing contraceptives in this way.

Changed Roles

GYNAECOLOGISTS

The increased number of women referred to gynaecologists for consideration of termination after the Act became law, a leading article [190] commented, ". . . startled those gynaecologists who had foreseen only a modest liberalising swing and who have been dismayed to see the figures leaping to the estimated 35,000 abortions under the Act in its first year. . . . Things were certainly easier for the gynaecologists before public and Parliament made their wishes known in the Act . . .", it continued, ". . . but they were much harder for women. . . ."

The increased demand bore especially heavily on the gynaecological out-patient facilities and beds in the NHS, where hitherto only small numbers of women with unwanted pregnancies had been assessed and operated upon. The situation was less difficult in Aberdeen and in Ayrshire, for example, where, prior to the Act, the less restrictive Scottish law had permitted liberal gynaecologists to make arrangements to meet a constant demand for therapeutic terminations. In England and Wales, the consultant gynaecologists discovered that they personally had to assess an unprecedented number of women requesting termination, on a large proportion of whom they later had to operate, with the result that they had to leave their registrars (residents) to see their other out-patients. In consequence, gynaecologists had to review the way in which requests for termination were handled so as to cope more efficiently with the increasing number of cases. In this situation, many gynaecologists wanted more information from general practitioners and, like Professor Rhodes, [191] requested fuller referral letters containing the family doctor's view and his assessment of the patient's circumstances. They called on medical social workers and health visitors to help and, in contrast, they less frequently turned to the psychiatrist, whose views on the desirability of termination were for the most part no longer necessary.

Many of the patients referred to gynaecologists for consideration of termination differed from their predecessors in being physically and psychologically healthier, and so appearing less deserving of the operation. Nevertheless, the gynaecologist often found that he had to spend a great deal of time investigating the women who were sent to him. Frank Denny, [192] describing 226 patients seen by himself and two colleagues in a London hospital between May and September 1968, pointed out that the 170 who were rejected for termination were turned down because no medical or social indication within the terms of the Act existed. But, as Professor Mac-Gillivray[193] noted, whether or not termination was carried out, suppport and after-care had to be provided, even though some women failed to take advantage of it.

One London gynaecologist, Lewis,[194] reviewing the figures for the first 8 months of the Abortion Act (22,256 terminations performed), observed that the whole character of the gynaecologist's work had altered because he (now) had to deal with two to four requests for termination at each outpatient session. "Rightly or wrongly, gynaecologists are doing many more termination operations than previously," he commented, "and I have made no mention of the large numbers of pregnancies that are being terminated in registered nursing homes for reasons of convenience and financial gain, masquerading as legal operations under the new Act." Lewis's article provoked a letter from Malcolm Potts,[195] who acidly observed: "If it is true that the 'whole character of the gynaecologist's outpatient work has altered', then it may be that some gynaecologists previously lived not in a fool's paradise but in a specialist's paradise, insulated from a grave and genuine medical need." Potts thought that one of the main effects of the 1967 Act had been "to enable women (and their general practitioners) to confront gynaecologists with what has always been a common and heart-searching problem". He considered that the age, parity, and marital status of women seeking abortion might have changed, but he did not think that the total number of induced abortions was any greater than 30 or 40 years ago. Richard de Soldenhoff,[196] a gynaecologist in Ayrshire, commented that he was "a little amazed at the howls of protest that it [the Abortion Act] is interfering with the ordinary work of units and outpatient clinics". He thought it unlikely that Ayrshire had better morals than other parts of Great Britain, and claimed that it had been possible to deal with the patients in the district expeditiously, admitting and discharging them within 2 or 3 days; he did not feel that the demand had made his waiting list longer or had interfered with the intake of patients into maternity beds. All told, the three gynaecologists in de Soldenhoff's area had performed some 120 terminations in the first year of the Act, helped greatly by the patients' general practitioners. "With this co-operation", he commented, "there is no time wasted and it does not take a genius to weed out the odd one in which this is not a justifiable procedure."

Peter Diggory,[175] a gynaecologist from Kingston, Surrey, described a personal series of 1000 consecutive cases of abortion carried out by himself or his junior colleagues from 1965 onwards. He pointed out that early in the series a large number of referrals came from other parts of the country, but that later on he had been forced to adopt a policy of accepting patients for NHS termination only if they lived in the catchment area of the hospitals concerned. Of the 1000 cases, simple curettage was performed in 77 per cent and hysterotomy in 16 per cent. There were few complications and none were serious. He thought that a more liberal policy in the NHS should be uniformly practised, and, to prevent the growth of private abortion clinics in London, Diggory advocated that such clinics be set up in the NHS.

PSYCHIATRISTS

The implementation of the Abortion Act brought about a marked alteration in the role of the psychiatrists. Prior to the Act, gynaecologists had tended to send patients to them when they did not know whether sufficient psychiatric, i.e. not purely "medical", grounds existed for termination to be justifiable. In such cases, the opinion of the psychiatrist often buttressed that of the general practitioner—or substituted for it—and was helpful to the gynaecologist in evaluating the patient's problem and in providing suitable "safeguards" under the case law of the Bourne decision. After the Act became law, and the number of women requesting termination rose, many gynaecologists, realizing that more than one other opinion regarding termination was no longer necessary, ceased to refer the majority of cases to psychiatrists. A good letter from a general practitioner who knew the patient well was sufficient as a basis for them either to perform the operation—e.g. in the case of some otherwise well-balanced single woman whose career would be ruined by having a baby—or to reject it, as when the grounds were flimsy because the pregnancy was merely inconvenient, or when there were no social factors arguing termination, or if the patient did not appear distressed. In the few cases in which the gynaecologist was uncertain, he would still sometimes refer the patient on for a psychiatric opinion, especially if she appeared to be psychiatrically ill or if relevant social factors were present, e.g. an unwanted pregnancy in a woman with six children and an invalid husband.

The more discriminating pattern of psychiatric referral supervened because gynaecologists, finding that pressure of work under the Abortion Act led to delays in appointments with the psychiatrist, tended to save "problem patients" for his consideration. In such cases, his opinion was of value, for in the course of his examination the psychiatrist, the gynaecologist felt, was often able to elicit material that was less likely to come to light in the more traditional gynaecological surroundings. Many cases he referred, the gynaecologist felt, would probably require continuing psychiatric support after the operation; even if they did not obtain this, an interview with a psychiatrist was frequently helpful in "sorting things out". After the Act became law, however, some gynaecologists ceased to refer cases because they felt the psychiatrist either always agreed or always opposed termination, a conservative gynaecologist/liberal psychiatrist or a liberal gynaecologist/conservative psychiatrist situation being established.

Speaking at a symposium on the working of the Abortion Act arranged by the Medical Protection Society in collaboration with the Royal College of General Practitioners and held in February 1969, P. H. Tooley[144] observed that, for patients who reached the psychiatrist, the criteria for termination were the same as before the Act. Sympathy—or lack of it—often determined the decision that was made, with the result that most abortions were done for the weak, the handicapped, and the immature. He thought that social stresses with which the patient was unable to cope were sometimes grounds for termination, as were a history of puerperal mental illness and a threat of suicide. He believed that termination was often advisable in older women with a "completed" family, but he advocated caution in advising it for rigid, over-conscientious personalities and in some unmarried girls who wished to continue with a pregnancy after obtaining support from their families. R. F. Tredgold,[144] speaking at the same symposium, thought that medical men should probably no longer make the decision on termination of pregnancy but should be able to leave the final decision to the mother, i.e. they should become advisors, not judges. He thought that the existing denial of responsibility probably promoted irresponsible behaviour, which might improve if responsibility was progressively reassigned.

GENERAL PRACTITIONERS

For the general practitioner, the implementation of the Abortion Act brought enhanced status. As indicated earlier, it was on his judgement that the gynaecologist now relied in the majority of cases. Formerly, his views on the case had ranked only equal with or had taken second place to the opinion of the psychiatrist, on whom the gynaecologist had often tended to rely in cases where he felt uncertain. Now the psychiatrist, as Hughes[197] pointed out, was usually no longer necessary. Only two medical signatures were needed on the form for abortion to be legal, and a gynaecologist could perform three abortions in the time the psychiatrist took to investigate one case. Nachshen[198] was not so happy: he pointed out that often in a perfectly healthy young woman, with no history of mental disorder, the general practitioner was being asked to agree to a termination of pregnancy on which the woman had already decided. Frequently she would not accept the general practitioner's opinion that termination was not advisable, and if the gynaecologist to whom he sent her concurred, she would frequently seek out privately a more liberal practitioner whose views approximated to her own, and would obtain a legal abortion under the terms of the Act. In these circumstances, the opinion of the family doctor was of little value; and he had either to let the matter rest or agree to well-nigh any request that came his way. Nachshen concluded: "The Abortion Act is destroying the conventional and time-honoured relationship between patient and doctor, wherein the doctor advises his patient as to what he considers to be the correct means of alleviating complaints and medical conditions. . . . Ultimately we shall lose our capacity for objective clinical judgement, and, with it, our self-respect."

NURSES

A substantial number of nurses became involved in termination of pregnancy after the Abortion Act became law in April 1968, and with the increasing number of patients seeking and obtaining terminations, the extent of nurses' involvement increased. Because of the conflicts aroused in her by the procedure—loyalties to her superiors, to her patients, and (perhaps) to her religion coming into opposition—the nurse's role was especially difficult.

A consultant psychiatrist,[199] writing by invitation in the *Nursing Mirror* in February 1966, drew attention to the emotional problems roused in a nurse by termination on psychiatric grounds. Was the procedure morally right? Should, in any circumstances, a baby be killed or denied birth? If so, under what circumstances was such an action permissible? Would not the availability of termination encourage promiscuity and carelessness, and so lead to yet more terminations with consequent further lengthening of the waiting period for other operations? Should help be given to an irresponsible, unstable girl that was not provided for a stronger, more conscientious woman, so that the latter might have to accept her (equally unwanted) pregnancy to the detriment of her own and her family's health? The consultant pointed out that, apart from her own ethical views, the nurse's attitude might be affected by reflecting what would happen to her friends or to herself when faced with an unwanted pregnancy.

The nursing staff of the operating theatre, the consultant observed, were in a difficult position. They were asked to act in opposition to their training and inclinations, which were directed towards saving life and helping with birth, and, whilst being expected to "clear up the mess" after the operation, had no one to whom they could express their feelings. Often they had no idea why the operation was being performed. The same applied to ward staff who frequently had to nurse patients who, relieved of their anxieties, demonstrated little sign of the symptoms which had led to the decision to terminate pregnancy. The ward nurse could readily conclude that the patient had "put on an act" and, by hoodwinking her medical attendants, had evaded the penalty of her misdeeds or her lack of foresight. Yet despite this it was important, the consultant insisted, that the nurse did not display any critical feelings she might have to the patient, for these could increase the latter's guilt and depression. Instead, whenever possible, she had to be prepared to help the patient with the mixed feelings of remorse and relief that were so often experienced after the operation. The nurse could be helped, the consultant thought, by being made aware of the law and of the problems of the individual patient. Whilst Roman Catholic nurses were within their rights to refuse to participate in any way in termination operations, the general principle of refusing to nurse patients whose illnesses were the results of conduct of which nurses disapproved—such as venereal disease, or alcoholic cirrhosis of the liver—seemed absurd.

Difficulties in regard to legal abortions were experienced in some degree by all levels of nursing staff, the juniors being concerned by their participation in procedures they found distasteful, and the seniors being troubled by the necessity for giving a lead in an uncertain situation.

EARLY TERMINATION PROCEDURES

Originally, as described in Chapter 7, dilatation and curettage was used to terminate the majority of pregnancies of less than 12 weeks' duration, and though this has been increasingly supplanted by vacuum aspiration, the situation for the theatre nurse has not very markedly changed. Dilatation and curettage is a messy, unpleasant procedure, especially when portions of the foetus become visible, and the nurse may find it disturbing, especially if she has religious objections or is fruitlessly trying to become pregnant herself. In recent months the development of larger curettes, whilst enabling termination by the vacuum method to be performed up to 16 weeks, has made the procedure a little less distasteful, though after the operation is completed the nurse may still have to clear up surgical towels with organic material adherent to them. Nevertheless, even when performed by a gynaecologist inexperienced in the procedure, a suction termination takes only 2 or 3 minutes longer than a dilatation and curettage, and is not very traumatic to observe.

Abdominal hysterotomy, on the other hand, can be a frightening procedure to watch, especially for nurses who are still in training. When the wall of the uterus is incised there is often a good deal of bleeding, and some nurses dislike seeing the removal of the foetus and the placenta. Doubts as to the ethicality of termination are mobilized, and the nurse may wonder why the patient did not seek a therapeutic abortion at an earlier stage. In one London teaching hospital, which was probably typical of many British general hospitals, operating theatre staff became anxious and started to express concern when terminations began on an appreciable scale, and a Roman Catholic theatre sister who participated in them became severely depressed. Nurses repeatedly checked the operating lists, counted the number of cases scheduled for termination, complained if the rota showed that they had a disproportionately large number to carry out, and on occasion refused to scrub for the operation. Reassurance was repeatedly sought from the senior nursing staff as to the ethical nature of the procedure and as to whether, after a hysterotomy had been performed, the foetus that had been removed was really dead. Sometimes nurses asked their seniors to check that this was so, and they objected to disposing of it.

In the course of a few months these misgivings settled down, and theatre staff found themselves able to dissociate their feelings from the task of termination. Much depended on their regard for the gynaecologists performing the operation: the fact that the latter were highly ethical, respected, considerate individuals made the nurse's burden of guilt appreciably lighter. Several continued to feel, however, that nurses in training were being excessively exposed to the sordid aspects of sexuality before having had a chance to observe the rewarding aspects of happy, successful childbirth. Others pointed out that the large number of terminations meant that little experience could be gained with gynaecological operations other than abortion, and it proved impossible to recruit a sister (i.e. a nursing supervisor) for the gynaecology theatre. In at least one hospital, Scarborough, 75 per cent of nursing staff refused to be involved in termination operations, and the remaining 25 per cent had to shoulder the burden of the increased work. [200]

Operating theatre nurses thus bore the brunt of termination operations in the first few months that the Act became operative. Their counterparts in the ward were less affected, apart from losing the chance of gaining experience with gynaecological illnesses other than legal abortions and of having to deal with the reactions of patients hospitalized for investigation of infertility who usually had had to be admitted to the same wards as those awaiting and recovering from terminations. The ward nurses found it hard to come to terms with legal abortions, for psychiatric and other notes were seldom made available, and they were left to draw their own conclusions. Much depended on a patient's background and the attitude she displayed. An unwanted pregnancy in a schoolteacher, a university student, or someone with whom the nurse could identify was usually regarded with compassion, but the same situation in a non-professional girl who appeared unconcerned or complacent about termination frequently provoked feelings of resentment —"Why should she get away with it?" This reaction was reinforced if the patient, pleading shortage of money or lack of time, showed no intention of attending the family-planning clinic to which ward staff routinely referred her for contraceptive advice. "Repeat" therapeutic abortions also provoked hostility, and many nurses found themselves in agreement with those gynaecologists who refused to perform more than, say, two successive terminations on psychiatric grounds.

Later Methods of Termination

As newer methods of termination were introduced in the hospital, stress began to revert from the operating theatre staff to nurses in the ward. Abortifacient paste injection and the intra-amniotic instillation of hypertonic saline were originally carried out in the operating theatre, but as more experience was gained the latter procedure began to be performed in the ward, and the majority of prostaglandin terminations did not require the use of an operating theatre at all.

In intra-amniotic termination procedures, nurses found it disturbing to watch the trocar and canula being pushed into the pregnant abdomen, and some thought of the pain and self-doubt that the patient was, they conjectured, experiencing. They wondered whether she would later regret having undergone the procedure, especially since, once the saline was injected, the die, as it were, was cast. Some nurses felt it was wrong to undergo termination when the "baby" was fully formed, and they disliked the entire procedure. Despite the premedication and the local anaesthetic that was administered, some women experienced pain with the method, and the nurse had to comfort them and usually had to be present at the miniature labour, ensuring that the 3 or 4 in. long unequivocably dead foetus—not infrequently damaged by the injection technique—was passed complete, together with the placenta. Disposing of the foetus and the afterbirth was for most nurses a particularly distasteful task. In some hospitals the ward staff nurse had to put six or more foetuses into bags every morning prior to incineration. The nurses noted with approval, however, that women who had undergone the experience of termination by the intra-amniotic injection of hypertonic solutions seemed to have had the "reality" of an abortion brought home to them and frequently took advantage of the arrangements that were made for them to attend family-planning clinics.

Prostaglandin terminations also were stressful for ward nurses. Assisting the physician to erect the drip was simple, but in Karim and Filshie's [160] trial of prostaglandin $F_{2\alpha}$, vomiting was a problem, and the severe diarrhoea developed by some patients necessitated the provision of a constant supply of bedpans. Most women aborted within 12 hours and were undisturbed by the pain of uterine contraction—which was relieved by pethidine —or by the experience of a prostaglandin-induced premature labour; but a fringe group of vulnerable individuals complained of severe pain, which was unrelieved by pethidine, and, distressed by the slowness with which their prostaglandin (an old batch) worked, disturbed the ward with their agitation and wailing, some requesting general anaesthetics. For the ward nurse as well as for the patient, its side-effects made the prostaglandin method somewhat repugnant; further, nurses disliked checking the foetus after delivery to ensure that it was complete, especially if, because it was biologically alive, they could see or feel its limbs moving. The labour was "dry", the "waters not breaking" as with a saline termination, and to some nurses appeared more traumatic than a saline induction. As with the former method, nurses found disposing of the foetus "absolutely horrible"; yet, as with the former method also, the nurses noted with approval that after a prostaglandin termination the patient usually was eager to take advantage of the opportunity to attend the family-planning clinic for contraceptive counselling.

Altered Attitudes

GYNAECOLOGISTS

Some of the reasons why many gynaecologists were opposed to the Act have been discussed in Chapter 2. Clearly, many did not wish to acknowledge the extent of the demand that they would have to meet when the Act became law, and they preferred to deny its magnitude since they perceived that it would involve them in a task that would be distasteful, unethical, and lacking in challenge. After the Act became law, the alteration that occurred in the role of the gynaecologists hardened the attitudes of the few who had been diametrically opposed to abortion on psychiatric grounds, softened the views of the many who, whilst unenthusiastic, were not markedly against it, and confirmed the liberal in their original beliefs.

Morally, two issues dominated the situation: (1) Is a foetus a human being and so to be accorded human rights?, and (2) Does a doctor have the right to punish a patient, in particular a woman, by withholding an abortion on grounds of "excessive promiscuity" or some other imagined shortcoming?[201] If the answer to the first question is "yes", it is difficult to decide at what point in its development the fertilized ovum attains human status; whilst if it is "no", abortion in certain circumstances is justifiable. Similarly, in regard to the second question, an affirmative answer would warrant denying a woman an abortion, whilst a negative one would imply that in some cases she was entitled to have one.

Gynaecologists like Professors McLaren and Donald who, as earlier noted, were in sympathy with the aims of the Society for the Protection of Unborn Children—an organization that would give an affirmative answer to the first question—continued strongly to oppose therapeutic abortion on psychiatric grounds after the Act became law. Thus Professor McLaren is reported to have stated: "I have not carried out an abortion on 'social' grounds and I never shall. I do not think we should be asked to cut out social problems with a surgeon's knife."[202] In a provocatively titled article "Abortion or modern obstetrics?", Professor McLaren[203] reiterated his objections to abortion for other than strict "medical" reasons. The general-hospital-based academic unit which he directed would abort, he said, for these or for rubella, but the terminations carried out for these reasons amounted to only four of five annually, a rate of 5 per 1000 deliveries, or one-tenth of the rate prevailing in Aberdeen. Professor McLaren admitted that he was seldom asked to abort to relieve social or economic pressure, "for it is widely known that this unit will not dispose of an unwanted pregnancy so that requests of that kind do not reach us". He claimed that the syndrome of "misery, anguish and despair" met with in Aberdeen by Professor Mac-Gillivray,[193] and taken there as an indication for termination of pregnancy, could be managed in Birmingham by admission to hospital, investigation, medication, help from a medical social worker, and, if necessary, psychiatric consultation. He believed that in the Midlands, the conservative line adopted by gynaecologists had led to an increased acceptance of contraception. In Glasgow, too, Professor Donald continued to perform very few therapeutic abortions—about 5 per 1000 deliveries per year—and, according to Professor McLaren, gynaecologists in Leeds and Liverpool also remained conservative.[203] Unfortunately, the NHS consultants who performed few or no terminations on psychiatric grounds were responsible for the flourishing private trade they tended to deplore, as well as for overloading their more liberal colleagues.

The majority of gynaecologists, however, slowly came to view termination of pregnancy on psychiatric grounds if not with approval, at least as being justified in many cases. "It is extremely distasteful for me to carry out this procedure," Professor Morris of London observed, "but I recognize there is no justification for not carrying it out."[161] Another London gynaecologist, Lewis,[194] noting that 22,256 terminations had been performed during the first 8 months of the Act and discussing the number of requests turned down (presumably far fewer than before the Act), observed: "Gynaecologists are discovering that conscience can work both ways. You may feel in one case that it would be wrong to operate; but equally you may feel in another that simply for humane reasons it would be wrong not to operate." Lewis thought that unless there was a remarkable change of heart by the permissive society, or contraceptive measures became universally accepted and applied, the high rate of operations would continue. "It is unrealistic", he said, "to expect a small section of the community—namely those trained to do gynaecology—to adopt within the framework of the law a moral attitude that is completely at variance with that of society as a whole." Many gynaecologists, originally conservative in their attitude, gradually became more liberal, influenced by the changed climate of opinion, and also perhaps by the knowledge that, in individual cases, if they did not perform the terminations requested, patients would readily obtain them quite legally elsewhere. Professor Rhodes, also from London, speaking at a medical society meeting, said that in the hospital in which he worked the Act had set a seal on a custom that had already been established, for the number of abortions performed there had risen steadily in the preceding 4 years.[191] He stated that he had a humanistic approach to the problem, and he declared that a large slice of medicine should be compassion; he performed two terminations a week, and he agreed with Sir Dugald Baird that deterioration in a patient's health as a result of guilt following termination was almost non-existent, and that neurotic and psychotic symptoms were no commoner after termination than after a normal delivery. Diggory[175] in his series of 1000 cases found subsequent remorse extremely rare, and Gross,[204] in a similar vein, pointed out there is no evidence that therapeutic abortions cause any more traumata than any other operation. Gross noted the tendency of both to produce a post-anaesthetic abreaction with weeping and depression, and he observed that, since the Abortion Act had become law the "average patient" referred for termination was healthy and mentally balanced. Such women resented being referred to a psychiatrist unless it was really necessary, and, relieved of the heavy burden of prejudice, were less likely to develop psychiatric sequelae. Friendly, sympathetic understanding coupled with reassurance contributed, he thought, to a complete recovery.

For those gynaecologists who were in favour of therapeutic termination, the passage of the Act into law came as a mixed blessing. In Aberdeen, Professor MacGillivray continued to exhibit the liberal attitude towards termination shown by Sir Dugald Baird. He thought that the problems of the gynaecologists of this orientation, who had formerly felt restricted by the law and since the passage of the Act had felt constrained to stem the tide of overwhelming applications for termination, were likely to resolve themselves once the administrative machinery was working efficiently. "The doctor who is concerned about the misery, anguish, and despair caused to his patient by an unwanted pregnancy", Professor MacGillivray[193] commented, "will take the trouble to make the necessary adjustments in his out-patient and in-patient facilities and, if by this means a satisfactory service cannot be provided, will press for more so that the terms of the Act can be properly applied." Following the publicity given to the liberal policy towards abortion practised in north-east Scotland, referrals of women by the general practitioners to the area increased: there were 150 terminations of pregnancy in 1965, 197 in 1966, and 280 in 1967. In Newcastle upon Tyne, another liberal abortion area, one well-known gynaecologist, Dorothea Kerslake, is reported to have personally performed over 400 terminations between April 1968 and February 1969.[202]

Clearly, attitudes regarding the Act continued to vary a great deal even after it had passed into law. Anthony Alment, Honorary Secretary of the Royal College of Obstetricians and Gynaecologists considered that it was impossible to get a common policy among specialists as long as the law remained open to interpretation. Whilst a few appeared to want "foetal abattoirs" run by co-operatives of doctors to provide an instant solution to a physical problem, he thought that the majority had been helped by the Act to understand more about environmental factors than ever before and now wanted to consider each case fully before deciding whether to operate. But since a gynaecologist spent much of his time trying to save life, it was difficult "to be a saviour and a destroyer in the same breath".[202]

The working of the Act was discussed at the Medical Protection Society's symposium held in London on 7 February 1969. Speaking of its legal implications, Sir Geoffrey Howe, QC, pointed out that though the doctor had the right to refrain from treatment, he did not have the right to refrain from consideration of treatment; it was his duty to discuss the question if he decided that abortion might be clinically necessary. Sir Geoffrey feared that the working of the Act might produce an unforeseen working rule of "If in doubt, terminate", since a continued pregnancy might produce adverse effects which might be the basis of a civil charge of negligence. He felt that when a doctor believed that termination was unnecessary, it was wise therefore for him to obtain a second opinion.[144]

GENERAL PRACTITIONERS

As far as general practitioners were concerned, the principal effect of the passage of the Act into law was to reinforce attitudes which had latterly become increasingly sympathetic towards women burdened with unwanted pregnancies.[33, 52] A few found the Act repugnant because it conflicted with their religious or ethical beliefs. Others objected because they thought the Act too loose in its terminology and made abortion so easy to justify that it could virtually be had on demand. This put them in a difficult position if they felt that termination was inadvisable, for often the woman would not accept their opinion and went elsewhere.

All shades of opinion were reflected amongst the family doctors. Margaret Dudley-Brown,[144] speaking at the February symposium, said that under the Act the general practitioner's duties were threefold: to know and understand its provisions; to apply this knowledge objectively; and to avoid using it if at all possible. Hughes[197]—and no doubt many others—thought this an extraordinary statement. In a letter to the editor of the *British Medical Journal* he commented: ". . . the Abortion Act is the law of the land and has already proved of immense benefit to many of my patients. It is there to be used and to be applied uniformly throughout the country. It is the antagonism to abortion reform of many doctors, particularly NHS consultants in certain parts of the country, that creates long queues for abortion . . .", and he concluded, more trenchantly still, ". . . If all doctors, general practitioners and consultants put their patients' welfare before their own religious and biased cobwebbed ideas on abortion, then the new Act would present no problems at all. A patient for termination of pregnancy would appear in hospital as an acute appendix does today, and would be dealt with as quickly and without question." Hardly surprisingly, these views raised violent objections. N. C. Lee [205] wrote that to say that he was disgusted by Hughes's letter would be a masterpiece of understatement. He observed: "I find the trendy assembly-line philosophy of the whole letter so utterly repugnant that it would take up valuable space to itemize my objections to it." Lee believed that an abortion destroyed a potential human being and that since the duty of the profession was to preserve life, it assumed the heaviest of responsibilities by destroying it. Such beliefs were not "religious and biased cobwebbed ideas", Lee declared, but were "the very stuff of medical ethics". D. C. Turk, [206] in a similar but somewhat less impassioned vein, drew attention to the assumptions that Hughes's views made it necessary to make—that objections to the liberal interpretation of the Act were necessarily religious, that being religious they were irrelevant to the present situation, that doctors who did not think like Hughes were more concerned about the peace of their consciences than about the welfare of their patients, that those who doubted the wisdom of the Act were biased, whilst only its enthusiastic supporters were capable of unbiased judgement and that that which was permitted by an Act of Parliament was *ipso facto* the best for all citizens. In contrast, E. F. Richard [207] wrote to say that he agreed with Hughes, and remarked that he thought a great deal of time was wasted by gynaecologists and psychiatrists in sorting out a problem which from the woman's point of view, and indeed the majority of the country, should present very few difficulties. Richard believed that the Abortion Act was the envy of Europe, and he thought that its only flaw was that a time limit—such as 13 weeks—had not been inserted.

One fact that after the Act became law indicated the liberal attitude of the majority of general practitioners towards abortion where adequate grounds existed was the greatly increased number of women they referred to gynaecologists for consideration of termination. The latter, as Lewis [194] observed, had failed to allow for general practitioners' attitudes. In liberal parts of the country, gynaecologists were deluged with requests; whilst, in more conservative areas, large numbers of patients were still referred, if not to local gynaecologists, to private facilities and to the Pregnancy Advisory Service.

Sara Abels,[189] honorary medical secretary of PAS, noted that of over 1000 women who had attended the London branch in the first 6 months after it had opened, 45 per cent had been referred by doctors, most of them general practitioners.

In regard to the attitude of the public, the 1-year termination figures spoke for themselves. Clearly, as Professor Huntingford[208] observed, termination for appropriate reasons was the will of the majority. Having endorsed the Act, most members of the British public, especially women, wanted their doctors to implement it in a liberal way. Yet, as Lynne Edmunds[209] pointed out, despite the passage of the Act into law, whether or not a woman with an unwanted pregnancy could get it terminated often depended on luck—the area of the country in which she resided, and whether she happened to have money available. When they found that abortion "on demand" was not available, many blamed the medical profession. Having decided that they wanted their unwanted pregnancies terminated, many women found the attitudes of conservative gynaecologists baffling and incomprehensible.

CHAPTER 9

Aftermaths: The Spring of 1969

THE first year of the Abortion Act ended on 26 April 1969, and during the months that followed, abortion and related subjects were seldom out of the medical or lay press for very long at a time. In the spring the occasional abortion deaths that occurred received extensive coverage, and doubts regarding the way in which the Act was working were repeatedly expressed, especially by those who had opposed its passage in Parliament. A series of General Medical Council Disciplinary Committee hearings on the professional activities of two physicians were followed by reports of overseas abortion-seekers arriving in London in droves, news which created a flurry of interest and speculation, especially in regard to terminations of pregnancy carried out in the private clinics. The way in which the Act was working was debated at the Annual Representative Meeting of the British Medical Association in July. This preceded the first unsuccessful parliamentary attempt to modify the Act. The defeat did not settle the controversy, though a British Medical Association Symposium on Legal Abortion in North East Scotland gave an indication of how the Act might be expected to operate in a few years' time.

Early Concern

The anxiety felt by some Members of Parliament in regard to the working of the Abortion Act became evident early in 1969 before it was even a year old. In February, Norman St. John-Stevas, Conservative Member of Parliament for Chelmsford and a self-styled "Catholic celibate" who had opposed the passage of the Act in Parliament, gave notice that he would use the device of the 10-minute rule to bring in a Bill "to improve the law concerning abortion and the status and rights of the medical profession in regard thereto". In his proposed new Bill he had three principal aims: (i) to rescind the medico-social clause which legalized abortion in the interests of the health of the existing children of the family; (ii) to strengthen the conscience clause whereby on this basis doctors could refuse to perform termination; and (iii) to provide a 6-month residential qualification so as to prevent foreign women from entering Britain to secure an abortion that was illegal in their own countries. "We are in an absolutely impossible position", St. John-Stevas asserted, "in that we have a law which is very permissive and which has created a demand that the profession is unwilling to fulfil. I am trying to get a better compromise than we now have," he went on, "I do not take the view that the law should not allow abortion in any circumstances. There are cases where for necessity the law should be permissive, but it should be restricted, not as permissive as it is now."[210]

Quick to defend the Act that the Abortion Law Reform Association had fought so hard to promote, Madeleine Simms[211] pointed out that what St. John-Stevas meant by "improving" the Act was in fact restricting and weakening it. She observed that only 4 per cent of the terminations carried out in the Act's first 5 months were performed on the basis of the "social" clause, and there was nothing to suggest that the conscience clause was being abused. Likewise, there was no solid evidence that large numbers of foreign women were coming to Britain for terminations which they were unable to get at home. Simms thought that St. John-Stevas's attempt to reform the law was predominantly a political exercise, and she felt that the demand for abortion would continue to rise until modern contraception caught up. Her views probably were endorsed by many of the public. Sir Geoffrey Howe,[144] speaking at the Medical Protection Society's Symposium on the working of the Act, said that he believed that the new law would be changed only if there was a run of inquests resulting from abortion operations, though he thought that there might be a revulsion of opinion if the number of abortions continued to grow at the rate then existing and if the proportion carried out in approved places continued at the level of 40 per cent.

In April 1969 Mrs. Jill Knight, a Conservative Member of Parliament, visited Lansing, Michigan, and told a Senate Committee on Health, Social Services, and Retirement there that London had become the "abortion capital of the western world". She was reported to have said that efforts were afoot to permit mercy killing of incurably ill and mentally deranged persons as a sequel to abortion law changes, and to have stated, "Once the principle has been accepted that innocent human life may be destroyed, there is nothing to prevent its extension to euthanasia, infanticide, and perhaps other cases as well."[212] At about the same time in London, Mrs. Renee Short, Labour Member of Parliament for Wolverhampton, North East, asked the Secretary of State for Social Services if he was satisfied with the operation of the Abortion Act in relation to the facilities afforded by the medical profession to women seeking termination of pregnancy. Richard Crossman replied that he was "by no means satisfied as far as private practice under the Act is concerned". He said he had requested additional information in regard to the private clinics, but he felt that it was too early to reach conclusions about the adequacy of National Health Service hospital facilities. Mrs. Short then asserted that in the NHS some consultant gynaecologists were issuing blanket refusals to undergo any terminations at all, even though they might have been referred and recommended by two or even three of their medical colleagues. She asked whether it was not high time that women were freed from the tyranny of certain sections of the medical profession. Would Mr. Crossman see what more could be done to see that the law was carried out? Mr. Crossman responded that Mrs. Short had pointed out an extreme danger that might occur in certain cases, but the danger he had mentioned (the question of whether the private clinics met acceptable standards) was, he felt, far graver.[213]

A Baby Dies in Glasgow

On 22 May 1969 a fatal accident inquiry at Glasgow Sheriff Court, Scotland, was told that a male child, believed to have been born dead in the gynaecological operating theatre of a NHS hospital in that city, had started to cry as it was being carried to the hospital incinerator.

> The mother, a student, later thought that she might have been impregnated at a party she had attended in August 1968, but as her periods were irregular she did not realize that she was pregnant until January 1969. She saw a consultant gynaecologist on the 15th of that month who accepted her statement that she had menstruated in August, and judged the pregnancy to be 26 weeks advanced. Together with another medical practitioner he certified that the continuance of the pregnancy would involve risk of injury to the physical or mental health of the pregnant woman greater than if the pregnancy was terminated, and that if the child was born it would suffer from such physical and mental abnormalities as to be seriously handicapped. The gynaecologist performed an abdominal hysterotomy on 20 January 1969, and the baby was delivered at 11.40 a.m. As it was pale and limp with no respiratory movements and no pulse, and as the cord did not bleed, the gynaecologist concluded that it was dead; two assisting doctors, the anaesthetist, and the theatre sister likewise saw no sign of life. The body was given to the theatre attendant to take to the incinerator for disposal; there, left in the open air, it was found by the incinerator attendant who "heard a whimper

from the bag". The baby was at once taken to the premature baby unit, where it was found to be blotchy, cold, and limp. Oxygen was administered but it died 8 or 9 hours later. At the inquiry, necropsy evidence suggested that the baby had been 32, not 28, weeks old; the jury concluded that death had been due to absence of attempts at resuscitation after the baby's birth, to its subsequent exposure to cold, and to prematurity.

Since there was a suggestion that in similar cases "in the no-man's land between the law of the Abortion Act and the law that says there is a right to life" resuscitation might not be carried out as vigorously as possible, the jury unanimously recommended: "(i) That in all cases where an infant of or approaching or about viable age, or apparently or possibly viable, is to be delivered by abortion, all facilities and resuscitatory methods applied in cases of ordinary birth should be adopted; and (ii) that legislation be introduced prohibiting abortion when the foetus is approaching or has reached the stage of viability." [214]

The director of the premature baby unit at the hospital subsequently estimated that the child's chance of survival at birth had been slightly less than 50–50. The case was unusual, a newspaper medical correspondent, Christine Doyle,[215] commented, in that neither the gynaecologist who performed the operation nor anyone else had had reason to suspect that the child might live, and it illustrated how close was the dividing line between a foetus with no chance of life and a premature infant for which all possible life-preserving measures had to be used. Whilst most terminations were performed between the 7th and 15th weeks, a minority—perhaps 5 per cent, she thought—were carried out after 20 weeks. It was very important, therefore, that women seeking abortion late in pregnancy should not mislead their doctor about its duration.

AN AMERICAN TRAGEDY

On 23 May 1969, at an inquest held at Hammersmith, London, it was revealed that an 18-year-old American married woman from Ohio had died in the Lady Margaret Nursing Home at Ealing, London, from respiratory obstruction whilst receiving an anaesthetic for a legal abortion.[216] The woman had wanted her pregnancy terminated after her husband had left her, and had been told by the Cleveland Clergy Consultation Service of the possibility of having this done in London. It later transpired that this group of clergy and rabbis was seeking to influence American public opinion against punitive abortion laws, and that the Cleveland group, which was run on the same lines as groups operating in New York, San Francisco, Philadelphia, Washington D.C., and Boston, operated for 24 hours a day and had, in the 5 months of its existence, advised nearly 500 married and unmarried women. The Reverend Fairley Wheelwright, a Unitarian minister and the chairman of the Cleveland Clergy Consultation Service, claimed that the organization always acted within the law, and he explained that its thirty-five consultants only suggested abortion as a last resort. Women expressing a desire to travel to Britain for terminations were given the names of sympathetic clergy or doctors in London, after which they made their own arrangements. [217] The "London solution" to an unwanted pregnancy was popular in the United States because of the activities of the counselling groups in large American cities, and because of the publicity given to London abortion facilities by American press, radio, and television. The Americans were confident that in London legal abortions would be performed under good conditions, and in Colorado, the only state to have had a liberalized abortion bill enacted, terminations were still extremely difficult to obtain. [218]

Doubts and Misgivings

On 31 May 1969, Edwin Brooks, the then Labour Member of Parliament for Bebington and sponsor of the National Health Service (Family Planning) Act 1967, told a symposium on contraception and abortion at the Neath General Hospital in Wales that those who, like himself, had supported the Abortion Bill had a duty to criticize those who abused it. He felt that it was wrong that certain doctors and gynaecologists were deliberately sabotaging the Abortion Act and in the process forcing women into the hands of "professional sharks". [219]

Early in June, Sir George Godber, Chief Medical Officer of the Department of Health and Social Security, injected a welcome note of objectivity into the debate regarding the working of the Abortion Act. Giving the National Birthday Trust Fund Dame Juliet Rhys-Williams Lecture at the Royal College of Physicians in London, Sir George said that whilst he hoped that eventually the Act would be justified by a fall in maternal deaths, a fall in illegitimacy, and a fall in perinatal mortality, he thought that "the greatest gain could be relief from distress not measurable in statistical terms". He drew attention to the great difference in the numbers of legal terminations taking place in different parts of the country—the instance varying from 1.1 per 1000 women in the Liverpool region to 6.5 per 1000 in the North West Metropolitan region of London—and he declared that Newcastle, with a rate

AFTERMATHS: THE SPRING OF 1969   133

of 2.7, of which 96 per cent were terminated under the NHS in the region and only 44 out of a total of 1271 were treated privately, came nearest to a stable service meeting the public need. (220)

Exactly a week later, P. H. Addison, secretary of the (British) Medical Defence Union, speaking at the annual meeting of the Canadian Medical Association in Toronto on 11 June, commented that the Abortion Bill was being interpreted much more liberally than had been intended, with repercussions in the utilization of hospital beds and the morale of nursing staff. He reiterated Jill Knight's assertion that London was regarded as the abortion capital of the world.

Later the same month, Laurie Pavitt, Member of Parliament for Willesden West and chairman of the Parliamentary Labour Health Group, returned to the assault on the nursing homes where non-NHS legal abortions were being performed. After praising medical staff for the way they were coping with the additional work produced by the success of the Abortion Act, he alleged that private abortion clinics, run at a profit, were taking valuable blood, plasma, and NHS consultants' time at the expense of the taxpayer. His attack followed complaints made by consultant pathologists, mainly in Greater London, that they were expected without warning to supply blood and other assistance when emergencies occurred in abortion clinics. Their protests arose out of the New Cross case described earlier (see p. 109). They disliked providing a makeshift service for people making money out of it, and were worried about the legal risks they had to take when they were called from work in an emergency and had to use blood which had been stored by the clinic in circumstances over which they had had no control. (221)

DISCIPLINARY HEARINGS

Early in June two medical practitioners resident in Britain appeared before the Disciplinary Committee of the General Medical Council for hearings in connection with their involvement in abortions. Many similar charges had been heard—of course—in earlier years, but through more extensive press coverage, those which followed the coming into effect of the Abortion Act created wider interest.

At this time, in 1969, forty-four of the forty-seven members of the General Medical Council were medically qualified; the President, Lord Cohen of Birkenhead, had been duly elected from amongst them. Eight, including the President, were nominees of the Queen, on the advice of her Privy Council or that of the Governor of Northern Ireland. Eighteen were the appointed representatives of eighteen universities in England, Wales, Scotland, Northern Ireland and Eire. Ten had been appointed by the Royal Colleges, the Society of Apothecaries of London and the Apothecaries' Hall in Dublin. The remaining eleven had been elected by the registered medical practitioners resident in the British Isles.

The Disciplinary Committee consisted of nineteen GMC members who were elected annually, each of whom usually served for three years. Two of the members of this Committee were of necessity lay members of the council, and six of the medical members of necessity were elected from the eleven members of the GMC representative of the registered medical practitioners. At its meetings, the President of the GMC, who was always a member of the Disciplinary Committee, took the chair.

On 5 June Dr. Patrick Uwaezuoke Aghadiuno, a Biafran physician from Lagos, Nigeria, appeared on a charge that he had been convicted of unlawfully procuring an abortion and had been sentenced to three years' imprisonment.

> Dr. Aghadiuno had pleaded not guilty at his trial and had given evidence in which he stated that he had used an instrument, but merely for the purpose of an examination, not to bring about an abortion. The jury, after three-quarters of an hour's consideration, had found him guilty of the offence as charged.
> Replying to the notice of enquiry, Dr. Aghadiuno wrote a letter maintaining that he had not been guilty of committing an abortion and urging the Committee to show mercy to him and to let him return to his people in Biafra who were in dire need of doctors. He was, he claimed, "not a criminal, but the victim of circumstances". At his hearing he addressed the Committee at length in regard to his version of the events leading to the conviction; later, having been informed by the Legal Assessor that the Committee was powerless to go behind the conviction, he repeated that he had acted in good faith with no intention to abort the patient or to do anything infamous against the profession or the laws of the country. Finally he implored the Committee not to erase his name from the Register.

The Committee, however, decided to direct the Registrar to erase his name from the Register.[222] Dr. Aghadiuno did not exercise his right of appeal under Section 36 of the Medical Act, 1956, and his name was erased on 9 July 1969. It was restored to the Register on 20 July 1970.[223]

At the same series of hearings, Dr. Gerald Ernest Moore of Heathfield, Sussex, appeared on a charge that with a view to obtaining patients or otherwise promoting his own professional advantage or financial benefit, he had advertised his services and those of institutions with which he was connected, thus being guilty of infamous conduct in a professional respect.[224]

AFTERMATHS: THE SPRING OF 1969

Evidence was given by Mr. G. R. Martin, Deputy News Editor of the *Sunday Mirror*, by Mr. Paul Ferris, a freelance journalist, and by Dr. Moore. Mr. Martin stated that he had been partly responsible for an article of 9 February headlined "Amazing World of Dr. Moore" which was written after he had had several conversations with Dr. Moore; the photograph in the article was taken from stock. Mr. Martin said that Dr. Moore had never asked him not to publish his name, but had explained that when it was published he had to be rather cautious. He admitted that Dr. Moore had not been prepared to pose for a photograph, and he agreed that as at the time the activities of the New Cross clinic and those of Dr. Moore, who was known to be its proprietor, were news, he had been determined to get an interview with Dr. Moore. Had the latter refused to see him or to say anything at all, Mr. Martin agreed, an article about Dr. Moore might still have appeared in the *Sunday Mirror*.

Paul Ferris told the Committee that he had been the author of an article published in the *Observer* of 9 February.[173] Before composing it, he said, he had had an interview with Dr. Moore at his (Mr. Ferris's) request, and had explained to the doctor that he wanted to write an article dealing not only with the inquest on the woman who had died after an abortion in the New Cross Clinic (see page 109), but also with the whole question of the abortion clinics. He was concerned that the case for the clinics should receive as fair a hearing as any case that might be against them as a result of the unfortunate death. Dr. Moore had been anxious not to be identified in a way that would reveal his name to the public and Mr. Ferris had told him that the information he provided could not be used in such a way as to keep Dr. Moore completely anonymous, but that he would not be identified by name to the public. Dr. Moore had thought it might be recognised by other doctors. Mr. Ferris explained that to write the article he had needed accurate information; in this context Dr. Moore was the obvious source. He agreed with Dr. Moore's counsel that the doctor had merely answered questions put to him and had not inflated his own personality or medical role.

Dr. Moore, giving evidence, told the GMC Committee that he had qualified as a dentist in 1949 and as a doctor five years later. After practising dentistry and working in junior hospital posts he returned to full time dental practice in June 1958. Two years later he had established a nursing home at New Cross which for some time functioned as an oral surgery unit. This nursing home was later mentioned in articles in the *Sunday Mirror* and the *Observer*. Dr. Moore told the Committee he had sold the nursing home and had no connection with it. He went on to explain that he had become interested in diagnostic processes and in geriatric psychiatry and had interests in several nursing homes amongst which was the Lady Margaret at Ealing. After the Abortion Act, 1967, came into force there was a decided increase in demand for beds at Lady Margaret and at other nursing homes, so that abortions began to constitute the majority of cases. Dr. Moore further explained that some years earlier he had become interested in the possibility of applying advances in electronics to medicine, especially computer recording and analysis. He became a shareholder and at one time a director of the Cavendish Biomedical Centre Limited, an enterprise which, incorporating a computer, was estimated to cost in all somewhere in the region of £250,000. Because of the cost a company was set up and in November 1968, a press release was made through a public relations firm. Under cross-examination Dr. Moore admitted that he had approved the release of the press hand-out for the purpose of advertising the existence and activities of the centre, so that the investors, which included himself, could get a return for their money.

The Disciplinary Committee considered the case *in camera* and decided that the facts alleged in the charge against Dr. Moore had been proved to its satisfaction. His counsel then addressed the Committee in mitigation. After further consideration of the case *in camera*, the Chairman said that the Committee regarded the facts in the charge with "grave concern". Dr. Moore had more than once made available for publication in national newspapers information about professional enterprises in which he was associated and had given personal details about himself so that widespread publicity had been given to his own professional sources and to institutions in which he had a professional and financial interest. The Committee judged him guilty of infamous conduct in a professional respect, but in view of assurances given on his future conduct they decided to postpone judgement for a period of one year.[224] The case was reconsidered by the Committee at its meeting in June 1970, but judgement was further postponed until November 1970, in order to give the practitioner—who was not present—a further opportunity to appear before the Committee and to satisfy them on certain matters related to his reappointment to the Board of the Cavendish Biomedical Centre.[223]

DANISH ABORTION-SEEKERS

On 2 July 1969, newspaper reports appeared that abortion trips to Britain at an inclusive fee of £120 were being organized by the Danish Association for the Individual and Society. Mr. Bjoern Seldel, the secretary of the Association, said that more than 150 women had made the trips since they had started 3 weeks earlier, and he explained that the Association had an agreement with a clinic in London which provided a bed and a doctor for an all-in fee of £85. This was below the clinic's usual fee but it had made a reduction for the Danes because of their numbers.[225] Two days later the front-page headline in the *Daily Express* read "Abortion Hotel. We've had 800 guests since September", with, below, a story of a small hotel in northwest London to which foreign women were conveyed by airport taxi-drivers who grossly overcharged and on occasion demanded money from the hotel for their delivery.[226] The following day, Mr. Seldel was reported to have stated that several private clinics in London had written to him quoting "all-in" fees ranging down to £50 if he could assure them of a regular supply of patients.[227] It transpired that London was popular with Danish women because they did not, as in Denmark, have to present a case, based on medical or social grounds, to a committee made up of a lawyer and two doctors, one of whom had to be the surgeon who would perform the operation, provided all three agreed. The much simpler British procedure made them feel less guilty. Further, most Danes knew English, they did not require a visa to come to Britain, and if complications developed after a legal abortion was privately performed they could, under the Anglo-Danish social service agreement, be transferred to a NHS hospital where free treatment was available. Complications, however, were unlikely, since the Association and the clinic did not accept women whose pregnancies were more than 3 months advanced. (225)

On 8 July 1969, Richard Crossman, addressing the House of Commons, said that he would "take a very grave view" if reports about the activities of some London abortion clinics were true. "I don't think it is very likely", he observed. He thought it would be most unwise to amend the Abortion Act because he had no reason to believe it was not working well through the Health Service. "There are minor defects which can be remedied", he said. "In a very small segment of the private sector concentrated in London, over which I have no control, things are taking place of which I do not approve." He added that since only very few doctors were involved, "it would be a grave thing if a small group were to discredit what I think is a considerable reform." (228)

Three days later Mr. Seldel announced that the Scandinavian women sent by his Association to London would be referred to gynaecologists' consulting rooms rather than direct to clinics. The new arrangement had apparently been made because the seven Harley Street gynaecologists with whom his Association co-operated had been perturbed by the publicity given to the Association's activities in the British press. The inclusive fee for gynaecologist, anaesthetist, and clinic would, Seldel said, remain at £85. (229) The following day it was disclosed that the British Embassy in Copenhagen, after investigating the Danish Association for the Individual and Society, had provided a confidential report for Richard Crossman.

Although it was rumoured that the Association had plans to send 30,000 women seeking abortion to London, the Embassy believed that in June and July about fifty women a week were actually arriving in the British capital for this purpose. (230) Answering a question from Mrs. Jill Knight in the House of Commons on 14 July, Mr. Crossman said that, in response to inquiries he had made, the seven London nursing homes concerned had denied any knowledge of an arrangement with a Danish organization to accept Danish women for abortions, and of any arrangement with taxi-drivers at airports. The replies showed that only four Danish women had had terminations performed in London between 1 July 1969 and 4 July 1969.(231) The story about the taxi-drivers turned out to be similarly exaggerated, for an investigation revealed that, of the 250 drivers at London Airport, seven, who were friendly with each other and who knew the addresses of the private clinics, had been responsible.(232)

A Further Death

On 3 July 1969 the Enfield coroner, Dr. David Paul, recording a verdict of death from natural causes in a 28-year-old mother of four who, when 18 weeks pregnant, had undergone an operation for termination in a NHS hospital, commented that the Abortion Act was "rapidly appearing to be a very bad law". The circumstances of the case were particularly tragic.

> The youngest of the patient's four children had abnormalities, and because of this and financial difficulties, her doctor sent her to a Family Planning Association clinic where she was fitted with an intra-uterine device. Unfortunately this failed and she again became pregnant in February 1969. Because of the social background and the patient's distress her family doctor wrote to a consultant gynaecologist about her on 14 May and asked "I wonder if you would agree that there are grounds here for termination". The gynaecologist replied on 16 May saying that he did not do abortions on social grounds and that there did not appear to be any medical indication. On 21 May the general practitioner approached a second gynaecologist who agreed on termination and performed it by abdominal hysterotomy, combined with sterilization by tubal ligation, on 4 June. By this time, however, the pregnancy was over sixteen weeks advanced; twelve and a half hours after the operation the patient collapsed and died from an acute heart condition which had previously been clinically undetectable.

The coroner was told that the more serious operation needed for a termination after the pregnancy had progressed had put a much greater strain on the patient's heart. He commended her general practitioner and the consultant who had operated, but commented "the disturbing thing is that a doctor, without seeing or examining a patient, has the absolute right to decline termination on the grounds of conscience or medical grounds".(233)

The British Medical Association Meeting

The Annual Representative Meeting of the British Medical Association, held in Aberdeen, Scotland, between 2 and 5 July 1969, was concerned *inter alia* with the working of the Abortion Act, and its debates on this and other topics were reported in the Association's journal.(234)

The first motion on the Act to be put forward at the meeting expressed disquiet concerning the way in which it was being implemented, and the proposer, D. F. Heath, alleged that there was dissatisfaction about its working not only in the profession but from the Secretary of State for Social Services, Members of Parliament, and many lay bodies. Commenting on the motion, J. S. Happel remarked that the Act had two shortcomings: firstly, it had been thought that the person in charge of the team carrying out an abortion should have consultant status; and, secondly, the special reference to the health of the other children in the family (the "social" clause) had gone too far in that any doctor, in reaching an opinion, would necessarily take into account the patient's total environment. Later, D. B. Brown, speaking as a gynaecologist, reiterated the BMA's original view that an abortion should not be carried out by any doctor but only by a consultant gynaecologist or one of his staff. Terminations should, he thought, be carried out only in a NHS or a service hospital "so as to do away with the private slur or smear on the profession". Gynaecologists who took a firm attitude against abortion for medical reasons should not, he felt, be allowed to train Britain's future gynaecologists. Kathleen Frith then pointed out that though it might be the ideal for one of the certifying doctors to be a consultant gynaecologist, if the modification in St. John-Stevas's impending motion was passed it would hinder the work of the Act. She believed that the profession should press for facilities to implement the Act as it stood and not press for a more restrictive Act.

Supporting the motion, Jean Laurie observed that it was unfortunate that the Abortion Act had become law before the Government had formed an adequate idea of what was required of a nursing home registered to perform terminations under it. She thought that the effects of the Act should be evaluated through an epidemiological investigation. A. Lyall said that both the profession and the public were showing increasing concern over so-called abortion on demand, which he thought resulted from the very lax interpretation of the "social" clause. Television interviews and reputable newspaper articles implied that "abortion on demand" was being performed, and it was said that one-day abortions were carried out in nursing homes where no questions were asked, but where large fees were demanded. Lyall thought that many young women who could ill afford the expense were being forced to go to nursing homes for terminations because of the shortage of NHS gynaecological beds, and he felt that an adequate number of such beds should be set aside for this in each area.

Expressing the British Medical Association's view, Ronald Gibson, the Chairman of Council, reminded his colleagues that during the passage of

Lord Silkin's original Bill in the House of Lords and later of Mr. Steel's Bill in the House of Commons, the Association had acted jointly with the Royal College of Obstetricians and Gynaecologists in the Committee stage on all the principles established in the Special Committee's Report which had been approved by the Annual Representative Meeting. Whilst a measure of success had been achieved, not all the principles laid down by the Association had been incorporated in the legislation; some of the existing problems were due to failure to take heed of the Association's advice. He thought two points needed emphasizing: firstly, it was difficult to express unequivocally in law the responsibility and clinical judgement attached to a team of doctors undertaking a therapeutic abortion; and, secondly, it had been felt that at least one member of the team should be of acknowledged competence, i.e. he should be a NHS consultant or the equivalent. Much of the criticism of the work of the Abortion Act could be said to have stemmed from omission of this latter proviso. The Association had warned the sponsors of the Bill that an Act of Parliament would not increase the trained personnel or the facilities available in the public sector, and that expansion of the private sector would be the inevitable result of making an abortion so much easier to obtain. He referred with approval to the amendment on the Abortion Act that was to be proposed by St. John-Stevas (see p. 144), and he mentioned that the Association had held discussions with him, as also with Sir John Peel, President of the Royal College of Obstetricians and Gynaecologists.

A second motion proposed by E. M. Jack moved "that we protest at the way the Abortion Act is working and at the decisions that gynaecologists, psychiatrists and family doctors are having forced upon them. We would suggest a more effective contraceptive service as a means of lessening the burden." J. H. Marks then moved an amendment "to delete the words 'and at the decisions that gynaecologists, pyschiatrists and family doctors are having forced upon them' ". He pointed out that the present Act was already discredited "largely due to the gross inadequacies of the state facilities and the greed of some of our weaker brethren". Nevertheless, decisions were not being forced upon doctors. Could it be that some doctors were unable to resist the demands of their patients or their general practitioner colleagues? He went on to ask: "Is much of the so-called force moral or financial blackmail with the patient threatening to change her doctor or the general practitioner threatening to send his private work elsewhere?" His amendment was carried by 162 votes to 99.

Later in the meeting, A. M. Spencer moved a motion regretting the Council's inability to achieve the complete confidentiality of information, which, under the Abortion Act, was statutorily reported to the Ministry of Health and Social Security. Replying, the chairman, Dr. Ronald Gibson, said that so far the Council knew of only one case in which confidentiality had been breached. They were watching the position and, as St. John-Stevas, who had been asked to include the matter in his Bill, had believed that he could not do so, the Council would continue to watch the situation.

PRESS COMMENTS

The discussion that took place at the BMA meeting was reported in the press, which was not slow to advance trenchant views. Struan Coupar and James Davies, writing in the *Daily Express* on the Abortion Act on 4 July, noted that some Members of Parliament felt that the Act was being abused, and particularly resented the money being made by the private clinics. The reporters traced this partly to the conscience clause (there should, they felt, be a list available of consultants who did *not* object to abortion on grounds of conscience) and partly to the difficulty, in some parts of the country, of finding a NHS bed. Commenting that Britain had become divided into distinct areas —some hostile to abortion, some favourable to it—they remarked "the anomalies produced by the situation have been staggering. In one case a 16-year-old mentally retarded girl who was pregnant through rape was refused an abortion—yet perfectly healthy women, fit in mind and body, had been granted them under the NHS." The real problem was, the reporters felt, that a minority of doctors actively opposed to abortion were determined not to make the Act work. Since 40 per cent of legal abortions were being performed privately, the clinics had a "captive market", and the cost of a private abortion—about £100 two years earlier—had almost doubled. They felt that the Abortion Act had had three main aims: (i) to give every woman, genuinely in need, the opportunity to have an abortion under the best conditions near her home through the NHS; (ii) to cut down the clientele of the high-priced "abortion doctors" in the big cities—particularly London; and (iii) to end the dangers of backstreet abortion. The Act, they thought, had failed in many cases in the first and second aims; it had only partially succeeded in the third. (235)

The following day an anonymous Harley Street doctor alleged that three unnamed physicians were making upwards of £300,000 a year each by arranging abortions in Britain for foreign girls. He said that the three were acting as "middle men", first discreetly advertising in Britain and abroad, next booking rooms in private clinics, and lastly arranging with surgeons to perform between ten and twenty operations a day. Whatever profits nursing home and surgeon made, the middle men obtained, the doctor thought, a handsome gain. [236]

About the same time an anonymous specialist, "Vaux", writing in the *Medical Tribune*, suggested that the "good faith" needed to certify the desirability of a legal abortion was often "bent" by the recommending private doctors or by the refusing NHS practitioners; if not, a genuine disagreement between doctors was involved. Of 500 British women seeking terminations seen by "Vaux", 380 had been turned down on the NHS, yet all had subsequently had legal abortions performed privately. Ninety had seen their NHS doctors (who were not Roman Catholics) and had learnt they were uninterested, "didn't want to know", or disapproved of abortions; none had had their cases assessed or had been referred elsewhere. One hundred and thirty-nine patients had seen a gynaecologist, having been sent with a strong recommendation (socio-psychiatric in 130 cases), and two had had no adequate history of these factors taken by the consultant surgeon—or he had invoked the conscience clause. In eighty of the remaining cases, the family doctor had written a "tepid" letter of recommendation, and neither he nor the surgeon had investigated the socio-psychiatric grounds for the case. "Vaux" concluded, "of course 'good faith' is not defined by the Act, but in practice, gross unfairness, if not law breaking, is occurring. Also the fat profits made by abortionists and clinics, privately, stem in part from the above abuses." [237]

D. M. Potts, [238] writing to the editor of the *Daily Telegraph*, emphasized the same point. The forthcoming parliamentary debate, he observed, seemed to be more concerned with fees than with the basic issues that were involved. Sir George Godber had pointed out that there was a sixfold variation in the incidence of abortion in different areas of England, yet the structure of the NHS tied women to certain hospitals where, in some instances, gynaecologists refused to perform terminations. Women in this situation had to seek criminal abortions or turn to private practice; the London Pregnancy Advisory Service tried to help them where necessary. "I think the first cause for complaint should be that patients are not obtaining satisfactory care under the NHS," Potts asserted, "I am more disturbed by the fact that a legal abortion, which was recommended by a general practitioner for a psychiatrically disturbed girl of 14, was refused than I am by the fact that some of my colleagues are making excessive sums of money (although I would prefer that neither happened)." He thought that if the geographical variations of the NHS could be eliminated, "most of the irresponsible fringe of private surgeons would find themselves unemployed".

On 13 July 1969, Paul Ferris [239] reviewed the general situation in regard to the "abortion racket", the emotive phase which, he observed, had come to connote a number of surgeons in the West End of London who were either very permissive over abortion, or charged high fees, or showed both tendencies. Permissiveness over legal abortion, however, Ferris commented, was quite widespread in the NHS as well as in the private sector; not all NHS gynaecologists agreed with Sir John Peel that women did not realize the risks involved in termination procedures. If the criticism was changed from "undue permissiveness" to that of "charging high fees", this stricture was also unjustified, for expensive private practice had always flourished in Harley Street. The Medical Defence Union had criticized the fact that patients were going to doctors who they felt were highly qualified but who in fact were not. However, of ten London doctors known to Ferris, who he estimated were performing between them at least 10,000 private abortions a year, only three were excludable on grounds of being inadequately qualified. The St. John-Stevas amendment, if it were passed, would give the Department of Health the ultimate power to decide which doctors should supervise abortions; the decision would be arbitrary and hard to defend; in addition it was opposed by Richard Crossman, who had pointed out that doctors had always demanded clinical freedom on abortion as in everything else, so that the Minister could hardly be expected to intervene in this area. Crossman thought that it was up to the profession to discipline its members, if it was necessary and if it was able to do so. Ferris believed that if the larger abortion clinics were sensible they would forestall criticism by taking more care. In any case, it would be an empty victory, he thought, to curb the private clinics, for a woman would rather be exploited than pregnant. The whole debate, Ferris aptly observed, was "littered with red herrings". The old taboos on abortion remained, the objection that more and more women were obtaining abortions being expressed in feelings of outrage over the marginal abuses that had developed. He believed that NHS abortion practice needed to be more uniform; that the private sector needed better medical standards; and that the problem of why so much abortion was necessary when contraception was available needed further study. The situation was far from perfect, he concluded, but was, he felt, infinitely better than it had been prior to the Act.

Speaking on the eve of St. John-Stevas's Bill, Mrs. Jill Knight, Conservative Member of Parliament for Edgbaston, declared emotively that abortion babies were being "burned alive". Mrs. Knight was referring to the death of the baby in Glasgow (see p. 130) and to Richard Crossman's statement in Parliament that 108 foetuses of over 28 weeks had been aborted in the previous year. She later admitted that she had no evidence to support her allegations and the Department of Health was unable to find any figures to support her contention that the 108 "viable" babies had been aborted in 1968. The Abortion Law Reform Association accused Mrs. Knight of creating a "scare story", and it was reported that even St. John-Stevas was "known to have been appalled" by her "hysterical" speech.[240] He later explained, responding to the article by Ferris, that in his view abortion, unlike other operations, was unique in that it involved two lives; this put it in a category by itself. His idea, he said, was for the professional bodies concerned to select lists of suitable doctors from which the Minister would choose. The effect of curbing the private abortionists would be to make abortion available only for strictly medical reasons; this would in turn, he felt, reduce the demand for abortion, which "grows more clamant as the law is relaxed".[241]

The First Attempt to Modify the Act

On 15 July 1969, after weeks of lobbying by the opponents and supporters of the Abortion Act, Norman St. John-Stevas, addressing a packed House of Commons, sought leave to bring in his Bill. This proposed that of the two doctors required to certify an abortion, one should be a consultant gynaecologist holding office under the NHS, and that the operation should be carried out under his supervision. Since the number of gynaecologists was limited, St. John-Stevas stated, he felt that doctors of equivalent status should be given ministerial approval from panels submitted by professional medical bodies. The community, he said, wanted neither a total ban on abortion nor abortion on demand; it wanted abortion to be available under the best conditions when a serious and genuine medical need existed. He pointed out that a minority of doctors were making huge fortunes out of the Act and were not observing proper standards of medical care. His Bill, which was supported by the Royal College of Obstetricians and Gynaecologists, the British Medical Association, and the Medical Defence Union, would stop much of the racketeering. He thought that the weakness of the Act was that there was no effective

Medical Termination of Pregnancy Bill, and 83 some weeks later against its third reading. However, something was probably attributable to the effect of the two speakers: a newspaper article commented: "Mr. St. John-Stevas, confessing humorously that an agnostic mother of nine would probably sponsor the Bill better than a celibate Roman Catholic, outclassed Mr. Steel."[244] The change in opinion should not, a leading article[245] observed, be over-emphasized, for when the same amendment was moved during the Committee stage of the original Bill, it was defeated by 13 votes to 11, so that the July figures represented a "swing" of only 2.7 per cent.

In contrast a leading article[246] in the *Observer* thought that the size of the vote—409 Members of Parliament—indicated that a backlash of opinion about the Abortion Act had occurred, and it commented that, in addition to the high prices and rapid turnover of the private clinics and the inadequacy of NHS provisions for abortion, some of the confusion had been produced by a lack of candour on the part of both sides in the controversy. Behind the lengthy arguments concerning the circumstances in which an abortion should be allowed was the basic disagreement between those who wanted no change in the law at all and those who wanted abortion on demand. Rather than argue their case, the article commented, the former had sought a compromise that was unrealistic and irrelevant. Abortion law reformers did not believe that abortions were ideal, and many would have preferred more comprehensive contraception. But basically most felt that every woman with an unwanted pregnancy had the right to decide for herself what to do. Many shared that view, including the *Observer*, the private clinics, many NHS doctors, and many members of the general public. The article noted that the recent alarm had been occasioned less by the question of abortion on demand than by the inadequate provision to meet the demand: if this could be rectified, it stated, the backlash of opinion should subside.

CONTINUING CONTROVERSY OVER LEGAL ABORTION

Instances of the basic controversy to which the article alluded were readily perceptible during the summer of 1969. "I am bound to view the whole of the Abortion Act with horror and dismay", wrote Lady Fergusson Hannay (Doris Leslie),[247] alluding to Jill Knight's (unfounded) assertion that aborted babies of 7 months were being placed alive in an incinerator (see p. 144). "I have found from my pastoral experience", wrote Hugh Robinson[248] from a Sussex vicarage, "that for many women the termination of pregnancy, however grave and urgent the medical and psychiatric reasons, check on it, and he considered that a responsible medical person, highly qualified and highly placed, was needed to check that the provisions of the Act were being followed.

Rising to ask the House to refuse St. John-Stevas leave to introduce his Bill, David Steel, sponsor of the Abortion Act, said that he did not do so because he regarded the Act as perfect, nor was he totally satisfied or complacent about the way in which it was working. He did so because the new Bill offered no solution to any real problems and would be a regressive measure. The limited evidence available suggested that the numbers of criminal abortions were being reduced, and the rate of legal abortion in Britain, 5 per 100 live births, was lower than the 6–8 per 100 in Norway, Sweden, Denmark, and Finland, countries which had roughly comparable abortion laws. It was nonsense to claim that London was the abortion capital of the world. The present problem, which had not been mentioned by St. John-Stevas, was the regional differences in abortion under the NHS: "it is the restrictive practices in cities like Birmingham", Steel said, "which in themselves stimulate the growth of private centres of abortion in London." The growth had little to do with foreigners. Whilst a small number of doctors were not giving the fullest medical attention to their patients, and were undoubtedly motivated by financial considerations, the Secretary of State had reserved powers to introduce ministerial regulations if he considered that the situation demanded it. Steel observed that the medical profession also had a responsibility, and as the GMC, in its rules of discipline, had as one of its definitions of infamous conduct the "abuse of financial opportunities offered by medical practice", he thought that the Council should take action where profiteering occurred. In advising the House to reject the Bill, he drew attention to four considerations: (i) the limiting of one of the two certifying doctors to a consultant would not check private abortions; (ii) the proposed amendment would cause delay for patients requiring terminations; (iii) the real need was for doctors in the Health Service to operate the Act in a balanced way—but the amendment, if successful, would create more areas like Birmingham instead of more like Newcastle; (iv) the amendment had been discussed twice in the House of Commons and twice in the House of Lords during the passage of the Abortion Bill. He saw no reason to depart from the original decision.[242, 243]

Leave to introduce the Bill was refused by 210 votes to 199—a majority of 11. The verdict came as a shock to the defenders of the Abortion Act, who had reckoned on a 3 to 1 majority. The number of votes for the amendment at first sight compared favourably with 29 against the second reading of the involved them in an agonizing decision, and the abortion itself a traumatic experience, bringing in its wake a crippling burden of guilt which persisted for many years." In contrast, Sir Dugald Baird, receiving the 1969 Martha May Eliot Award for achievement in the field of maternal and child health, said in New York that a liberal policy of therapeutic abortion was "a necessity". His own practice from 1938 to 1965 had convinced him that the patient herself was usually the best judge of whether the pregnancy should or should not be terminated, and in over 20 years in Aberdeen only two patients had received psychiatric treatment for emotional disturbances which might have been related to termination of pregnancy. The tragedy of thalidomide, Sir Dugald said, had been a factor stimulating the change in public opinion that had led to the Abortion Act. The legislation was a forward step, and was supported by many of the younger men and women of Britain; nevertheless, resistance to the Act in the medical profession remained, and many doctors were opposed to termination on social grounds—such as substandard housing, overcrowding, sickness in other children, alcoholic husbands, elderly or bedridden parents, and the economic necessity for some mothers to work— in contrast to pure "medical" indications.[249]

The legacy of humane gynaecology, excellent clinical care, and an active research programme bequeathed to Aberdeen and its surrounding area by Sir Dugald Baird was demonstrated in a symposium in that city held as part of the 1969 annual scientific meeting of the BMA. As mentioned earlier (see p. 22), Aberdeen was years ahead of England in relation to experience with legal abortion, so that experience in north-eastern Scotland provided an indication of the way in which the Abortion Act might later work. The symposium was reported in the *British Medical Journal*[250] and elsewhere.[251]

Therapeutic Abortion in North-eastern Scotland

Professor Ian MacGillivray, opening the symposium, observed that the Abortion Act had not greatly changed the legal situation in Scotland, where a liberal interpretation of the law had been possible since 1956. Being an isolated area with a relatively stable population, the north-eastern region provided an opportunity to study the effect of the abortion law as if it had been in operation for a number of years. What was needed in his country, he thought, was not a change in the law, but a change in the attitude of doctors. In Aberdeen, a retrospective review of all pregnancies terminated since 1956 had been carried out, and a prospective study was in progress in which every woman referred for termination of pregnancy was being examined and investigated by a team of gynaecologists, psychiatrists, psychologists, and social workers. The team was endeavouring to discover why women requested—and obtained—terminations, what kind of women they were, and what subsequently happened to them.

In Scotland, Professor MacGillivray observed, the overall rate of legal termination in women aged between 15 and 44 was 2.4 per 1000. This was the same as the average for England and Wales if private abortions were excluded. The overall rate of abortion in the latter two countries was 4.0 per 1000 but 1.6 per 1000 were due to private abortions, performed mainly in north-west London, where the overall rate was 19.2 per 1000 with only 2.5 women per 1000 having terminations under the NHS. Elsewhere in England, Liverpool with 1.3 per 1000 women, Sheffield with 1.3, and Birmingham with 1.5 stood out as regions where the abortion rate was lowest, the rates being similar in NHS hospitals. The abortion rates in Scotland ranged from 4.9 per 1000 women in the Inverness region to 1.6 in Glasgow. Almost all the Scottish terminations were performed under the NHS. In Aberdeen about half the women referred for terminations had them performed. The number carried out was increasing, but this was due to the mounting number of illegitimate pregnancies.

LEGITIMATE AND ILLEGITIMATE BIRTHS

G. P. Milne, a senior obstetrician and gynaecologist, next explained that the birth rate in north-eastern Scotland was falling; whilst the total number of legitimate births in 1958 was 3059, in 1968 it had fallen to 2561. Although there might be other influences, such as emigration and an ageing population, he felt that the pill had been the major factor in the fall. Termination of pregnancy did not account for the lower number of births: the number of abortions performed had been steady in married women for some years, rising only from 83 in 1958 to 92 in 1968. In contrast, terminations in unmarried girls had risen from 9 out of 172 in 1958 to 123 out of 380 in 1968. In other words, the current problem was the group of women who were illegitimately pregnant, of whom one-third had had their pregnancies terminated.

SOCIAL CHARACTERISTICS

Some of the social characteristics of women seeking abortion were described by Jean Aitken-Swan of the Medical Research Council's Medical Sociology

Unit at Aberdeen, who explained that the gap between the numbers of women referred and the numbers terminated had been increasing since 1966. In 1968 just over half of all the women applying—single and married—had had terminations; not all the remainder were refused, for 11 per cent had changed their minds or had had spontaneous abortions. Just over half of the women referred in 1968, were married compared with 90 per cent in 1963; in this group, abortion was performed most frequently in older women with five or more children, and sterilization was often carried out at the same time. In the unmarried group, in contrast, demand had been increasing since 1963 with a steeper rate since 1966, and it amounted to 150 referrals a year in 1969. The greatest demand came from students, unmarried professional women, and trained nurses. The biggest rise in therapeutic abortions had been the sevenfold increase among students—12 out of 13 students referred in 1963–5 compared with 63 out of the 89 referred in 1966–8. Amongst schoolgirls, 51 out of 70 referred in 1963–5 had had abortions compared with 195 out of 317 in 1966–8. In 1967–8 teenagers had made up half the total in contrast to less than a third 4 years earlier.

INDICATIONS FOR TERMINATION

These were discussed by K. J. Dennis of Aberdeen. He explained that in 1967 about 50 per cent of therapeutic abortions in married women had been carried out for social or socio-psychiatric reasons, medico-psychiatric or strictly medical grounds applying in the remainder of the cases. Since 1956 the proportion of social reasons had tended to increase whilst medical grounds had become less common. In the 11 years up to 1967, terminations of illegitimate pregnancies had risen from single figures to almost eighty a year, the principal grounds being social or socio-psychiatric. The proportion of women seeking and obtaining an abortion was highest (68% in 1967) in married women (or women who had ever been married) who had an extramarital (or illegitimate) pregnancy. He thought that the Abortion Act did not readily cover termination of illegitimate pregnancies for social reasons in unmarried girls.

PERSONALITY FACTORS

P. C. Olley of Aberdeen, who had studied the psychiatric aspects of women seeking therapeutic abortion using Catell's sixteen personality factor test, reported that single girls requesting terminations had "accident prone" personalities, i.e. they were impulsive, absent-minded, changeable individuals with a stubborn streak. These traits were especially marked in those who had had previous illegitimate pregnancies. Approximately three-quarters of these girls, though not less intelligent than the others, had, like their partners, taken no contraceptive precautions; married women with illegitimate pregnancies resembled the single girls, but others with legitimate but unwanted pregnancies tended to be insecure, anxious, serious, and "burdened with a load of care". Olley commented that ". . . it appears that superior intellectual ability by itself has little part to play in the avoidance of illegitimate pregnancy", and he concluded that personality factors predisposed both to pregnancy and the desire for termination.

Factors Determining Legal Abortion

The factors determining whether legal abortion was performed had been studied by C. McCance, who concluded that those women who most badly wanted an abortion were the most likely to get one. The existence of anxiety, depression, and social factors influenced both the psychiatrist and the gynaecologist, but in over a third of cases the psychiatrist was not clear of the general practitioner's views, and in over half the gynaecologist was unaware of them. This happened because the family doctor often did not state his opinions, and the resulting poor communication meant that the decision to terminate not infrequently rested on the woman's acting ability and her capacity effectively to put her case.

A sociologist working in Aberdeen, C. Farmer, next outlined the findings of an investigation in progress since December 1968, in which he had studied the effect of the Abortion Act on the selection of women for legal abortion. The number of women asking for terminations had risen, and family doctors were referring them to hospital without selection, almost as a matter of right. In consequence, the work load on consultants had increased, and this seemed likely to continue until education increased or other policies changed. Doctors were not in favour of giving contraceptives to single girls who—though more sexually active than formerly—did not seek them.

Methods of Terminating Pregnancy

The methods most commonly used to terminate pregnancy were described by W. T. Fullerton, an Aberdeen gynaecologist, who compared abdominal hysterotomy with hypertonic saline, curettage, and suction evacuation techniques. The method selected, he observed, depended on the surgeon's preference, the stage of pregnancy, the necessity for sterilization, the cost of the longer hospital stay needed for abdominal surgery, and the morbidity associated with the various techniques. Abdominal hysterotomy was sometimes associated with thrombotic complications, but could be easier than vaginal termination in the multipara; saline induction was sometimes complicated by sepsis which could threaten subsequent fertility; and curettage could be followed by lacerations. Procedures were being improved, he said, so as to reduce the delay before termination; this should always be carried out as early as possible.

A. I. Klopper, a second gynaecologist, then described a method of terminating pregnancy with saline to which had been added oestriol sulphate. Possibly this mimicked the naturally occurring situation in which a fully grown baby signalled its readiness for delivery—and perhaps played a part in initiating labour—by transmitting a hormonal message.

CONCLUSIONS

Summarizing the symposium, Professor MacGillivray observed that more terminations were being performed in Aberdeen as a result of the rising illegitimacy rate. Nevertheless, abortion was not obtainable on demand in north-east Scotland, and terminations were being carried out and their effects investigated in good faith without monetary gain.

CHAPTER 10

Summer and Autumn

THE defeat of the first parliamentary attempt to modify the Abortion Act did not reduce concern over the way in which it was operating in the private sector. In late July a series of hearings by the General Medical Council's Disciplinary Committee on the activities of four physicians kept interest in private abortion arrangements high. In August the publication of a lecture by Sir George Godber, the Chief Medical Officer, stimulated a reaction from those who favoured a conservative interpretation of the Abortion Act. Pregnancy tests became freely available at chemist's shops in September, and in November Baroness Summerskill proposed that when a single woman sought an abortion, the man who had impregnated her should be fined if termination was performed or should be made to support the child if the pregnancy went to term. In the same month a psychiatrist acquitted of a charge of advertising stated that he had told the Disciplinary Committee that he believed that there should be abortion on demand. Interest in family planning continued unabated and, in parallel with this, a recurring preoccupation with the efficiency and safety of oral contraceptives became evident. In December the continuing inadequacy of NHS facilities for legal abortions in some parts of the country led to the founding of the first all-abortion clinic in Birmingham.

EFFECTS OF THE DEFEAT

It might have been supposed that the parliamentary defeat would have reduced interest in the operation of the Abortion Act, but this was far from being the case. On 17 July 1969 it was reported that an investigation into the working of the Act had been ordered by the Royal College of Obstetricians and Gynaecologists following reports that some practitioners were amassing fortunes by performing termination operations (see p. 141). The College and the British Medical Association were concerned that the activities of these individuals might bring the reputation of the profession into disrepute; the

300 members and fellows of the College were requested to submit detailed reports of their experiences since the Act became law, so that a review could be prepared for transmission to Richard Crossman.[252]

On 20 July 1969 a doctor who had until recently been practising as a NHS dentist in Brixton, London, but who was reported to be performing terminations at private nursing homes and providing lunch-time consultations for women seeking abortions (sic), said that the provision in the Act that two registered medical practitioners must approve a termination before it could be carried out was being unduly abused by some West End doctors and private London clinics. The doctor who made the accusation was said by a newspaper reporter to have spent only 5 minutes with one patient; she was a 21-year-old student nurse from the West Indies earning £14 a week whom he sent to a private nursing home where she was to pay £80 for her unwanted pregnancy to be terminated.[253]

M. J. Henry,[254] whose letter to the editor of the *Medical Tribune* was published on 24 July 1969, found the narrowness by which the St. John-Stevas amendment had been defeated "depressing", and "even more depressing" was the fact that the BMA and the RCOG had supported it. He noted that the medical hierarchy appeared to be disturbed about the way in which abortions were being carried out in the private sector and he commented: "The hypocrisy of this attitude is so blatant that I marvel at their temerity." Henry pointed out that it was acceptable to charge similar fees for other operations, such as tonsillectomies and the ligation of varicose veins, and he thought it would be interesting to have an inquiry into the necessity for procedures such as cosmetic surgery and the implantation of hair. St. John-Stevas's amendment, if it were ever adopted, would make the Abortion Act unworkable, and he trenchantly observed: "The immorality, and I use the word deliberately, of sabotaging an Act of Parliament, which besides relieving the misery of hundreds of women [statistically unproven] has halved the hospital admission rate for criminal abortions [statistically proven] is appalling." He thought that what was needed to make the Act work better and more evenly through the country was the provision of more facilities and staff. "The latter", he said, "I am afraid will be difficult to find, and perhaps it is a case of waiting for the old diehard reactionaries of the RCOG to retire and a whole new breed of humane gynaecologists to take their place."

Garth Jones[255] was in favour of the Abortion Act being changed "to cope with the present scandal of private abortions", but he felt that the BMA and the RCOG were wrong in attempting to insist that terminations should be performed by a consultant or an individual of equal status. Both bodies, he thought, were making a rod for their own backs, for the demand for abortion was hardly likely to decrease, and if the BMA and the RCOG were successful in their attempts, the entire abortion demand would be directed solely on NHS consultants and NHS hospital beds, to the detriment of both. Jones thought that the Act as it stood was a bad Act, and in view of the aims of the social clause (he saw them as "to permit doctors to consider the mental, physical, and social pressures resulting from too large a family and to prevent poor social conditions from deteriorating into chaos") he found it "ludicrous" that almost 50 per cent of abortions were performed on healthy single women. He advocated a new social clause and suggested that it contained (i) a residential qualification (6 months); (ii) a minimum number of children (that is, two or three) before being eligible for a purely social abortion; and (iii) a compulsory assessment of the pros and cons of sterilization by the doctors concerned, and, if thought fit, an offer (refusable) to the successful applicant of such an operation under the NHS. Jones cautioned that whatever steps were taken to change the Act, the views of general practitioners—who were intimately concerned with the problem—ought to be canvassed.

On 15 July 1969 Richard Crossman reported that in the period 27 April 1968 to July 1969, 46,714 notifications were received of abortions performed in England and Wales, of which 1055 operations had been on girls under the age of 16. The following week, on 21 July, his figures showed that the general feeling that a tiny minority of doctors were performing the vast majority of terminations was accurate. He revealed that in the first 11 months of the Abortion Act, ending on 1 April 1969, 1293 doctors carried out fewer than 50 abortions, 80 did between 50 and 99, 23 performed between 100 and 199, 9 between 200 and 299, 3 did between 300 and 499, and 8 performed 500 or more.[256] The stage was set for new developments.

FURTHER DISCIPLINARY HEARINGS

On 21 July 1969, Dr. Herman Peter Tarnesby of Harley Street, London, to whose book *'Abortion Explained'* reference has earlier been made[5] appeared before the GMC Disciplinary Committee. The hearing received considerable press publicity and Dr. Tarnesby was charged that "with a view to attracting patients and promoting his own financial benefit he had contributed or provided written, oral and photographic material for publication in the German magazine *Stern,* published in Hamburg, and that in relation to the facts alleged he was guilty of infamous conduct in a professional respect". The material was alleged to include (1) particulars of cases in which he had successfully terminated pregnancies in women who had come from Germany for the purpose; (2) details of the circumstances in which he would be ready, under the terms of the Abortion Act, to terminate pregnancies in other women from Germany; and (3) particulars of the costs and fees involved. (257)

On 27 April 1967, the day the Abortion Act became law, Dr. Tarnesby had appeared on a television programme dealing with the working of the Act. Soon afterwards he was contacted by the *Sunday Times*, who on 5 May published a question-and-answer interview between him and one of its representatives. After this appeared Dr. Tarnesby was approached for further information by a representative of *Stern*, which on 12 May published an article in which it was stated that the doctor, who had originally come from Germany, had earned many distinctions in England and was famous as an obstetrician. He had had, it declared, "mountains of correspondence" from his earlier homeland in regard to whether the new British law on abortion could help German women in distress. Dr. Tarnesby had replied that every foreign girl could buy a ticket to London in order to have her pregnancy terminated, but that foreigners had to pay cash and that in London the total cost was some 1,000 to 1,500 DM (£100-£150). Moreover, a citizen of the Federal Republic could be punished in Germany for an abortion which was legally carried out in another country. Dr. Tarnesby wrote a letter about this article to *Stern* on 24 May though this did not appear in print until 22 September. Meanwhile he supplied further material to *Stern*, but before its next article appeared he sent the magazine a telegram "Please do not print any matter suggesting advertisement of my practice, and do not give my address or that of clinics used". *Stern*'s second article, which was published on 11 August, contained *inter alia* a photograph of an embryo said to be 10 weeks old and to have been aborted by Dr. Tarnesby, three case histories of abortions and a photograph of an operating theatre and an operating team with the caption "Abortion for 1,300 to 2,300 DM. Dr. Tarnesby with operating team and patient". The article also contained another photograph of the doctor, giving his name.

At the hearing Dr. Tarnesby explained that he had been born in Germany and had come to Britain in 1939 when 18 years old. He had qualified in 1947 and had later acquired additional qualifications in psychiatry and gynaecology; he had contributed to radio and television programmes—in some of which his name had been mentioned—and had had articles and books published. After the publication of the article in the *Sunday Times* he said he had been contacted by a representative of *Stern* who had asked for further information. After *Stern* had published its article on 12 May he wrote to the magazine "to protest, particularly about the implication that the law was being broken, and that I was aiding and abetting in the breaking of criminal law, and that women were unnecessarily harassed and frightened". Dr. Tarnesby explained that he had dual nationalities and could have been arrested in Germany if he had broken that country's law. Later, he went on, he had misgivings about the letter and it was agreed with *Stern* that it should not be published; however, it appeared in print four months later. Prior to this, however, *Stern* had approached him again asking him to contribute to a "serious coverage of the problems of abortion" and had named Cardinal Heenan, Dr.

Heinemann (then the West German Minister of Justice) and other prominent people as contributors. Dr. Tarnesby explained that he had provided details of the British Abortion Act, and had given examples of cases where he had considered it was permissible to terminate pregnancies as well as examples of cases where he felt it was not permissible. When the article appeared, he said, it did not give any examples of the latter cases and had distorted his observations as well as increasing his estimate of the cost of an abortion from his figure of £92 minimum (920 DM) to 1,300 DM. Dr. Tarnesby explained that he had not been very happy about the photographs being taken but had reluctantly agreed; the object was to contrast the good conditions in Britain with the dismal conditions in illegal abortion dens in Germany. The embryo had been in the bottle for many weeks or many months, and he could see no objection to a photograph of an embryo appearing in a serious article. He denied ever having seen the photograph of himself in his consulting room and having given permission for it to appear. When he heard that the article was to be published without his having seen it, he said, he contacted the representative of *Stern* immediately but was informed that the article had been set up and that it would be very expensive to alter; he replied that this was not his concern, but he could get nothing from the *Stern* representative other than reassurances to the effect that there was no need to worry as the article was in the best of taste. Following this, Dr. Tarnesby said, he realized he could not stop the article being published and he sent the telegram referred to earlier.

Replying to cross-examination Dr. Tarnesby stated that his personal fee for performing a termination averaged between £20 and £25 per patient and he said that he had done about fifteen cases a week since the Abortion Act had come into force. He denied that he had ever received as much as one hundred guineas for an operation, but he conceded that abortions were a remunerative side of his practice. More than half his patients were foreign and five or six a week came from Germany. He had frequently given factual information to newspapers, he said, but he never expected them to quote his name: he had expected the same standards from *Stern*. He explained to the Chairman of the Committee the reasons for his assertion in *Abortion Explained* that "the number of semi-legal abortion runs into thousands" and he also answered further questions about fees.

Before considering *in camera* whether the facts alleged in the charges were proved to the satisfaction of the Committee, the Chairman announced that he wanted to make it clear in public that the Committee would not be influenced by any views it might hold on the rights or wrongs of abortion or the working of the Abortion Act. Confining its judgement to the facts alleged against Dr. Tarnesby, the Committee found that they had been proved with the following exceptions: (i) it had not been found proved that he had made information available indicating that he had become a distinguished specialist in gynaecology and obstetrics in England; (ii) it had not been found proved that he had been in any way concerned with the *Stern* caption which gave in prominent type the cost of the operation for abortion; (iii) it had not been found proved that he had made available for publication a photograph of himself sitting at a desk and (iv) it had not been found proved that the ten-week-old embryo in the photograph had been aborted by him. Dr. Tarnesby's counsel then placed before the Committee a large number of testimonials showing the esteem in which for many years Dr. Tarnesby had been held by an important section of his professional colleagues and observed that in the existing climate of medical opinion Dr. Tarnesby was not the first and would not be the last doctor, as a result of being anxious to see that the press were accurately informed about medical matters, transgress. After further consideration *in camera*, however, the Committee found Dr. Tarnesby guilty of infamous conduct in a professional respect, and directed the Registrar to erase his name from the Register. [257]

Pending his appeal to the Judicial Committee of the Privy Council, which was heard on 1–4 June 1970, Dr. Tarnesby's name remained on the Register. In the appeal he claimed that he had been the victim of publication against his will; that the Committee's decision had been unsupported by evidence and was defective in law; and that the penalty imposed was disproportionate to the gravity of the offence. An Order in Council dated 28 July 1970 approved the advice of the Judicial Committee that the appeal against the determination of the Disciplinary Committee that Dr. Tarnesby had been guilty of infamous conduct in a professional respect ought to be dismissed, but stated that the direction of the Disciplinary Committee should be varied to one of suspension of registration for twelve months. In accordance with this decision Dr. Tarnesby's registration was suspended for a period of one year, beginning on 29 July 1970. [223, 258]

On 24 July 1969, Dr. Henry James Sloan of Jersey in the Channel Islands, who admitted that he had deceived three women into believing that he had performed abortions when he had not, appeared before the GMO Disciplinary Committee charged with infamous conduct in a professional respect. [259]

> It was alleged that in three cases in June or July 1967 Dr. Sloan had prescribed tablets and given injections at a fee of 10s. 6d. to women who had consulted him regarding termination of pregnancy, and had told them that the tablets and injections would produce a miscarriage. Further, in August 1967 he was alleged to have accepted £50 and £60 from two of the women for performing or arranging for an abortion to be carried out, and had subsequently given them a general anaesthetic, telling them (untruthfully) on their recovery that a termination had been performed. He had told the third woman, it was stated, that he had had her urine tested and that she was pregnant, when in fact she was not.
> It was explained that the first patient consulted Dr. Sloan in June 1967 because she wanted her pregnancy terminated. After several visits, when the tablets and the injections he later gave her had produced no effect, she asked

whether he knew of a doctor who could terminate the pregnancy. Dr. Sloan said he had a specialist friend "Carl" who was coming to Jersey on holiday, and promised to make arrangements with him to perform the operation; at Dr. Sloan's request she brought him £50 to pay for it. When she arrived at the surgery for the operation Dr. Sloan told her that the "specialist" was upstairs, and gave her an injection after which she lost consciousness. On coming round, she found blood between her thighs and padding in her vagina. Dr. Sloan assured her that all was well and explained that two packs had been inserted, one of which would come away in a few days and the other should be removed in 3 weeks. The patient returned 3 weeks later asking whether the pregnancy had in fact been terminated; Dr. Sloan said that if she wanted to see "it", it was in a bag upstairs. A month later she returned yet again because she had felt internal movements and her abdomen had become larger. Dr. Sloan initially told her that she had a "phantom pregnancy", then later said that she must have had twins and must still be carrying one of them. In November she consulted another doctor who found that she was pregnant; she subsequently gave birth to a child.

The case of the second patient was very similar except that she found it hard to accept that an abortion could have been performed during the brief time she was unconscious after the injection. Dr. Sloan allayed her suspicions by telling her that she could see "it" upstairs if she wished. Subsequently she returned saying she believed she was still pregnant. Her suspicions were confirmed by a visit to another doctor. She then asked Dr. Sloan for her £60 back but he told her that he would write to the "specialist", who would contact her direct. She later gave birth to a child. In the case of the third patient Dr. Sloan had charged 12s. 6d. for each visit; he arranged for a urine test as a result of which he told her that she was pregnant. He then arranged for her to meet "the specialist" on 4 July and again on 11 July, and when the latter did not appear Dr. Sloan explained this by saying that bad weather had prevented his coming to Jersey. She then consulted another doctor who found she was not pregnant at all.

Dr. Sloan, a married man with four children, had qualified in 1949 and had settled in general practice in Jersey. He said that he had gone through the motions of performing an abortion firstly to reduce the patients' anxiety, secondly to prevent them falling into the hands of professional abortionists, and thirdly because of his own religious beliefs. He told the Committee that after a psychic experience in 1966, when his brother, a medical student in Belfast, was drowned and came to him whilst sitting in his chair, he joined the "Greater World Church", a spiritualist church with tenets, including those on abortion, resembling those of Roman Catholicism. Dr. Sloan explained that he attended "automatic writing" meetings once a week and received messages from a Chinaman called Sung Ling; he said that he was assisted in diagnosis by Saint Benedict and clained that some sick children for whom he had prayed had recovered completely. Whatever the result of the inquiry was, Dr. Sloan said, he intended to retire from medical practice and to devote himself to the business of the Greater World Church. He regarded the fees he had collected as "blood money"; it was still in his surgery, he claimed, and he had intended to return it. He agreed in the main with a statement he had made in September 1968, to the St. Helier police who had found that "Carl" did not exist. Since he had observed that 60 per cent of women who had missed a period were not pregnant, Dr. Sloan said, he habitually arranged urine tests, then gave tablets and later administered injections: failure to menstruate in forty-eight hours was diagnostic of pregnancy. He felt that such pregnancies were a tremendous social problem in which no-one was interested. He had thought that the first of the three patients was a suicidal risk, and as he had found that many women who said they would have their unwanted babies adopted later wanted to keep them, he tried in such cases to get the pregnancy as far along as possible, so as to reduce the risk of suicide. It was a question of "leading them up the garden path", as it were, for their own good.

The Committee found Dr. Sloan guilty of infamous conduct in a professional respect in relation to the facts proved against him in the charge, and directed the Registrar to erase his name from the Register.[259] Dr. Sloan's appeal to the Judicial Committee of the Privy Council was heard on 16-17 March 1970. It was dismissed by an Order in Council dated 29 May and his name was erased from the Register with effect from 1 June 1970.[223]

On 29 July 1969, a further GMC disciplinary hearing connected with abortion took place, the sixth to be heard in full since the Abortion Act had become law. Since Dr. Arthur George Bell, the physician involved, had committed an offence in New Zealand, his case received little publicity in the lay press. The charges were that in 1966 at Waipukurau in New Zealand Dr. Bell had unlawfully used an instrument on a woman with intent to procure an abortion; and that in March 1968, the Supreme Court of New Zealand had found him guilty of procuring the abortion of the woman and had sentenced him to 2 years' imprisonment.[260]

> In May 1968, Dr. Bell had appeared before the New Zealand Medical Council, which had ordered his name to be erased from the New Zealand Medical Register with effect from 28 August 1968. It had then applied to the Supreme Court of New Zealand for an order for Dr. Bell's name to be erased from the British Register since it had no power to order this itself.
> At the Disciplinary Committee hearing Dr. Bell did not seek to deny the facts alleged against him in the charge. The Committee, whilst fully aware that Section 33(1) of the Medical Act, 1956, related only to convictions in the United Kingdom, according to established principle treated the conviction in New Zealand as prima facie evidence and found the facts proved. It was then addressed by Dr. Bell's Counsel, who observed that no money had passed to the doctor and that there was no suggestion that he was in practice as an abortionist; indeed, in sentencing him at his trial, the Judge had stated that he regarded it as an isolated offence.

After considering the case *in camera*, however, the Disciplinary Committee found Dr. Bell guilty of infamous conduct in a professional respect in relation to the facts proved against him in the charge and directed the Registrar to erase his name from the Register.[260] Dr. Bell did not exercise his right to appeal and his name was erased from the Register 28 days later.[223]

On 30 July 1969, Dr. Parviz Faridian, a Persian-born physician of Earls Court, London, appeared on a charge that he had been a director of, and had had directly or indirectly a controlling and a substantial financial interest in, a company which had advertised services connected with the practice of medicine. [261]

Through two intermediary companies, Nurses Night and Day Ltd. and Parviz Holdings Ltd., Dr. Faridian was stated, at the material times, to have had a controlling interest in the Langham Street Clinic Ltd. (a private nursing home where many legal abortions had been performed). It was further alleged that the clinic had sought to attract patients and thereby to promote its own (and its directors') financial benefit by advertising its services to women wishing to rid themselves of unwanted pregnancies, and by offering financial inducement to medical practitioners to refer or introduce women to the clinic. The clinic was alleged to have circulated some fifty letters to medical practitioners in Western Germany in and after December 1968, offering 200 DM (about £20) for each patient sent to the clinic with a view to termination of pregnancy under the Abortion Act. Finally it was alleged that the matron of the clinic had advertised its services in the British Broadcasting Corporation's television programme Panorama on 17 March 1969. She had stated that patients came to the clinic for terminations of pregnancy from many countries including Germany, where similar operations were illegal, and that the procedures were performed by "top specialists" and "under the right conditions".

Dr. H. N. Young, a general practitioner from Leicester, gave evidence that he had referred a patient to the Langham Street Clinic, which he had seen advertised in the *British Medical Journal*. The discharge note he received was followed by the arrival of a registered letter containing four five-pound notes with the sender's name given as the Langham Street Clinic. He had forwarded the money to his medical defence society. Mr. Leslie Toulson, a journalist employed by the *Sun*, then told the Committee that, accompanied by a photographer, he had visited the clinic by appointment and had subsequently written an article which was published in the *Sun*. Mr. Jack Saltman, a BBC television producer, also gave evidence that he had visited the clinic, and had met a lady described as the matron, who later appeared in the Panorama programme. Both Mr. Toulson and Mr. Saltman admitted that they had had no contact with the accused physician.

Dr. Faridian, who described himself as a general practitioner with a list of about 4500 patients, explained that Nurses Night and Day Ltd. had been formed in 1962, then Parviz Holdings Ltd., and lastly the Langham Street Clinic Ltd. In October and November 1968, he said, he had developed recurrent depression with bronchitis and asthma, which had necessitated continuous medical attention. Because of his ailing health he had resigned from the Langham Street Clinic Ltd. on 8 November 1968, and from Nurses Night and Day Ltd. on 7 January 1969. He stated that he had operated at the Langham Street Clinic under consultant supervision but had not carried on medical practice after the beginning of December 1968. Dr. Faridian denied all knowledge of the letter sent to German doctors and said that if he had known about it he would have prevented it being sent, for he strongly disapproved of this action. He also had no knowledge that the matron of the clinic was being approached by the British Broadcasting Corporation with a view to her appearance on a television programme and he said that he would strongly have disapproved if he had known that the Panorama programme mentioning the Langham Clinic was to be broadcast. Similarly he did not know of the article that appeared in the *Sun*, of which he also disapproved. He told the Committee that he had sold the shares he had held in Nurses Night and Day Ltd. and in the Langham Street Clinic Ltd. Under cross-examination Dr. Faridian conceded that he was a sleeping partner in all the companies, though he said he did not advise or assist in running them; he received £2000 to £3000 a year as a director of Nurses Night and Day Ltd.

Evidence was then given by Mr. Felix Onyesoh, the Secretary of the Langham Street Clinic Ltd., and by Mrs. Leila Burstoft, formerly a secretary in Nurses Night and Day Ltd., who in 1968 had helped to organize the operation at the Langham Street Clinic. Mrs. Burstoft explained that following conversations with an *au pair* girl she had decided to send the letter to the German doctors; she agreed that it advertised the services of the clinic. She did not consult Dr. Faridian, or anyone else before sending the letter; and she left the clinic in December 1968.

The Committee judged that the facts alleged against Dr. Faridian had been proved to its satisfaction. In mitigation, his Counsel observed, since the autumn of 1968 Dr. Faridian had had a severe depressive mental illness which had had the effect of preventing his actively running or being in control of the Langham Street Clinic since its incorporation. The Clinic, Dr. Faridian's Counsel suggested, had become a Frankenstein monster turning on its creator by developing a life of its own through the misguided zeal of its servants or agents and doing what was wrong against a medical background though not obviously wrong against a commercial one. None the less, the Disciplinary Committee judged Dr. Faridian to have been guilty of infamous conduct in a professional respect and directed the Registrar to erase his name from the Register.[261]

The sentence of the Committee was not put into action pending the hearing of Dr. Faridian's appeal to the Judicial Committee of the Privy Council, which took place on 20–22 July 1970. An Order in Council dated 29 July approved the report of the Judicial Committee that the appeal should be allowed and the determination of the Disciplinary Committee set aside.[223] This was the first time ever that the Privy Council had reversed a decision of the Disciplinary Committee of the General Medical Council to have a practitioner's name erased form the Register.[262]

Aftermaths of Sir George Godber's Lecture

The hubbub that had been created at the time St. John-Stevas made his first attempt to modify the Abortion Act soon died down, and the dispute regarding the way in which it was working, having temporarily lost its news value, disappeared from the newspapers. A statement made by the Canterbury Group Hospital Management Committee that the treatment of patients under the Abortion Act was delaying the admission of some gynaecological cases on the waiting list,[263] for example, aroused little interest.

Early in August, however, the partial text of Sir George Godber's Dame Juliet Rhys-Williams Memorial Lecture, to which reference has earlier been made,[220] was published in the *Lancet*.[264] An annotation[265] in the same issue commented on the hope that Sir George had expressed that the Abortion Act would reduce maternal mortality, illegitimacy, and "distress not measurable in statistical terms", and observed that in any assessment of its effect on self-induced or backstreet procedures, a reliable baseline for criminal abortion would be of value. The annotation drew attention to an article by Goodhart[266] in which he had suggested that the frequently cited figure of 100,000 legal abortions a year (see p. 2) prior to the Abortion Act was too large. However, whilst Goodhart's paper was useful in eliminating estimates far in excess of 100,000 cases, it commented, his own figure of 15,000–20,000 criminal abortions annually seemed unrealistically low.

On 13 September a letter published in the *Lancet* by a Birmingham psychiatrist, Howard White,[267] expressed disquiet at the published part of Sir George's speech. "It was apparent to many of us that any abortion law demanding a real risk of physical or psychological disorder to justify a legal termination would fail to meet the demands of a large group of women whose only objection to their pregnancy is on grounds of convenience", White wrote. "It was entirely inevitable and foreseeable that such women would seek illegal abortions." He found it "odd" that Sir George Godber hoped that this situation would be solved by the Abortion Act, and "disturbing" that termination of an unwanted pregnancy was an NHS service women had a right to expect. If the Government wanted abortion on demand, White said, it should induce Parliament to legislate accordingly. He thought it was unlikely to be successful. Meanwhile it was becoming increasingly difficult for those who tried to interpret the Act in a conservative way.

Sir George Godber[268] immediately responded that a large proportion of the women who died after illicit abortions had had four or five children and were over 30 years of age. Whether or not their objection to pregnancy was on grounds of "convenience", they were sufficiently disturbed to risk their lives. In his lecture, he pointed out, he had explicitly stated that abortion on demand had not been legalized; he had not said that any woman was entitled to an abortion if she wished it nor had he advocated any illegal procedure.

Sir George said that he knew that the profession was trying to interpret the Act conscientiously, but he thought it was necessary to face the fact that widely differing interpretations of the Act were being followed in different areas "and even in different departments of the same area". The result was not only that departments felt to be "liberal" were being overloaded, but also that women were having recourse to termination at private clinics or by consultation with backstreet abortionists or by their own hands.

A gynaecologist, Professor J. S. Scott,[269] whose letter to the *Lancet* was published on 27 September, deplored the fact that the full text of Sir George's lecture had not been published, and said that he agreed with Professor Stallworthy that it was incorrect to assume that every abortion notified to the Minister of Health was *ipso facto* legal. He observed that, despite Sir George's[268] rejoinder, the fact that he had said in his lecture that arrangements to terminate unwanted pregnancies "should be part of the medical service which women in a given area have a right to expect" was difficult to interpret under the Abortion Act. Professor Scott believed that the situation since the Act represented the greatest threat to professional freedom since 1948 (the year of the inception of the NHS, and he said that he was alarmed to find a senior administrator (Sir George) passing judgement on clinicians by his remark that the situation in Newcastle upon Tyne in regard to termination, where of the 2.7 per 1000 women who were aborted 96 per cent had had their pregnancies terminated under the NHS, came nearest to a stable service meeting a public need. He closed by observing that Dame Juliet Rhys-Williams, in whose memory Sir George's lecture had been given, had herself been fundamentally opposed to abortion for social, economic, or personal reasons.

PREGNANCY DIAGNOSTIC SERVICES

With the development of rapid, cheap, accurate tests of pregnancy (see p. 85), confidential testing had been steadily increasing since the Abortion Act became law, and on 15 September 1969 a new service was introduced in 11,000 chemists' shops throughout Britain. On that date the Pharmacy and Professional Services Laboratory in north-west London, which had hitherto been performing about 1000 tests weekly by mail order, made kits available to women over the counter, and for a fee of £2 any woman could get a reply by post within 24 hours. The new arrangements immediately increased business at the laboratory by one-fifth.[270]

Commenting that it seemed likely that pharmacists would soon be giving the results of pregnancy testing direct to the public, a leading article [271] pointed out that though the latex agglutination test was about 98 per cent accurate when carefully performed, and though no great skill was required to carry it out, there were sound reasons for arguing that a doctor was the right person to make the diagnosis. Firstly, a clinical assessment was necessary, since further investigations might be needed if an abnormality was suspected. Secondly, women who intended to continue the pregnancy needed advice on antenatal care, and it was important that those who intended to seek termination should see a doctor rather than an abortionist. Thirdly, women who were not pregnant but who had felt that they might have been probably required advice on contraception or infertility as the case might be. The leading article thought that women used the postal service partly from reticence, partly from the belief that, especially if they were single, they would receive an unsympathetic hearing from their general practitioner, and partly because, in London and other large cities, many were not registered with doctors under the NHS. If doctors themselves performed the tests, they were not remunerated by the NHS, and they were not allowed to charge for doing it; yet if the profession was sincere in its opposition to laymen making the diagnosis of pregnancy, it had to show a greater willingness to accommodate women who did not wish to "wait a few weeks" to know the worst—or the best—about their condition.

FINE THE FATHER!

Speaking at a debate in the House of Lords on 29 October 1969, Baroness Summerskill commented on the working of the Abortion Act and said that the father of the child of a woman seeking an abortion should be fined. "We need to establish a new social code", she said, "to ensure that a man responsible for impregnating a woman by negligence is also guilty of an offence against the society which subsidizes the National Health Service." [272] The Baroness later explained that she thought that many girls were reluctant to go to the courts because of pressure from their families and possible publicity; as things stood, the girl suffered, the State paid for an abortion under the NHS, and the man who was responsible "gets off scot-free". She thought that it should be made possible for the women to name the men who had made them pregnant to "confidential courts", each composed of two or three people of undoubted reliability, where they could, in strictest secrecy, produce appropriate evidence. Action could then be taken against the father

—a heavy fine could be imposed if an abortion was performed, or payment under an affiliation order could be made mandatory if the pregnancy was completed.[273]

Lord Wilson, the Lord Advocate, replying to the debate, described Baroness Summerskill's suggestion as "diverting", and said that whilst he did not know what the English law would make of it, he was horrified to reflect on the difficulties which would arise in Scotland, especially in regard to the law on corroboration. "I cannot", he commented, "regard this as a serious suggestion or one which should be given effect to."[272]

FAMILY PLANNING

As mentioned earlier, the discovery by gynaecologists that a high proportion of the patients whose pregnancies they had legally terminated under the Abortion Act had employed no form of contraception (see p. 112) re-emphasized the importance of education in birth control in particular and in family planning in general. The National Health Service (Family Planning) Act 1967 referred to England and Wales, and the corresponding law for Scotland, the Health Services and Public Health Act 1968, came a year later. Further, Gardiner[274, 275] pointed out, the Secretary of State for Scotland was able, because of the economic situation, to postpone the implementation of the act concerned with family planning, thus denying the 5 million people resident in Scotland—10 per cent of the population of the United Kingdom—the benefit of a service. In the light of the work carried out in Aberdeen by MacQueen,[80] it was surprising that other parts of Scotland lagged so far behind the north-eastern area.

In July, the proceedings of a symposium on Personal and Community Factors in Fertility Control, held at Brighton, Sussex, in September 1968, were published. Discussing sociological factors, Claire Russell and W. M. S. Russell[276] observe that the evidence from mammalian societies suggested that social inequality and social violence were responses to high population density, and were capable of reducing the population for more than a generation. This, by sparing natural resources, could save such resources from irretrievable depletion. Population crises had occurred throughout history, but the current crisis was especially dangerous because modern weapons, as well as destroying individuals, could lastingly destroy natural resources on an unprecedented scale. Voluntary reduction of human birth rate provided an alternative form of population control, which could make enduring world peace possible. Edwin Brooks,[277] speaking at the same symposium, drew attention to the political and economic factors in fertility control. He regarded the Papal encyclical *Humanae Vitae* as "a disaster of our times", and he explained that he was not persuaded that the world of the Early Fathers, remote across a gulf of fifteen centuries, had the right to legislate morally for the world of today's fathers and mothers. The objections that had existed to contraception had been invalidated by medical science and the resultant world growth of population. Public attitudes to contraception had changed in Britain in recent years, Brooks said, but he felt that the opposition to the Family Planning Act (which he had sponsored) was based on reservations and anxieties resulting from the emancipation of women as workers and as sexual partners. He believed that the Family Planning Act would be more widely implemented by local authorities when suspicions were allayed and when its obvious financial benefits became more apparent. He felt that a comprehensive and clinical domiciliary service was needed; the Family Planning Act, he pointed out, was not hostile to large families as such, but was a device for avoiding unwanted pregnancies. Whilst it might reduce the birth rate, it should enlarge freedom by ensuring that only the consequences desired followed sexual relations; and it should halt the "steady and alarming" increase in illegitimate births.

M. S. Emerson,[278] speaking on personal factors in fertility control, drew attention to the importance of the patient's attitude to contraceptive advice. She felt the doctor must be prepared to spend time listening to the patient's problems, and must demonstrate a positive attitude towards contraception so as to allay the patient's anxiety and guilt. If the patient was married, the form of contraception chosen should be acceptable to her husband. Whether married or not, however, contraception was an important aspect of preventive medicine. This was particularly the case in single women if abortion and illegitimate pregnancies were to be avoided. Miriam Moore-Robinson[279] next spoke on future prospects in fertility control, starting by delineating areas where stricter applications of contraception might be applied. In Britain, she observed, 250,000 unwanted pregnancies were conceived every year. Moore-Robinson described the qualities of the ideal oral contraceptive, and went on to discuss the qualities of chlormadinone acetate, the "third-generation" (low-dose continuous progestin) pill. Lastly, she dealt briefly with research in contraceptive methods—injections, post-coital preparations, and immunology. Finally, Hilary Hill[280] discussed the vital role of education in birth control. She pointed out that it was necessary to educate the educated (the doctors) so that they in turn could teach the present generation of parents, grandparents, and children about reproduction and birth control. Physicians taught health visitors, nurses, and social workers; they spread their ideas to colleagues, to individuals, and to groups. Hill felt also that youngsters should be educated in fertility control before it became an intense personal concern. Doctors who had had an inadequate undergraduate education in contraception, she pointed out, could attend courses arranged by the Family Planning Association. In addition, educational aids were sometimes of value.

In July also, Malcolm Potts, secretary of the International Planned Parenthood Federation, told a conference in Cambridge that the pill should be available commercially and that family-planning clinics should be easier of access, "more like fish and chip shops". He said that the preponderance of people in the upper social classes who attended the clinics was worse than in the 1930s, and he thought that one of the main reasons was the attitude of the doctors who "examined every orifice", had "long faces", and "tried to delve into patients' sex lives". "The way some FPA doctors carry on implies that barbers should examine the scrotum of every man to whom they sell condoms", he said. Potts, himself a member of the FPA, listed his "seven commandments" of contraception as follows: (1) whatever his speciality, the doctor must keep family planning in mind; (2) the family-planning clinics should be open at more suitable times, the patients should not be kept waiting, and the doctors should take off their white coats and "solemn faces"; (3) no distinction should be made between married and single women seeking advice; (4) the doctor should not alarm the patient about the pill—it was safer than pregnancy or other contraceptives; (5) there should be more research into family planning; (6) a more sensible attitude should be adopted towards abortion, "less of the hysteria we have seen at the BMA meeting"; and (7) an attempt should be made to get the Government interested in population policy.[281]

Hilary Hill[282] quickly wrote on behalf of the FPA and the 1200 doctors working in its clinics to protest about the remarks attributed to Malcolm Potts. A pelvic examination, Hill observed, was mandatory if a diaphragm or an intra-uterine device was prescribed, and a pre-pill vaginal examination might exempt the pill from the suspicion that it had been associated with an unsuspected pathological condition, as well as providing an opportunity to take a cervical smear and to allay the patient's anxiety. FPA doctors did not have "long faces", and the reason that the clinics were restricted in their hours of opening was that they were dependent on charity for the availability of their premises; she thought it was a tribute to the FPA doctors that they manned the clinics week after week at times which were as inconvenient to themselves as they were to the patients. Saroja Ramaswamy,[283] writing as a practising gynaecologist and an active FPA doctor, also deplored the comments attributed to Potts, which he thought represented the height of irresponsibility. Ramaswamy pointed to the research being done on the long-term effects of the pill, and he insisted that a vaginal examination—"through the 'vaginal orifice' and nothing else"—was "basic good medicine" and was necessary before advising on contraception. He listed six women with significant diseases which he had diagnosed in less than a year in the three FPA clinics in which he worked.

Humphrey Arthure,[284] whose letter to the editor of the *Lancet* appeared on 6 September, pointed out that the number of terminations under the Abortion Act was steadily increasing, and that few women realized that contraceptives could be obtained free for medical reasons or for social reasons if financial need existed. Those practitioners who performed NHS terminations of pregnancy had become aware that it was difficult to make a sharp distinction between medical indications and social need. Since an unwanted pregnancy should be recognized as an illness, greater efforts should be made to prevent it, and no distinction should be made between medical and social needs for contraceptives, which he felt should be freely available on the NHS. In addition, Arthure believed, there should be a centrally organized campaign of public education on sex matters and on the prevention of unwanted pregnancies, including instruction in schools in both sexes.

On 13 October, Richard Crossman[285] declared in the Commons that he would have liked to make the Family Planning Act mandatory on local authorities rather than discretionary, but it was no use doing this, he observed, unless simultaneously sufficient money was supplied to implement it. The shortcomings of the legislation were later referred to by Professor Peter Huntingford[286] speaking at a meeting of the International Planned Parenthood Federation held in Budapest. The Family Planning Act restricted the services freely available to those provided by the local authorities, the Professor said, whilst the hospital services responsible for maternity and gynaecological care had no obligation to give contraceptive advice, and, furthermore, did not have the financial resources necessary to provide it.

Despite the shortage of money to which Professor Huntingford referred, a few British hospitals have for some years endeavoured to provide family-planning services. The late Professor Nixon established the first contraceptive clinic in a London teaching hospital in the post-natal department of University College Hospital as long ago as 1952. Ten years later Sir Dugald Baird,[287] amongst others, was advocating the same provisions. In 1966 S. J. Steele[83] drew attention to the need for contraceptive services after abortion. In July 1968, Caroline Woodroffe[288] observed, FPA central London branch lay workers began to visit a municipal hospital to provide information and advice to mothers and to women who had undergone sterilization and abortion.

The scheme, which has recently spread to other hospitals, developed out of a request to the FPA by a consultant gynaecologist for a visiting service for his inpatients. As a result, FPA officials had interviews with the matron, the hospital secretary, and the superintendent of midwifery. Subsequently, one of a team of five lay workers visited the four wards involved every week. As most mothers stayed in for a week, and as patients who had been sterilized stayed in for an average of 2 weeks, the worker would usually see up to thirty patients in one 2–2½-hour session. Wearing ordinary clothes, she would interview patients at the bedside, offering help and information about contraceptive services. She encouraged each patient to visit her local FPA clinic or to consult her general practitioner, who, the lay worker had previously checked, was willing to see the patient for this purpose. The lay worker supplied leaflets with maps of local FPA clinics and their hours of opening; she also provided FPA pamphlets such as *Sex in Married Life* and *Growing Up – Facts About Sex for Boys and Girls* which were translated as necessary into several languages. Of 313 hospitalized mothers seen over a 3-month period ending in February 1969, 30 per cent of those at risk refused information. Others were more appreciative, and the lay workers, through the local health department, sent the names of those who wished to attend FPA clinics to the health visitors before they paid their statutory post-natal visit.

In 1967, Woodroffe pointed out, 117 FPA clinics were held in hospital premises; yet only 3 per cent of new referrals came from the hospitals—which were reluctant to assume responsibility for a service which they felt it was the task of the local authorities to provide. Clearly, Woodroffe observed, family planning had to be accepted by patients and staff as an integral part of post-natal care. A good relationship between doctors, nurses, and FPA workers—"you be sure to see the family-planning lady when she comes round"—was vital if the latter were to be accepted as part of the team, so as to function with maximum efficiency.

In 1969, Barbara Laws [289] states, the senior gynaecologist of the Whittington Hospital in north London succeeded in having a doctor appointed as a clinical assistant for two sessions a week devoted to family planning. One session was spent visiting patients in the gynaecological and post-natal wards, so that advice on contraception could be given after abortions and postnatally. The other session was spent in a clinic adjoining the post-natal clinic, where, with the assistance of a trained FPA nurse, patients were seen by appointment. Apart from providing advice and practical help—inserting IUDs, fitting diaphragms, and so forth—patients were given information on the location and times of opening of their local FPA clinics. Care was taken to suit the method to the individual, and the majority of women were grateful and co-operative; in particular, the Roman Catholic patients appreciated help with calculating the "safe" period. This type of arrangement, though more costly than the visiting of wards by FPA lay workers, had the advantage that a high proportion of patients could be given practical help at their first interview with the doctor.

The need for hospital-based family planning to supplement the local authority services was appreciated by the Ministry of Social Security. In December 1969, John Dunwoody, the then Under-Secretary of State for the Department of Health and Social Security, revealed that Richard Crossman had written to the hospital boards and the teaching hospitals making proposals in this regard. He had asked them to investigate their arrangements for providing family-planning services and to acquaint him with the developments they proposed so as to make an effective service available to all women patients. The hospitals themselves, his letter observed, could often provide this service most effectively and at the time it was most needed. Crossman suggested that the regional hospital boards should consult with their hospital management committees and gynaecologists to decide whether the hospitals should give advice on family planning or whether it should leave the task to voluntary organizations. [290]

On 27 November the FPA took a great step forward when the Duke of Edinburgh opened its new national office, called the Margaret Pyke Centre in memory of one of the Association's best-known pioneer workers. The Centre combined a national administration base for co-ordinating FPA activities in London and the provinces with research and training facilities. It had a family-planning bookshop with over 200 titles, two clinic units with consulting and examination rooms, and a group teaching unit with a one-way screen. The Centre also contained a subfertility clinic and a laboratory where cervical smears, pregnancy diagnosis, and sperm counts could be performed. Research studies in progress were focusing on the acceptability of medically approved contraceptive methods and on ways in which greater numbers of patients could be seen at the clinics without lowering the standards of care. To this end, nurses were being trained to take over some of the tasks usually performed by a doctor—for instance, the preparation of cervical smears. In addition, the Margaret Pyke Centre was implementing a programme for educating doctors, nurses, and medical students in contraceptive techniques. One hundred and seven training sessions for doctors and eighty-eight for nurses had been held since June; of those trained, 77 per cent were from overseas and 23 per cent came from Great Britain. [291, 292]

In his speech the Duke referred to the steady growth of the Association from a one-room office and 20 clinics in the entire country when Mrs. Pyke joined it as its secretary in 1930 to 400 clinics in 1954 when she became its chairman. In November 1969, 3 years after Mrs. Pyke's death, it consisted of 950 clinics, increasing at the rate of 2 clinics a week, where 1200 doctors, 6000 nurses, 8000 voluntary workers, and a staff of 100 working in 52 branches were caring for half a million patients. The Duke commented that it was a most impressive record. He went on to refer to the 1967 United Nations Resolution that it was the inalienable right of people to have the size of family they wanted (see p. 42), and he said that even the enormous effort made by the Association was not sufficient in view of the number of illegitimate children born and the number of abortions being performed. The Duke briefly reviewed family planning from the statistical, the socio-economic, and the evolutionary standpoints, and he referred to the cloud of accumulated moral and social attitudes, many reflecting the anxieties and uncertainties of human existence through most of its history, which he said hung over the whole subject. He mentioned with approval Arnold Toynbee's question as to whether the end of man in the religious sense was to populate the earth with the maximum number of human beings or to lead the best kind of life that the spiritual limitations of human nature allowed. In the end, the Duke thought, the most important consideration was the individual, and unless the individual was prepared to hand over freedom of choice to the State, the effort had to be made to educate and enlighten so that an intelligent choice could be made. [293]

In December 1969 the resignation of Hilary Hill, the Medical Director of the FPA, was announced. In a statement at an unofficial meeting of FPA doctors on 15 December, Hill referred to the considerable authority formerly vested in her which had latterly been so "eroded" that it had become impossible for her to work effectively. She was afraid that the trends then extant might lead to a less professional service and to an impairment of the relationship between clinic doctor and patient. Commenting on the affair, a leading article[294] observed that family planning involved far more than fitting contraceptive devices and prescribing the right pill. Patients might need to discuss their psychosexual problems or other medical matters arising out of their contraceptive needs. Examinations, such as a cervical smear, were sometimes necessary; and there was the question of treating failure to conceive as well as that of helping with problems in the marital relationship. Such a comprehensive service required a properly trained medically qualified individual with time to interview each patient and to assess her needs. The leading article expressed the hope that the committee of inquiry which had been formed by the FPA under the chairmanship of Lord Platt to examine its medical structure and function would "recognize the value of a sympathetic unhurried approach to a subject which patients still find embarrassing".

In January 1970 the Conservation Society—an organization concerned with the impact of population size and growth on the environment of which the President was Yehudi Menuhin—sent a statement to the Prime Minister of the United Kingdom calling for a government policy to stabilize the size of the population. Even at the current low level of growth, the statement said, a child born in 1969 was likely to see the population of Britain nearly double in its lifetime. Adverse effects would include huge urban areas, overcrowding of recreation areas, restriction on the freedom of movement, and loss of peace and solitude. The statement claimed that over half of the Roman Catholic parents in Britain used methods of contraception not sanctioned by their Church. "Thus the Roman Catholic Church's teaching does not command the general assent of its own members in Britain, and there is no justification for allowing the fear of opposition from this quarter to influence public policy." The Society pointed out that only a fractional reduction in the average family size of 2.5 would bring the country in sight of stabilizing the population, and it said that the first priority of the Government was to ensure that Britain had a comprehensive family-planning service. [295]

Later the same month, Richard Crossman, in a written answer to a Commons question, said that he welcomed the action of the Independent Television Authority in removing the ban on advertising family-planning services. The Health Education Council, he revealed, was actively considering the possibility of making television fillers for free showing in public service time, though publicity for local services was a matter for the local health authorities. They had to decide to what extent their limited resources should be spent on advertising existing arrangements or expanding their services, for which, he felt, there was an urgent need.[296]

ORAL CONTRACEPTIVES

Throughout 1969, interest continued to be expressed in the efficacy and safety of oral contraceptives. On 22 May the Committee on the Safety of Drugs, which had become fully operational on 1 January 1964, under the chairmanship of Sir Derrick Dunlop, and which was noted for its impartiality as well as for the excellence of its advice to the pharmaceutical industry on the marketing of drugs, advised all doctors that sequential oral contraceptives appeared to be less effective than combined preparations. However, it did not recommend their withdrawal because they were more effective than non-oral methods, and because on occasion they constituted the only oral contraceptives that patients could tolerate.[297] According to Poller and Thomson,[298] however, sequential contraceptives, like combined preparations, caused an increase in blood-clotting factors VII and X in women who took them, a finding suggesting the existence of an equal risk of thrombosis.

Early in June, Butler and Hill[299] reported on a clinical trial of conception control using a daily dosage of 0.5 mg of the "third-generation" progestogen-only oral contraceptive, chlormadinone acetate. In over 1642 cycles in 208 women, the incidence of "unwanted occurrences" was lower than with combined oral contraceptives, except that persistent heavy or irregular bleeding occurred in thirteen women and another thirteen became pregnant.

G. A. Christie,[300] the Medical Director of Syntex Pharmaceuticals (which manufactured chlormadinone acetate), commented that the results of the trial were in keeping with those of other investigations, but he thought that perhaps because calendar packs were not employed, the rate of pregnancy had been unduly high. However, a further British trial by Geraldine Howard et al.[301] in 260 who also took 0.5 mg of chlormadinone acetate daily and completed 2080 cycles, again revealed a substantial pregnancy rate, with a use-effectiveness of 8.6 per hundred women years and a method failure of 5.2. An annotation[302] subsequently commented that the new agent was simpler to use, and appeared to be safer, than earlier preparations, but expressed misgivings regarding its efficiency as a contraceptive.

On 11 December the warning that $1\frac{1}{2}$ million women in Britain received from Professor Scowen, the new chairman of the Committee on Safety of

Drugs, that they should only take oral contraceptives containing less than 50 μg of oestrogen,[303] temporarily boosted confidence in chlormadinone "mini-pills", but on 20 January 1970 it was reported from California that Syntex had suspended tests on it in the United States due to the "adverse effects" it had produced in beagle dogs.[304] The announcement, a Syntex marketing director immediately declared, was "virtually without relevance" in Britain,[305] but 2 days later its sales were banned in France. On 23 January, supplies of chlormadinone acetate were stopped for approximately 7000 women taking it in New Zealand,[306] and the following day the drug was generally withdrawn from an estimated world market of 100,000 women. The "adverse effects" the dogs in California had exhibited were hyperglycaemia and the development of breast nodules (to which beagles are especially susceptible). Despite the difficulty of extrapolating findings from animals to man, Syntex preferred to err on the side of extreme caution in the emotive climate that by then prevailed in regard to oral contraceptives.[307] In Washington, for instance, Hugh Davis had just alleged that the widespread use of oral contraceptives "had given rise to health hazards on a scale previously unknown to medicine",[308] and Roy Hertz had told a Senate monopoly sub-committee on 15 January that women were engaged in a "grim race" with laboratory animals to determine the safety of the pill.[309] In Britain, whilst on 22 January the Royal College of General Practitioners cautioned women not to panic, pointing out that the risks of taking it were far lower than those of being involved in a road accident,[310] on the same day seven East London ambulance drivers decided to be sterilized because they did not trust the pill.[311] None the less, Syntex did not rule out the possibility of reissuing chlormadinone if further tests exonerated it.[312] Further, a leading article[313] in the *British Medical Journal*, pointing out that it did not affect blood-clotting factors and was less hepatotoxic than its predecessors, commented that the evidence that had brought it under suspicion was slender. It was to be hoped, the article stated, that neither the Food and Drug Administration in the United States, nor the Committee on Safety of Drugs in Britain, would ban it, though improved compounds should continue to be sought.

Throughout the autumn the controversy regarding the safety of oral contraceptives was never absent from the media for very long. Gynaecologists, family doctors, psychiatrists, and others deplored the adverse publicity the pill received, for they knew that a few weeks after each new "scare" there would be another wave of requests for terminations of pregnancy from women who, frightened by the adverse reports, had stopped taking the pill. Aviva Wiseman,[314] the director of a family-planning clinic, remarked in fact that the greatest side-effect occasioned by the pill had been rumours and adverse publicity. The list of major hazards associated with the use of oral contraceptives, even after the exhaustive studies that had been performed, Martin Vessey[315] observed, was short, and there was strong evidence that the thrombo-embolic phenomena with which they were sometimes associated were only one-third as frequent in pill-users belonging to blood group O as in users belonging to other blood groups. Furthermore, a study carried out in Manchester by Kay et al.,[316] reported on 6 December, showed that amongst 32,000 women who were prospectively surveyed there was a highly significant deficiency of non-smokers and an excess of heavy smokers in the group which was taking the pill. The importance of this last finding is hard to assess, but it seems that cigarette smoking, long known to be associated with coronary thrombosis, for example, might be playing a significant role in increasing the propensity of women taking oral contraceptives to develop thrombotic phenomena.

On Friday, 5 December, David Frost, a well-known English television personality, presented a programme on the pill in which Victor Wynn, a consultant in human metabolism, was ranged against Malcolm Potts and an unnamed gynaecologist. Wynn, supporting his case with charts, graphs, quotes, and authoritative sources, made ten points against the pill, alleging that it could be a significant contributing factor in thrombosis, cancer, infertility, premature ageing, overweight, personality changes, and harmful genetic effects. At this stage Milton Shulman,[317] a television commentator, remarks: "If I were a woman on the pill I would have been rushing to my medicine chest and flushing my supply down the loo." Potts and his gynaecologist colleague did their best to rebut Wynn's charges, especially those concerning cancer, genetic effects, and infertility. Yet in spite of their vigorous defence, Shulman commented: "I would hazard a guess that many women watching the programme gave up the pill that evening and that many more resolved not to start taking it." The programme was unfair to Wynn's opponents, Shulman thought, because Wynn was allowed more than half the time, uninterrupted, to set out his case; his opponents had not been informed that he would present a barrage of statistics and thus did not have counter-statistics ready to hand; and they were seated amongst the audience rather than being placed, like Wynn, on the platform with Frost.

This commercial network programme, as well as references to the pill in the BBC's regular television feature 24 Hours, was responsible for creating a telepanic" which erupted on 12 December when Professor Scowen issued his committee's warning regarding the dangers associated with taking oral contraceptives containing more than 50 µg of oestrogen. His statement meant that only 11 of the 20 oral contraceptives on the British market could be taken with relative impunity, and women swamped doctors and family-planning clinics with telephone calls concerning the dangers associated with the pill.[318] The doctors were rightly incensed because the public had been informed of the dangers before they themselves—immersed in coping with outbreaks of influenza—had been notified.[319] The unfortunate situation had developed, D. H. Ennals,[320] the then Minister of State, Health, and Social Security, explained in the Commons on 15 December, because though the Committee had planned to inform the doctors first, they had felt it appropriate to follow their usual practice of consulting the manufacturers before taking important action concerning them. Manufacturers were accordingly told in confidence of the Committee's decision on Wednesday, 10 December, but the information "leaked" within 2 hours, and the following day the *Daily Express* carried a prominent headline on the subject. This brought pressure for a statement from the press, radio, and television, as well as from patients and doctors, and a decision was taken for one to be released. Caspar Brooks, Director of the FPA, which, having an estimated 400,000 women on oral contraceptives, was heavily involved, called an emergency meeting which ordered a rush printing of a new information leaflet *Change to Lower Risk Pill* to circulate to FPA patients. Later the situation became so urgent that the FPA announced it was telephoning advice to patients to its fifty-two branch secretaries up and down the country covering its 950 clinics. Women were told not to panic, and those who were taking high oestrogen content pills were advised to employ alternative methods of contraception if they decided to discontinue them. It was also announced that in FPA clinics patients would initially be given 1-month rather than 6-month prescriptions for the pill so as to conserve supplies.[318]

Shirley Summerskill, the medically qualified Labour Member of Parliament for Halifax, long an opponent of the pill, lost no time in condemning "high-dose" oral contraceptives, and declared that as "women should not be expected to be guinea-pigs any longer" such pills should be banned at once.[321] In the Commons she twice requested that an inquiry be made into the adverse effects of oral contraceptives, but this was twice refused by the Minister of

State, Health, and Social Security, who pointed out that a good deal of research was already being carried out by the Medical Research Council, the FPA and the Royal College of General Practitioners. He thought that "a good deal of alarm and despondency" about the use of oral contraceptives had been created by statements in the public media. Meanwhile several pill manufacturers announced that they would bring out low-dosage oral contraceptives the week after the Committee's statement. [322] Professor Scowen, [323] tardily providing the statement in the medical journals on 20 December, explained the reasons for his premature release of information to the public and noted the Committee's regret that this had been necessary. "The Committee", he said, "apologized to the profession as a whole that things have occurred in this inappropriate order through no fault of its own."

On 27 December many references to the affair were to be found in the *British Medical Journal*. The first leading article [324] referred to the "hullabaloo" over the Committee's announcement, and commented that "official committees set up to inform the medical profession should communicate their information simply and solely to the profession". "Where matters of life and death are concerned," the leading article continued, "as they are with the 'pill' and have been in several of the committee's previous reports, a press conference is an entirely inappropriate means of expressing the committee's views. The committee was not set up to educate—let alone alarm—the public. . . ." The article commented on the role and function of the Drug Safety Committee, and observed that the medical profession ought to have been provided with an account of the numerical basis on which it had reached its conclusions, especially as its opinion conflicted with work that had earlier been reported. Endeavouring to assist its readers, the *British Medical Journal* published a further leading article [325] "Switching pills" and a review [326] "Changing oral contraceptives" in the same issue. This also contained, however, a selection of thirty-one letters that the editor had received from all parts of the country by the time the *Journal* had gone to press. It printed a section, including a further explanation from Professor Scowen, under the heading "Publicity and the pill". [327] Most correspondents were incensed at the way in which, without doctors having been given prior warning, information had been communicated directly to the public on the television and in the press, and they complained bitterly about the Committee's maladroitness and discourtesy.

G. M. Swyer, [327] an acknowledged authority on oral contraception, was particularly indignant, and commented on the Committee's apparent contempt for doctors in not releasing the factual data from which its conclusions were drawn. He pointed out that not only were ethinyloestradiol and mestranol —the two oestrogens used in oral contraceptives—dissimilar in potency, the former being twice as strong as the latter, but also no account appeared to have been taken of the progestogen component. With great self-control, Swyer remarked: "It would be unlikely, to say the least, if this were irrelevant, since some progestogens have intrinsic oestrogenic activity or have oestrogenic metabolic products while others have quite markedly anti-oestrogenic activity." He thought that if the Committee on Safety of Drugs had not taken these considerations into account when reaching its conclusions, the chances were that they were invalid. It was "ludicrous", he felt, that, as the medical correspondent of *The Times* had observed, the list of oral contraceptives "recommended" by the Committee included the two chlormadinone acetate-alone preparations, which trials in Britain had demonstrated were associated with high rates of pregnancy, and that a woman taking high-oestrogen pills should be advised to "go and discuss the matter at leisure with her doctor" who had not been given any factual information on the basis of which to advise her. He further thought that, unless she was in possession of a great deal more information than others, Shirley Summerskill's call for a ban on high-oestrogen pills had reflected "a degree of irresponsibility and contempt of the medical profession which is altogether intolerable in a public personage".

M. C. N. Jackson,[328] a family-planning clinic medical officer, wrote to the editor of the *Lancet* in a similar and very practical vein. She pointed out that by placing the whole emphasis on the oestrogen component of oral contraceptives, the Committee on Safety of Drugs had caused "widespread and needless apprehension and confusion". Doctors had been placed in a very difficult position, for it was known that overloading with the progestogenic component of the pill could produce adverse effects such as increasing weight, acne, dryness of the vagina, headaches, bloating, irritability, loss of libido, and depression. Many of these symptoms could be alleviated by the prescription of an oestrogenic pill of greater effect, yet what was to be done in the light of the Scowen Committee's recommendations? Should the women put up with their difficulties on a low-oestrogen pill? Should they adhere to the more oestrogenic contraceptive which suited them well? Or should they give up oral contraceptives altogether? Jackson wondered which of these alternatives posed the greatest risk, and she noted that the Scowen Committee had given no guidance. She observed that the "angels"—the low-risk pills—were listed on the basis of their oestrogen content alone, and that no distinction was made on the type or amount of the oestrogen, nor on the character or amount of the progestogen content—even though the first six pills listed contained progestogens which were metabolized to oestrogens in the body. No clear indication was given as to the point at which the increased oestrogen content was linked with thrombosis, and it seemed that a number of well-tried and useful products with a fractionally larger dose of oestrogen (0.08 or 0.075 mg instead of 0.05 mg) were to be thrown away to make room for new, hastily produced, largely untried, and possibly unbalanced products produced by firms which had no "angels" to put on the market.

A fitting climax to the issues on the safety of oral contraceptives that had been raised—and which, as mentioned earlier, were ventilated yet again at the governmental hearings in Washington, D.C. in January 1970[308, 309]— was a report, published on 30 January, that a £417,000 law suit had been filed against G. D. Searle & Co., the manufacturers of Ovulen, by a woman who had developed a pulmonary embolus after taking this drug.[329] The news post-dated an otherwise up-to-date authoritative statement in an article by Potts and Swyer[330] in the January 1970 issue of the *British Medical Bulletin*, which was entirely devoted to "Control of human fertility". The article stated that the risks associated with the use of oral contraceptives were small, the death rate being of the same order of magnitude as deaths due to cricket or football, below that from swimming, using lifts, travelling on the roads, and far below that resulting from the use of alcohol and tobacco.

ABORTION CLINICS

As mentioned earlier, the reluctance of certain members of the medical profession to implement the Abortion Act had led to pressure on facilities and to a demand that more adequate provisions be made under the NHS. The most concrete expression of this demand was that abortion clinics should be established in regions where NHS terminations were difficult to obtain. The issue was discussed at the annual representative meeting of the BMA which was held early in July 1969.

At the debate on gynaecological services the following motion was moved: "That in view of the considerable demand made on gynaecological beds by the National Health Service as a result of the Abortion Act, expansion of gynaecological services is imperative to cope with the total volume of obstetric and gynaecological requirements."[331] A further motion that was attached requested "That the Council press the Department of Social Security to provide the extra facilities in all areas to ensure that the provisions of the

Act can be fulfilled without detriment to other gynaecological patients". M. R. Sheridan, moving the motion, explained that he was concerned with the problem of the private abortion clinics and those who worked in them, since it was felt that the problem would resolve itself very rapidly when the Department of Health and Social Security was persuaded to honour its commitments. The Act had been introduced and made into law to help thousands of women who genuinely required their pregnancies terminated. He drew attention to the problem of women from poor families or girls without private means who, under the Act, could not in many areas obtain the service which was recommended to them. These patients, he said, could not go on a waiting list and did not have a priority over other cases; they did not even have a service. Sheridan thought that in every area special units, properly equipped and staffed, should be provided; given these facilities, he was sure that there were sufficient gynaecologists, trained and in training, in sympathy with the Act and its implications, to make it work. Two other practitioners supported the motions, which were both carried.

H. Gordon, of Kingston upon Thames, next moved "That the Government does provide centres for abortion situated throughout the country to facilitate early treatment and to prevent cases of this nature blocking gynaecological units. The moneys for this should be in addition to that already provided for the hospital service." It would be an advantage, Gordon thought, if practitioners were enabled to refer patients requiring this form of treatment to a centre where they would know in advance that they would receive sympathetic consideration; there was no difference in concept, he felt, between a family-planning clinic and an abortion centre. The motion was opposed by Derek Tacchi, a Newcastle gynaecologist, who said that abortions could be satisfactorily performed only in well-staffed gynaecological units with full ancillary services. He did not want to see "abortoria" set up under the NHS. Myre Sim and Lewin also opposed the motion, which was lost.

J. M. W. Sedgwick next moved "That the Minister of Health and Social Security be asked to direct gynaecological departments which facilities should be curtailed in view of the extra work load created by the greater number of terminations of pregnancy that are now performed without additional facilities having been provided in anticipation of this extra work load". He said that most gynaecologists were doing more abortions than they were before the Act, and he felt that the situation was causing hardship—and even danger—to patients. Sedgwick stated that he had used the word "direct" in the sense of a direction signpost, and an amendment proposed by A. E.

Malone to substitute the words "suggest to" for "direct" was carried. Kathleen Frith spoke sympathetically of the "wretched pregnant women... for whom the Act was created", and pointed out that the number of pregnancies had not increased since the Act; for every abortion which was done cleanly in hospital, a maternity bed was set free. G. R. Outwin supported Kathleen Frith's remarks, observing that references to overloading gynaecological departments in this context were a misconception—even if a woman was aborted three times during what would be the normal period for a pregnancy there would still be a saving of workload in the obstetric departments. After further discussion the amended motion was lost.

Towards the end of July, Alan Golding, a senior official of the Pregnancy Advisory Service, writing in *Marriage Guidance*, said that NHS abortion clinics should be established throughout Britain by the Minister of Health. Such clinics would, he stated, eliminate almost all the abuses under the Abortion Act.[332] Two months later Frank Denny, consultant gynaecologist to the Chelsea and Kensington group of hospitals in London, writing in a booklet *Marriage Guidance*, noted that of 41,496 abortions notified in England and Wales between August 1968 and May 1969, the majority—24,745 cases— had been dealt with in NHS hospitals as a burden on the taxpayer, and the figure could well increase annually. Denny commented: "If it is not the intention by law to have abortion on demand in this country, then the present Act requires amendment. If, on the other hand, it is the will of people and Parliament, that it should be on demand, then the law should clearly state this and there should be set up proper abortion centres, under the NHS, to deal only with these cases." The pressure of abortion demands on hospitals was so great, he said, that if all such cases were given top priority, gynaecologists would end up dealing exclusively with these patients, and women suffering from gynaecological illnesses would have little hope of obtaining early treatment.[333]

On Monday, 1 December, the Calthorpe Nursing Home, the first clinic in Britain to deal solely with abortions, was opened in Birmingham. The privately run clinic, which was set up despite medical and religious opposition, had eighteen beds and a staff of twenty-eight. A rota of surgeons working 6 days a week were capable of performing 100 abortions weekly at a flat rate fee of £65 per case. In licensing the clinic, which was a converted old people's home, Richard Crossman stated that he had considered assurances that every patient would stay in for at least 24 hours, and that there would never be more patients than beds in a 24-hour period. The Calthorpe project had grown out of the Birmingham Pregnancy Advisory Service, which was receiving about 100 inquiries each week about abortions (see p. 107). Perturbed by the 11 per cent rate of illegitimacy in Birmingham, the shortage of NHS facilities, and the cost and inconvenience of going to London for a private abortion, Martin Cole and his PAS colleagues had raised the money from private sources to buy the lease of the clinic building and to erect a new operating theatre. The Calthorpe Nursing Home planned to cater for women up to 14 weeks pregnant and hoped in time to reduce its fees. Cole and his associates were anxious to demonstrate that a private clinic could operate properly without charging excessively—its fees were about half those charged in London. [335] However, 2 weeks after the Calthorpe Nursing Home opened, David Hay, a consultant gynaecologist in Manchester, alleged that it had offered a young woman doctor a salary of £24,000 a year for working a 9-hour week—three 3-hour sessions during each of which she was to perform about eighteen abortions. Martin Cole later said that the figure had been £20,000 a year, which he felt was a "reasonable annual salary for someone of consultant status who will have full-time responsibility for every patient in the Home". In fact, the salary was nearly four times that of a full-time NHS consultant—an indication of the disinclination of many members of the medical profession to involve themselves in such work and of the financial rewards available to those willing to undertake it. [336]

CHAPTER 11

Winter: The End of the Beginning

AFTER Christmas, fresh rumours began to circulate about arrangements allegedly being made to cater for abortion-seekers from America. Not inappropriately they immediately preceded the second parliamentary attempt —no more successful than its predecessor—to amend the Act. The figures that became available at this time made it possible to review the working of the Abortion Act in the first 18 months of its existence. Interest in abortion and related subjects persisted unchecked, and in May 1970 the difficulties created for gynaecologists by the Act were clearly revealed when the Royal College of Obstetricians and Gynaecologists published the results of a questionnaire sent out to ascertain their experiences with it.

American Interest in London Facilities

Late in December it was reported that Eric Moonman, the then Labour Member of Parliament for Billericay, was to ask the Secretary of State for Social Services what consultations had taken place between his department and the Los Angeles based firm American Medical Enterprises Incorporated regarding the purchase of a British hospital for use as a private abortion centre, and whether approval for such a centre had been given. Declaring that his source was "confidential but utterly reliable", Moonman stated: "My information is that the Harley Street nursing home will be used for abortions. I understand that other hospitals are involved as well." He envisaged "jumbo jet" facilities being "laid on" to cater for American women seeking abortions in Britain. Stanley Balfour-Lynn, the medically qualified managing director of the Harley Street Clinic and general executive of American Medical Enterprises in Europe, at once hotly denied Moonman's allegations. Not a single abortion had been performed in the Harley Street Clinic in the last 10 years, he declared, though to be a complete clinic, it had

had to be registered under the Abortion Act. The Clinic was extremely well known and had an excellent reputation. The £4.2 million Euro-dollar bond issue raised by American Medical Enterprises through a Dutch subsidiary, and underwritten by the London firm of G. S. Warburg, was purely to finance hospitals, not nursing homes, and the company's expansion was not to be confined to Britain.[337] The following month Moonman issued a full apology, in which he stated that the information he had been given was "wholly erroneous", and he said that he greatly regretted having given currency to it. He stated that he fully accepted that it had never been the practice to carry out abortions at the Harley Street Clinic and that neither the Clinic, nor Dr. Balfour-Lynn, nor American Medical Enterprises Incorporated had ever had the slightest intention of using it for abortions in future. "The Harley Street Clinic", his statement ended, "is concerned with acute surgical and medical cases and has specialized in major cardiac surgery and cardiac resuscitation. It is intended that these specialized services will be further developed in the future." The *Daily Telegraph,* in which a report of Moonman's question had appeared, published and associated itself with his statement and expression of regret.[338]

Late in January 1970 it was reported that an American professional abortion service, the London Agency Incorporated, had begun to operate in Springfield, Boston, and Hartford. According to J. C. Stothert, a lawyer representing the three member corporations, the agency was selling a "package deal" to pregnant women in America who, for a total cost of approximately £500, were flown to London, had their abortions, and were flown home.[339] According to a news comment on the BBC network, the terminations were being carried out at more than one centre and a "very reasonable" profit was being made. The organizers thought the arrangements represented "an absolutely solid situation"; they felt that the United States was "very backward" and that Britain had "given a great social lead" with its "sound and progressive approach" to therapeutic abortion. Two weeks later it was reported that Robert Quinn, the Massachusetts Attorney-General, had asked the State Supreme Court to rule whether the London agency was violating state laws, and that summonses had been served on J. C. Stothert.[340] Within a few days, Sir Gerald Nabarro, Conservative Member of Parliament for Worcester South, was questioning Richard Crossman in the House of Commons about the scheme, and asking whether this "highly undesirable" traffic had not been encouraged by the "dreadfully permissive" abortion laws. "Are you really saying in your reply", Sir Gerald asked, "that you are prepared to encourage such an undesirable form of invisible export?" Mr. Crossman responded that in his view it would be quite unjustifiable to include an abortion as part of a "package" tour. As for policy in general, the position in regard to admitting foreigners for abortions was no different in principle from admitting them for any other private operation. It was not Governmental policy to exclude foreign visitors who came to England for private medical and surgical treatment, Richard Crossman said. He told Sir Gerald that the question of whether or not the abortion law was working well or badly was quite different from the question of whether foreign visitors should be allowed to come to Britain to use the system of private practice. [341]

Meanwhile, early in February, the legal adviser of the Langham Street Clinic, where 9000 private abortions had been performed in the preceding 16 months, complained to Scotland Yard that taxi touts were operating at London Airport and charging foreign girls £30 or more for the drive from Heathrow to central London. About two dozen touts whose weekly earnings averaged £200 were thought to be responsible; the money far more than compensated for the small amounts they were fined if they were apprehended. The legal adviser further complained that the touts were taking Langham Street Clinic patients to other clinics so that they could collect a fee. The Langham Street Clinic, a report revealed, was charging foreign women an average of 150 guineas for an abortion; English girls were charged an average of 140 guineas, of which the surgeon and the clinic each took 45, the remainder being divided up between the two doctors who authorized the abortion and the other medical help needed during the operation. [342]

Modifying the Abortion Act—The Second Attempt

Two months after St. John-Stevas's first attempt to modify the Abortion Act was defeated, Norman Chisholm [343] wrote to the editor of the *British Medical Journal* stating that in his view the "seemingly innocuous and apparently sensible" suggestion that one of the two medical practitioners signing the certificate for the abortion be a consultant gynaecologist was "a retrograde step". It represented, he thought, a "despicable attack" on the competence of "the other" general practitioner, and he pointed out that, by restricting the Act to a minority of the profession, many of whom were opposed to it on religious or other grounds, the legislation would be crippled.

In the House of Commons, on 3 November, St. John-Stevas asked the Secretary of State for Social Services whether he would appoint an independent commission to inquire into the working of the Abortion Act. Crossman refused, but St. John-Stevas alleged that there was widespread professional and public anxiety about the working of the Act. As abortions were running at more than 1000 a week, and as his Bill had been only narrowly defeated, was there not a case for a substantial inquiry into the whole issue? Richard Crossman said he did not think so; he pointed out that during 1969 the proportion of abortions carried out in National Health Service Hospitals had risen from 56 per cent in the first quarter to 65 per cent in the third. He thought that St. John-Stevas would agree that it was the activities of the private sector about which they were alarmed, and that he would welcome the increased proportion of abortions performed in NHS hospitals. David Steel then congratulated Crossman on "resisting the invitation to set up yet another independent committee", but wondered whether he would agree that a report from the Department of Health and Social Security on the working of the Act and the difficulties which had arisen in some parts of the country might be of assistance. Crossman replied that he felt that such a report would be useful, and he explained that he had asked the British Medical Association and the Royal College of Obstetricians and Gynaecologists to send out questionnaires on the basis of which he might be able to issue a report.[334]

On 17 November, the results of a Gallup Poll undertaken for the Society for the Protection of Unborn Children (see p. 21) was announced.[344] According to this, 63 per cent of people believed that termination of pregnancy should be permitted in particular circumstances, 18 per cent felt it should be available on demand, and 13 per cent thought it should never be allowed. St. John-Stevas, announcing the findings, said that the Society's campaign against the Act would continue. It would concentrate on securing an impartial inquiry and on amending the legislation to ensure that the operation was carried out under the supervision of a NHS gynaecologist or a doctor of equal status, and it would eliminate the "social" clause. To bring in consultant gynaecologists would stop the flow of women coming from abroad for private abortions and would curb other abuses. The proposed amendment, John Haward, Under-Secretary of the BMA said, had the support of the BMA and of the RCOG. St. John-Stevas believed that the findings of the poll supported the two main objectives of the Society for the Protection of Unborn Children. The results showed, amongst other things, that 77 per cent of people thought that, when deciding on abortions, Members of Parliament should take the views of the BMA and the RCOG into account. Seventy-seven per cent of people believed that abortions in Britain should be available only to residents, and 62 per cent thought that it would be a good thing to make a consultant responsible in all abortions.

A leading article [345] in the same issue of the *Daily Telegraph* that reported the Gallup Poll findings observed that they suggested that public opinion was "overwhelmingly convinced" that abortion on demand was a bad idea and that the public was "extremely doubtful" about the value of the Abortion Act. There was a general feeling that too much abortion was going on, complicated, on the one hand, by the view that too much was being performed at public expense, and, on the other, that not enough took place under the relatively safe conditions of the NHS. The leading article thought that the whole subject was surrounded by "strong but obscure sentiments of shame and an infinity of ill-defined doubts". It thought that there was much to be said for an amending bill "confining the right to authorize abortions to highly qualified consultants who would not be exposed to the temptation to engage in a commerical racket". Three days later, another leading article [346] in the *Medical News Tribune* also commented on the results of the Gallup Poll. It posed the question as to why, if the public was in favour of NHS abortions and the BMA and the RCOG also favoured them, the private clinics were flourishing. The answer, the leading article said, was perfectly clear—too many NHS consultants were interpreting the Act, especially in some parts of the country, in an unduly restrictive fashion; this was driving patients to the private clinics. If they really wanted to be in charge of all abortions, such consultants should show they appreciated the new law; instead of "trying to turn the clock back", they should perform terminations where these were indicated under the terms of the Act.

On 25 November 1969 St. John-Stevas initiated a motion in the House of Commons which called on the Prime Minister and the Secretary of State for Social Services to set up a committee to carry out an impartial independent inquiry into the working of the Abortion Act. This would, he hoped, clarify the facts of the situation, and reveal the effects of the Act on the health, as well as on the legal, social, and moral life of the nation. Early in December it was reported that more than 100 Members of Parliament of all parties had signed the motion. [347] In addition at this time, B. G. Irvine, the Conservative Member of Parliament for Rye, introduced his Abortion Law (Reform) Bill in the Commons; he wanted to ensure that one of the two doctors required to certify that an abortion is allowable should be an NHS consultant gynaecologist or a doctor approved by the Home Secretary. [348]

Whilst St. John-Stevas was marshalling the opponents of a liberal interpretation of the Abortion Act, however, there were signs that others believed that the Act should be interpreted very freely indeed. This was shown by the evidence given at a hearing of the General Medical Council's Disciplinary Committee on 26 November on the case of Dr. Reginald Geoffrey Bird, whose original hearing on 24 July 1969 had been adjourned until that date. Dr. Bird, a psychiatrist practising in Harley Street, London, was charged with infamous conduct in a professional respect in that, with a view to attracting patients and promoting his own financial benefit, he had contributed or provided written, oral and photographic material to the German magazine *Stern* published in Hamburg. [349]

> The GMC Counsel said that the charge arose out of three matters: firstly a letter that Dr. Bird wrote to *Stern* on 25 May 1968; secondly an interview he gave to two of its representatives at which he allowed his photograph to be taken, and thirdly an article "To London for an abortion—a report on German women who travel to England in order not to have a child" which had appeared in *Stern* on 11 August 1968, and which referred to Dr. Bird, cited part of his letter, disclosed some of the information he had given in the interview and showed the photograph of him taken on that occasion. The article referred to Dr. Bird's liberal views on the new British abortion law and stated that during a two-week period in Harley Street he had been consulted in regard to certifying the medical necessity of terminating pregnancy by twenty-four German women, fourteen of whom were unmarried; in every case the opinion that was asked for was granted. Dr. Bird had emphasized in the article that he would never recommend an abortion but had added "when a woman comes to me she has already made up her own mind and basically I can only assent to her decision".
>
> The Registrar of the General Medical Council wrote to Dr. Bird asking for an explanation. Replying, Dr. Bird stated that he had practised as a consultant psychiatrist and a partner in general practice since 1964. He had specialized in psychiatry since his registration 10 years earlier and was a senior hospital medical officer in psychiatry; he had become deeply interested in the social and psychiatric aspects of abortion. Dr. Bird went on to explain that he had become concerned when a German journalist had told him in May 1968 that German women who had had abortions performed legally in the United Kingdom were liable to be prosecuted on their return to Germany, and that an article stating this had recently appeared in *Stern*. Although few of his patients came from Germany and he had no direct connection with that country, Dr. Bird's letter to the Registrar said, he had written an indignant letter to *Stern* on 25 May 1968, saying that in twenty-four cases with which he had dealt in a short period there were, in his opinion, grounds for lawful termination of pregnancy and that it seemed monstrous that these women should be liable for prosecution on returning to their native land. Dr. Bird's letter added that he did not ask *Stern* to omit his name or address should the letter be published; it did not appear and he forgot about it for several weeks.

In his letter Dr. Bird went on to explain that he had later discussed the subject of abortion with a representative of *Stern* and with an individual who was introduced as the editor of the magazine. He had gained the idea that *Stern* planned to publish a symposium on abortion which was to contain the views of the West German Minister of Justice, of Cardinal Heenan, of a prominent woman lay Catholic and of Dr. Tarnesby (see pages 154–7) as well as his own. Dr. Bird said in his letter that he had been prepared to participate in the project provided that he was able to see and to approve a copy of the proposed article before it was published; to this the *Stern* representatives expressly agreed. In fact, Dr. Bird's letter said, he was not given the chance to approve the article which, when he saw it, "horrified" him; had he seen it prior to its being published, he stated, he would never have agreed to its publication. "Superficial, popularized and misleading", it gave an "alarmingly false, unbalanced and selectively biased" account of his approach to abortion. A protest he had made to the editor of *Stern* resulted in a cablegram to the effect that whilst it had originally been planned to send him the article for perusal this had not been possible because of "deadlines"; they prayed his forgiveness. Dr. Bird's letter explained that had he been able to see the article as had been promised he would have been able to prevent publication of the offending material; the promise had made him less wary than he should have been, but though in some respects he had lacked prudence there had never been any intention on his part to attract patients or to promote his own financial benefit.

Giving evidence at the Disciplinary Committee's hearing, Dr. Bird amplified the account given in his letter. At his counsel's request the Committee listened for 90 minutes to a tape recording of the interview between Dr. Bird and the editor and the London representative of *Stern* of which they were given a thirty-nine-page transcript. Continuing his evidence, Dr. Bird said that *Stern* had lost the whole spirit of the article, which had been doctored to suit popular readership. It was just "an account of abortion in London with a few remarks of Dr. Bird's tacked on the end". As a result of it about two patients a week for six weeks had come to see him but he had ensured that none were given a consultation. The photograph which he regarded as something of a joke had been inserted to contrast the open nature of abortions in England with the "underground" attitude in Germany.

Having deliberated the matter *in camera*, the Disciplinary Committee announced that the facts alleged against Dr. Bird had been proved to its satisfaction. Nevertheless, it had not formed the opinion that he had been influenced primarily by a deliberate intention of attracting patients or promoting his own benefit; for this reason they found him not guilty of infamous conduct in a professional sense. Dr. Bird said later that he was delighted with the verdict, and stated that he had told the Committee that he believed that there should be abortion on demand. [350]

On the morning of 27 November 1969, a group of youthful feminists, calling themselves the Woman's Liberation Movement and the Woman's Liberation Workshop, demonstrated outside the Royal Albert Hall in London, where the Miss World beauty contest was being held. They objected to the contest, they said, because it degraded women into "just a man's plaything". Some demonstrators wore flesh pink sashes labelled "Mis-laid" and "Mis-fortune"; one, wearing a sash labelled "Mis-conception", carried a banner "Demands free abortion for all women". [351]

In Parliament, meanwhile, Mrs. Renee Short asked the Secretary of State for Social Services what improvements he intended to introduce into the operation of the Abortion Act to ensure that all women in every regional hospital board had equality of treatment. Crossman replied that officers were making a series of exploratory visits to selected areas of the country to study the effects of the Act on the hospital services: he would consider what further action should be taken in the light of their findings. Edwin Brooks then asked whether he was aware of allegations that in certain parts of the country women were denied abortions unless they simultaneously agreed to be sterilized. The Health Secretary said he had not heard of the allegation but he would investigate it. Responding to a further question from Brooks, he said that the number of women sterilized between 27 April 1968 and 30 June 1969 in NHS hospitals in England and Wales was 9491; the corresponding figure for Scotland was 1054. [352] Diane Munday, secretary of the Abortion Law Reform Association, later commented that the stories of sterilization had probably been very much exaggerated. The Registrar-General's statistics showed that of women presenting for abortions, 21 per cent of women in England and Wales and 37 per cent of those in Scotland were sterilized; of those who had undergone this procedure, 75 per cent had five or more children. [353]

Towards the end of January 1970, as the time approached for the second reading of Irvine's Abortion Law (Reform) Bill, the Abortion Law Reform Association issued a four-page review on the first 18 months of the Abortion Act. [170] Prepared from official statistics, the review contained the Abortion Act statistics, the grounds on which abortions had been performed, the problems—"real" and "exaggerated"—that had developed, the Act and the community (the death rate, the effect on emergency hospital admissions, and on illegitimacy), the number of consultants available to work the Act, and the safeguards against abuse. The "real problem", the review observed, was unequal availability of abortions in different regions of the country; the "exaggerated" one was that of abortions in foreign patients (about 6% of total abortions performed). The death rate of legal abortion in the first year of the Act (21 per 100,000) was slightly lower than the maternal mortality rate (24 per 100,000). A comparison of two periods of one year, one before and one after the Act became effective, showed that abortion emergency admissions fell from 5178 in the period January 1966 to December 1966 to 3445 in the period October 1968 to September 1969. Although there were 555 consultants in gynaecology and obstetrics in England and Wales in 1968, their full-time equivalent, the report observed, was only 436 consultants, of whom some were opposed to abortions on conscientious or religious grounds and others were extremely conservative in the indications they accepted for abortion. Thus the number of consultants left to work the full provisions of the Act was unknown, and the regional variations that had developed showed that more, not fewer, doctors were needed to undertake abortions. Fewer doctors meant delays and later, more dangerous terminations, which required longer periods in hospital. When such delays occurred, desperation might impel women to turn to criminal abortionists with the resultant increased danger and a tendency for emergency abortion admissions to rise again. There were far more stringent safeguards against abuse, the report pointed out, than before the Act since (i) two doctors, rather than one, were required to certify an abortion, (ii) private nursing homes now had to be specially inspected and approved, and (iii) abortions had to be notified to the Chief Medical Officer.

Furthermore, at the behest of the Abortion Law Reform Association, 1705 electors in 100 constituencies were questioned by National Opinion Polls. These findings, published on 29 January, at a time when more than 76,000 legal abortions had been performed, 54,142 in NHS hospitals, showed that 55 per cent of those questioned thought that there should be no tightening up of the existing laws, including the "social" clause. Forty per cent said that the law should be left as it was; and 15 per cent said that the law should make abortion easier to obtain. Thirty-eight per cent believed that the law should be changed to make it more difficult to get an abortion; and 7 per cent were undecided. The views of the responders were not affected by their political opinions, but religion played a part, for 53 per cent of Roman Catholics believed that abortion should be made harder to obtain, whilst those of other religions shared the general view that the law should be left unchanged. Most of the respondents thought it right to allow abortion if the pregnancy was likely to damage the woman's physical or mental health, taking account of her circumstances. The highest support (77%) was for abortion on the ground that there was a substantial risk that the child would be born seriously deformed; the lowest (61%) was for the "social" clause, i.e. abortion permitted on the grounds that the health of the woman's existing family might be affected if the pregnancy was allowed to continue.[354]

Commenting on these findings, David Steel, the sponsor of the 1967 Abortion Act, remarked that they were especially significant at a time when another attempt was being made to restrict the working of the Act. They showed that the public agreed that the proposals being made by people who had always opposed abortion reform would only have a damaging effect on the working of the law.[354] Diane Munday, speaking for the Abortion Law Reform Association, stated that public opinion was still firmly behind the Act, but she thought that there was a desire to bring it into disrepute. Opponents of the Act, she said, had a vested interest in avoiding action over the current influx of foreign women coming to Britain for abortions; she thought that the way the GMC was "dragging its feet" over the "undue financial gain" being made by many doctors out of these women made it appear that there was a "professional conspiracy" to keep things as they were. She was afraid that if the press continued to sensationalize stories about foreign women "coming to Britain in their droves" for abortions, public opinion could change and swing against the Act. This would be, she declared, a "devastating tragedy" for women everywhere, because many countries were looking to Britain for a lead on abortion legislation.[355]

On 6 February, R. G. Bird,[356] a psychiatrist to whom reference has earlier been made (see p. 188), published a spirited attack on the proposal to amend the Abortion Act. He drew attention to the mounting demand for abortion (an increase of over 400% in the NHS), the constant pressure on private clinics, the probable continuing traffic in backstreet abortions, and the growing irritation of women compelled to plead their cases in crowded out-patient departments, and to seek permissive doctors and liberal surgeons. Bird observed that women did not request abortions "just for fun", and he pointed out that but for the Abortion Act in its first year, up to 70,000 unwanted babies would probably have been born, half of them to unmarried mothers. In his own series of 500 private patients, more than 80 per cent unmarried, 300 had been disowned or rejected by the man responsible for their condition. Their babies would have been a burden on the taxpayer if taken into care. They would have been disadvantaged at the outset of life, and would probably have later contributed to the unhappy, the neurotic, and the delinquent. Little regard was paid by the opponents of abortion to the women made happier or helped out of their misery and conflict; similarly, the fact that the rate of emergency admissions for abortion in London was falling rapidly was ignored. Bird said that there was evidence of frank law-breaking in some doctors who did not consider cases properly, and he believed that a number of pregnant women were driven into the clutches of professional abortionists by "rigid, ambivalent, or indifferent doctors" as well as by those medical practitioners with ethical objections or those who would only recommend termination on strictly "medical" grounds. Bird thought that the need for an opinion from a consultant gynaecologist was impractical, and that a consultant psychiatric opinion was irrelevant, since the average family doctor could assess a patient—whom he was much more likely to know—as competently as a psychiatrist. The support given to the move to amend the Bill by the BMA and the medical defence organizations was, Bird stated, irresponsible, ignorant and a departure from their normal functions. The RCOG seemed to want to maim the Act. Bird thought that the basic opposition to abortion was religious, and Roman Catholic in particular. He believed that the establishment of subsidized privately run abortion clinics was called for where the operating fee for a straightforward abortion would be about £25 and the total fee about £60.

A *Sunday Times* editorial,(357) published on 8 February 1970, commented that abortion aroused strong emotions. The campaigners who lost the frontal assault on the Bill in 1968 had never tired of trying to undermine the Act by amendment. "They have every right to tunnel away," the editorial remarked, "but it should be clear that repeal rather than reform is the purpose of these elegant legislative manoeuvres." The editorial noted that B. G. Irvine's Abortion Law (Reform) Bill, under which abortions would be permitted only if performed under the supervision of an NHS consultant gynaecologist or his equivalent, and one of the signatories of the form permitting an abortion would have to be one of the specialists supervising or performing the operation, would almost certainly restrict the number of abortions carried out. The editorial, as the Abortion Law Reform Association's review (see p. 190) had commented, observed that the effective number of NHS consultant gynaecologists available to work the Act was smaller than the figures suggested. If passed, Irvine's Bill would exaggerate existing regional inequalities in abortion, would delay the operation, and, by driving women to backstreet abortionists, would increase the number of deaths. The editorial felt that if Irvine's proposals were accepted there would be a great deal of human misery which the abused Abortion Act had successfully prevented. "No other piece of social legislation in recent years has suffered from such exclusive concentration on its admitted, but marginal, abuses and deficiencies and such neglect of its successes", the editorial commented. "It has cut the abortion emergency admissions to hospital. It seems to have reduced the illegitimacy rate. It has saved the physical and mental health of innumerable women." The editorial concluded by observing that the campaign against the Abortion Act was sustained not by the facts on the working of the Act but by moral considerations for the foetus. These must be respected, it stated; but so must the lives and rights of the women who had to bear children.

Four days later, on the eve of the second reading of Irvine's Bill, an *Evening Standard* editorial[358] re-emphasized the points made by the Abortion Law Reform Association and the *Sunday Times*. It commented that the Bill purported to be concerned with safety, though the history of abortion since the passage of the 1968 Act showed that legal abortion was perfectly safe as it was; if there were any shortcomings they could only be rectified by closer inspection of non-NHS premises and by "mopping up those rackets that anyway operate outside the law". The Bill, the editorial stated, was not really about safety; its effect would be to make abortion harder to obtain, which would in turn decrease the safety of abortions and cause misery to thousands of women. "Let the Act act", said an editorial[359] written in a similar vein in the *Medical News Tribune*. "The Abortion Act is one of the finest, most humane and far-sighted pieces of legislation in the twentieth century", it claimed. "We sincerely hope that the wrecking amendment proposed once again by its implacable opponents will fail anew in the House of Commons today."

General practitioners for the most part tended to support the Act. A National Opinion Poll conducted on behalf of the Abortion Law Reform Association showed that 66 per cent of family doctors in the British Isles believed that the Abortion Act should be left as it was or amended to make it easier for a woman to obtain an abortion; only 28 per cent wanted an abortion to be made more difficult to obtain.[360] A group of general practitioners with practices in Bedfordshire, Devonshire, Glamorganshire, Lancashire, Yorkshire, and London wrote to the editor of the *Medical News Tribune* to record their disapproval of the attempts being made to amend the 1967 Abortion Act. They commented that though the gynaecologists who were supporting moves to restrict its operation to themselves were sincere in their beliefs, they were mistaken in suggesting that this would be for the public good. The general practitioners made the telling point that the specialists in a hospital had only to see the patients through 9 months of pregnancy, and for him abortion was an admission of failure; the family doctor, on the other hand, had "to give support and treatment to the woman and her family sometimes for 20 years or more and see the real damage that can be caused to all concerned . . .".[361]

The supporters of Irvine's Bill did their best to make capital out of alleged shortcomings in abortion arrangements in private clinics. The Society for the Protection of Unborn Children held a Press Conference in London on 8 February 1970 at which "Yvonne", an unmarried girl of 18 who had travelled from Birmingham to a private nursing home in West London for an abortion, related her experiences.

> Yvonne said that when she was 4 months pregnant her parents decided to see a social worker, who asked if she had £125 in notes. When her father undertook to borrow the money, an interview with the doctor who would do the abortion was arranged at his house the following evening. When, later, Yvonne arrived at the nursing home, she was taken to a ward with nine or ten other girls and instructed to undress. A nursing sister collected an envelope containing £125 in notes from her and also collected envelopes from the other girls, counting the money afterwards. Yvonne then went to the operating theatre where she was told to lie on one of three tables. She was not examined by the doctor or by the anaesthetist who had given her the injection prior to the operation.
> Yvonne was still bleeding and in pain when she left the nursing home with her boyfriend and caught the train back to Birmingham. Three days later she was taken to hospital by ambulance as an emergency, where she was given antibiotics for an infection and where an operation to clear her womb was performed. Yvonne later claimed that her abortion operation in London had been "inefficient and incomplete", though the doctor who had performed the operation and the matron of the nursing home denied her charges. A doctor at the West London nursing home claimed that conditions were very good and that the rate of illness was 75 per cent lower than in comparable NHS institutions.[362]

Tape recordings which lasted for an hour and contained the voices of Yvonne, her father, a NHS hospital consultant who cared for her after her abortion, and another consultant who interviewed the Birmingham doctor who had performed the operation were sent to Richard Crossman, Sir George Godber, and B. G. Irvine.[362] Mrs. Jill Knight, long an opponent of the Abortion Act, claimed at a press conference that "backstreet abortion butchery" had been legalized.[363] Captain Kerby, Conservative Member of Parliament for Arundel and Shoreham and an opponent of the Abortion Bill, had meanwhile asked the Secretary of State for Social Services for up-to-date figures on abortion. In a written answer, Richard Crossman revealed that Walker Park Hospital, Newcastle upon Tyne, where 411 abortion operations had been performed in the first 9 months of 1969, and the Langham Street Clinic, London, where 5130 terminations had been carried out in the same period, headed the lists; they had had no deaths. During the whole of

1969, NHS hospitals had performed 33,150 operations under the Abortion Act with twelve deaths; the corresponding numbers for the private clinics were 20,863 and three.[364] For the Langham Street Clinic, P. Stanley, the legal and business consultant, was reported on 12 February to have said that even if Irvine's Bill was passed it would not make the slightest difference to the abortions the Clinic carried out. "If a woman is pregnant and she has the one hundred and forty guinea fee she will get her abortion", he said. "Effectively in many parts of the National Health Service and certainly in the private sector", he added, "there is abortion on demand for women who feel they need it." In the 17 months the Langham Street Clinic had been licensed, 9200 abortions had been performed without a single death or a serious complication. "Our record in this sense", Stanley claimed, "is better than that of National Health Service terminations."[365]

On Friday, 13 February 1970, the second reading of the Abortion Law (Reform) Bill took place in Parliament. The same day fourteen uniformed nurses who supported the Bill lobbied Members at the House of Commons. Their leader, Miss Elizabeth Mott, handed Mr. Irvine a letter which she said represented the views of 200 nurses. They claimed that babies being aborted were often alive at birth, and said that during an abortion there was often a "severe mental strain" on nurses.[366] B. G. Irvine, introducing his Bill, said that it had the backing of the BMA and of the RCOG. He explained its provisions and he claimed that though it had been alleged that its intention was restrictive, there were 1618 doctors in England and Wales and 269 in Scotland who had had specialized gynaecological training, as well as 50 professors and their deputies who specialized in gynaecology, so that there should be no difficulty in getting an adequate number of doctors to deal with the problem. He referred to one girl who had been "desperately ill" for 6 weeks after spending 3 hours in a clinic, and he mentioned another who had likened clinic conditions to Piccadilly Circus. Irvine stated that a consultant had telephoned him that morning to say that he had had three cases of severe septicaemia in girls from one of the clinics. Girls should, he thought, spend at least 3 days under observation after an abortion. Mrs. Renee Short then drew attention to the editorial headline in the *Evening Standard*, "Abortion Reform?" (see p. 194), and said that this was really the crux of the whole thing. B. G. Irvine was not seeking to reform the Act meaning presumably to improve or to make progress. "What he really wants to do is to repeal the Act to make it ineffective," she declared, "but he does not have the courage to say so." The majority of the public and most doctors, she claimed, were in favour of the Act, and the majority of doctors who were in the closest contact with patients were satisfied with the way it was working. Since the Abortion Act had been passed, the most encouraging thing had been that the percentage of terminations carried out under excellent conditions in NHS hospitals was steadily increasing. The total number of abortions had fallen from nearly 80,000 to about 54,000, Mrs. Short declared. The fact that between 6 and 7 per cent of women having abortions in the first year of the Act were foreign did not make London the abortion capital of the world.

St. John-Stevas, supporting Irvine's Bill, observed that standards of care in the private sector were not as high as in the NHS. He emphasized that Mrs. Short's percentage figure of foreign women having abortions in London represented over 3000 patients, which he felt was a minimum number. He pointed out that the abortion rate of 54,000 a year represented a threefold increase, and he predicted a future rate of 100,000 annually. The new Bill might reduce abortions but this was not, he stated, its specific and sole aim; its intention was to get rid of "legalized rackets". John Dunwoody, the medically qualified former Under-Secretary for Health and Social Security, observed that the Bill would decrease the number of private abortions and increase the demand on NHS hospitals, which were already under considerable pressure. It might produce an increase in backstreet abortions, and the proposal that the Secretary of State should approve practitioners would place a difficult and invidious responsibility on Richard Crossman, who would have to make a distinction between individual doctors. The standards demanded of approved places had received considerable attention in the past year, and all but one had been inspected. There were grounds for dissatisfaction about the operation of the Act in the private sector, but this was being very closely watched; the Act was working reasonably well within the NHS. David Steel, sponsor of the 1967 Act, then remarked that it did not follow that because the RCOG and the BMA supported Irvine's Bill, the House of Commons had to accept it. Because of the pressure from these bodies, it was unfair to suggest that amendment of the 1967 Act would be widely welcomed by the medical profession. The Right Honourable A. L. N. D. Houghton, Labour Member of Parliament for Sowerby, commented that much of the publicity about foreigners coming for abortion and about taxi touts was propaganda from other countries to effect a change in their own abortion laws. At this point the debate was adjourned. The Bill accordingly went to the bottom of the list of private members' Bills with no chance of further progress.[367, 368]

The Act at 18 Months

In the first 18 months of the Abortion Act, i.e. between 27 April 1968 and 28 October 1969, 65,241 legal abortions were performed in England and Wales, 39,927 (61%) in NHS hospitals, 25,152 (38%) in approved places, and 162 elsewhere. In an important paper published in February 1970, Diggory et al.[369] analysed trends that had developed. Drawing attention to the increase, quarter by quarter, that had occurred in the number of terminations performed, they pointed out that in the first half of the second year the rate of increase had declined. The proportion of NHS terminations, they commented, had risen from 60 per cent of the total in the June quarter of 1968 to 65 per cent in the December quarter of 1969, the increase in the number of terminations being less marked in private cases. Further, regional discrepancies in the availability of NHS abortions had narrowed: in Sheffield there had been an 80 per cent increase, Liverpool had had a 70 per cent increase, and even Birmingham—where feelings against abortion were high—had had an increase of 50 per cent. The work load that the 65,241 terminations had imposed amounted to 120 abortions per gynaecologist each year, or 74 per each gynaecologist in the NHS. In the first 6 months of 1969, they noted, there had been a slowing down of the illegitimacy rate, which had previously risen steadily since 1958 (see p. 38). This was due, the three writers felt, to the fact that 47 per cent of all the abortions carried out during the first 18 months of the Act were performed on unmarried women who would otherwise have given birth to unwanted children. They commented that the fact that the Act had not had an even more marked impact on illegitimate births could be taken as indirect evidence of the extent of unregistered private abortions prior to 1968. They thought that, since the Act, there had probably been a transfer from private abortions to the official statistics.

To evaluate the Act, Diggory et al. observed, it was necessary to ascertain the extent to which legal abortion had replaced criminal abortion, and also the number of private therapeutic abortions being carried out prior to the Act. The total number of hospital admissions annually for abortion (spontaneous and criminal) was known, and had steadily risen from 69,410 in 1961 to 79,600 in 1967; since there were no special factors likely dramatically to affect the numbers of spontaneous abortions, the increase could normally be taken as an indication of an increasing rate of criminal abortions. Diggory had made personal estimates of the numbers of privately performed therapeutic abortions, and he believed that this might have risen from some 12,000 in 1961 to about 17,500 in 1967. The figures for 1968 and 1969 were much smaller, perhaps, because, after the Act was passed, many abortions, hitherto performed privately, were done under the NHS, and because some doctors, who had formerly performed terminations in their consulting rooms, were unable initially to obtain sufficient beds in approved clinics. The conclusion Diggory and his colleagues reached was that though it had become customary to portray the Abortion Act as a revolution in medical practice, it could more accurately be portrayed as the continuation of a trend which had existed for at least a decade before the Act had been passed.

The article went on to study the medical and sociological effects of the working of the Act as it affected the specialist and the general practitioner. In practice, Diggory and his colleagues observed, the grounds for terminations had changed very little—the new law was really the old Bourne decision case law made statutory. The difference was that, for the first time, the outcome of the woman's request had altered because the average gynaecologist had had to confront the woman personally. He had been made to appreciate the distress occasioned by an unwanted pregnancy and by and large had tended to respond in a humane manner. Fears that legal abortion would prove dangerous had not been justified, but many practical questions remained unanswered and research was required to solve them. Diggory and his colleagues drew attention to the shortcomings of the form used to notify terminations, and observed that women being referred for non-NHS abortions by the pregnancy advisory services in Birmingham and London were not typical of those who had hitherto used the private abortion facilities. The three authors remarked the indifference of women presenting for abortions to the use of contraception and pointed out that, as shown by Japan and eastern Europe, improvements in contraceptive practices could occur when abortion law was liberalized; they deplored the inadequate provision made for family-planning services by the local authorities. Finally, Diggory *et al.* emphasized that the Abortion Act was working satisfactorily. It had worked particularly well, they thought, in that, by placing the decision in the hands of physicians, needless delays in obtaining abortions (such as had occurred in Scandinavian tribunal proceedings) had been avoided. The major point that emerged from their review, they stated, was the need to improve the contraceptive services.

Further Developments

Family planning continued to receive considerable publicity in the early months of 1970. By the year 2009 the world's population would double to 7000 million if current growth rates continued, a United Nations demographic year book estimated. Whilst the rate of increase was greater in the earth's developing regions, it was also appreciable in the more industrially advanced countries in Europe and elsewhere.[370] The estimate given at this time for the population of Britain in the year 2000 was 68 million.[371] Speaking on 6 February at the Anglican Church Assembly held in London, Canon Hugh Montefiore asked the delegates whether "far from contraception being forbidden, should it not be regarded as a positive duty? ... The world desperately needs a view of sexuality concerned primarily with neither pleasure nor reproduction, but with personal relationships", he declared. "People assume they have a right to have as many children as they think fit. What moral right have they to act as they please in this matter?", the Canon wanted to know. "Something must be done to halt the curve of rising world population", he continued. "The ecumenical movement demands that we speak the truth in love, as we see it, even when it conflicts with the official views of our Roman Catholic friends."[372] Mrs. Winifred Taylor,[373] writing to the editor of the *Sunday Times*, pertinently pointed out that the slogan "No woman should bear a child she does not want" ought to be replaced by "No couple should risk conceiving a child they are not prepared to bring up". "This at least places the responsibility where it belongs—on the parents", she said. Speaking to a House of Commons sub-committee on 11 March, Richard Crossman, the then Secretary for Social Services, said that he believed that Britain could contain a larger population, but he stressed that there were too many people who did not make adequate use of family-planning facilities. He had no objection, he said, to providing contraceptives "free" on the NHS; it made no difference whether this was done on medical grounds or for social reasons.[371] A few days later the Family Planning Association, at its London headquarters, opened its first public information bureau designed to cater for people with all kinds of sex problems—contraception, divorce, infertility, sterility, venereal disease, and so forth.[374] This coincided with an FPA and a Health Education Council campaign to stop young people having unwanted children. Posters bearing a picture of a "pregnant man" clutching his bulging abdomen with the caption "Would you be more careful if it was you that got pregnant?" were released for display on the walls of a thousand local authority clinics. [375]

The disadvantages of illegitimacy were disputed by a number of individuals who opposed the Abortion Act. Criticizing Bird's [356] views on the rectitude of providing abortion for women desirous of ridding themselves of unwanted pregnancies (see p. 192), a letter written by A. S. Franklin [376] implied that treatments other than abortion should take precedence over it, that the deliberate destruction of unwanted life was not the purpose for which many individuals had become medically qualified, that the prevention of an unwanted pregnancy was better than its "cure", that adoption catered for very many unwanted children, and that satisfying the demand for abortion tended to increase it. [376] Mrs. D. Robb, [377] writing to the *Daily Telegraph*, observed that though the rising illegitimacy rate (about one-third of which consisted of children born to people living with the spouses of others) was deplorable, it was a mistake to suppose that it was invariably due to promiscuity. She thought that "truly promiscuous" women seldom became pregnant, and pointed out that illegitimacy was not necessarily a permanent condition since many girls, disliking "shotgun weddings", waited until after the birth to marry, whilst others had their babies adopted. Mrs. Robb thought that society should "stop straining at the gnat of premarital sex, whilst swallowing the camel of extramarital affairs, with all the misery and poverty they bring to innocent wives and families". Richard Crossman, however, felt that the fact that 20,000 of the 76,000 terminations carried out in England and Wales during 1968 and 1969 prevented illegitimate births was a partial justification for the Abortion Act. [378] His view, predictably, was shared by Diane Munday, the general secretary of the Abortion Law Reform Association, who observed that it was necessary to look at the figure of 20,000 in relation to the illegitimacy rate and the fact that it was falling for the first time in a decade. Though it was unfortunate that the need was there, she said, it was better that women with unwanted pregnancies should get NHS abortions than go to backstreet abortionists or produce unwanted children. [378] Equally predictably, many were opposed to abortion for this reason. Mrs. Jill Knight said that she was totally against "this business of knocking them off if they are not wanted. There have been many many lives which began as illegitimate births", she said, "which later went on to be successful lives and also extremely happy ones." [378] Four different correspondents wrote to the editor of the *Daily Telegraph* strongly protesting against Crossman's views. [379] St. John-Stevas, addressing a teacher's meeting in London on 11 March, declared that

Richard Crossman's statement that 20,000 illegitimate children would be alive if it were not for the Abortion Act could only mean that the Government viewed pregnancy in unmarried women as sufficient grounds for abortion, and said that the Prime Minister should relieve Crossman of his post, since he had shown a callousness totally unfitting him to be in charge of the social services. [380]

The advantages and disadvantages of various forms of contraception continued to be debated. On 11 March, Alistair Breckenridge, a consultant physician at the Hammersmith Hospital, speaking at a conference held by the Chest and Heart Association of London, questioned whether oral contraceptives, by altering the hormonal balance, might not remove the "natural protection" of female pill-users against heart attacks. [381] In the public generally, a surprising degree of ignorance in regard to the pill was revealed by a National Opinion Poll conducted early in 1970 for the *Daily Mail*. The findings, published in March, showed that one person in three either knew of no dangers associated with the pill, or thought there were done, whilst one woman out of four taking it was unaware of any hazard to her health. Nearly 40 per cent of those questioned thought (mistakenly) that the pill was more dangerous than pregnancy. [382] In the United States, Mrs. Phyllis Piatrow, an advocate of birth control, told a Senate Committee that the concern that had developed regarding the safety of the pill meant that about 100,000 unwanted babies would be born in 1970. [382] The doubts that had been raised stimulated the development of alternative methods of contraception, especially 3- and 6-month injections of progesterone, which were effective as contraceptives but could adversely affect menstruation and subsequent conception. [383, 384] The warning given in December 1969 by the Committee on Drug Safety [323] that the risk of thrombosis was greater with high-oestrogen oral contraceptives (see p. 173) resulted in a 10 per cent reduction in the $1\frac{1}{2}$ million women in Britain estimated to be taking the pill, but about half of these were thought to have resumed taking it by March 1970. This was due in part to the reassurance given by experts on the subject such as Richard Doll and Malcolm Potts. [335, 386] Doll, in particular, observed that figures from an American survey showed that women using other forms of contraceptives had intercourse on average seven times a month in contrast to the average of nine with those on the pill. He commented, "Women who use the pill are more sexually active than others. I would say the reason is that they are more relaxed and at ease." [387]

As an alternative to contraception, sterilization procedures, female and male, continued to be improved and to become increasingly popular. In September 1969 Steptoe and Imran[388] described the technique and results of the aspiration termination and laparoscopic sterilization of 101 women over a 1-year period. Aspiration termination had become accepted as one of the safest methods available up to about the 16th week, the two authors observed, the optimum time to carry it out being about the 8th week, since not larger than a No. 12 Hegar dilator was required, the risk of accidentally perforating the uterus was small, aspiration could readily be performed, and blood loss was minimal. The indications for terminating pregnancy were not the same as those for sterilization, they pointed out, but there were many patients of high parity in whom a further pregnancy was undesirable. The technique of sterilization by diathermy and division of the isthmus of each ovarian tube was described by Steptoe as far back as 1967, and has been previously mentioned (see p. 52). Essential features, Steptoe[389] observed, included an adequate pneumoperitoneum induced with carbon dioxide, a fibreoptic laparoscope, a high-frequency diathermy apparatus, a special coagulation forceps with an appropriate trocar and cannula, and a partial Trendelenburg position. The procedure could be carried out under general or local anaesthesia. Most patients required only 9 hours in hospital in contrast to an average stay of 10 days for sterilizations carried out by abdominal hysterotomy. In 500 patients laparoscopically sterilized by Steptoe, the subsequent pregnancy rate was 0.2 per cent (one broad ligament ectopic pregnancy) and complications (mainly accidental damage to epigastric vessels) occurred in 0.8 per cent. Laparoscopic sterilization thus was more effective than earlier methods, such as the Madlener and the Pomeroy techniques (see p. 52), as well as being safe and economical of hospital beds. In a postal survey conducted by Steptoe, in which 278 replies were received from 350 patients sterilized for 12 months or longer, 98 per cent of responders were pleased that they had been sterilized, a view shared by 92 per cent of their husbands; 72 per cent had not been disturbed by the operation for more than 3 days, and 57 per cent said they enjoyed intercourse more than they had done before the procedure. The technique has the advantage over operations on the male that after laparoscopic sterilization, coitus without contraceptive precautions can be allowed within a week, in contrast to the 2-month delay that ligating or resecting a section of the vas deferens necessitates. In February 1970 Liston et al.[390] published the results of tubal electrocoagulation and division under laparoscopic control in 760 patients treated at the Royal Infirmary in

Edinburgh. They concluded that laparoscopic sterilization was "an invaluable technique for pregnancy control". As an alternative, "ovariotexy", i.e. operative burial of the ovary beneath the peritoneum in a silastic bag, was described by Wood and Leeton [391] of Melbourne, Australia. The procedure was, they claimed, effective in the six patients in whom the operation had been carried out, and, unlike earlier methods, had a greater possibility of reversal. For sterilization in male patients, vasectomy continued to increase in popularity, and a questionnaire sent by the Simon Population Trust to 1092 men, of whom 1012 (93%) responded, showed that 99 per cent would recommend the operation to others, that 73 per cent thought that their sex lives had improved, that two-thirds had had no side-effects, and that more than half felt that their marriages had become more harmonious.[392] The legality of sterilization in terms of the British law was briefly considered in a leading article.[393] This concluded that though the law had not changed very much, public opinion had demanded that the category of "just causes" had extended, so that private rather than public policy had become the relevant consideration.

On 24 February 1970, a Disciplinary Committee hearing on the case of Dr. Christopher Michael Swan, formerly a general practitioner in Hackney, London, which had been adjourned from November 1969, and before that from July 1969, reawakened interest in illegal "medical" abortions, though most of the charges were concerned with drug and other offences. Dr. Swan was charged with having been convicted of a series of charges (to which he had pleaded guilty) at the Central Criminal Court on 2 January 1969, and of having been sentenced to 15 years' imprisonment.[394]

> Amongst a number of charges of misprescribing and misdirecting amphetamines, of conspiring with other persons to contravene the Drugs (Prevention of Misuse) Act, 1964, of conspiring with other persons to assault one man and for unlawfully soliciting one man to murder four others Dr. Swan had been charged with having aided and abetted one woman (a midwife) to procure the miscarriages of two other women (Irish girls who had paid him to have their unwanted pregnancies aborted prior to the midwife's unsuccessful attempts with a syringe).
> After his sentence Dr. Swan had given notice of appeal; on his behalf it was submitted that he had been unfit to plead at the time of the trial and that a new trial should be ordered. The submission was not accepted and his appeal was dismissed. At the Disciplinary Committee's hearing his Counsel observed that only after the trial had it emerged that Dr. Swan had suffered from a mental disorder: even when he was a student those who had charge of him suspected he was suffering from schizophrenia. He was unable to be present at the Disciplinary Committee's hearing because he was in Broadmoor (a special hospital for mentally ill criminals).

After considering the case *in camera* the Disciplinary Committee directed the Registrar to erase Dr. Swan's name from the Register. [394] Dr. Swan did not exercise his right to appeal and his name was erased 28 days later. [223]

Attitudes towards legal abortion continued to arouse sporadic interest, and many gynaecologists continued to regard the Abortion Act ambivalently. A few, like Professor Stallworthy, [395] examining the marked increase in abortions that had occurred with liberalization of the law in Japan, Hungary, and Romania, saw in the increasing number of terminations in the United Kingdom a threat of "national suicide", and agreed with Professor Donald that Britain was "only a starter in the abortion race". Most gynaecologists continued to dislike performing terminations, especially in the increasing numbers being referred, because they detested destroying life and felt they had not been trained for this purpose. They particularly objected to the fact that as many as five out of seven women requesting abortions had employed no contraception at the time they had become pregnant. Many gynaecologists felt that when the Abortion Act had been debated their advice to codify the existing Bourne decision case law so as to keep abortion restrictive, and to push contraception, should have been heeded. The logical alternative, they thought, would have been to provide abortion on demand. Instead a middle course had been pursued—the flood gates had been opened, no additional facilities or money had been provided, and contraception had been promoted too little and too late. The politicians and the public, they felt, were appalled by the number of abortions that were having to be carried out, and objected to individuals making money out of performing them privately. Whilst some gynaecologists objected to the possibility of any medically qualified individual from a non-surgical discipline setting up an abortion clinic, others were glad to be relieved of some of the burden, and conceded that practice in performing terminations could make their less well-qualified colleagues adept at this procedure. The small but increasing number of referrals for second or even third terminations after "repeat" pregnancies in women too feckless to practise contraception was another cause for concern.

On 25 March David Steel, sponsor of the Abortion Act, published the report of his working party on the operation of the Act and sent it to Richard Crossman. The rules needed tightening up, the report said, so as to check "any abuses by a small minority of the medical profession". It considered that too many terminations were being done in "approved places", that some terminations were not being notified, and that "blatant overcharging" was occurring. The report recommended that the form of notification (see Appendix I, p. 275) sent to the Department of Health on private terminations should include details of fees charged; that the nationality, date of entry into Britain, and the passport number of foreign women visiting Britain for abortions should be entered on the form; that both the doctors who signed the certificate authorizing an abortion should actually see the patient; and that medical officers of health in the local authorities should check clinics to make sure that all the terminations performed were being notified.[396] C. B. Goodhart,[397] a member of the Society for the Protection of Unborn Children, commented that the proposals were well intentioned and sincere, but he doubted whether they would be able to stop the rackets that were going on since the rules would have to be administered by the people whose activities they were designed to control. He advocated that independent medical referees be specifically appointed to ensure that applications for abortion were dealt with in the best interests of the mother and her child, in strict accordance with the law. Such referees would not do abortions themselves but would authorize them where indicated.

Psychiatrists, by contrast, appeared to be satisfied in the main with the principles embodied in the Abortion Act, and few psychiatric opinions disagreeing with it appeared in print. What did appear were the findings of an excellent study by Pare and Raven,[398] who had followed up 321 patients referred for consideration of termination of pregnancy to the Department of Psychological Medicine at St. Bartholomew's Hospital, London. Two groups of patients—a "psychiatric" series of 271 and a "gynaecological" series of 82 who had not been referred for a psychiatric opinion—were reviewed 1–3 years after referral. Of 250 patients followed up in the "psychiatric" series, the larger and the more significant termination had been recommended in 130. Two did not undergo the operation, but of the remaining 128, all but 2 patients (terminated because of mental illness in their husbands) were glad, despite occasional mild guilt feelings, that they had had it performed. In contrast, of the 120 patients in whom terminations were *not* advised, only 59 (49%) continued the pregnancy and kept the baby (43 had abortions elsewhere, 14 had the baby adopted or fostered, and 4 had stillbirths), this course of action being followed by two-thirds of the married women, but by only one-third of single women or those who were estranged from their husbands. The stress of continuing an unwanted pregnancy was much greater in the latter two groups, particularly in girls whose boyfriends or families did not support them. Absence of such support usually meant that the child was adopted, and in some women led to the development of psychiatric symptoms. In contrast, patients whose boyfriends or families stood by them did reasonably well and frequently kept the baby. Among the patients who continued the pregnancy one-third (16) subjectively felt the burden of a further child, regretted that the pregnancy had not been terminated, and admitted to feelings of resentment towards the baby. The two investigators thought that in six of these patients their pregnancies should undoubtedly have been terminated; their ability to cope with an extra child had been overestimated, for at follow-up they had depressive and/or phobic reactions. Pare and Raven questioned 136 consecutive patients about contraception. The vast majority, irrespective of religion or marital state, had either used no contraceptive device or had employed an unreliable method; there was little evidence of an "unconscious" desire to get pregnant, but lack of contraceptive education appeared to be a big factor, since only nine patients (7%) ever used a cap or an oral contraceptive, either regularly or occasionally.

Pare and Raven commented that their findings confirmed the view that the stress of bearing an unwanted child can produce psychiatric symptoms, especially in overburdened multiparae and in single girls lacking support. Wanted terminations were followed by remarkably few psychiatric symptoms, and of those who were refused, more than a third (37%) obtained an abortion one way or another, which also was followed by few psychiatric sequelae. Whilst 57 per cent of married women kept the baby and reared it themselves, only 25 per cent of single girls did this, and of all the unmarried women who came to the hospital seeking termination, 86 per cent got rid of the baby in one way or another. In retrospect it was easy to ascertain those patients who should have had a termination and to learn to identify such patients in the future, Pare and Raven remarked; but it was far more difficult to find which terminations had been unnecessary. Their study emphasized yet again the inadequacy of contraceptive measures taken by married and single women alike.

General practitioners, for the most part, also seemed convinced that the Abortion Act was necessary and, when properly administered, was ethical and humane. "The reason life is better for general practitioners under the 1967 Abortion Act is that the situation in which a patient in distress over an unwanted pregnancy comes to seek advice is now more like a normal medical item of service", commented John McEwan[399] in a constructive article setting out the task of the family doctor in relation to the Act. The most important thing, McEwan observed, was not to reject a patient because of the type of problem she had. He discussed some of the common problems encountered by family doctors in connection with legal abortion, outlining the pre-operative and post-operative steps that were necessary in the majority of cases.

In 1969 the total number of terminations notified as having been performed in England and Wales was 54,819, and during the new year the rate continued to increase inexorably. In January 1970, 4398 abortions were reported, and in the 5-week period up to 3 March the number notified was 7182, a rate of 75,000 abortions annually. The figure for the next 5 weeks was even higher, suggesting the equivalent of 80,000 abortions a year.[400] The unexpected increase in abortions was probably attributable to the pill "scare" of December 1969, when the Scowen Committee had warned women off high-oestrogen oral contraceptives and two television programmes had given wide publicity to anti-pill advocates (see p. 175). On 25 April the Scowen Committee published a statement[401] providing the data on the basis of which it had issued its warning and drew attention to the report of an investigation carried out on thromboembolic disease and the steroidal content of oral contraceptives made by Inman et al.[402] The investigation was based on 1305 reports of thromboembolism occurring in women taking oral contraceptives, which were submitted to the Committee on Safety of Drugs between 1 January 1965 and 30 June 1969. Whilst the cases that were reported were probably only a small fraction—perhaps 10 per cent—of those which had occurred, there were no grounds, the Committee thought, for believing that they were an unrepresentative sample. If all oral contraceptives carried the same risk of thromboembolism, the Committee observed, the reports they received should have been distributed over the different products in strict relation to the frequency with which they had been used. When the frequency of use was assessed from estimates of sales made available to the Committee, it showed that for twelve differently constituted oral contraceptives (which included fifteen different brands) marked differences in the numbers of reports existed. Amongst five products (Lyndiol; Conovid-E, Previson; Ortho-Novin 2 mg, Norinyl-2; Ovulen; Novacon) which contained 150 or 100 mg of oestrogen in combination with five different progestogens, all but one (Conovid-E, Previson) showed a substantial *excess* of observed reports. In contrast, amongst seven products (Lyndiol 2.5; Norinyl-1; Volidan; Anovlar; Gynovlar; Norlestrin; Minovlar, Orlest) which contained 75 or 50 mg of oestrogen in combination with five different progestogens, five (Lyndiol 2.5; Anovlar; Gynovlar; Norlestrin; Minovlar, Orlest) showed a substantial *deficiency* of observed reports. In short, the findings were that with 150 mg of oestrogen the reports were double those expected, with 100 mg they were 20 per cent in excess, and with 75 and 50 mg they were 18 and 21 per cent below expectation. The findings were in alignment with those obtained from reports made in Denmark and in Sweden, and thus were even more convincing.

In December 1969, when the Committee had issued its early warning, it stated the overall figures showed that deaths from pulmonary embolism were three times higher in women taking preparations containing 100 mg than in those who were taking 50 mg of oestrogen. The number of women on these two doses were equal and together they covered 80–90 per cent of the market. The change from 100 mg to 50 mg could reduce the total mortality by 50 per cent, a by no means negligible figure in view of the fact that an estimated $1\frac{1}{2}$ million women were taking oral contraceptives. For venous thrombosis with or without pulmonary embolism a reduction of dosage from 100 mg to 50 mg of oestrogen could be expected to reduce the incidence by 25 per cent. The same was true for the less frequent but dangerous arterial thromboses that occurred. In view of the importance of these findings and their relevance for reducing mortality and morbidity, the Committee had felt, it stated, that an early warning was imperative and that it could not delay publication until detailed analysis of individual preparations, which would take months, became available. Whilst going some way to assuage the criticisms made at the time of the Committee's initial warning, there seemed no reason, in view of its report, why some of the facts quoted should not have been incorporated in its original pronouncement.

In summarizing their findings, Inman et al.[402] commented that in the United Kingdom a positive correlation between the dose of oestrogen and the risk of pulmonary thrombosis, deep vein thrombosis, cerebral thrombosis, and coronary thrombosis had been found. A similar association was found for venous thrombosis and pulmonary embolism in Sweden and Denmark. No significant differences could be detected between sequential and combined preparations containing the same doses of oestrogen, nor between ethinyloestradiol and mestranol. The investigators believed that certain discrepancies in the data suggested that the dose of oestrogen was not the only factor related to the risk of thromboembolism—there was a significant deficit in reports associated with the combination of mestranol 100 mg, with norethynodrel 2.5 mg (Conovid-E, Previson), and a significant excess of reports associated with the combination of ethinyloestradiol 50 mg with megestrol acetate 4 mg (Volidan). An excess of reports also occurred with other combined preparations containing megestrol acetate (Novacon).

The increased demand for abortions did not go unnoticed, for on 23 March it was reported that a group of London taxi-drivers had set up a pregnancy advisory service, The Langham Pregnancy Advice Bureau, with headquarters in London's West End. The bureau, which had started work 2 weeks earlier, was said already to have dealt with twenty young women. A large number of London taxi-drivers were said to have been issued with bureau business cards and were promised a "cut" for every girl they sent. The "consultation fee" for advice was 4 guineas and it was alleged that by means of a panel of doctors and nursing homes, clients who were adamant about their wish for an abortion could have one and be home again in a matter of hours. The Langham Street Clinic, the largest private abortion clinic in the world with forty beds and an average of twenty abortions a day, at once sought through its solicitors an injunction against the bureau to prevent it using the word "Langham" in its title.

Shortly afterwards it was reported that applications to open abortion clinics in the Harley Street area were being refused. A few days later the Department of Health and Social Security, on behalf of Richard Crossman, demanded assurances on eight points be sent to him by 13 April from the private nursing homes approved for abortion as a precursor to the renewals of their approvals which were due on 26 April. These points were: (i) that no patient was discharged after an operation without receiving any necessary medical help or advice; (ii) that no patient would be discharged prematurely simply because she did not have enough money to cover the cost of the necessary stay; (iii) that in all cases the doctor who performed the operation would advise the patient when she could safely leave; (iv) that if on discharge a patient still required medical attention, everything possible would be done to see that it was forthcoming; (v) that if suitable transport was not available on discharge, the nursing home would arrange it; (vi) that homes would neither advertise abroad nor employ touts to solicit patients at London Airport; (vii) that adequate arrangements be available for dealing with emergencies: appropriate medical cover, blood-transfusion facilities, anaesthetic suction apparatus, and presterilized instruments were always to be on hand; and (viii) that records be kept of the time and date of all operations and that these registers and the nursing homes themselves be open to inspection at any time by department officers. These assurances had been necessitated by complaints made to Richard Crossman that abortions had been performed in private clinics, in some instances without prior medical examinations, sometimes only a few minutes after the patient had arrived, that patients had had to walk downstairs or to proceed unaided to a waiting room after recovering from an anaesthetic and had been prematurely discharged.[403] Unfortunately, the tightening up of standards insisted on by Richard Crossman, in combination with the activities of the taxi touts, led to an increase in the charges for private abortions in London—from a former fee of £80 to a new fee of £100 in many cases, the head of the Calthorpe Nursing Home reported.[404]

On 5 April the Abortion Law Reform Association for the first time sent details of a case of a woman refused a NHS abortion to Richard Crossman, the Minister for Social Services. The Association was subsequently notified that a Ministerial inquiry had been ordered. Mrs. Diane Munday, the Association's secretary, explained that she had become concerned about the barrage of anti-abortion "horror stories" published by the press and consequently had decided that she would depart from the Association's usual practice. "The real scandal of the [Abortion] Act is represented by a case such as this," she said, "not by the things that have been making the headlines."

> Mrs. F., the 43-year-old woman concerned, was in poor health, having undergone a pneumonectomy at the age of 25. She had had two daughters aged 11 and 7 and during the second pregnancy, having developed varicose veins and hypertension, had spent the final 6 weeks in hospital. In May 1969 she and her husband were extremely distressed to learn that she had again become pregnant and they asked their doctor for the pregnancy to be terminated on the grounds of her poor health (she found the care of her two children a considerable strain), her age, and her medical history during her second pregnancy. The doctor recommended an abortion—at the time she was by her own reckoning 8 or 9 weeks pregnant (she had always been meticulous about recording the dates of her periods)—but when, 3 weeks later, she was seen by a consultant gynaecologist at a large hospital, to her amazement he insisted that she was 4 months pregnant and he refused to recommend an abortion because it would be a risk to her health. Mr. F. explained that he and his wife were ignorant and had accepted what the consultant said; they did not think of having a termination performed privately since they thought the consultant must be right.
>
> In late November a second gynaecologist examined Mrs. F. and immediately admitted her to the antenatal ward. She had such marked hypertension that her own life and that of the unborn child were considered to be in danger. Mr. F. left his job to look after their daughters. Early in 1970, when the baby was 2 weeks overdue according to the first gynaecologist, the ward doctor decided the baby was not due for another 2 weeks. Since Mrs. F. was losing weight it was decided to induce the birth and the child, a boy, was born by forceps delivery. He was a mongol and the health visitor told the parents that he was 37 weeks old when born and premature; thus when seen by the first gynaecologist, Mrs. F. had been 13 weeks pregnant.

The birth of the child and the fact that he was a mongol had seriously affected Mrs. F.'s physical and mental health, the report stated. Her husband had formally complained to the management committee of the hospital. "We *do* feel bitter," he said, "surely the Act was supposed to help people like my wife?"[405]

The Act and the Gynaecologists

On 30 May 1970 the RCOG published the findings of a questionnaire containing fourteen items (some with several subitems) which in July 1969 they had sent to 570 consultant gynaecologists in England and Wales.[400] Two reminders had been sent out during the autumn of 1969 and by mid-January 1970 returns had been received from 450 respondents. The questionnaire, which was designed to elicit information on the experience of gynaecologists in connection with the first year of the Abortion Act, also sought their opinions on a number of related issues.

The report noted that many respondents had had difficulty in completing the forms, a circumstance which not only affected the value of the returns, but also revealed a serious defect in the secretarial and statistical facilities available in gynaecological departments. Further, whilst the number of terminations performed during the first year of the Act were known, the number carried out in the previous year was less certain, and little information was available on patients considered for termination but rejected. In half of all departments, records of complications following terminations were not available, and there was virtually no follow-up information on women in whom termination had been refused. The facts and opinions yielded by the questionnaire were based on 27,331 operations to induce abortion carried out in 233 departments in England and Wales, i.e. on 75 per cent of the terminations notified between 27 April 1968 and 30 April 1969.

The principal findings were as follows:

1. Ninety-four per cent of respondents had no conscientious objection to the termination of pregnancy "in all circumstances".
2. Fifty-eight per cent thought that the Abortion Act legislation should be amended to restrict certain categories: if "social indications" and "existing children of the family" were regarded as synonymous, 47 per cent of the gynaecologists felt that restriction of socio-economic indications was desirable. Twenty-eight per cent believed the Act should be left unchanged. Only 6 per cent favoured extension of the categories of indica-

tions for terminating pregnancy, and 92 per cent were opposed to abortion on demand.
3. Fifty per cent of respondents believed that abortions should be induced only in NHS hospitals, but 48 per cent disagreed.
4. Eighty per cent thought that abortions should be induced only by or under the direction of consultant gynaecologists in the NHS.
5. Forty-eight per cent of respondents thought that separate units should be set up under the NHS for therapeutic abortion, but 50 per cent did not agree with this, and 39 per cent said that they would not be prepared to work in such units (21% stated that they *would* be willing to work in NHS abortion units).
6. Seventy-two per cent stated that none of the patients reported to them for termination of pregnancy were seen instead by staff of below consultant rank; a further 20 per cent said that less than 10 per cent of patients referred were seen by junior staff.
7. Nineteen per cent of respondents stated that they did not delegate abortion operations to junior staff; 28 per cent delegated less than 10 per cent, and 16 per cent delegated between 10 and 25 per cent of patients to staff of below consultant rank.
8. Sixty-six per cent stated that their juniors shared their views, whilst 17 per cent found junior staff more permissive and 13 per cent found them less permissive.
9. Fifty-four per cent of respondents judged themselves "average" in permissiveness in comparison with their colleagues.
10. Fifty-eight per cent believed that if the number of abortions increased, recruitment of doctors into gynaecology would be affected, the majority feeling that there would be a reduction in the number and quality of entrants.
11. Forty-four per cent of respondents had "occasionally" encountered reluctance from nursing staff in regard to termination procedures (21% had met with it "sometimes", and 12% had experienced it "frequently"), the principal problem being nurses' religious views. Twenty-seven per cent had "occasionally" met with reluctance from medical and other staff (9% "sometimes" and 5% "frequently"), the commonest problem being anaesthetists' attitudes.
12. Seventy-nine per cent of the responding gynaecologists stated that in situations where the number of terminations had increased, this was due to the fact that the Abortion Act had become law; 59 per cent said that

the increase was *not* due to their increased awareness of social and economic problems (though 26% thought it was); 88 per cent attributed it to the greater number of patients being referred; 58 per cent stated that the attitude of their psychiatric colleagues had not changed (though 28% thought that it had); and 69 per cent denied that the greater number of pregnancies being terminated was due to a change in the amount of influence exerted by psychiatrists (18% said that it was).
13. In 1968–9, as mentioned earlier, 233 departments of obstetrics and gynaecology reported that 27,331 terminations of pregnancy had been carried out in contrast to 12,109 terminations performed in 206 departments in 1967–8. In regard to "spontaneous" abortions and incomplete abortions the report calculated that 220 departments dealt with 53,128 cases in 1968–9 in contrast to 51,701 dealt with by 213 departments in 1967–8.
14. In 1968–9, 809 complications were encountered in contrast to 232 in 1967–8. The most numerous were retained products (mentioned by 43 departments), pelvic infection (mentioned by 40), haemorrhage (encountered by 36), and uterine perforation (mentioned by 26). In 1968–9, 8 maternal deaths occurred in relation to termination of pregnancy (suicide, 2 cases; pulmonary embolism, 2; intravasation of abortifacient paste, 1; anaesthetic catastrophe, 1; acute myocarditis, 1; and no cause assigned, 1 case).

Discussing the findings, the report noted that the number of legal abortions carried out in England and Wales had increased steadily: 55,000 were performed in the year to May 1969, the rate rose to the equivalent of 75,000 per annum in the 5 weeks up to 3 March 1970, and in the next 5 weeks it had reached a level in excess of 80,000 annually. Since 60 per cent were being performed in NHS hospitals, the inference was that either gynaecologists were becoming more liberal or that the number of cases qualifying for the operation was increasing. The results of the questionnaire showed that the great majority of consultant gynaecologists had modified their outlook and practice only to a very limited extent after the Act was passed, and that about a third of the terminations carried out in 1968–9 (and also in 1967–8) had been performed by about 10 per cent of consultants and their teams in a small number of departments. Wide variations in different regions of the country were due not only to difference in medical opinion, the report stated, but to variations in demand, in public outlook, and in local circumstances, such as the reluctance of nurses and anaesthetists to be involved in abortion procedures.

The majority of the consultant gynaecologists had stated that the increased number of terminations being performed was due to the passage of the Act and to the resultant increase in referrals rather than to a change in their attitudes. There was no evidence that the operation of the Act in its first year had led to a significant change in the number of cases of spontaneous abortion requiring admission to hospital or that the number of fatalities associated with all types of abortion in England and Wales had been reduced; this confirmed the experience of most other countries. Over 13 per cent of the responding gynaecologists had commented on the adverse effect of the Abortion Act on their other hospital work, mentioning that admission of patients with other conditions had had to be postponed and drawing attention to the time necessary to assess new referrals for termination; this, they said, could seriously dislocate other work and interfere with teaching. As a result some gynaecologists had adopted the easier course of terminating every pregnancy on request—a procedure which, though time-saving initially, often involved urgent admission and the denial of operating time to other patients.

The questionnaire had not provided very reliable information on the complications of legal abortion, but the death rate (eight patients) in the 27,331 terminations performed, at 0.3 per 1000, was higher than the maternal mortality rate (including abortions, criminal or otherwise) for all pregnancies in England and Wales at the comparable time. Amongst the 54,000 (54,819) induced abortions performed in 1969, the death rate was fifteen, which revealed a similar state of affairs.

Most gynaecologists felt that the principal difficulty they had encountered in implementing the Act had not been its wording but its interpretation. Though the legislation as passed stated that abortion was legal only when two doctors "acting in good faith" decided it was justified because of certain defined medical indications, the legislators, the press, and a small group of agitators had, since its enactment, fostered the idea that it provided for abortion on demand or for social or economic reasons *per se*. Even the Secretary for Health and Social Services had expressed satisfaction that during 1969 the Act had prevented the birth of 20,000 illegitimate children, though nothing in its wording indicated that an extramarital conception justified termination of pregnancy. Though whilst it was under discussion the supporters of the Act had repeatedly assured both Houses of Parliament that abortion on demand was not their object, once the Act had become law, the report stated, the public had been encouraged to believe that any woman could have a pregnancy terminated if she wished it and that gynaecologists had a duty to apply their surgical skills when told to do so, irrespective of their expert judgement. This the report considered had created uncertainty and even resentment in the minds of women, probably accounted for their widespread irresponsibility and failure to take contraceptive precautions, and had caused considerable disquiet amongst consultant gynaecologists.

Overall, the responses to the questionnaire had shown that about 10 per cent of consultant gynaecologists were inducing abortion freely, that about 6 per cent objected to performing abortions in any circumstances, and that the remainder—the majority—were trying to make the Act work, interpreting it as it seemed best to them in the light of their knowledge and their duty to serve patients according to their needs. In implementing the Act the gynaecologists were facing difficulties which included inadequate time for the consideration of requests, the rival claims on time and beds of other gynaecological patients, and the reluctance of some members of the nursing and medical staff to co-operate in termination procedures. In addition, gynaecologists were constantly under pressure from politicians, administrators, patients, and their relatives, as well as from some other members of the medical profession, to act in a way that they felt was unethical and not strictly in the interests of their patients. Despite the fact that the Act had set out the circumstances in which a pregnancy *might* be terminated legally rather than when it *must* or *should* be terminated, gynaecologists and their Royal College were being assailed by the press and by other opinions that they were not doing what they were told. Gynaecologists had nevertheless felt their responsibilities under the Act so acutely that 72 per cent had personally seen every case referred, and a further 20 per cent had delegated less than 10 per cent to junior staff; nearly 50 per cent performed terminations themselves if this was decided on, and whilst those who judged themselves less liberal than their colleagues were worried that they were overloading the latter, the more permissive gynaecologists were concerned because in spending time performing terminations they feared they were neglecting other patients. Whilst as conscious as any other group of doctors of the urgent need to regulate fertility, both from the point of view of family well-being and from that of population control, most gynaecologists rejected abortion on demand and felt that termination of pregnancy was only a short-term solution, which offered a woman little protection from further mistake or misadventure, and did not necessarily safeguard her physical and mental health. Easy abortion in other countries had encouraged unplanned pregnancies, the report stated, so that it was important to determine to what extent this was happening in Britain, especially in young single girls. Not only were better contraceptive facilities needed, but also better education and better motivation. The urgency and complexity of the problem had prompted the College to set up a working party with representatives from other disciplines to study all the aspects of planned and unplanned pregnancies.

The most pressing problem arising from the Abortion Act, the report concluded, was that its interpretation by those called upon to operate it differed from that held by many legislators and members of the public. The time had come, the report stated, for them to decide whether what they really wanted was abortion on demand. If not, this should be made clear, so that the medical profession could continue to judge the issue dispassionately. If abortion on demand *was* what they wanted, the Act should be modified and provision for its application should be made which would not involve coercion of unwilling gynaecologists or encroachment upon beds and the other facilities of hospital gynaecological departments to the detriment of non-abortion patients. Making abortion on demand legal would not make it ethical, the report observed. Obstetricians and gynaecologists, it stated, were not to be regarded as technicians whose function was to apply their technical skills irrespective of their knowledge and experience; they had a right to freedom of professional judgement and action which they were anxious to exert in applying the Abortion Act as it stood at present, as wisely and reasonably as possible, bearing in mind that their overriding concern was to offer such advice and treatment as would be in the best interests of the women who sought their help.

A leading article[406] in the same issue of the *British Medical Journal* in which the report appeared found it "in several ways disquieting". The number of terminations carried out was rising steadily, it observed, and though there was variation in the way patients and doctors interpreted the legislation, it was disconcerting to find that a third of terminations were being carried out by a tenth of consultants (or their teams). The remaining 90 per cent of gynaecologists varied sufficiently in their attitudes towards legal abortion for members of the public in some areas to be genuinely worried about having their pregnancies terminated, whilst elsewhere every request was apparently being granted in order to save time for teaching commitments and for the care of other patients. Many people, the article observed, were unreasonable and lacking in foresight, and as such were liable to neglect contraceptive measures "and to think abortion will brighten their day as harmlessly as a shampoo". It was thus possible, up to a point, that the more readily abortion was made available, the longer would be the queues for it. But despite this, the article concluded, "more effort could well be devoted to educating the public on the facts of contraception, family planning and abortion, for ignorance about them is still remarkable".

The Act at Two Years

In the first six months of 1970 the number of abortions notified in England and Wales was 38,824, an annual equivalent of just under 80,000 cases. The Abortion Law Reform Association, reviewing the first 2 years of the Act, noted that the grounds under which abortions had been performed had hardly varied since it had come into effect and that the regional variation in abortion operations had continued, Birmingham with 2.1 and Wessex with 2.9 NHS abortions per 100 live births reporting fewer legal terminations than Newcastle (7.4) and London (7.3) (this could have been due in part to the disparity between facilities in the different regional hospital board areas). ALRA commented that hopeful trends following at least in part from the Abortion Act included: (1) decline in London Emergency Bed Service abortion admissions; (2) greater priority being accorded to family planning; (3) decline in some kinds of preventable handicap, e.g. muscular dystrophy; (4) greater willingness to adopt hitherto unacceptable babies; (5) decline in the illegitimacy rate; (6) impetus for abortion research; and (7) beneficial impact on community health. The principal problems, the Association observed, were the difficulty in obtaining abortion in some areas and its consequences, the excessive profiteering and substandard practices of a minority of medical practitioners and the attitudes of nurses. Commenting on the situation abroad, ALRA remarked the encouraging attitude the World Medical Association had shown in adopting the British-sponsored Australian-drafted "Declaration of Oslo"—a statement based on a resolution with a "conscience clause" permitting abortion as a therapeutic measure provided it was endorsed by two doctors and performed by a competent doctor in approved premises—and the progressive liberalization of abortion laws that had occurred in British Commonwealth and former Commonwealth countries as well as in the United States. [407]

CHAPTER 12

Abortion Problems in Other Countries

THE English experience with legalized abortion must finally be compared with the situation elsewhere in the world. In this regard the status of abortion in Europe, in Japan, in the United States, and elsewhere is of interest.

Europe

From the standpoint of abortion, Tietze[140] has observed, Europe can be conveniently divided into three parts—the west and south, the north, and the east.

In western and southern Europe, which with some 300 million inhabitants contains half its constituent countries, abortion is in general permitted on strict medical indications only, a state of affairs resembling that obtaining in the majority of North American states. Exceptions are Switzerland, where for more than a decade the abortion laws have been liberally interpreted by the medical profession, and Great Britain, where the case law stemming from the Bourne decision was eventually codified and developed into the Abortion Act. In western and southern Europe, relatively few therapeutic abortions are carried out, and illegal abortions are believed to be very common, though there is no reliable evidence that, as has been claimed, the number is equal to or greater than the total number of live births.

In northern Europe, the Scandinavian countries have for some years permitted abortion on socio-medical, humanitarian, and eugenic grounds, i.e. cases where the pregnancy had resulted from a criminal assault; where the child, if born, would suffer from grave physical or mental defects; or where the birth would endanger the mother's physical or mental health. The laws on abortion were liberalized in Iceland in 1935, in Sweden in 1938, and in Denmark in 1939. After the Second World War, the laws were further relaxed in Sweden in 1946 and 1963, in Denmark in 1956, in Finland in 1950, and in

Norway in 1960. The Swedish experience is especially relevant for the number of legal abortions, which stood at 400 in 1939, rose to over 6300 in 1951, declined between 1956 and 1963, and rose again to an estimated 9600 cases in 1967.[408] In Denmark, the same course of events occurred. But whereas in Sweden the mortality of legal abortion was 257 per 100,000 cases between 1946 and 1948, from 1960 to 1966 it fell to 39 per 100,000. These unduly high rates were probably mainly due to the Swedish practice of referring candidates for abortion to the Royal Medical Board, the deliberations of which often imposed lengthy delays and led to terminations being performed unduly late; though up to 97 per cent of all abortion requests were granted, permits often took several weeks to come through, so that many terminations were performed between the 12th and 24th weeks of pregnancy.[409] The Danish procedure was also cumbersome (see p. 136), and many terminations were not carried out in Denmark until the 4th month. These late operations had an appreciably higher mortality than abortions performed in the first 3 months of pregnancy, and, in addition, women in Scandinavia were perhaps less fit than those in eastern Europe.[408, 410] Unfortunately, despite the legal provisions that were made, some Scandinavian women continued to resort to illegal abortions and, as mentioned earlier (p. 67, reference 135), the criminal abortion rate did not fall as much as had been hoped for when the new laws were brought in. Further liberalization and simplification of the law was apparently desirable. Norway was opposed to this, it announced in August 1969, despite the fact that the Nordic Council had recommended co-ordination of legislation between the Scandinavian countries.[411] In contrast, Sweden announced in October 1969 that a committee appointed to draft new legislation was in favour of "abortion on demand" up to the 12th week in cases where a birth would be "unreasonably burdensome" for the mother; the provision could be added to the existing law, which would be retained.[412] In March 1970 the Danish Parliament passed a law granting abortion to girls under the age of 18 who were able to demonstrate that they lacked the money, time, or maturity to care for a baby.[413]

In eastern Europe, abortion has long been permitted if not actually "on demand", at least on broad social indications. "Ironically it is not in the humanitarian nations of Scandinavia but in the Communist states of eastern Europe that abortion is considered to be a question of individual freedom", Peck[414] observes. "In the USSR, East Germany, Hungary, Poland,

Czechoslovakia, Romania and Bulgaria, abortion laws were proclaimed on the basis of the right of the individual woman to decide the outcome of her pregnancy." Abortion was legalized in Russia in 1955, and in Bulgaria, Hungary, Poland, and Romania in 1956; Czechoslovakia followed suit in 1957, and Yugoslavia in 1960. As in the West, by far the greatest number of legal abortions were performed on married women who already had children, for multiparity, for overcrowded housing conditions, and because of the need or desire of working women to continue to go to work.

In Hungary, where abortion on demand up to 3 months of pregnancy obtained, the number of abortions rose from 16,300 in 1954 to 170,000 in 1962, yet its death rate declined from 5.6 per 100,000 in 1957–8 to 1.2 per 100,000 in 1962–3. In Czechoslovakia, the rate of 3.1 deaths per 100,000 abortions in 1958–62 dropped to 2.5 per 100,000 cases during 1963–7.[410] Commenting on an account by John Stephen on abortion and polyclinics in eastern Europe, Malcolm Potts,[415] the Medical Secretary of the International Planned Parenthood Federation, stated that, except in Hungary, abortion was not available on demand, but contraceptives were available and that their use was increasing, and that though there were differences of opinion on abortion laws—not surprising since many of the practising doctors in eastern Europe were Roman Catholics—most doctors adopted a point of view as liberal as, or more liberal than, the 1967 Abortion Act. He thought that many eastern European doctors had watched the alteration in the British laws with sympathy, and he believed that Stephen had received an unfortunate impression of experience in eastern Europe concerning abortion. The death rates were extremely low, and the complication rate did not reach the 10 per cent noted by Stephen. In Hungary, amongst 23,000 abortions performed, 23 women experienced early complications such as bleeding and pyrexia, and the number of women readmitted to hospital after the operation was 20 per 1000. There had been an increase in the prematurity rate, which could be correlated with the number of induced abortions. John Stephen[416] disagreed with almost all these observations. He thought that Roman Catholicism was a "red herring", and he pointed out that though in eastern Europe condoms and coitus interruptus were used, oral contraceptives and more sophisticated methods of contraception were just not available. He thought that doctors there had watched the British Abortion Act, not with sympathy, but with interest to see what the position in Britain would be in 5–10 years' time, hoping that it would not reach the position that obtained in their own countries but fearing that it could well do so. Stephen reiterated his view that the complication rate reported to him in Bulgaria—10–12 per cent complications with incomplete abortion, salpingitis, and uterine perforation (in 0.1–0.2%) in that order—was probably typical of eastern Europe, and he mentioned that gynaecologists in Romania had noted an increase in spontaneous abortion in the second trimester and in placenta praevia, which they felt was due to frequent previous abortions. He thought that prematurity was not connected with abortions but was due to women continuing to work too late in their pregnancies.

The generally low rate of mortality attending legal abortions in eastern Europe was almost certainly due to the majority of terminations being performed in the first trimester of pregnancy—it was prohibited after the 3rd month except for strict medical reasons, and it was also forbidden when the woman had undergone an induced abortion during the preceding 6 months. [410]

The effect of the liberal abortion policy in some eastern European countries was that the number of abortions rose so steeply that in some cases it exceeded the number of live births. In Hungary in 1967, for example, there were 187,500 abortions compared with 148,900 babies born alive. This suggests that, as in Czechoslovakia, abortion was being used as a substitute for contraception. [134] The fall in birth rate produced by its liberal abortion laws led Romania, which in 1965 had had a legal abortion rate of 24.7 per 1000 population, to enact a more restrictive statute in 1966, under which, to warrant an abortion, the unwanted pregnancy had to threaten the woman's life, or had to be in a woman over the age of 45, or in one with four or more children, or associated with the risk of a deformed child, or resulting from rape or incest. After the new law came into effect, the birth rate increased from 13.7 per 1000 population in the fourth quarter of 1966 to 38.4 per 1000 in the third quarter of 1967. In 1968 Bulgaria followed suit, imposing slightly less drastic restrictive clauses on its hitherto liberal abortion laws. [407] In Czechoslovakia, however, legal abortion was seen as being a necessary evil until the public became educated in contraception; a poll held amongst 1889 women attending the gynaecological departments of half the district hospitals in the Czech region (two-thirds of Czechoslovakia) revealed that the responders felt that the declining population and the low birth rate could be solved not by repealing the liberal abortion law (in 1968, 46 pregnancies were interrupted for every 100 live births) but by improving social and economic policy to benefit families with children and by making more information available on methods of birth control. [417]

In European terms the British abortion rate, with 37,736 cases terminated in the first year of the Abortion Act, amounted to only 5 patients operated on for every 100 live births and was quite low. Comparative figures per 100 live births were: Denmark 6.7, Sweden 7.9, Poland 32, Czechoslovakia 44, and Hungary 126. Clearly, London was not "the Abortion Capital of the West" as some critics of the Abortion Act had alleged.[418]

Japan

The alarming rate of population growth in Japan led the Government in 1948 to pass the Eugenic Protection Law under which abortion was made permissible if a pregnancy could seriously affect the woman's health from the physical or economic viewpoint. This was so broadly interpreted as to amount to abortion on demand, and in 1949, when there were 2,690,000 live births, legal abortions numbered 246,000. Six years later the number of abortions notified to the authorities had risen to 1,170,000, though it is possible that as many as 40–50 per cent were not reported by Japanese doctors, some of whom were anxious to minimize their income tax. Without induced abortion M. Maramatsu, quoted by Greenhill,[419] believes, the number of live births in Japan for 1955 would have been twice or more the number that were actually registered. Subsequently the numbers of reported legal abortions declined, and by 1967 had fallen to 748,000. Tietze and Lewit[408] have observed that this was the year after the birth rate had dropped precipitately, perhaps because traditionally girls born in 1966, the "Year of the Fiery Horse", were bad-natured and difficult to marry off! It seems possible, however, that the declining number of abortions was due at least in large part to an increase in contraceptive practices. In Japan, abortion—except for medical reasons—was prohibited after the 3rd month, and the mortality, as in eastern Europe, was very low—in the region of 1–4 deaths per 100,000 terminations. In 1969, according to the Japanese Health and Welfare Ministry, about 1 million abortions were performed, 743,000 by gynaecologists and the rest illegally. Since women still received hospital treatment for the complications of the latter, criminal abortions had not been eliminated but it was believed that they had been greatly reduced.

In the spring of 1970 pressure began to grow for revision of the liberal abortion laws, Professor Watanabe of Jikei University, Tokyo, observed, addressing a meeting at the Fourth Tokyo–New York Medical Congress. The net reproduction rate had remained below 1.0 since the Eugenic

Protection Law had been passed and it was feared that the population might become senile and that there would be insufficient people to meet national needs. Government agencies were studying the stricter abortion laws enacted by other countries.

The United States

In the United States, as in the United Kingdom prior to 1968, abortion is a major medico-social problem. In recent years the situation has aroused considerable concern, and individual states have approached the issue in separate ways.

 SIZE OF THE PROBLEM

The number of abortions that take place annually in North America is hard to ascertain, but at a Conference on Abortion sponsored by the Planned Parenthood Federation and the New York Academy of Medicine held at Arden House in 1955, a committee estimated that the annual total of illegal abortions might be between 200,000 and 1,200,000. Thirteen years later Schwartz[141] estimated that between 1 and 1½ million abortions were being performed every year, or 3 for every 10 live births. Whilst 30 years ago it was believed that deaths from criminal abortions in the United States might amount to 5000–10,000 annually, it now seems probable that fewer than 1000 women a year die from this cause: in 1965 the National Centre for Health Statistics listed 235 fatalities resulting from illegal abortions. According to Peck,[414] the fact that between 1958 and 1964 puerperal deaths fell by 11 per cent whilst deaths from septic abortion rose by 31 per cent supports the widely held belief that the number of illegal abortions is rising significantly. In 1969 some 350,000 women required hospital care after botched abortion attempts; over 8000 of these died.[420] During the same year Beck et al.[421] reported the information brought together by the first federally sponsored Workshop on Abortion, which was held under the auspices of the National Institute of Child Health and Human Development and the National Institute of Mental Health. The title of the Workshop, "Abortion, a National Public and Mental Health Problem", as well as its size and scope, left no doubt of the significance of the abortion issue in the United States.

American Abortion Laws

A. F. Guttmacher [422] has pointed out that modern statutes are all traceable to the English law of 1803. This designated abortion a statutory offence, but its gravity depended on whether or not the foetus had "moved". Abortion before "quickening" brought a penalty of 14 years in indentured labour overseas, whilst abortion after this time constituted legal manslaughter and was heavily punishable—in some cases by hanging. In North America, Connecticut was the first state to pass a law against abortion, outlawing it in 1821 if it was performed after quickening by means of poison; in 1930 instruments were added to the ban. In 1828 New York made abortion legal "to preserve the life of the mother", but in 45 out of the 50 states, Ingram [423] observes, the laws governing abortion were enacted during the decade following the Civil War. At this time moral and religious fervour against the results of "sinful" activities was intense, surgery was dangerous, and manpower was urgently required to advance the nation's frontiers and to serve the needs of industry. [420] These considerations no longer apply, and within the last two decades the legal profession has demonstrated its belief that the laws on abortion should be liberalized. In 1954 the American Law Institute in its Model Penal Code proposed that abortion should be permitted (i) when continuing the pregnancy would gravely impair the physical health of the mother; (ii) when the child might be born with a grave physical or mental defect; or (iii) if the pregnancy had resulted from rape, incest, or other felonious intercourse, including intercourse with a girl below the age of 16. This code was subsequently endorsed by many religious professional groups, including the New York Council of Churches, the Episcopal Diocese of New York, the Federation of Protestant Welfare Agencies, the New York Civil Liberties Union, the New York Academy of Medicine, the Californian Medical Association, the American Medical Women's Association, and the Student American Medical Association.

According to J. M. Ingram, [423] the desirability of reforming legislation on abortion was advocated as long ago as 1904, when Judge Anna Kross advocated a change in the law and condemned the "universal indifference, both lay and professional" with which abortion was regarded. Her attempt was unsuccessful, as were its successors led by Taussig of St. Louis in the 1930s, and the legal changes advocated by the Planned Parenthood Federation of America in 1942 and 1955 were never implemented. Within the last decade, however, interest has returned, and many individuals, professional and lay, have expressed their case for liberalization of the law. Relevant reviews have been provided, amongst others, by Greenhill,[419] Simon,[145] Hall,[424] Roemer,[139] Schwartz,[141] and Tietze and Lewit.[408] In 1964 J. P. Greenhill observed that "legitimate" therapeutic abortions carried out chiefly to maintain the health or life of a pregnant woman had decreased, but he noted that psychiatric grounds, and to a lesser extent foetal indications, had kept the number of therapeutic abortions high. Greenhill believed that therapeutic abortion and sterilization constituted "an international problem comparable to an epidemic disease", and he declared that the United States could be of considerable help in underprivileged areas of the world where there was "enormous overpopulation", though he did not specify how. Alexander Simon's viewpoint, also published in 1964, has been mentioned earlier (see p. 80). R. E. Hall, writing in 1967, charged that the practice of abortion in American hospitals was "inequitable, inconsistent and largely illegal", and he observed that the basic reason was that it was an aspect of twentieth-century medicine that was governed by nineteenth-century laws. The comprehensive review provided the same year by Ruth Roemer, an attorney in California, is of especial interest in that it affords a legal perspective and the article by Schwartz, which appeared in 1968, affords an appropriate psychiatric counterpart. The worldwide overview provided by Christopher Tietze and Sarah Lewit in 1969 has been mentioned earlier (see p. 223).

Attitudes Towards Abortion

In the United States, as in the United Kingdom, there is evidence that in the last two decades there has been a progressive liberalization of attitudes towards legal abortion, which has been reflected in the views and experiences of the public, the gynaecologists, the psychiatrists, and the medical profession in general.

The Public

As far as the general public is concerned, religious affinities have continued to exert an influence on the moral issues of therapeutic abortion. The Roman Catholic Church was and has remained opposed to the procedure, the Protestant Church has cautiously endorsed it where appropriate grounds exist, and the Jewish Law—as Rabbi Martin J. Goldman[425] has observed— has been the most liberal of all. Because of the restrictive laws and the anxiety and repugnance with which many members of the American medical profession viewed therapeutic abortion, a series of barriers had been built up by the 1950s which had made hospital abortions difficult to obtain. Prior to this time, it had generally been sufficient for the attending physician to state in writing that the abortion was necessary, though often a supporting letter from one or two colleagues was also required. In the early 1950s, however, hospitals began to form committees to evaluate cases to be operated upon, a procedure which conferred an aura of respectability on the situation, protected the hospital's reputation, delayed treatment, and drastically reduced the number of terminations performed. Some hospitals, according to Schwartz,[141] even prided themselves on having virtually eliminated all therapeutic abortions, especially those carried out on psychiatric grounds. Between 1963 and 1965 only about 8000 therapeutic terminations of pregnancy are thought to have been performed in American hospitals.

In 1965, as part of the National Fertility Study which centred on factors associated with reproduction and contraception, the members of a national probability sample of 5600 currently married women under the age of 55 were asked a series of questions on abortion after they had provided detailed accounts of their pregnancies and their contraceptive practices. After an open-ended question on her feelings about interrupting a pregnancy, each woman was asked if she would endorse an abortion in the following circumstances: if her health was seriously endangered, if the woman was unmarried, if the couple could not afford another child, if they did not want any more children, if the woman had good reason to believe the child might be deformed, or if the woman had been raped. Based on the responses to these questions, Westoff et al.[426] reported, married women in the United States in late 1965 overwhelmingly favoured abortion if the mother's health was threatened; they were evenly divided in the case of deformity or rape, and they were overwhelmingly opposed if the woman was unmarried, could not afford another child, or did not want further children. The two commonest combinations were rejection of all grounds except health, and acceptance of deformity, rape, or health with rejection of the other three reasons. Nine per cent rejected all six grounds, whilst 5 per cent, accepting them all, appeared to favour abortion on demand. The most favourable attitudes towards abortion were held by educated older non-Catholic white women living in urban areas in the North-east or the Far West who had worked since their marriage. White Catholic women in the Mid-West and the South, and non-white women in the rural areas of the South, were opposed to abortion, especially if they belonged to fundamentalistic sects such as the Baptists, had had a limited education and did not work outside the home.

In 1965 also, C. L. Harter and J. D. Beasley[427] carried out a survey concerned with induced abortions in New Orleans, Louisiana, a state with a long firmly established Catholic tradition. Two groups were studied: one was a representative sample taken from 540 women who were, or had at one time, been married and/or women who were, or had at one time, been pregnant, aged between 14 and 45 who had been questioned in an earlier survey; 483 who were either Catholic or Protestant were included. The second group consisted of 65 out of 90 women discharged from the Tulane gynaecological service of the Charity Hospital of New Orleans with a diagnosis of abortion. All patients were interviewed, and each was asked to answer a seven-item questionnaire dealing with the grounds on which abortion might be considered justifiable. As might have been anticipated, the Catholics were more opposed to termination of pregnancy than the Protestants, but both ranked the reasons for refusing abortion in the same order. Ninety-five per cent thought abortion unjustifiable if a woman wanted no more children, 82 per cent were opposed to it on the grounds that the woman had too many children, 60 per cent did not accept the belief that abortion was every woman's right, and 41 per cent would not endorse it for mental illness in the mother, but only 31 per cent would not allow it for rape, and only 24 per cent opposed it for somatic illness in the woman or the child; only 24 per cent would not grant abortion because of incest. Harter and Beasley thought that their second group of patients—those discharged from the Charity Hospital—were at "high risk" of having attempted an abortion, and they observed that 94 per cent were non-white; because of this they compared the women in the group with the non-whites and with the lower class in the representative sample. Of the latter only three—all non-white Protestant women—admitted attempting abortion, though this lower class had undergone a total of 1536 pregnancies (a rate of 2 abortion attempts per 1000 pregnancies). In the "high risk" group, 7 out of 65 patients admitted abortion attempts (a rate of 28 attempts per 1000 pregnancies). The two investigators provided brief histories of the ten patients who had attempted to procure an abortion, and concluded that attitudes on whether a woman should have an abortion varied greatly, depending on the circumstances surrounding the pregnancy. They thought that the opinions they had been given were truthful, and that the incidence of criminal abortions in New Orleans was probably low since the small number of women admitted to the Charity Hospital with abortion complications implied that either only very few were being performed or that highly skilled abortionists were at work; the impoverished financial status of the patients, they believed, precluded the latter probability. On the whole, women in New Orleans were, they felt, conservative, the majority believing that abortions should be allowed only for mental illness, incest, physical ailments, and rape; most would oppose unrestricted liberalization of the abortion laws. Finally, they concluded, the data suggested that those who had attempted induced abortions might not have done so if they had had adequate family-planning information or services.

In California, meanwhile, Sherwin and Overstreet[428] comment, the rubella epidemic of 1964–5 and the charges of unprofessional conduct subsequently preferred by the State Board of Medical Examiners against nine San Francisco physicians who had performed abortions on the indication of first-trimester rubella, awakened public interest in the issue of legal abortion. The findings of a sample poll carried out early in 1966 by the Field Research Corporation showed that only 25 per cent of people favoured very restrictive abortion laws, whilst 65 per cent were in favour of liberalizing them.

Reference was made earlier (see p. 55) to the study of life events and acceptance of pregnancy carried out in Omaha, Nebraska, by Helper et al.[102] In six small groups of between twelve and thirty women stemming from divergent religious, socio-economic, age-structure, and pregnancy-status backgrounds, all agreed that two circumstances especially threatened the woman's adjustment to pregnancy: rejection of the pregnancy by the putative father and the experience of having had a previous child who was defective or seriously disturbed. By implication, women in these situations would probably be more liberal towards abortion. In December 1967, Peyton et al.[429] in Lafayette, Indiana, decided to survey women's attitudes towards abortion in the senior author's private gynaecological practice; of 3100 patients aged between 20 and 60 who were asked to complete, anonymously and voluntarily, a thirty-nine-item questionnaire, 2070 responded. They were mostly Caucasian middle-class permanent residents of Indiana from an equal distribution of agricultural, industrial, and university families. Ninety-two per cent were married; 78 per cent were Protestant (1607 women versus 349 Catholics and 114 of other faiths); 75 per cent were under the age of 45; 74 per cent had two or more children; 70 per cent wanted no further children; and 53 per cent considered themselves capable of being pregnant again. The data showed that approximately 80 per cent of respondents favoured abortion if advisable on grounds of a threat to life or health, though amongst the Catholic women only 56 per cent would endorse an abortion if life was imperilled, and only 50 and 45 per cent respectively would accept it if continued pregnancy would seriously impair mental or physical health. Most respondents (65%) were in favour of legal abortion if there was a 1 in 5 chance of a child being abnormal, but only half (48%) favoured it if the child's chance of being abnormal was 1 in 10; again, much smaller percentages (37% and 26%) of Catholic women would endorse abortion for these reasons. Most of the respondents, both non-Catholics and Catholics, opposed abortion for socio-economic reasons, though 83 per cent favoured it if the mother-to-be was mentally retarded. Most respondents—a higher proportion of non-Catholics than Catholics—endorsed abortion for rape. About half (1025) of those responding felt that the foetus had a right to life from the time of conception, and of these 76 per cent (778) felt that a legal abortion should never be permitted. Ninety-three per cent felt that a doctor should have the right to refuse to perform a legal abortion; 88 per cent felt that a pregnant woman should not abort herself even if a safe method existed; 76 per cent felt that the decision for an abortion should rest with a combination of the mother, the father, the doctor, and the consultant; and 58 per cent thought that contraceptives should never be made available to unmarried women.

Though interesting, the data from three of the four studies [426, 427, 429] are biased by the small number of unmarried or never-pregnant women included (none in the National Fertility or the New Orleans study and only 8% in Peyton's investigations), and in all except the Californian survey the absence of opinions from males—who, after all, make the laws—is conspicuous. An investigation by Lawrence Lader,[430] chairman of the National Association for the Repeal of Abortion Laws, has filled in some of the gaps. For over 500 women who wrote appealing for help after the publication of his book *Abortion* in 1966, Lader arranged consultations with carefully screened east coast gynaecologists and subsequently sent each woman a 50-item questionnaire to complete anonymously. He based his findings on the original letters and the 282 completed questionnaires that were returned. Fifty-three per cent of his sample were single and 38 per cent were married, the majority of the latter (72%) having had more than one child; 73 per cent were under 31 years old; and there were over 51 per cent Protestants, 28 per cent Catholics, and 16 per cent Jews. Twenty-three per cent had family incomes of less than $5000 a year; 43 per cent had family incomes between $5000 and $10,000 a year; and the annual family income of the remaining 32 per cent was greater than $10,000. Sixty-seven per cent had had at least one year at college; 46 per cent were employed full time; and 27 per cent were students.

Ninety-three per cent had never had an abortion before. Seventy-two per cent claimed that they had been using some birth-control technique at the time of impregnation. Seventy-two per cent consulted a doctor after becoming pregnant: of the latter, 43 per cent offered some advice and 30 per cent opposed abortion. Eighty-two per cent of the women eventually secured an abortion.

Surveying the women's feelings about their abortions, Lader found that 55 per cent were "glad without reservation"; 33 per cent were "not happy but knew that the abortion was necessary"; 8 per cent were "satisfied but doubtful"; and only 0.1 per cent regretted having had it. Eighty-two per cent reported no damage from the abortion; 11 per cent said they had been affected emotionally; and 2 per cent said that they had had physical sequelae. Forty-four per cent found the operation painless; 29 per cent experienced moderate pain; and 24 per cent called the operation painful; 76 per cent experienced no unpleasant consequences within 3 days of the operation. Thirty-three per cent paid less than $300 for the abortion; 37 per cent paid between $300 and $500; and 25 per cent paid more than $500 for it. Fifty-nine per cent felt that the abortion had had no effect on their marital or sexual relationship; 30 per cent reported some effect; and whilst 9 per cent mentioned an improved relationship, 9 per cent broke off from their partners and 10 per cent noted increased caution, fear, or reduced sexual activity. Seventy-eight per cent stated that they would have another abortion if again faced with the same situation; 13 per cent would not consider another abortion; and 5 per cent were undecided.

As Lader remarks, the findings convincingly refute the myth that guilt and physical damage frequently follow an abortion. The pain that some women experience during it was due to the employment of local anaesthetics. Many told him of their difficulties in securing help, some sharply complaining that physicians who had provided them with birth-control advice were totally unhelpful when the techniques they had advocated failed. From the information he received, Lader found that help was often difficult to obtain, even in states such as Colorado and California where the law had been liberalized. The regard in which American doctors who help with the problem can be held is illustrated by the reputation of Dr. Robert Spencer, who died at Ashland, Pennsylvania, in early 1969, having in his 45 years of medical practice performed by his own admission more than 100,000 illegal abortions, for none of which he charged more than $100. Students at the East Coast Women's College frequently referred to him as "the Angel of Ashland".[431]

"I always figured a doctor is supposed to help people, to help the living", Dr. Spencer once said.

GYNAECOLOGISTS

In the United States, as in Britain, gynaecologists in general were opposed to therapeutic abortion, their dislike of the procedure being reinforced by medical ethics, the law, and—in some cases—the Church. Within the last 5 years, however, a few gynaecologists have become more vocal, and have pointed to the shortcomings of much of the legislation on abortion and the adverse consequences of practices based on it.

Reference has earlier been made (see p. 225) to the Model Penal Code proposed by the American Law Institute under which a licensed physician would be justified in terminating a pregnancy if he believed that there was a substantial risk that continuance of the pregnancy would gravely impair the physical or mental health of the mother, or that the child would be born with grave mental or physical defect, or the pregnancy resulted from rape by force, or incest. In 1965 R. E. Hall,[432] a New York gynaecologist, reporting the results of a postal survey sent to 2285 obstetricians and/or gynaecologists in New York State, observed that 85 per cent (1152) of the 1350 respondents expressed preference for the more liberal abortion statute embodied in the Model Penal Code.

Edwin M. Gold,[433] a second New York gynaecologist, writing in the spring of 1966, observed that though 1–1½ million assumed-to-be illegal induced abortions were estimated to be performed in the United States every year, the corresponding number of legal abortions was only 18,000. Further, whilst national vital statistics revealed an 11 per cent decline in puerperal mortality, from a rate of 38 per 100,000 live births in 1958 to 34 per 100,000 in 1964, the number of abortion deaths due to sepsis increased by 31 per cent. In his own study of therapeutic abortion in New York City in the period 1943–62, Gold noted, the number of therapeutic abortions performed had declined from 5.1 per 1000 in 1943 to 1.8 per 1000 in 1962, whilst abortion as a cause of puerperal deaths had concomitantly increased by 60 per cent; by 1964 abortion was the major cause of puerperal mortality in New York City, accounting for almost half (46%) of the seventy-four puerperal deaths. In addition, marked ethnic and socio-economic disparities were operating in regard to therapeutic abortion, the Puerto Ricans, the non-whites, the poor, and the patients in voluntary hospitals having much less chance of having this procedure performed than the white and the more well-to-do patients who could afford private hospital care. Commenting briefly on the reported effects of criminal abortion in Latin America and of legal abortion in Hungary, Gold aligned them with his own findings, and observed that medicine had a responsibility "not only to equalize the opportunities for therapeutic abortion, where indicated, regardless of ethnicity, socio-economic status or hospital practices, but also to develop a practical public health programme designed to reduce the incidence of and legal sequelae of criminal abortion". He thought that existing United States abortion laws, which resembled the New York State Law (unchanged since 1881), were restrictive and archaic, and he quoted with approval the Model Penal Code. He felt that efforts by medical, legal, and lay groups to amend the legislation had to be continued, and from a public health aspect, he thought, sex education was needed in which the dangers of criminal abortions could be stressed; improvement and expansion of family-planning facilities were also required.

Later in 1966, Sherwin and Overstreet[428] decided to seek specific information about the individual attitudes and practices of gynaecologists and/or obstetricians in California. They mailed questionnaires to 943 board-qualified practitioners and had 748 (over 81% of 913 possible replies) returned, a rate of response suggesting that concern over the problem was considerable. Ninety-one per cent wrote that they believed that abortion was justifiable if there was imminent risk of maternal death; 87 per cent favoured it for definite risk of shortened maternal life; and 67 per cent supported it for psychiatric certification of suicidal risk; these three indications were legal under the (then) existing California law. More interesting were the indications that were not then covered by the law: 83 per cent favoured abortion for forcible rape or incest; 77 per cent approved of it for significant foetal abnormality; 72 per cent favoured it for risk of impairment of the mother's physical or mental health; but only 21 per cent favoured abortion "for purely socio-economic reasons". The findings suggest that the responding gynaecologists were not illiberal about therapeutic abortion in general, though, like most of their colleagues elsewhere in the world, they objected to performing it on socio-economic grounds.

In November 1966 J. R. Willson,[434] lecturing at Temple University School of Medicine in Philadelphia, reviewed the entire problem of abortion from the standpoint of a gynaecologist. He pointed out that the majority of societies throughout history had devised means of limiting family size—contraception, abortion, and infanticide all having been used for the purpose. Although the early leaders of the Church in Rome did not proscribe abortion, the present stand of the Catholic authorities gradually developed, and the physicians—through their education and training—had tended to adopt a similarly rigid attitude. Thus the belief had grown up that pregnancy must be preserved if the birth of a live child could be anticipated, no matter what effect this had on the mother, the family, or the community, and this had resulted in an unreasonable limitation of therapeutic abortion. Since women often found it difficult to obtain either contraceptives or legal abortions, they were driven to seek criminal operations: one-third of the maternal deaths in some states and two-thirds in large cities were due to induced abortions. Willson pointed out that therapeutic abortion was not by any means new, and he observed that as successful treatments for some diseases which had hitherto merited termination of pregnancy had been discovered, other grounds for inducing abortion had emerged, notably pressures generated by socio-economic factors and the changed pace of life. He commented:

> ... It is essential that we become concerned with the kinds of people who are being born into the world today. Can children born of physically healthy but emotionally crippled parents be expected to develop normally and to lead happy, useful and productive lives? What chance does a sixth or eighth illegitimately conceived child of a mentally incompetent, indigent woman have of becoming a responsible citizen? Why should we insist that an embryo with only a slight chance of developing into a reasonably normal individual must be preserved because its mother is healthy and her life is not endangered by the pregnancy? Are we ready to become involved with personal and community problems produced by such pregnancies or shall we continue to hide behind the convenient platitude that life, no matter how inadequate it may be, must not be destroyed?
> Few physicians in this country have really faced up to the problems relating to abortion. Until recently the obstetrician–gynaecologist was about the only one who had to make a decision because other doctors dodged the issue by referring their patients. We did little better. Those of us who wanted to avoid any involvement could do so by telling the patients that abortion was not permitted in our hospital. Sometimes, however, we salved our consciences by telling the patient where she could be aborted legally with greater risk and much less competency. Dr. Timanus, a practising abortionist in Maryland for many years, reported that 401 of 5210 patients he had aborted were M.D.s, nurses, or had been impregnated by M.D.s or medical students, and most had been referred to him. He also stated that many of his other patients were referred to him by physicians practising in the area.
> The strong negative attitude of physicians against induced abortion does not necessarily represent the general feeling in our society and it certainly does not reflect the reaction of a woman with an unacceptable pregnancy. . . .

Willson discussed some of the more recent indications for therapeutic abortion which were replacing the earlier "medical" indications. Amongst foetal indications he referred to maternal rubella, mumps (possibly), and drugs such as thalidomide, to which the mother had been exposed. Psychiatric indications, he observed, had risen to 80 per cent of the total; he thought that in these patients psychiatric consultations should be provided, and he pointed out that though the risk of suicide was often used to justify a therapeutic abortion and to satisfy the hospital committee, many terminations on psychiatric grounds were really performed because of socio-economic factors, because it was felt that a child born of psychotic parents would stand no chance of developing normally or because legal abortion was easier than supporting an emotionally disturbed woman through pregnancy, labour, and the puerperium. Contraception raised complicated issues: in some countries, notably Japan, abortion had been used as contraception, and in other instances failure of contraception denoted failure to use a method rather than failure of a method. Humanitarian grounds such as rape and incest also justified therapeutic abortion and appropriate psychiatric help.

The results of therapeutic abortion, Willson observed, depended on the emotional stability of the woman, the reasons for the operation, and the conditions under which it was performed. He believed that physicians and gynaecologists had to stop (i) leaving the problem of abortion to social workers and legislators, (ii) ignoring the individual and social problems of unwanted pregnancies and rationalizing this with euphemistic phrases, (iii) forcing women to consult criminal abortionists, and (iv) performing illegal but approved abortions in hospital because their colleagues provided acceptable reasons. Instead the doctor had to show his concern about the problems of abortion by (i) *understanding* that the woman felt that the unwanted pregnancy had placed her in an untenable social, economic, or psychological position—for which doctors had often been partly responsible through their failure to provide contraceptive advice and premarital counselling; (ii) *educating* medical students on sexuality and the social implications of women having too many children, as well as teaching lawyers, social workers, and other physicians that unwanted pregnancies could be prevented; sex education in schools was also necessary; (iii) *taking action* to obtain reform and liberalization of the law in abortion so that subterfuge could be abandoned and therapeutic terminations done on appropriate grounds; and (iv) *preventing*, through contraception and where necessary legal abortion, the need of many women to have recourse to criminal abortionists.

The principal points of Willson's lecture have been considered in some detail since his wise, prescient, informed, liberal, therapeutic attitude presaged the course that was followed in subsequent years by a number of American states as well as in Britain and other countries.

In early 1967 *Modern Medicine* concluded a nationwide survey of the attitudes physicians held towards abortion. Of 40,089 respondents 86.9 per cent favoured liberalization of the law; even though the obstetrician–gynaecologists were the group most opposed to such a move, 83.7 per cent of them favoured it on grounds similar to those proposed in the Model Penal Code. The journal pertinently pointed out that no case had ever been reported of a conviction of a physician for abortion in a licensed hospital; one practitioner only in Pennsylvania had been brought to trial for performing a therapeutic abortion and he was found not guilty.[435]

R. E. Hall,[424] surveying abortion in American hospitals generally in November 1967, observed that it was the outmoded restrictive and inequitable nature of the laws on abortion which had led to shortcomings in hospital practices. The inequities chiefly concerned psychiatric illness and maternal rubella, he observed. The therapeutic abortion boards established by many hospitals in the mistaken belief that they were required by the Joint Commission on Accreditation of Hospitals were serving mainly as medical tribunals, he stated, and were rendering moral judgements which were more academic than humane, so that the number of therapeutic abortions had been reduced. Hall felt that the public health aspects of abortion had too long been overlooked: 1 million cases of cholera a year would create a public scandal, he pointed out, or even a million cases of rickets; but 1 million abortions a year were "embarrassingly ignored". He recommended that the American Public Health Association consider three important approaches to the problem: (i) the promotion of sex education in schools, (ii) the pursuit of an active contraceptive programme, and (iii) the sponsorship of abortion law reform.

In 1968 the American College of Obstetricians and Gynaecologists endorsed the Model Penal Code of the American Law Institute. This was the same year that the American Public Health Association urged the repeal of all abortion laws, Beck *et al.*[421] observe, and the year after the American Medical Association and the American Psychiatric Association had endorsed the Model Penal Code.

Psychiatrists

In December 1965 the Association for the Study of Abortion sent a questionnaire to all the members of the American Psychiatric Association in regard to their attitudes towards therapeutic abortion. Crowley and Laidlaw,[436] reporting the results in May 1966, stated that 5289 psychiatrists from the United States had responded (40.6% of the total membership). Whilst only 23.5 per cent favoured abortion "on demand", more than 85 per cent considered abortion justifiable (i) when the life of the mother was endangered, (ii) when the physical health of the mother might be impaired, (iii) when there was a significant risk that the mental or emotional health of the mother might be jeopardized, (iv) when there was a significant risk that the child would be born mentally or physically defective, (v) when the pregnancy had resulted from rape or incest of a girl under 16, and (vi) when the pregnancy had resulted from rape or incest of a girl over 16. Summarizing these results, Crowley and Laidlaw observed that over four-fifths of those who had responded "favoured liberalization of the legally permitted bases for interruption of pregnancy. In addition letters and comments revealed an intense interest in the matter, not only in regard to the welfare and interests of the individual woman but also in regard to the welfare and interests of the child to be and that of the community to which both mother and child looked for support. Canadian and foreign psychiatrists differed little from their American colleagues." In June 1966, Thomas Szasz[437] acutely observed that if it was moral to practise contraception it was moral to have an abortion, at least in early pregnancy when the foetus could not lead an independent existence, for since it was then an integral part of a woman's body, she had the right to decide what to do with it.

In view of these opinions it is not surprising that amongst the 40,089 physicians responding to the poll reported by *Modern Medicine* early in 1967, the psychiatrists, of whom 94.6 per cent approved, were the group most in favour of liberalization of the abortion law.[435]

In June 1967 the Council of the American Psychiatric Association approved a Position Statement on Abortion.[438] This stated:

> Pregnancy and childbirth are a happy and rewarding experience for most women. The carrying of pregnancy to term and the experience of motherhood fulfill many of the deepest personal and biological needs of most women and in addition reinforce the joy of her marital relationship and increase her pride of identity with her family and her community.
>
> However, we as psychiatrists recognize that pregnancy can constitute a grave threat to the life or mental health of certain women with emotional or mental illness or disordered emotional development. Abortion can likewise constitute a threat to the mental health of certain prospective mothers.
>
> As in other medical situations, therapeutic recommendations relative to abortion should take account of the religious beliefs of the woman and her family.

In view of the above, the American Psychiatric Association supports an abortion on medical grounds when:

1. There is substantial medical evidence that continuance of the pregnancy will threaten the health or life of the mother, or
2. There is substantial medical evidence that the infant will be born with incapacitating physical deformity or mental deficiency, or
3. There is substantial medical evidence that continuance of a pregnancy resulting from legally established statutory or forcible rape or incest will constitute a serious threat to the health or well-being of the patient.

Arthur Peck,[414] addressing a divisional meeting of the American Psychiatric Association in November 1967, reviewed the situation in regard to abortion in Scandinavia, eastern Europe, and Japan, and concluded that the pressure of public opinion in the United States would probably be directed increasingly towards social rather than medical indications for termination of pregnancy. He thought that whilst physicians in North America were often described as social conservatives, they might in some ways be in advance of the public on the question of abortion. However much one argued the case from the standpoint of Szasz, i.e. that the woman had the right to decide whether or not to continue her pregnancy, she needed the skilled services of her physician to terminate it; thus no amount of social, ethical, and economic considerations could remove it from the special interest of the medical profession and the emotional reactions and attitudes of the latter towards it would influence their behaviour towards abortion policy. Peck instanced the physicians' fear of the physical and the psychiatric sequelae of abortion, both of which he felt were exaggerated, and probably based in part on guilt, in part on fear of loss of public approval and position, and in part on anxiety about being overwhelmed to the point of being unable to function as a physician. He pertinently concluded: "Abortion upon request is so foreign to attitudes fostered in physicians during their medical training that conflicts arise not only between physicians and those pressing for widespread legal abortion but also within the physicians most directly involved in the abortion process. Some of these attitudes are inferred from physicians' current practices with therapeutic abortions and some from the nature of their writings on the subject."

In March 1968 Richard A. Schwartz[141] provided a psychiatric perspective on abortion. Contrary to public supposition, he observed, most abortions took place in married women over 30 years of age who had been impregnated by their husbands and had had three or more children. On the other hand, abortions were also in demand for unwanted pregnancies in unmarried women—in 1963 one-quarter of a million illegitimate children were born. Yet planned parenthood was vitally important in preventive psychiatry: Freud, Karl Menninger, and others had stressed its role in reducing psychiatric morbidity. Schwartz pointed to the problems engendered by out-of-wedlock pregnancy, the birth of huge numbers of illegitimate children, the problems of fostering out and caring for them in institutions, and the difficulties created for the child, the mother, and society by the (then) existing situation. Arguments for reform of the abortion laws included those centred on public health (the avoidance of unsafe illegal abortions and of deformed children being born following maternal rubella), demography (excessively large birth rates in slums and undesirable areas: New Jersey, Rhode Island and Massachusetts all had population densities greater than Japan), poverty (half of all families with an annual income of less than $3000 had four or more children, compared with only one-quarter of the families earning $10,000 or more per year), and civil liberties (deprivation of the right of a woman to obtain an abortion through medical channels to safeguard her life and her health). Schwartz saw religious beliefs and the (mistaken) theory that abortions were detrimental to mental health as the main obstacles to reform.

In May 1969 Professor R. B. Sloane,[439] studying the problem of unwanted pregnancy in the *New England Journal of Medicine* by carefully examining British, Scandinavian, and American experience, reached the conclusion that there were no clear-cut psychiatric indications for therapeutic abortion. The risk of precipitating or exaggerating an existing psychosis was, he commented, slight and unpredictable, and suicide was rare. Nevertheless, women who sought abortions, he observed, could prove unsatisfactory mothers if forced to continue their pregnancy to term. Their symptoms could subside more rapidly if they were granted their wish, and there was little evidence that new psychiatric illness appeared after therapeutic abortion. Professor Sloane thought that a changed abortion law should, as in Britain, include a "social clause". This would, he said, "facilitate a more candid appraisal of the problem as a therapeutic rather than a medico-legal one".

In October 1969 the Group for the Advancement of Psychiatry (GAP) published its authoritative statement *The Right to Abortion: a psychiatric view*.[440] Whilst motherhood in the right circumstances was hard but rewarding work, GAP observed, an unwanted pregnancy could become "a lifetime sentence, an ordeal emotionally destructive to the mother and disastrous for the child". Yet once pregnant, a woman's freedom of choice disappeared, and if she did not wish to continue the pregnancy her desire for an abortion was regarded as a crime. This was surprising in view of the overpopulation problem; it stemmed partly from religious attitudes such as the Roman Catholic Church dictum of the inviolability of life, even though when life began was uncertain. Further ambiguities were that some contraceptives, such as IUDs, probably acted as abortifacients, and that wealthy women always had safe medical abortion available, whilst their less affluent sisters had to resort to illegal abortions with their attendant risks and complications. Women disagreeing with Roman Catholic beliefs should not be prevented by laws based on them from having therapeutic abortions, GAP observed; to deny a woman the termination of an unwanted pregnancy could be to deny her the joy of a wanted pregnancy later on. The limited gain in sexual morality produced by old-style abortion laws was far outweighed, GAP thought, by the adverse consequences on the mother and the child, for whom foster parents were difficult to find. Modern therapeutic abortions were safe and had few complications; the psychiatric sequelae that occasionally followed abortion were usually linked with sterility caused by infection acquired at illegal operations. GAP believed that the Liberalized Abortion Law (the "Model Code") proposed by the American Law Institute was unsatisfactory since it contained too many indefinable phrases, no consistent valid psychiatric indication for termination existed, and in areas where it had been applied the result had been a reduction of the number of therapeutic abortions and a restriction of them largely to affluent women. Accordingly, GAP proposed, abortion, where performed by a licensed physician, should be made legal— though a doctor should be expected to exercise medical judgement and should have the right, on conscientious grounds, of refusing to terminate a pregnancy. This "broad change in social policy" was proposed, GAP stated, "not as a final step but as a current appropriate measure".

OTHER PHYSICIANS

In many American states, as in Britain, medical practitioners who were not gynaecologists or psychiatrists adopted a position midway between the conservatism of the former and the liberality of the latter. After the 1964–5 California rubella epidemic, when nine gynaecologists were charged with unprofessional conduct, concern over abortion rose sharply in California. In March 1966 the House of Delegates of the California Medical Association, representing some 20,000 physicians in that state, passed a resolution expressing "its belief in the broadening of the therapeutic abortion laws".[428]

The poll, carried out and reported by *Modern Medicine* early in 1967 to which 40,089 physicians responded, indicated that the majority (86.9%) favoured liberalization of the laws on abortion. As might have been anticipated, 93.3 per cent of non-Catholic doctors approved of liberalization, whilst only 49.1 per cent of Catholic physicians supported it. The grounds on which therapeutic abortions were considered justifiable were: substantial risk of maternal death (75.6%); following rape or incest (75.1%); direct positive evidence of foetal abnormality (71.6%); substantial risk to mother's physical health (69.7%); possible foetal abnormality (62.7%); substantial risk to mother's mental health (60.6%); substantial risk of maternal suicide (58.4%); and substantial risk to mother's emotional health (44.5%). Illegitimacy was considered an adequate reason for therapeutic abortion by 29.1 per cent of the respondents, and socio-economic grounds were considered adequate for termination by 26.6 per cent, but abortion at the request of the pregnant woman was only supported by 14.3 per cent of the respondents. Finally, 962 (2%) of those responding felt there should be *no* law on abortion, and 2605 (6%) felt, in contrast, that none of the reasons cited above should be legal, i.e. all induced abortions, for any reason whatever, were wrong.[435]

In June 1967 the policy statement on therapeutic abortion adopted by the American Medical Association had a considerable impact on legislatures and hospitals alike. The cautiously worded statement ran as follows:

> The American Medical Association is cognizant of the fact that there is no consensus among physicians regarding the medical indications for therapeutic abortion. However, the majority of physicians believe that, in the light of recent advances in scientific medical knowledge, there may be substantial medical evidence brought forth in the evaluation of an occasional obstetric patient which would warrant the institution of therapeutic abortion either to safeguard the health or life of the patient, or to prevent the birth of a severely crippled, deformed or abnormal infant.
>
> Under these special circumstances, it is consistent with the policy of the American Medical Association for a licensed physician, in a hospital accredited by the Joint Commission on Accreditation of Hospitals, and in consultation with two other physicians chosen because of their recognized professional competence who have examined the patient and have concurred in writing to be permitted to prescribe and administer treatment for his patient commensurate with sound medical judgment and currently established scientific knowledge. Prior to the institution of a therapeutic abortion, the patient and her family should be fully advised of the medical implications and the possible untoward emotional and physical sequelae of the procedure.
>
> In view of the above, and recognizing that there are many physicians who on moral or religious grounds oppose therapeutic abortion under any circumstances, the American Medical Association is opposed to induced abortion except when:

(1) There is documented medical evidence that continuance of the pregnancy may threaten the health or life of the mother, or
(2) There is documented medical evidence that the infant may be born with incapacitating physical deformity or mental deficiency, or
(3) There is documented medical evidence that continuance of a pregnancy, resulting from legally established statutory or forcible rape or incest may constitute a threat to the mental or physical health of the patient;
(4) Two other physicians chosen because of their recognized professional competence have examined the patient and have concurred in writing; and
(5) The procedure is performed in a hospital accredited by the Joint Commission on Accreditation of Hospitals.
It is to be considered consistent with the principles of ethics of the American Medical Association for physicians to provide medical information to State Legislatures in their consideration of revision and/or the development of new legislation regarding therapeutic abortion.

The statement, the American Medical Association emphasized, in no way infringed the rights of physicians to express opposing views and to practise their beliefs, and it did not suggest that physicians should act contrary to their personal consciences. All segments of the population were becoming restive in regard to abortion practices, the American Medical Association pointed out, and it observed that change and reform in this area were inevitable. The new policy was, it felt, "a reasonable and conservative approach" which would provide the American Medical Association with a position of leadership in this important contemporary problem. [441]

The American Public Health Association adopted a more liberal position, expressed in a resolution it adopted at its ninety-sixth annual meeting in November 1968. [442] The resolution declared:

It is generally accepted that individual women and couples should have the means to decide, without compulsion, the number and spacing of their children. This personal right has been supported and enhanced through governmental action at all levels. The APHA and many other groups have joined with public agencies to secure this right, and to make widely available those services that will provide a range of choice of contraceptive methods consistent with personal beliefs and desires. However, contraceptive methods among users vary in effectiveness and suitability. Pregnancies sometimes occur due to rape, incest, and difficulties in obtaining contraceptives or because of contraceptive failures.

In order to assure the accepted right to determine freely the number and spacing of their children, safe legal abortion should be available to all women. Further, the provision of abortion within the usual channels of medical care will reduce the well-known adverse health effects of illegal abortion.

The American Public Health Association urges that access to abortion be accepted as an important means of securing the right to space and choose the number of wanted children. To this end, restrictive laws should be repealed, so that pregnant women may have abortions performed by qualified practitioners of medicine and osteopathy.

R. H. Williams,[443] delivering the president's address at the meeting of the Association of American Physicians held in Atlantic City, New Jersey, on 6 May 1969, drew attention to the Japanese use of abortion and the fact that Britain, Sweden, and other countries had liberalized their abortion law to distinct advantage. He observed:

> Our enormously restrictive abortion laws cause extensive mental and physical suffering as well as major social, economic and other problems. Our laws have not prevented abortion; about one million are performed each year. Of those who have abortions ten per cent are eventually hospitalized and 5000 to 10,000 die. Eighty per cent are performed on married women impregnated by their husbands. They are chiefly thirty to forty years of age with an average of two or more children. Some groups condone abortion when performed before "life begins" or before "the soul enters the body"; some select "quickening" as the time of soul entrance. As Lederberg has emphasized, life began many centuries ago. Quickening only symbolizes a very early phase of the recapitulation of phylogeny by ontogeny.
>
> Experience shows there is almost no mortality and very little morbidity from abortions performed by competent physicians in a licensed hospital. Eighty-six per cent voted that the criminal abortion laws should be made inapplicable to licensed physicians and to women under the care of a physician. Almost all voted that such an abortion should be carried out in an accredited hospital and that physicians and others objecting to abortion should not be required to engage in it. The major basis for abortion should be the mental and physical status of the mother and child, and the effects on social, economic, and other conditions pertinent both to the family and to society. . . .

In November 1969 at the AMA clinical convention in Denver, a move to liberalize abortion practice was rejected, but in the spring of 1970 the Board of Trustees recommended the adoption of a resolution stating that the decision to perform an abortion be regarded as a matter solely for the woman and her physician, it being understood that no physician or hospital should be obliged to carry this out where conscientious objections existed.[444] This new attitude, the Board of Trustees observed, had become necessary because several states had amended their laws to permit abortions for reasons other than therapeutic (in the old sense) and, as a result, many American physicians could not perform a legalized medical prodecure without violating AMA policy. As expected, a heated debate took place and over 50 speakers expressed widely divergent points of view. Spokesmen for several thousand Roman Catholic physicians declared that they would be forced to resign from the AMA if a liberal abortion policy was adopted. The final resolution, slightly modified from the reference committee's recommended wording, was as follows:

Whereas, Abortion, like any other medical procedure, should not be performed when contrary to the best interests of the patient since good medical practice requires due consideration for the patient's demands; and

Whereas, the standards of sound clinical judgement, which, together with informed consent should be determinative according to the merits of each individual case; therefore be it

Resolved, that abortion is a medical procedure and should be performed only by a duly licensed physician and surgeon in an accredited hospital acting only after consultation with two other physicians chosen because of their professional competency and in conformance with standards of good medical practice and the Medical Practice Act of his State; and be it further

Resolved, that no physician or other professional personnel shall be compelled to perform any act which violates his good medical judgement. Neither physician, hospital, nor hospital personnel shall be required to perform any act violative of personally held moral principles. In these circumstances good medical practice requires only that the physician or other professional personnel withdraw from the case so long as the withdrawal is consistent with good medical practice.

In the end only 26 physicians wrote to resign their AMA membership following the adoption of the revised abortion policy. The AMA replied to each separately, stating that its new position did not permit abortion on demand and urging that each physician should reconsider his resignation since it was "entirely possible for a physician to be unequivocally opposed to abortion and yet in good conscience be a member of an organization that has revised its abortion policy for various reasons, provided his freedom not to perform an abortion remains respected and protected by that organization".[445]

Sexuality and Contraception

In the United States, as in other advanced countries, a sexual revolution has taken place in which teenagers have figured prominently. In America, as in Great Britain, increasingly disinhibited behaviour and neglect of contraception by adolescents are producing an increasing number of unwanted pregnancies. Professor J. E. Owen[446] has drawn attention to the extremely high birth rate which, occurring in the decade following the Second World War, is responsible for the present unusually large number of American adolescents—the United States now has some 18 million children aged between 13 and 17. Lax child-rearing practices, inadequate supervision from parents who often work during their children's formative years, co-educational schools, and the effect of advertising and films have led a proportion of American children to fail to develop controls and to become prematurely preoccupied with sex. Many premarital pregnancies occur mainly in consequence of factors in the home, the majority of the 2070 women questioned in the study carried out in Indiana by Peyton et al.[429] believed. Ninety-one per cent thought that permissiveness regarding early dating and late hours was responsible; 86 per cent believed that lack of home training was to blame; 67 per cent attributed them to innocence and/or ignorance towards getting pregnant, venereal disease, or having guilt feelings; only 45 per cent of the respondents blamed movies or television and only 41 per cent thought they were due to current magazines and novels. As a result of unwanted pregnancies, many marriages are "forced": 1 in 3 teenage brides is pregnant on her wedding day, and 1 in 6 brides above that age is in the same condition. Half of all American girls marry before the age of 20 and have their last child by the age of 29. "Forced" and premature weddings, due in appreciable proportion to unwanted pregnancies, are associated with a high rate of marital breakdown: 20 per cent of American marriages end in divorce; a quarter of a million American children have their lives disrupted by divorce or separation every year; and one-third of delinquents come from such homes.

Frank J. Ayd,[447] reviewing the problem of the teenager and contraception from a psychiatric standpoint in May 1969, noted that "a sinister coalition of permissive morality and commercial fostering of the prurient inclinations of youth has produced a copulation explosion". He pointed out that in the last decade there had been an increasing amount of sexual intercourse among juveniles with, in addition, a drop in the age of the first sexual experience so that pre-teen intercourse was not rare. Many girls, he stated, were having repeated carnal experiences, often with a succession of partners. The result was a rise in illegitimate pregnancies, abortions, and venereal diseases, together with "the incalculable psychological harm which is the inevitable consequence of adolescent promiscuity". Ayd discussed the problem of whether to give birth control advice to adolescents and noted that they were unlikely effectively to employ contraception because of their emotional immaturity and impulsivity. For single teenage girls in whom an intra-uterine device was seldom suitable, oral contraceptives were frequently prescribed; yet their use, he thought, had many risks—physical, psychological, and social. Ayd pointed to the side-effects of the pill such as thrombosis and sterility (?), and he noted that frequent indiscriminate intercourse carried a greater risk of venereal disease and of carcinoma of the cervix. He believed that there was "reason to fear that the policy of contraceptives for teenagers ultimately may undermine the stability of the nation, for a country is as stable and strong as the families of which it is composed". Regardless of why a girl engaged in sexual intercourse, he stated, it seldom, if ever, led to permanent commitment to one man; ultimately, the girl was rejected by her lover and a series of such experiences shattered her self-image when she realized, sooner or later, that she had become a sex object used by others for their gratification and had not been treated as a person. He thought that many teenagers who indulged in sexual intercourse would not develop the emotional maturity and capacity for self-restraint necessary to make a happy and stable marriage. Ayd declared that self-restraint was necessary for health, and he quoted Thomas à Kempis to this effect, transposing to adolescent girls by implication the comments that the latter had made on the deleterious consequences of self-indulgence in men. Ayd concluded that physicians should not prescribe contraceptives for young girls but should seek to encourage in their patients "an aspiration to a certain nobility of behaviour—with all the cost involved".

It is interesting to contrast Ayd's view on contraception—that of a Catholic psychiatrist—with the views expressed by Alan F. Guttmacher, a gynaecologist who in 1969 was President of Planned Parenthood—World Population, and was an authority on the Jewish attitude towards birth control.[422] Guttmacher, speaking at the American Medical Association's twenty-third clinical convention held in 1969 in Denver, Colorado, told his audience that the sexual revolution that had occurred—part of which was, he thought, the movement towards a single, rather than a double, standard of sex—was a good thing. He felt that the current generation were not as promiscuous as their parents had been, because their relationships were more geared to one individual. He advocated giving sexual advice and oral contraceptives to certain unwed minors—even including 14-year-old girls—but stressed that each case had to be viewed individually on its merits.[448]

The intransigent attitude adopted by the Catholic Church to methods of contraception other than abstinence and the "rhythm method" has earlier been noted. Fortunately, other religions were less opposed to less frustrating and more effective techniques of conception control, the need for which was lucidly expressed in an article in the *Journal of the Kansas Medical Society* by Gerry Weichmann.[449] His article, in many ways an American counterpart of the article published 2 years earlier by Sir Theodore Fox,[73] drew attention to the Universal Declaration of Human Rights reaffirmed by the United Nations in 1968 (see p. 42). Weichmann went on to examine the population problem in the political, the socio-economic, and the scientific dimensions, discussed methods of conception control, including abortion and contraception, and considered the possibility of conception control programming.

The medical profession in the United States, as Peel and Potts [76] have pointed out, were years in advance of their British colleagues in regard to professional interest in contraception. Robert Dale Owen produced *Moral Physiology*, the first book to be published on birth control in America, in 1830; 2 years later Charles Knowlton published his *Fruits of Philosophy*, the work which, in its English edition, featured in the Bradlaugh–Besant trial held in London in 1877. In the United States, as in Britain, the birth-control movement attracted a number of eccentrics, but in the New World it was supported by several eminent physicians—A. M. Mauriceau, R. T. Trall, Edward Bliss Foote, Edward Bond Foote, and Alice B. Stockton. The Comstock Act of 1873 made it illegal to send information on contraception through the mail, but in 1882 Peel and Potts observe, an article on contraception appeared in the *Michigan Medical News*, and in 1888 a symposium number on contraception was published in the *Medical and Surgical Reporter*. The British medical press, in contrast, continued to condemn birth control for the next 40 years. In 1921 Abraham Jacobi, in his presidential address to the American Medical Association, advocated contraception be practised on economic, social, and medical grounds. In the same year a similar plea was put forward at the Church Congress in the English city of Birmingham by Lord Dawson of Penn, the king's physician. In America at the time, as in Britain, some inspired members of the laity were trying to initiate family-planning facilities; Mrs. Margaret Sanger, who produced a widely read pamphlet *Family Limitation*, founded the first birth-control advice centre in Brooklyn in 1916, and 11 years later she organized the first World Population Conference in Geneva, which attracted an international group of physicians and scientists. Two bodies, the International Medical Group and the International Union for the Scientific Study of Population, resulted from this. In 1948 Margaret Sanger assembled delegates from twenty-three countries to form the body which subsequently became the International Planned Parenthood Federation.

Whilst it might be thought that the long history of medical interest in contraception might have facilitated instruction of American medical students in sexuality and birth-control techniques, this has not altogether been the case. Further, Mudd and Siegel [450] observe, despite the formal courses in sex education which have been established, the average student is deficient in sex knowledge and in the capacity for understanding his own sexuality; in consequence he is inadequately prepared to cope with the sexual problems he encounters in medical practice. Mudd and Siegel administered an anonymous ninety-five-item written questionnaire to 397 male medical students at the University of Pennsylvania: the results showed that the students were more experienced sexually than the college-educated men studied by Kinsey but that they had a strong desire for education in sexuality. Convincing evidence was found that, especially in the early stages of his medical school career, the student's sexual anxieties inhibited his professional objectivity.

All the methods of contraception utilized in Britain are employed in the United States and two, oral contraceptives and vasectomy, are of especial interest. In March 1970 an estimated $8\frac{1}{2}$ million women were taking oral contraceptives, though a poll taken after the hearings of the Senate Small Business Monopoly Subcommittee in January 1970 (see p. 174) on the dangers of taking the pill showed that 6 per cent of users had stopped ingesting it and 23 per cent had considered giving it up. Whilst the hearings were of undoubted value, many family-planning authorities were afraid that the great advantages of the pill might be overshadowed by its comparatively slight dangers.[451] The Food and Drug Administration wrote to all physicians in the United States advising them to discuss the risks of the pill with each patient, and, early in April, the Government announced that it would order a hundred-word statement on the danger of oral contraceptives to be included in every packet sold. The statement cautioned that oral contraceptives were powerful, effective drugs which should not be taken without a doctor's continued supervision; it mentioned possible side-effects such as abnormal blood-clotting, and it advised regular examinations by a woman's doctor. Finally, it warned women to beware of severe headaches, blurred vision, leg and chest pains, an unexplained cough, and irregular and/or missed periods.[452] A week later Mrs. Roberta Meinert, aged 29, of Brooklyn, was awarded $251,000 (£104,000) for intestinal damage attributed to Enovid, an oral contraceptive manufactured by G. D. Searle & Co. of Chicago. The drug had caused an intestinal thrombosis for which Mrs. Meinert had had to undergo two operations.[453]

Male sterilization by section and/or ligation of the vas deferens has long been practised more widely in the United States than in the United Kingdom and in 1970 a total of 75,000 men was considered likely to undergo the operation. Voluntary sterilization is legal in all fifty states (though Connecticut and

Utah restrict its use to medical necessity), but there i[s under]standable medical and lay reluctance to perform or to und[ergo it.] At one clinic operated by the Margaret Sanger Resea[rch, New] York, a man can apply, and after passing a medical and [examina]tion can be sterilized. (454)

 Unwanted Pregnancies and Unwanted Children

Within the last 5 years there has been an increasing recognition of the problems created in a woman by an unwanted pregnancy (439) as well as an increased awareness of the deleterious consequences to a child born as a result of such a situation, (141) and, in the long run, the problems that such mothers and children create for society. (120, 141) In a young teenager an unwanted pregnancy can produce a cycle from which frequently she is unable to escape: repeat pregnancies, dropping out of school, subsistence on welfare and failure to become a productive individual—the "unwed mother's syndrome". Over fifty projects throughout the United States are reported to be struggling with this problem.

As far as the child of an unwanted pregnancy is concerned, Grunebaum and Weiss (455) have emphasized, its future welfare deserves more thought and study than has been thus far accorded to it. In a letter to the editor of the *New England Journal of Medicine* they referred with approval to the pioneer study of Forsmann and Thuwe, (120) and they pointed out that the ethical dilemma of the unwanted child had often been avoided by the belief that society adequately provided for such children either through adoption or through foster care. This was not the case, Grunebaum and Weiss pointed out, especially for the child of a mother of low socio-economic status; such children were often unadoptable and became the responsibility of the State. Every child born, the two authors observed, was entitled not only to be alive but to reasonable prospects for growth and opportunity. It was therefore of the utmost importance that public policy concerning abortion took into account the future welfare of explicitly unwanted children, and that studies on their development should be encouraged.

 Changes in the Law

Impelled by public opinion, consciousness of the shortcomings of existing legal codes, and the example of other countries, from 1967 onwards different states began to liberalize their abortion legislation. By January 1969, Ingram[423] observes, five states—Colorado, North Carolina, California, Georgia, and Maryland—had modified their laws to conform with the principles expressed in the Model Penal Code (see p. 225). Each state chose to add certain provisions of its own, some of which were useful, whilst others were of dubious value. Nevertheless, despite the changes in the law, many hospitals continued to make legal abortions difficult to obtain, Lorry Plagenz[456] reported in July 1969. Unnecessary impediments were erected, valid requests for termination were refused, residence requirements were enforced, and though the numbers of legal abortions performed increased, far too few were carried out, and it continued to be easier for a wealthy woman to get her unwanted pregnancy terminated than it was for her counterpart with more limited means. The same inequity had been described 2 years earlier by a New York gynaecologist, R. E. Hall.[424] Within the next 3 months four additional states—New Mexico, Arkansas, Kansas, and Oregon—had liberalized their laws.[423] By April 1970, three further states—Alabama, Hawaii, and New York—had followed suit, and abortion on reasonably liberal grounds was legal in twelve American states in addition to the District of Columbia and Puerto Rico. Massachusetts, New Jersey, and Pennsylvania continued to prohibit "unlawful" abortion without defining what this was.[457]

COLORADO

On 25 April 1967, Colorado passed the first liberal abortion law in the United States. The new legislation, which was sponsored by Richard D. Lamm, a Democratic Member of the Colorado House of Representatives, who was later joined in sponsoring the Bill by Carl Gustafson, a Republican Member from Denver, had its approval facilitated by the successful passage 2 years earlier of a law providing birth-control information for indigent women. Lamm, writing with a gynaecologist and a psychiatrist, has described the careful preparation that was necessary to steer the Bill through opposition to a successful conclusion.[458] The Bill stated that a committee of doctors could approve an abortion if the woman's life was in danger, or if there was serious impairment of her mental or physical health, or if it was likely that the pregnancy would result in the birth of a child with grave and permanent physical deformity or mental retardation, or if the pregnancy had resulted from rape (including statutory rape) or incest.

William Droegemueller et al.[459] have described the first year of experience with the new law. They observed that, amongst other requirements, legal abortions had to be performed in accredited hospitals, that each participating hospital had to have a special board consisting of three licensed physicians which had to consider each case presented and had unanimously to recommend termination, and that the new legislation made it a crime for any person to perform an illegal abortion. Should a woman die from such an illegal operation, the new law stated, the person performing it was guilty of murder and would be punished accordingly. Soon after the Colorado legislation was passed, it received a good deal of national recognition through radio, television, and newspapers. In consequence, members of the University Department of Obstetrics and Gynaecology in Denver were flooded with telephone calls and letters from physicians, parents of prospective patients, and prospective patients asking for help in terminating unwanted pregnancies. Eventually, in September 1967, the University of Colorado Medical Center announced that it would not accept a patient for therapeutic abortion from outside the state, except for foetal indications. Perhaps, because of this, the danger that Colorado would become an "abortion Mecca" did not materialize. Of the state's 52 accredited hospitals, 23 elected not to perform abortions and of the remainder 21 appointed therapeutic abortion boards and carried out legal terminations; 3 hospitals appointed boards and had had no requests, and a further 5 were about to appoint boards in the near future. Four hundred and seven terminations (11.6 per 1000 live births) were performed in the first year of the new law. This represented an eightfold increase over the fifty-one known legal abortions carried out in the previous year. Of the 407 patients, 278 (68%) were Colorado residents and 269 (66%) were single, divorced, or widowed. Psychiatric indications, on the basis of which 291 (72%) patients underwent legal abortions, were the commonest grounds, followed by foetal indications in 47 (11%) and rape in 46 (11%). Almost half (46%) the legal terminations were performed on patients whose family incomes were below $6000 a year. Dilatation and curettage was used on 236 patients (58%), usually before the 12th week of pregnancy; after the 14th week amniocentesis was commonly employed, this method being used in 108 women (26.5%). Thirty-four patients (8.4%) underwent abdominal hysterotomy and 29 (7.1%) had hysterectomies. Droegemueller et al. commented that the Colorado law had worked well in its first year of operation, its main disadvantage being the false hopes it generated in people both outside and inside the state. The three authors favoured a restriction on therapeutic abortions, except for medical reasons, to pregnancies of less than 20 weeks of gestation, and they believed that a residence requirement would make it possible to administer the law more equally and expeditiously.

Psychiatric reactions to the new law were provided by Heller and Whittington,[460] Stanfield,[461] and Whittington.[462] Describing their experiences at the 124th annual meeting of the American Psychiatric Association held in Boston, Massachusetts, in May 1968, Heller and Whittington[460] praised the uncommon skill and adroitness displayed by the political leaders who had accomplished the passage of the Bill, and commented that following its enactment the medical community was unprepared. Nevertheless, the Colorado Medical Society soon put out guidelines which interpreted the law and suggested appropriate procedures, and the Colorado Psychiatric Society formed an Abortion Committee which also published guidelines for its members. Psychiatrists were advised to resist pressure for an abortion, to identify the source of the pressure, to perform a comprehensive investigation of each case, and to assess the potential efficacy of psychotherapy. Amongst 224 women whose pregnancies were legally terminated in the first 9 months of the new Act, 151 (68%) had the operation performed for psychiatric reasons; six cases of depression occurred. Heller and Whittington concluded that few clinical guidelines for advising legal abortions existed, though they identified a major clinical subtype amongst unemancipated teenagers, and they commented that lower socio-economic groups under-used therapeutic abortion.

In April 1969, Clyde Stanfield[461] presented a paper to the Nebraska State Medical Association Meeting in which he described some of the problems he had encountered as a psychiatrist member of a therapeutic abortion committee in a large metropolitan private hospital and as a psychiatrist-consultant examining applicants for termination at several private hospitals. In the first 2 years of the Colorado abortion law he had found that therapeutic abortion boards (i) often refused to deny legal abortion to patients from other states, (ii) were more impressed by psychopathology antedating pregnancy than by agitation and depression during it, (iii) were more favourably disposed to approve abortion in patients permanently incapacitated for pregnancy or in those who had tried through sterilization and/ or psychiatric treatment to avert recidivistic irresponsibility over getting pregnant, (iv) had sometimes combined indications for termination (psychiatric, medical, foetal) when one alone would have been insufficient, (v) had avoided automatic validation merely because of claimed use of lysergic acid diethylamide (LSD), and (vi) had become aware that many district attorneys favoured psychiatric indications for abortion as a way of avoiding certification of rape or incest. Stanfield concluded, however, that ". . . Colorado's implementation of the new Abortion Law had been clearly conservative and frustratingly disappointing to many desperate applicants. It may have raised therapeutic abortion to a safer and more honest entity, but it has by no means made it easier, less expensive, or [more] predictably available than did our old law. . . ."

H. G. Whittington,[462] another psychiatrist who, at the American Psychiatric Association's 125th annual meeting in Miami Beach, Florida, described 2 years' experience with the Colorado Abortion Law, was also unhappy with it. He said he had addressed himself to the question of whether the abortion law programme had been successful in preventing mental and emotional illness in the Colorado population, and to this end he had sent letters to 196 women who had requested abortions at Denver General Hospital between 31 March 1967 and 17 December 1968. Sixty-two of the 196 women had been denied abortions, 60 on psychiatric grounds. Eventually thirty-one of the patients who had received an abortion returned Whittington's questionnaire (only 1 of the 51 women located who had been refused abortions returned it). Eighty-seven per cent of these thirty-one said that they were happy (45% "very happy", 42% "fairly happy"); 87 per cent said they were in better mental health (68% "definitely", 19% "probably"); 25 (81%) said they would make the same decision again, 2 said they would not, and 4 were uncertain. Whittington observed that whilst the findings suggested that the women who had responded felt their health and happiness had benefited by the operation, they did not help to establish which women with unwanted pregnancies would develop psychiatric illnesses as a result of them, and they did not clarify the long-term effects of therapeutic abortion. He thought the abortion committee, which usually consisted of older men sitting in judgement on a young woman who was not allowed to appear but whose case was presented in documents from other physicians, was unconstitutional and a poor social instrument. The "liberalized" abortion procedure was still extremely cumbersome, time-consuming, and expensive. "We are not able to define the line between personal misery and psychiatric illness", Whittington stated. "It is ironic that psychiatry, which espouses the concept of individual freedom, should be caught up in a cruel legalistic hoax that forces women to have unwanted babies, rationalized on the basis that it is all right for them to suffer because they will not become mentally ill." He concluded that women in Colorado were less deprived of their liberty than had formerly been the case, but he thought that the present law and the operation of the system was unjust and unequal. Because the Colorado statute had been hailed as "liberal", pressure for reform had slackened, and an air of complacency had settled. Whittington believed that psychiatry should dissociate itself from participating in certifying the need for an abortion; the procedure should be covered by medical practice acts in each state, as with any other medical procedure.

Others were disconcerted by the results of the Colorado abortion law. A. F. Guttmacher [422] commented that the eightfold increase in legal abortions which had occurred in its first year of operation was not as much as it sounded, and the report by Droegemueller *et al.* [459] observed *inter alia* that hospitals in small and medium-sized towns were performing very few legal abortions. Representative Lamm, commenting on the variation that had been noticed between legal terminations done in Denver and those performed elsewhere, stated: "Too many hospitals, private as well as public, are concerned about their images. And the boards of directors don't want to jeopardize their sources of income. Nobody wants his hospital to be labelled an abortion mill.... We are only reaching a small number of women seeking abortions", he went on, "the legislature produced a bill that would help about five per cent of them but the doctors and the hospitals have turned it into a three per cent bill". [456] Don Arnwine observed that it had probably become more difficult to get a hospital abortion than it was before the law was passed, because of the official and public scrutiny. [456] An article in *Life* in March 1970 commented that the Colorado legislation was regarded by a Denver doctor as "a rich lady's law". Even with correct documentation, 12 out of every 13 requests for abortion were rejected, the article observed, and in the first 2 years after the legislation was enacted, less than 800 legal abortions were performed. This compared with an estimated 9000 women who in the same period underwent illegal abortion. One of the law's original sponsors regarded it as a failure, and was reported to be pressing for its repeal. [420]

NORTH CAROLINA

Within 2 weeks of Colorado's enactment of its new abortion law, North Carolina passed its own law, which was adopted on 9 May 1967. J. M. Ingram [423] remarks that the political climate of the state was almost ideal for the passage of abortion legislation, for all bills were ratified into law by the North Carolina General Assembly without the necessity (and political risk) of the governor's signature, and the population was largely Protestant. R. A. Ross, reviewing the history of North Carolina's abortion law in his discussion of the paper by Droegemueller et al.,[459] commented that the first law on abortion had been passed in 1881. In 1930 a medical school contraceptive clinic was established, the same year that a eugenics board and a sterilization board were founded. In 1960 the first county-organized oral contraceptive clinic came into existence, 3 years before the permissive sterilization law was enacted.

The new law was sponsored and supported by individual laymen supported by individual interested physicians; the state medical society did not participate in any official way. The legislation permitted abortion when there was a substantial risk that continuance of the pregnancy would threaten the life or gravely impair the health of the woman, when there was substantial risk that the child would be born with grave physical or mental defect, or when the pregnancy was the result of rape or incest (the said alleged rape having been reported to a law-enforcement agency or a court official within 7 days of its having taken place). The woman (or if she was a minor, her parents or her husband) had to give written permission for the abortion to be performed, had to have resided (except in emergency when her life was endangered) in North Carolina for at least 4 months, had to have the operation carried out in a hospital licensed by the North Carolina Medical Care Commission, and had to be certified prior to the operation being performed (except in emergency) as meeting the new legal requirements by three doctors of medicine not engaged jointly in private practice, one of whom was the person performing the operation. No physician or hospital was required to be a party to any abortion, and reporting was voluntary.

North Carolina insisted, however, on policing by the medical profession. The Committee on Maternal Health of the Medical Society of the State of North Carolina solicited the co-operation of all licensed physicians in the state in 1969, asking them to report therapeutic abortions and providing for this purpose a document designed to elicit information of value in evolving the concepts for acceptable abortion practice in North Carolina. The Maternal Health Committee also recommended that each hospital establish a committee on therapeutic abortion, the membership of which, it declared, should ideally comprise five physicians, and the transactions of which should be recorded and preserved in a confidential file.[463]

Discussing the working of the new law, R. T. Parker[459] pointed out in commenting on the paper presented by Droegemueller et al. that in the Duke Medical Center during the 5 years 1961–6 a total of 37 therapeutic abortions were carried out, 21 on medical, 11 on psychiatric, and 5 on foetal indications. The residency clause had reduced out of state requests to a reasonable number, and though the total abortions performed in the hospital had risen by 230 per cent in the first year, the relative frequency of different indications had not altered. The responsibility of the physicians practising under the new law was (i) to avoid the rigidity which had existed under its predecessor, (ii) to accept liberalization and (iii) to protect the family. J. R. Ashe, discussing the paper given on changing aspects of abortion law at Hot Springs, Virginia, in February 1969, by J. M. Ingram, described experience with the new law in more detail.[423] Examining the therapeutic abortions performed between 1 July 1966 and 30 June 1967, and those carried out between 1 July 1967 and 30 June 1968, Ashe noted that 53 abortions were performed during the first year and 98 in the second; the rate of therapeutic abortions to live births thus increased from 1.7 per 1000 in 1966–7 to 3.1 per 1000 in 1967–8. R. A. Ross, speaking after Ashe, put the North Carolina abortion law into historical perspective and commented on the disturbing "double standard" regarding the indications for therapeutic abortions (and sterilization) which existed in many hospitals and communities.[423] Finally, O. H. Jones observed that the State Obstetrical and Gynaecological Society, despite discussing the old law for several years, had never been able even to agree on the need for revision; the prevailing attitude had been to "let sleeping dogs lie", with the result that the new legislation had been brought in by laymen rather than by doctors. He thought this had been just as well, but he was concerned that the legislator who had introduced the Bill had openly stated that in his opinion in the future the law would continue to be liberalized until any woman could get an abortion for any unwanted pregnancy. He thought this was society's problem rather than primarily the gynaecologist's, though he felt he was not accepting his professional responsibility when a pregnant, single, usually young, girl came to his office and having been advised by him to go to a home for unwed mothers said: "No, I will not have this baby, I will find someone to do an abortion". He was concerned that hundreds of thousands of women had criminal abortions each year, some of them ending in tragedy; it was the responsibility of organized medicine and the obstetrician-gynaecologists to assume leadership and to advise legislators on problems of this kind.[423]

CALIFORNIA

Following repeated attempts, beginning in 1961, to change the law on abortion, the Californian Therapeutic Abortion Act, which was adopted on 1 May 1967, was passed by the California legislature in June 1967 and became effective on 8 November 1967. Whilst the Bill was pending, Governor Reagan stated that he would veto any abortion legislation that contained foetal deformities as an indication, and the Bill as passed omitted these. It provided that abortion was permitted under two general conditions: (i) when there was a substantial risk that continuance of pregnancy would gravely impair the physical or mental health of the mother, or (ii) when the pregnancy resulted from rape or incest. There was no residency requirement, but the abortion—which was permitted up to the 20th week of pregnancy—had to be approved by a hospital committee of two licensed physicians (three if the proposed termination was to be performed after the 13th week of pregnancy) and had to be carried out in a hospital approved by the Joint Commission on Accreditation of Hospitals.

Russel and Jackson,[464] reviewing the first year's experience with the new law, described the background of the measure—the thalidomide tragedy, the California rubella outbreak, the upsurge in the use of contraceptive pills and IUDs, the "sexual revolution", the "population explosion", and—above all—the charges of professional misconduct made against nine respected San Francisco obstetrician-gynaecologists by the State Board of Medical Examiners in 1966 because they had performed hospital-approved therapeutic abortions on the indication of first-trimester rubella. The data collected during the first year of the new Act showed that of the 477 accredited hospitals in California, 230 had had abortions carried out within them in 1968. Of 5488 applications for termination, 5045 (91.9%) had been approved by hospital abortion committees and a total of 4865 (88.6%) had been performed. Danger to mental health accounted for applications from 4812 women (88% of the total applicants); 4459 (92.7%) were approved. Rape or incest accounted for 407 requests (7% of the total applicants); 349 (85.7%) were approved. Danger to physical health was responsible for the remaining 269 applications (5% of total applicants) of which 237 (88.1%) were approved. Of those whose pregnancies were terminated, the vast majority (98%) resided in California and were white (89%); most (73%) were under 30, about half (53%) had never been married; and for half (51.5%) the pregnancy was their first. It was noteworthy that the San Francisco Bay Statistical Area, which had 23 per cent of the state's births, performed 64 per cent of the abortions, whilst the Los Angeles Metropolitan Area, with 44 per cent of the state's births, performed only 18.8 per cent of the abortions. Rape accounted for 3.5 per cent of legal abortions in the San Francisco Bay Area, whilst in the Los Angeles Metropolitan Area this indication was responsible for 17 per cent of terminations. In addition, a higher percentage of the total applications received in the San Francisco Bay Area was approved (94.6%) than in the Los Angeles Metropolitan Area (84.4%). The San Francisco Bay Area had approximately 31 abortions per 1000 live births in contrast to 5 per 1000 in the Los Angeles Metropolitan Area, so that there appeared to be some impediment to application of the law in southern California.

Commenting on this variability, Russel and Jackson observed that differences had occurred from community to community and from hospital to hospital within the same community. Contributing to it they felt was: (i) "a certain vagueness", legislatively speaking, over "mental" and "physical" health, designations which were not accepted uniformly by hospital staffs; (ii) lack of knowledge by hospital staff, social workers, and others of the exact provisions of the law; (iii) lack of acceptance by some physicians of the law as written due to (a) some regarding it as insufficiently liberal, (b) some resenting the omission of foetal indications, and (c) some being opposed on religious grounds to abortion or contraception; (iv) concern that the District Attorney's offices were prosecuting *all* abortions; (v) the belief, based on past experience, that the State Board of Medical Examiners would interpret the law ultra-restrictively; (vi) the idea that hospital accrediting bodies in granting certification had a certain "acceptable" incidence for therapeutic abortion; (vii) uncertainty over medical and hospital coverage via insurance and medicaid; (viii) financial costs and "red tape"; and (ix) the fear of hospital administrators and staffs that their hospitals would become known as "abortion centres". The California Therapeutic Abortion Act had, nevertheless, Russel and Jackson believed, made several positive contributions. These included (i) the establishment of hospital-based therapeutic abortion as a "legal entity"; (ii) the provision of medical care for over 5000 women, many of whom would otherwise have sought criminal abortions; and (iii) focusing social attention and professional concern on a significant social and public health problem.

Leon Marder,[465] in a paper given in May 1969 at the 125th anniversary meeting of the American Psychiatric Association, described the experience of the Los Angeles County—University of Southern California Medical Center's Therapeutic Abortion and Sterilization Committee with 147 of the patients it had approved for legal abortions. He commented on the need to identify suicidal risks, the unique problems presented by patients' need to exaggerate their symptoms, and the fact that referral to the Committee in itself could reduce the intensity of their symptoms. He drew attention to the resistance of the residents and nurses towards abortion and the difficulties created by the Committee's original over-conservative criteria. Few of the patients reviewed by the Committee developed serious post-abortal difficulties, but several women whose pregnancies were terminated by amniocentesis and who passed the products of conception in bed or in the toilet (rest room) were upset by seeing tissue and a formed embryo or foetus. Attempts to evaluate the effect of rejection of requests for therapeutic abortions were difficult because of hostility developed by many of the applicants, and, in fact, the Committee's philosophy changed gradually in such a way that, whereas, originally, psychiatric evaluations and recommendations for termination were questioned, later it was its failure in certain cases to recommend abortion that gave rise to concern. Most patients were relieved of anxiety and depression when these had developed under the stress of an unwanted pregnancy, and they reported improvement in their relationship with others, together with improved living situations, following their terminations. Marder, like many of his psychiatric colleagues, felt that therapeutic abortion should come under the code of medical practice and should be removed from the criminal statutes.

In July 1969 P. B. Thurstone[466] presented the experience of a single medical centre, San Mateo County General Hospital, over a 1-year period from 1 January 1968 to 31 December of that year. During this time, the 249-bed hospital which was affiliated with the Stanford University School of Medicine received 60 applications for therapeutic abortions of which 55 were approved and 52 were carried out—a frequency of 98 per 1000 live births. All but two of the applicants were residents of California, 90 per cent of those terminated were white, and 83 per cent were unmarried, separated, or divorced; 87 per cent of those operated on had their pregnancies terminated on psychiatric grounds. Thurstone concluded that her figures showed that there had been a marked increase in the number of legal in-hospital abortions in California, this being particularly true for terminations performed on psychiatric grounds. The findings, she thought, suggested "a changing emphasis toward the application of preventive medicine rather than mere survival through completion of pregnancy". Physicians were now able, she considered, to help many pregnant women whose health was threatened by pregnancy in a way in agreement with the World Health Organization's definition of health as "... a state of complete physical, mental and social well-being and not merely the absence of disease and infirmity...".

A leading article [467] in the issue of the *Journal of the American Medical Association* that contained Thurstone's report briefly discussed the question of termination of pregnancy on psychiatric grounds, and expressed the hope that though a flexible interpretation of the law on abortion should be possible, the law should stop short of endorsing abortion on demand. The article commented that a study of the patients whose requests for termination of pregnancy were rejected might well be revealing, and it emphasized the need for more systematic information to be gathered. Kummer, [468] writing on the situation in California in the summer of 1969, declared that he thought that complete liberalization of the abortion law was imminent. Like Guttmacher [422] and others, he objected to Governor Reagan's veto on therapeutic abortion for foetal indications, and he drew attention to the charge of unprofessional conduct against the "San Francisco Nine" (see p. 229) which led to sentences varying from "public reprimands" to suspension of medical licences for 1 year—findings and penalties which were overturned on appeal to the Superior Court. Kummer also mentioned the case of Dr. Leon Belous, who was convicted of conspiracy to perform abortion for having sent a patient to an unlicensed practitioner who allegedly performed a clandestine abortion in the state; this case also was heard by the Supreme Court, which on 9 September 1969, "handed down the most far-reaching decision, even surpassing the Bourne case". In reversing the conviction of Dr. Belous of conspiracy to perform abortion, the Supreme Court stated *inter alia* that the law under which he had been prosecuted was unconstitutional because it infringed upon "the woman's right to life and to choose whether to bear children. The woman's right to life is involved because childbirth involves risks of death." Despite the discrepancy of abortion practices between the north and the south of California, and the fact that psychiatrists sometimes had to state that a suicidal risk was present where none existed, so as to convince doubting abortion committees of the need for termination, Kummer believed that a wider acceptance of abortion by the public and the medical profession had taken place, and he declared that the possibilities of liberal interpretation of California's abortion law had extended to the point where any woman wanting her pregnancy terminated could be accommodated. He commented that early in pregnancy several leading hospitals were performing abortion on a modified outpatient basis, and he thought the time was at hand to challenge the requirement of inpatient hospitalization consultants and a committee. Like other investigators, [422, 441, 462, 465] he wanted the decision to abort to be left to the patient and her physician.

Some were not as convinced as Kummer regarding the efficacy with which the California Therapeutic Abortion Act was operating, though these views, admittedly, were expressed before the Supreme Court's decision of 9 September on the Belous case. A. F. Guttmacher[422] observed that, lacking a eugenic clause, the Bill was a "mongrel" and had given concern to many physicians. With an estimated 50,000–100,000 illegal abortions being performed annually in the state and 80,000 as the likely figure, California's first-year total of 5045 legal abortions gave a decrease in criminal abortions of only about 6 or 7 per cent. E. W. Overstreet quoted by Kummer,[468] George Cunningham,[456] and others pointed out that some hospitals were making abortions unnecessarily difficult, whilst others were refusing to carry their share of the load. Poorer patients were discriminated against, overcharging was occurring (as much as $500 for a legal abortion that, like a dilatation and curettage, should cost $150–$200), and the situation was driving some patients to the courts where they were questioning the constitutionality of restrictive abortion laws. In April 1970 it was reported that John Gwynne, a young Los Angeles physician, had for the past year exhibited a sign in his window stating "Community Service Center and Women's Abortion Clinic", where he and his colleagues performed twenty abortions daily on patients approved for abortions by an examining psychiatrist. The centre was raided by the police a week after it was opened, but though Gwynne was charged with breaking the law he was released without bail and promptly reopened his centre. Five years ago few practitioners would have dared such a challenge; currently the winds of change are bolstering the abortion law reformers.[469]

GEORGIA

On 27 February 1968 the new Georgia Abortion Law, which had failed in earlier sessions, was adopted, and, Ingram[423] remarks, passed the House easily despite its length, complexity, and strong provisions, though it barely survived a stormy session in the Senate. After 6 weeks on Governor Maddox's desk the law, which had been introduced by laymen and which was supported openly and vigorously by the Medical Association of Georgia, became operative. It made abortion legal on maternal or foetal indications as well as in cases of forcible or statutory rape. "Bona fide" state residence had to be certified in writing by the patient and her physician. Consent to termination from the patient only was required, and a clause was included to exclude the unreasonable demands of a "vindictive husband". The constitutional or other rights of the foetus could be defined by the Supreme Court at the request of the Solicitor-General or a relative of the child, abortion being prohibited if court rules were violated. Two consultants and a hospital board were necessary, and a full record of consultations, consents, and certificates of abortion had to be filed, not only in the hospital notes, but also with the Department of Health; failure to comply with this provision made abortion criminal.

Ingram[423] remarks that preliminary reports from the Georgia Board of Health showed an extremely conservative use of abortion under the new law: in 6 months, 57 therapeutic abortions were reported, 23 for foetal indications, 19 on psychiatric grounds, 14 on medical indications, and 1 for rape. The Board of Health, as well as acting as a recipient for data, also had the right to take disciplinary action.

MARYLAND

In 1968 the first Bill introduced into the Maryland legislature would have repealed all state law in regard to abortion and would have left it as "solely a medical procedure and therefore performed by physicians subject to the standards of medical practice". This Bill was defeated and a modified Bill, which was introduced by laymen, supported openly both by the State Medical Society and by individual physicians, was adopted on 25 March 1968. It made abortion legal on maternal and foetal indications as well as in cases of forcible rape: incest was not provided for, but this was covered on grounds of foetal consanguinity. Therapeutic abortion was prohibited after 26 weeks of gestation; hospital-board approval was required, and the boards were required to report yearly to the Joint Commission on Accreditation and to the State Board of Health on the number of requests, authorizations of requests, indications for granting authorizations, and number of abortions performed. A conscience clause was provided and a penalty was set for failure to report.

A. F. Guttmacher,[422] amongst others, commended Maryland on this forward-looking step, and commented in February 1969 that the Johns Hopkins and Sinai hospitals in Baltimore appeared to be allowing their staffs relatively great licence to perform the abortions they considered to be justified. Describing the preliminary results of the new law at the 92nd annual meeting of the American Gynaecological Society in New Orleans in May 1969,

A. C. Barnes, in discussing the paper by Russel and Jackson, gave some preliminary findings.[464] As in California, workers in Maryland had found that hospitals varied a great deal as to whether or not they would undertake therapeutic abortions; the total number done in Maryland would, he thought, approach the number done in California in the first year of the latter state's Therapeutic Abortion Act (5045), but he felt that attention—rather than focusing on the total—should be directed towards deaths from criminal abortions and teenage illegitimacy rates. Barnes thought that the medical profession's responsibility in regard to criminal abortions was more than the mere accumulation of statistics, and he felt that in Maryland, as in California, ten times the current rate of therapeutic abortions would have to be performed if criminal abortions were to be significantly reduced; in Maryland these accounted for one-third of the maternal mortality. He also felt that teenage illegitimacy presented a grave problem and was "one of the worst of the ills that can befall a community", and he observed that to speak of a 12- or 13-year-old as "mother" was to miss the concept of motherhood. He pointed out that the Deputy Commissioner of Health of the City of Baltimore had appeared before the Maternal Welfare Committee of the local Medical Society, where he had scolded the medical profession for not doing enough therapeutic abortions, and had recommended counselling for pregnant girls under the age of 16. Barnes believed that the medical profession was living through a period of transition and that attitudes and practices which had become engrained would have to change. "Discussions of morality", he said, ". . . should not mislead us. Morality is a matter of opinion, whereas teenage pregnancy and out-of-hospital abortions are a matter of fact. . . ." He thought that he and his colleagues were "but scratching the surface of what must become a new dimension of obstetric care . . .".

In April 1970 it was reported that Maryland had become the most progressive American state regarding abortion law in that legislators had passed a Bill which made abortion entirely a matter between the patient and her doctors. A clause was included to ensure that a physician was not obliged to perform an abortion if his conscience did not allow it; nevertheless, a flood of women from other states requesting abortion was expected.[470] Johns Hopkins Hospital in Baltimore, another report stated, had started a streamlined outpatient clinic where an applicant for abortion approved by the hospital's review board arrived at 10.00 a.m. and was discharged a few hours later; the cost was $90–$100 depending on the drugs used.[420]

Other States

In Kansas in November 1968, M. M. Halley[471] discussed the development of the state's laws on abortion and pointed out the advantages of liberalizing them on the lines suggested by the Kansas Judicial Council—which proposed broadening of the circumstances under which abortion could justifiably be performed—and the Kansas Medical Society—which recommended removing abortion from the domain of criminal law and according it a status similar to other medical procedures.

In Ohio, in December 1968, Perr *et al.*[472] reported the findings of a poll answered by 220 members of the Ohio Psychiatric Association which revealed that only 6.4 per cent of Ohio psychiatrists considered the abortion law of their state adequate and that 77.7–90.5 per cent were in favour of termination of pregnancy on maternal and foetal grounds or in cases of rape and incest. The following month, Copeland *et al.*[473] reported on seventy-four therapeutic abortions carried out at the Ohio State University Hospital over a 7-year period from 1 January 1959 to 1 January 1966; during the same period there were 55,660 live births, so that the ratio was 1.3 abortions per 1000 deliveries. Clearly an extremely conservative policy had been followed in Ohio, and Copeland and his co-workers emphasized the need to liberalize the laws.

In March 1969 New Mexico and Arkansas adopted liberalized abortion legislation; they were followed in this in April by Kansas and in May by Oregon. The development of abortion laws in these four states were briefly described by Ingram,[423] but it is too soon for experience of the laws in action to have been gained. Most of the new abortion laws broadly followed the pattern laid down by the American Law Institute.

In the summer of 1969, physicians in Delaware,[474] Massachusetts,[475] and Alaska[476] were calling for liberalization of the laws on abortion in their respective states. By the middle of April 1970 three more states—Alabama, Hawaii, and New York—had liberalized their legislation in this regard. Hawaii's law was as liberal as Maryland's but, unlike the latter state's, had a residency requirement. The New York Abortion Law Reform Bill, passed after much discussion, became operative on 1 July 1970. It allowed a woman and her doctor to decide whether to terminate a pregnancy of 24 weeks or less, abortion after that time being permitted only to save a woman's life.

In the first 2 months of the new Bill 16,000 women underwent legal abortions in New York State, 10,500 pregnancies being terminated in New York City. Four deaths occurred, but only one was connected with abortion.

Immediately the Bill became operative, requests for abortion flooded hospitals all over the state: applications outstripped operations by over 5 to 1 and by late July most hospitals with abortion services had lengthy waiting lists; accordingly they limited their facilities to state residents, established abortion quotas and refused to take patients over 12 weeks pregnant. Since, in addition, many Catholic and orthodox Jewish gynaecologists would not perform terminations, much confusion ensued and many women were denied necessary operations. The well-to-do flocked to out-of-town hospitals for abortions costing $500, but in the city the problem of coping with the indigent was acute. The Planned Parenthood Federation advocated inexpensive "freestanding" abortion clinics located close to hospitals, and one gynaecologist, M. Bergman, successfully practised office suction terminations under local anaesthesia at a fee of up to $100. *In toto* it seemed that the English experience of excessive demand and inadequate and unevenly distributed facilities was being replicated in New York. [477]

Canada

In this country, though pressure of public opinion forced liberalization of the abortion laws in August 1969, the medical profession has remained ultraconservative in its attitude to therapeutic termination of pregnancy.

K. T. MacFarlane of Montreal, commenting on the Canadian abortion situation in the spring of 1969, emphasized the "theological objections" and the "innate distaste" of the medical profession towards "wasteful destruction".[459] A new problem for the profession, he observed, was how to deal with a sexually enlightened population which demanded abortion because they wanted it or felt they did. The Criminal Code of Canada permitted legal interruption of pregnancy only to preserve the life of the mother, though on occasion this had been liberally interpreted. Nevertheless, over a 25-year period which he had analysed in 1961 only 122 therapeutic abortions had been performed in the Montreal General Hospital and the incidence of such operations showed a progressive downward trend from 12 per 1000 gynaecological admissions to 0.8 per thousand latterly. As medical grounds for termination had diminished, psychiatric grounds, as seen in situations such as Colorado, had become more prominent: he could not "escape the horrible thought that we are somewhat hypocritical as a profession if we clutch at such a straw to meet the problem of abortion on demand". The role of the psychiatrist in recommending therapeutic abortion was being reappraised, MacFarlane said, because the less clearly defined psychiatric problems presented difficult decisions which some psychiatrists did not like being forced to make. He thought that the majority of Canadian gynaecologists would welcome constructive changes in the law governing abortion, so that artificial interruption of pregnancy could become legal when it was deemed that its continuation would be hazardous to mother or child.

In February 1969 R. A. H. Kinch et al.[478] described the findings of a study in Western Ontario in which they had compared 149 white unmarried mothers with 99 married mothers from a similar age group and population. The youngest unmarried mother more often came from a broken home, and this was more likely to have happened before she was 10 years old but there were no other statistically significant differences in socio-psychological background. The results suggested that unmarried women with unwanted pregnancies were not usually emotionally or psychiatrically disturbed; it was thus no longer possible to preserve the comfortable stereotype of low socio-economic status, low mentality and promiscuity for an illegitimate pregnancy, for it had invaded a younger age group in the higher social classes. Kinch et al. went on to describe the operation of a specially staffed pediatric prenatal clinic as an integral but minor part of an adolescent care clinic in a children's hospital. Its overall aim was to help the young person to emerge from the experience with as positive an image of herself as a mother as possible, which, they said, "may mean denying ourselves the right to deny this young woman what may be an essential biologic and emotional need".

In May 1969 C. P. Harrison[479] of Vancouver, assessing the topic of abortion in general, and its relevance to the pregnant teenager in particular, commented that abortion did not "enjoy the guarantee of reasonable medical certainty which comes with widespread medical practice" and stated that neither the salvage of maternal lives nor the reduction of maternal morbidity by abortion had been demonstrated. He thought that "no focus of objective medical reality" for abortion was discernible, and that teenage pregnancy was "the product of social pathology: parental neglect, lack of love, insecurity, poverty, ignorance and violence". "The pregnant teenager", Harrison declared, "is caught by the hypocrisy of a society which condones her promiscuity and condemns her pregnancy. To abort the teenager because of this hypocrisy is not only foolish, it is irrelevant as far as the future welfare of the girl is concerned." By and large, he thought, the pregnant teenager did not want an abortion; the suggestion and the pressure came from parents or boy friends. "Continuation of the pregnancy provides for an irresponsible act a responsible outcome", he stated, "and the care, counselling and affection that the continued pregnancy ensures is of therapeutic value. . . ."

Further disapproval of legal abortion was expressed in a comment in the *Canadian Medical Association Journal* in August 1969 by "A. D. K.", who said that much of the information he had received on the operation of the Abortion Act in Great Britain had been outspokenly critical of the abuses which had attended the legislation since it had become operative.[480] Amongst the phrases he had gleaned were "London, the Abortion Capital of the World, unscrupulous doctors making a killing, nursing homes proclaiming their licenses under the Act, NHS hospitals overcrowded with abortion-determined patients, gynaecologists obliged to spend a disproportionate amount of their time discussing abortions to the neglect of patients with pressing gynaecological problems, the reluctance of the nurses (and) the ethical crisis in the British profession". "A. D. K." said he had encountered the "medico-legal tangle" of the death of the baby aborted in Glasgow (see p. 130). He thought that the death of the child (and presumably the Abortion Act too) was "a nasty business" and he said that he hoped that Canadian legislation and the action of physicians would not confront the Canadian medical profession with such dilemmas.

The New Canadian Law

In August 1969 the Canadian Parliament amended the Criminal Code to make abortion legal if a three-member hospital committee certified that continuance of pregnancy would endanger a woman's life or health.[481] The new law, which was permissive only, did not impose any responsibility on hospitals to provide abortion services or on doctors to perform therapeutic abortions; in effect it merely legalized what had been going on for years in some hospitals which had had "termination committees" that recommended therapeutic abortions when a woman's life was threatened by the continuation of a pregnancy. Membership of these committees, however, had formerly seldom included psychiatrists; after the law was amended psychiatrists were given a role on the new therapeutic abortion committees and, growing more flexible, began to exercise it. A nationwide survey carried out by the Canadian press indicated that an increasing number of therapeutic abortions began to be performed, though Roman Catholic hospitals, doctors and nurses were loath to participate in them.

The new legislation, however, did not work in the way many people had wanted and expected, reported Gerald Waring.[482] It had removed the stigma of illegality from abortions performed for therapeutic purposes, he said, but had not provided a satisfactory service for women requiring terminations of pregnancy, and might even have decreased the availability of such operations by casting the hospitals and their therapeutic abortion committees in an active rather than a passive role. Only 235 authorized therapeutic abortions had been approved in six provinces in 3 months, the inference being that women were either consulting backstreet abortionists or flying to Europe for legal terminations there. Not only the "free abortion" activists were disappointed, but also a proportion of the general population, both men and women, including many liberal reformers who felt the failure of their legislation the more keenly because of the passage of the Abortion Law Reform Bill in New York State. Blame for the situation was apportioned to the government for its lethargy, to hospitals for their failure to provide facilities and to the medical profession for its disinclination to implement the new code.

P. G. Coffey,[483] discussing the problem in January 1970, explained that he was opposed to therapeutic abortion on moral grounds, though he added that from a medical standpoint few indications other than psychiatric ones existed and that psychiatrists disagreed on the benefits and adverse effects of the procedure in individual cases. He did not believe that legal terminations reduced backstreet abortions; rather, the reverse happened. He felt that in caring for a pregnant woman a doctor really had two patients on his hands, even though one was very tiny: it could not be morally right to kill one patient in the hope of improving the lot of the other. Commenting on these views, R. N. Borsch[484] observed that Coffey had dealt with the problem of therapeutic abortion on religious grounds, and that morality encompassed a broader cross-section of life than that considered in Coffey's letter. What of the problem of dealing with an emotionally crippled youngster who was the product of an unwanted pregnancy, Borsch asked, whose mother had unsuccessfully attempted to obtain first a legal and then a criminal abortion? " 'The life' which was mercifully 'saved' is now severely handicapped with little likelihood of ever reaching normality", Borsch observed. "What about the mother who has had to be shackled with a pregnancy which she did not want or, as happens in many cases, is financially unable to support?" he went on. "Her husband (as is usually the case) resents the 'life' and adds further to his wife's rejection of the baby. Also what happens to the increasing number of unadoptable children? These are but a few of the many moral issues."

The opposition to therapeutic abortion expressed by Coffey was echoed by several other physicians. P. B. Walsh[484] pointed out that two of the principal arguments in favour of broadening the abortion laws were that the conceptus at an early stage was not a human being and that the mother and/or father did not want it. Regarding the first, he thought that advances in technology would enable medicine to offer survival to foetuses from the 20th week of gestation onwards, and in regard to the second, he thought that it signified a "flagrantly negligent attitude towards the laws of nature". The real issue, Walsh stated, was "to make the public realize that one reaps what one sows and that any abortion legislation must be limited to contraception education". C. P. Harrison[485] wrote to say that the argument Borsch had advanced in his letter to justify therapeutic abortion was the same that had been used by Hitler's regime to justify its euthanasia programme with the resultant death of 270,000 mental defectives in Germany. It was a retrograde step, Harrison thought, to apply the argument to the uncertain situation of the unborn child. "Surely," he said, "we are not expected to believe that Dr. Borsch's difficulty with the emotionally crippled youngster is sufficient justification for eliminating that youngster?" Hardly surprisingly, Borsch, [485] replying to Harrison's letter, could not follow his reasoning at all. Cezar Heine[485] writing from a Lutheran Theological Seminary, said that he feared that broadening the abortion law might give it the force not only of permissiveness but of command. "This is, of course, a predictable outcome of liberalization", he observed. "Not only are we to be uninhibited about performing abortions, but we are labelled poor citizens if we are inhibited. Will a threat of legal consequences soon be heard as a result of non-compliance? It is clear that the law is supposed to set our standards of living . . . what is permitted by law becomes the code of behaviour. . . ."

It seems clear that the Canadian public had good reason to blame the tardy implementation of their new law on the recalcitrance of some members of the medical profession.

Israel

The law in this country, a residuum of the days of the British Mandate, specifies that abortion is not permissible except to save the prospective mother's life or to preserve her health. A physician who performs an illegal abortion is liable to imprisonment for 14 years, whilst a woman who procures a miscarriage on herself is liable to 7 years of imprisonment. These laws, however, were not enforced by the British, nor have they been applied by the Israelis; in the rare cases where death has resulted from the performance of an abortion by a physician, he has been charged with "medical negligence". As a result of this lenient application of the law and an enlightened medical viewpoint, many reputable Israeli doctors will perform terminations not only on medical grounds but also for such indications as adultery, rape, intercourse between minors, desertion by a father, unmarried status, inadequate income of the potential parents, inadequate housing, inability to educate a child properly, large families, and prostitution. The operation, in government hospitals, must be approved by the medical director and two department heads; in Kupat Holim (sick fund) institutions each case is considered individually by a special committee.

According to Erwin Raban, director of the Tel Hashomer Maternity Government Hospital and president of the Committee for the Study of Maternal Mortality, in cases where the reasons for abortion are not medical, physicians make every attempt to convince the woman not to have an abortion, trying in many instances to arrange medical help, partly because it is governmental policy to encourage large families. Nevertheless, if a woman insists on abortion, this is carried out by a doctor. Currently, Israel has a population of almost 2.8 million people, and during each of the years 1966, 1967, and 1968 there were about 47,000 live births; in the same period there were an estimated 26,000 abortions, 1200 of which were carried out in hospitals and nearly 25,000 of which were performed privately. During the years 1966–8 there was only one death (the result of an air embolism) after an abortion operation, and morbidity amounted to only 0·1 per cent, so that the abortion mortality and morbidity rate in Israel has recently been almost zero, though one-third of all pregnancies have ended in abortion. Nevertheless, Erwin Raban observes, a considerable number of patients with late after-effects are seen; these include incompetence of the internal uterine os, intra-uterine adhesions, and tubal occlusions causing sterility.[486]

Australia

In this country, which has approximately 12.2 million people in its six states and two territories, the annual rate of abortion has been stated to be as high as 115,000,[487] whilst the number of illegal abortions performed yearly has been estimated as approaching 70,000.[488] A survey of public opinion carried out in April 1969 revealed that over 60 per cent of the population considered that abortion should be legalized if the woman's physical or mental health was threatened, if mental or physical deformity was likely in the child, if the pregnancy had resulted from rape or incest, or if the mother was mentally defective or mentally ill.

Despite these statistics, many members of the medical profession in Australia, as in Canada, were reluctant to sanction liberalization of their abortion laws. A London Newsletter published on 20 September 1969 emphasized the abuses which, in the writer's view, had followed the introduction of the British Abortion Act—package deals for foreign clients, advertising of abortion services, expensive clinics where "abortion on demand" was available and varying professional standards (of termination) in separate parts of the United Kingdom.[489] "Abortion might be regarded—resulting as it does from failed contraception—as unintelligent, irresponsible (and) potentially harmful as well as immoral", the writer commented. "An unsatisfactory 'image' of abortion", he thought, "could be augmented by charging a stiff fee for even NHS abortions—related to the applicant's or her husband's earnings—which could be doubled in the event of future request for termination. Advice to these women concerning effective contraception is particularly relevant in the United Kingdom, where surveys have revealed a high rate of conception in unmarried girls who have made no attempt whatever at contraception."

A week later a further Newsletter reviewed the situation regarding induced abortion in Victoria, Australia's second most populous state.[490] There 80 per cent of doctors thought that abortion should be legalized if there was a significant risk of foetal abnormality and almost the same percentage believed that the law should be liberalized, though in a vote taken on 14 July the Victorian Branch of the Australian Medical Association signified that they were opposed to abortion if the grounds were solely that the pregnant woman requested it. The Victorian police had customarily been quick to prosecute medical practitioners who performed abortions, but in a case brought to trial before Mr. Justice Menhennitt in May 1969, the learned judge found the accused physician not guilty and handed down a verdict closely resembling the decision reached in the Bourne case (p. 8) which he had earlier reviewed. His judgement was soon put to the test when Bertram Wainer, a migrant from Great Britain, publicly declared that he had performed three terminations—one in a 22-year-old girl who had threatened suicide; one in a 47-year-old mother of nine; and one in a girl who alleged rape. The police seemed in no hurry to prosecute Wainer, indicating perhaps the beginning of a more liberal attitude towards therapeutic abortion.[488]

On 25 October 1969, the *Medical Journal of Australia* in its Editorial[491] entitled "The Abortion Debate" referred to two articles appearing elsewhere in the same issue—one by R. C. Bretherton[492] in favour of abortion law reform and one by B. A. Smithurst[493] which was opposed to it. Smithurst, like the writer of the London Newsletter[489] and "A. D. K." in Canada[480] reviewed the working of the British Abortion Act in a negative way. The Editorial[491] commented that (i) it was "not the prerogative of the medical profession as such to determine the moral standards of the community or to frame the laws governing these standards" and (ii) that "the community could not fairly impose upon a doctor as a professional duty a course of action that is repugnant to his personal conscience or seriously at variance with his professional judgement—as the procurement of an abortion can be". Nevertheless, the doctor's continuing duty was to help his patient in one way or another, the Editorial stated. Thus "if the patient's health or welfare is seriously threatened he must surely do something about it or give the patient the benefit of a second opinion".

LIBERALIZATION OF THE LAW

On 8 January 1970 South Australia gave a lead to the rest of the nation when its Abortion Reform Bill, which had been debated for a year, became law, thus making abortion legal under certain conditions in 71 hospitals throughout the state. Such abortions, which normally required the approval of two doctors (except in emergency in remote areas), could be granted on two grounds: (i) where continued pregnancy would involve the woman in greater risk of her life or greater danger of physical or mental damage than if the pregnancy was terminated; and (ii) where there was a substantial risk of the child being born with mental or physical handicap.[487]

In February 1970 it was reported that a full-scale state enquiry had been launched in Melbourne to investigate allegations that seven senior policemen from the Victoria Homicide Squad had been engaged in an abortion protection racket involving many thousands of dollars over the past 17 years.[494] The board of inquiry was told that the police had provided cover for the abortionists—medical and otherwise—in the form of non-intervention, by taking no action over complaints received, and in other ways. The outcome of the inquiry, which was front page news in the Melbourne press, was thought likely to lead to liberalization of the law on abortion.

Though other states were slow to follow South Australia's example, awareness of the abortion issue was widely evident. In March 1970, a comment "Illegitimacy and Ignorance"[495] proposed that interested individual doctors conducted tutorials on sex education and contraception to teenagers in afterschool classes. Roger Wurm[496] advocated the same approach, suggesting that education of married couples as well as of teenagers in the 12 to 13, 14 to 16, and 17 to 20 age groups could cut down the need for abortion. These approaches, though eminently worth while, seem unlikely to the present writer to solve the issue, which, the title of Wurm's article implied, was "Abortion: condescension or prevention".

New Zealand

This country has a population of almost 2.8 million, i.e. about the same as that of Israel. The law permits abortion where the life or health of the mother is thought to be endangered by pregnancy, but medical opinion in regard to therapeutic abortion—to judge by an extensively referenced article by H. P. Dunn,[497] a senior Auckland gynaecologist—has remained opposed to the procedure.

In October 1968 Dunn discussed fifty-eight cases of therapeutic abortion performed during the preceding 8 years in the National Women's Hospital, and concluded that it was doubtful whether any incontrovertible medical reasons for the operation existed. He thought that non-medical factors were the probable reason for its increasing incidence and, after surveying the position in other countries, discussed social considerations, criminal abortions, eugenic, medical, and psychiatric indications, eventually advocating an ultra-conservative, not to say reactionary, line in regard to legal terminations. Thus Dunn recommended that the law on abortion should not be liberalized, that if the law was changed a local branch of the Society for the Protection of Unborn Children (see p. 21) should be founded, that therapeutic abortions should be reported on approved forms and discussed at Perinatal

Mortality Conferences, that hospitals where the operations were performed should appoint therapeutic abortion committees constituted from staff appointed by rota who should see the applicant, that one member of the committee should be nominated to speak for the unborn child, that jury rules should be followed (i.e. no action to be taken without a unanimous verdict), that the obstetrician should recognize that he alone was in charge of the case, that the work (of abortion) was of "such seriousness and danger that it should never be passed on to junior staff to perform, even for teaching purposes", and that therapeutic abortions should be notifiable and should be performed only in hospitals (not necessarily public) licensed for this purpose.

In June 1970 it was announced that a Society for the Protection of Unborn Children had been established in New Zealand "to combat the threat of legalized abortion". The president was Professor A. W. Liley and the secretary was H. P. Dunn.[498] It is clear that the liberalization of the abortion laws that had taken place elsewhere in the developed countries of the world was meeting stiff opposition in New Zealand.

Appendix I

The Abortion Act—Form of Notification

IN CONFIDENCE

SCHEDULE 2

ABORTION ACT 1967

NOTIFICATION TO THE CHIEF MEDICAL OFFICER OF AN ABORTION
PERFORMED UNDER SECTION 1 OF THE ACT

I, ...

(Name and qualifications of practitioner in block capitals)

of ....

....

(Full address of practitioner)

hereby give notice that I terminated the pregnancy of

....

(Full name of pregnant woman in block capitals)

of ....

....

(Usual place of residence of pregnant woman in block capitals)

(Ring appropriate number)

The grounds for terminating the pregnancy were certified as—

1. the continuance of the pregnancy would have involved risk to the life of the pregnant woman greater than if the pregnancy were terminated;
2. the continuance of the pregnancy would have involved risk of injury to the physical or mental health of the pregnant woman greater than if the pregnancy were terminated;
3. the continuance of the pregnancy would have involved risk of injury to the physical or mental health of the existing child(ren) of the family of the pregnant woman greater than if the pregnancy were terminated;
4. there was a substantial risk that if the child had been born it would have suffered from such physical or mental abnormalities as to be seriously handicapped.

In case of emergency
The grounds for terminating the pregnancy were—
5. it was necessary to save the life of the pregnant woman; *or*
6. it was necessary to prevent grave permanent injury to the physical or mental health of the pregnant woman.

Place of termination
The pregnancy was terminated at: 1. N.H.S. hospital
                                                        2. Approved place
                                                        3. Other place
(Ring appropriate number)

(address) ....

....

on (date) ....

Signature of practitioner who terminated pregnancy

....

In all non-emergency cases, particulars of the practitioner(s) who joined in giving the certificate required for the purposes of section 1 should be shown below in the appropriate space(s)—

If the operating practitioner joined in giving certificate, insert at A particulars of the other certifying practitioner.	A. Name .... Address.. Qualifications ....
If the operating practitioner did not join in giving certificate, insert at A & B particulars of the two certifying practitioners.	B. Name .... Address.. Qualifications ....

THE ABORTION ACT—FORM OF NOTIFICATION

	For official use only
Other information relating to the termination (Items 1 to 8 to be completed to the best of the knowledge and belief of the operating practitioner):	

1. N.H.S. Number of woman...............
2. Maiden name of woman...............
3. Date of birth of woman...............
4. Marital status of woman:
       1. Single   2. Married   3. Widowed
       4. Divorced or separated   5. Not known
           (Ring appropriate number)
5. Occupation ....
   NOTE: (a) If woman is married, specify husband's occupation ....
          (b) If woman is unmarried, specify her own occupation ....
6. Date of woman's last menstrual period...............
7. Previous pregnancies of woman:
       Number of live births...............
                       stillbirths...............
                       abortions...............
       If applicable, date of last termination of pregnancy under the above-mentioned Act
8. Number of woman's existing children*...............
9. Date of admission to place of termination of pregnancy
10. Date of discharge from place of termination of pregnancy
11. Grounds for termination of pregnancy ....
    (a) Medical condition of woman:
        Obstetric disease (specify)
        Non-obstetric disease (specify)
    (b) Suspected medical condition of foetus (specify)
    (c) Non-medical grounds for termination of pregnancy (specify)

*Children mean a woman's natural children and any adopted, foster or step-children up to the age of 16 years living with her.

APPENDIX I

	For official use only

12. Type of termination of pregnancy:

    1. Dilatation and evacuation

    2. Hysterotomy—abdominal

    3. Hysterotomy—vaginal

    4. Hysterectomy

    5. Vacuum aspiration

    6. Other (specify)..
       (Ring appropriate number)

13. Was sterilization performed?..

14. Complications or death prior to notification:

    1. None

    2. Sepsis

    3. Haemorrhage

    4. Death

    5. Other (specify)..
       (Ring appropriate number)

15. In the case of death, specify cause..

....

....

NOTE: This form is to be completed by the operating practitioner and sent in a sealed envelope within seven days of the termination of the pregnancy to the Chief Medical Officer, Ministry of Health, Alexander Fleming House, Elephant and Castle, London, S.E.1.

Appendix II

Patient's Follow-up Questionnaire

Dear

We are investigating the after-effects of the treatment you received at King's College Hospital. It would help us a great deal if you would answer the questions below and if you would add any comments you consider relevant. Your reply, which will be kept strictly confidential, will be used anonymously for research purposes in conjunction with information provided by other patients with similar problems.

Please place a tick in the appropriate space and comment where relevant.

1. Has the treatment helped you physically?   Yes .... No ....
   If "yes", in what way?
2. Has the treatment had bad physical effects?   Yes .... No ....
   If "yes", what bad effects?
3. Did the treatment help you mentally?   Yes .... No ....
   If "yes", how?
4. Has the treatment had bad mental effects?   Yes .... No ....
   If "yes", what bad effects?
5. Did the treatment help your circumstances?   Yes .... No ....
   If "yes", how?
6. Did the treatment make your circumstances worse? Yes .... No ....
   If "yes", how?
7. In regard to having had the treatment are you:
                    Glad .... Sorry .... Undecided ....
8. Do you reproach yourself for having had the treatment? Yes .... No ....
   If "yes", are your self-reproaches:
                    Slight .... Moderate .... Severe ....
9. Have your attitudes been altered by the treatment?   Yes .... No ....
   If "yes", in what way?
10. What would you have done if you had not had the treatment?
11. Please add any comments you feel are relevant and attach separate sheets if necessary.

Thank you very much for your help.

                                            Yours sincerely,

Appendix III

Illustrative Cases

THE histories of six women whose unwanted pregnancies were terminated on psychiatric grounds and who were followed up by means of the questionnaire shown in Appendix II are now outlined to illustrate the considerations raised in Chapter 6. It will be noted that the questionnaire, which was mailed to the patients a minimum of 6 months after termination, was kept deliberately vague so that no secrets would be betrayed were it to fall into the wrong hands.

CASE I

Miss A., a 23-year-old student, was admitted to hospital after taking an overdose of ergot, progesterone, and oestradiol. She was 8 weeks pregnant and though she said that she had wanted to rid herself of the pregnancy, she was, in fact, so depressed that she did not care whether she lived or died. The 29-year-old single Welsh labourer who had been responsible for her condition had forced himself upon her, she said, against her wishes, and the act of intercourse—her first—had been unaccompanied by contraceptive precautions. He left soon afterwards and Miss A., becoming anxious when she did not menstruate, came to London to get help. She saw six general practitioners who were unsympathetic and refused her a legal termination; eventually she reached a woman doctor who treated her with tablets and injections without any effect on the pregnancy. Prior to admission, Miss A. was living in lodgings by herself and was short of money; she pictured herself as formerly being a quiet, rather aloof person with few friends, who was not gregarious but tended to be suspicious and overparticular; she said she was conscientious in regard to her work, but admitted that she readily became upset and was very lonely.

Miss A.'s father, a gentle, kindly shopkeeper, had latterly developed cardiac symptoms which had caused her to return to England from overseas. Her mother, a chronic migraine sufferer, had always dominated her father's life, and throughout their married life had greatly resented having to live with her husband's parents; 4 years earlier the patient's mother had developed a suicidal depression in which she left home, refusing to return until her mother-in-law left. The situation was eventually resolved by the patient's parents retiring to the Channel Islands. The two eldest siblings, both professional men, were always held up to the patient as examples to emulate, but her younger brother, something of a ne'er-do-well, unbeknown to their parents, was supporting his own 2-year-old illegitimate child. As a little girl Miss A. had felt extremely isolated and she believed that her parents had little love for her. She was shy and apprehensive and did not do very well at school due to truancy and a disinclination to work. Nevertheless, she obtained six O-levels and one A-level, subsequently proceeding to a school for children's nurses. She then found work as a clerk, and began to study at a night school for an external degree, but changed to pottery before transferring to an art college where she stayed for 2 years, leaving when her mother had her breakdown. Subsequently she held various shop jobs before going overseas for 18 months, when she was reasonably happy. Her menarche occurred at the age of 15 but she had few friendships with boys, regarding the physical aspects of sexuality as "horrible". Despite this she desperately wanted to be married and to have babies. She concentrated on "platonic" affairs with married men. At the age of 16 she began to suffer from fainting attacks which were attributed to petit mal; she was put on hydantoin, became quite severely depressed, and took an overdose of aspirin in a suicidal attempt; she saw a psychiatrist on one occasion but did not continue to attend.

A diagnosis of a depressive state with drug overdosage caused by an unwanted pregnancy in an intelligent but insecure girl with a family history of mental illness and a personal history of instability, petit mal, and a suicidal attempt was made. There was no possibility of a relationship with the man responsible for the pregnancy, and its continuation would have made Miss A.'s situation even more difficult. Termination on psychiatric grounds was recommended.

Termination was carried out by vacuum aspiration under general anaesthesia; blood loss was 100 cc. Subsequently Miss A. was put on oral contraceptives which suited her well and on which, 4 months after the operation, she had gained 4 lb in weight. Followed up by questionnaire 8 months after her termination, Miss A. said that the operation had "served as a severe reminder, and has made me a more responsible and understanding person". She went on to explain: "It would have been very difficult for me if I had not had the treatment, as I should have kept my child myself— I believe there are enough unwanted children without me making things worse". She said that she was glad she had had the treatment, and stated that she did not reproach herself. She commented: "My attitudes have altered as an indirect result of the treatment. I have always believed that abortion, providing it is not misused, is a good thing for the times we live in—and since it happened to me I believe in it more strongly." Had she not had the operation, "I would have had the child and looked after it myself—though I would certainly not have married its father." She went on to say: ". . . I feel sure that if abortion was looked upon as an accepted treatment it would cause far fewer suicides—mental breakdowns and permanent mental damage caused by a feeling of guilt—which I found could easily be caused by the attitudes of the doctors that I saw. Also it would put all the backstreet abortionists and do-gooders out of business. I saw a woman who tried to help me with pills—but apparently these could have been permanently damaging. If it could be brought into the open and looked upon as something not to be ashamed of, and made available to any girl, then I am sure that the necessity [for abortion] would decrease. It is rather like not allowing a child to have something he wants—only because he's not allowed it—but if he knows all about it and can look at it and understand, then the desire is not there from the beginning."

CASE II

Miss B., a 26-year-old unmarried art teacher, was referred when approximately 12 weeks pregnant. She had a moderately severe depressive reaction of about 1 month's duration characterized by suicidal ruminations, tearfulness, concern regarding the future, impaired concentration, reduced working efficiency, self-reproach, restlessness, sweating, initial insomnia, broken sleep, lethargy, and anorexia. Her pregnancy had resulted from intercourse without contraceptive precautions with a 30-year-old chance acquaintance at a party, where both had had too much to drink; she had no means of tracing the man, nor did she wish to see him again. She was living alone in an apartment near her work, had few friends, and pictured herself as being customarily an imaginative, readily hurt girl, with a number of obsessional traits. Her interests centred round her work, and she had always been inclined to be moody.

Miss B.'s father had been invalided out of the Army with psychoneurosis, and during the patient's childhood had quarrelled continually with her mother, who herself had had a nervous breakdown and had received electro-shock therapy; the patient's mother had severe migraine, played up her disability as much as possible, and was apprehensive and excitable. As a result the patient, an only child, could never communicate with either parent, and belaboured by the mother a great deal, could never bring friends home. Two maternal aunts, in addition to her mother, had suffered from depressive psychoses. In early life Miss B. was a robust, tomboyish child who was disturbed by a tonsillectomy performed when she was 7. Subsequently she walked in her sleep, bit her nails, and was shy, and very self-conscious in regard to her obesity; she was called "Tubby" all through her schooldays, but passed a scholarship at 11 and later obtained five O-levels at grammar school. She then went on to art college for 3 years and later did a year at a teacher-training college prior to obtaining a post as an art teacher which she had held for 4 years when she became pregnant. Her menarche occurred at the age of 12; later she began to go out with boys and had one steady relationship which lasted for 2½ years. The year prior to her referral she had a serious friendship with a 30-year-old art student, which got on to a sexual footing, but in which adequate contraception was practised; his rejection of the patient 4 months earlier had evoked a depression from which she was suffering when she went to the party at which the act of intercourse which resulted in her pregnancy occurred. She had suffered a head injury at 16 following a fall at netball—she was in hospital for a week and off school for 2 months—and also had had two further minor head injuries prior to her referral. Since these accidents, she said, she had been nervous, irritable, tense, depressed, and lacking in self-confidence.

A diagnosis of a depressive reaction of moderate severity occurring as a result of an unwanted pregnancy in a single girl with a strong family history of mental illness and a personal history of neurotic traits and minor head injuries was made. There was no possibility of a relationship with the man responsible for the pregnancy, and as its continuation would have led to the patient losing her job, and as no support could be expected from her parents, termination on psychiatric grounds was recommended.

Termination was carried out by vacuum aspiration under general anaesthesia; blood loss was minimal. Followed up by questionnaire 7 months after the operation, Miss B. said it had relieved her anxiety and tension. Asked whether the operation had helped her circumstances, she explained, "As I live alone in a bed-sitter it would have been necessary for me to give up my work. I feel that I am the sort of person who would be quite unable to cope with the hardship that this would [have] produce[d]." She said that she was glad she had had the operation, stated that she did not reproach herself for it, and added that her attitudes had not been altered by it. Had she not had it she "would have been compelled to seek unprofessional advice". She commented, "although there are probably many cases where the treatment is not advised and which still result in a happy conclusion, I cannot but feel that there are many cases such as my own where a normal pattern of life would have been impossible had I not had the treatment. It is difficult to say with absolute certainty (such a long period having elapsed since the treatment) what action I may have taken. In retrospect I still feel that I may

ILLUSTRATIVE CASES 283

have been driven to the extremes which (before I learned I would be accepted for treatment) I was seriously considering at that time." Miss B. apologized for her delay in returning the questionnaire, explaining that she had been away. She concluded her letter, "I should like to express my deepest thanks to you again. I am now enjoying a very full and happy life."

CASE III

Mrs. C., a 27-year-old housewife, was referred when 14 weeks advanced in her second pregnancy. She had a moderately severe depressive illness of about 6 weeks' duration characterized by tearfulness, retardation, self-reproach, disinterest, tension, anxiety, and concern regarding the care of her 7-month-old baby; however, she had had no suicidal feelings and her appetite and sleep had been unaffected. The pregnancy had resulted from neglect of contraceptive precautions, though neither the patient nor her husband wanted another child. They were living in a small house with the patient's mother, and before her baby's birth their relationship had been so bad that Mrs. C. had left her husband and returned to her parents' house. Prior to her illness she pictured herself as a good mixer with many interests, such as ballet, swimming, the theatre, and reading. She had some obsessional traits, but had never been inclined to be moody, nor did she smoke or drink very much.

The family history was relevant to her condition. Her father, a 67-year-old accountant, had married late in life and suffered from recurrent depressive episodes which on occasion had necessitated electro-shock therapy. During these episodes his extreme hypochondriasis imposed such severe stresses on his marriage that his wife, who could not stand his illness, frequently threatened to leave him. When Mrs. C. returned to her parents' house to have her baby, her father was once again ill, but both she and her mother thought he was "play-acting" and took little notice of his condition. Soon afterwards he collapsed in the front room and was admitted to hospital where he died 2 weeks later, during the time the patient was in labour, though she was not informed until 2 days after she had had her baby. The patient's 55-year-old mother, an excitable, forceful woman, had suffered from Sydenham's Chorea, but had been close to the patient. Like Mrs. C., she had reproached herself a good deal following her husband's death, understandably so in view of her reaction to his final symptoms, but, unlike Mrs. C., she did not connect her husband's death with the birth of her son. The patient, an only child, was born and brought up in a northern English city, in happy circumstances with adequate affection. There was a strong family history of mental illness, for a paternal uncle was a recurrent depressive and his daughter had epilepsy, whilst a maternal sister, like Mrs. C.'s mother, was said to be unusually nervous. In early life Mrs. C. was extremely shy and wet the bed until she was 12 years old. She attended school as a day girl, going to two elementary schools prior to the age of 11 and then spending 8 years at a grammar school where she passed eight O- and three A-levels. She was generally regarded as "swotty" and was never particularly popular. She went to university on a grant and at the age of 22 obtained a BA in English and French. She then started on an MA but since she could not manage to pay for the course, studied child care for 18 months. Subsequently she took a degree in social studies at another northern university but, following her marriage, did not work. Her menarche began at 14, and a year later she began to go out with boys, eventually meeting her husband at the age of 20. They were engaged on and off for 5 years, both their parents disapproving of the liaison and feeling it was unsuitable; eventually they married suddenly but the relationship was always insecure. The patient's husband, who had had little sexual experience, was impotent for the first 3 months of the marriage, so that her first pregnancy was welcomed as evidence that their sexual functions were normal. Mrs. C. had a difficult pregnancy with stomach ache and sickness, and latterly became so upset and miserable that she returned to her parents' home. She said that her labour had been "awful" and she described 4 days in a maternity home followed by a painful forceps delivery and the subsequent news of her father's death.

A diagnosis of a depressive illness of moderate severity occurring as a result of an unwanted pregnancy in a highly educated housewife with a strong family history of mental illness and a personal history of neurotic traits was made. In view of her marital status and the lateness of her pregnancy, both the gynaecologist and the psychiatrist tried to persuade her to accept it, promising both gynaecological and psychiatric support. Mrs. C., however, remained adamant that she did not want the pregnancy to continue and she made it clear that she greatly feared another labour, having apparently connected her first labour with her father's death. In view of her depressive state, and the factors in her background, a decision was made to terminate the pregnancy on psychiatric grounds.

Termination was carried out by vaginal hysterotomy. At operation the uterus was anteverted and about 15 weeks in size. The cervix was dilated and the membranes ruptured, showing dark brown liquor. The cervix was dilated to 12 Hegar and the bladder was dissected up and the cervix was divided up to the internal os anteriorly. The uterine contents were evacuated and the patient was given a 2-pint blood transfusion to compensate for a moderately severe blood loss at one stage amounting to about 800 cc. Convalescence was uneventful. Followed up by questionnaire 9 months after the operation Mrs. C. said the treatment had helped her physically and had left no adverse physical effects. She felt it had helped her mentally and said: "I felt it to be absolutely necessary at the time and having the operation was a great load off my mind." She said the treatment had had no bad mental effects. She did not feel it had helped her circumstances or made them in any way worse. She said she was undecided in regard to having had the termination and explained that she reproached herself to a moderate extent over having had it. She said that her attitudes had been altered by the treatment and remarked: "To some extent, I feel that if I were facing the same problem now, I would decide against the operation but I did feel it was the only thing to do at the time." Had she not had the treatment she would "probably have tried my own methods of 'treatment' at home, since I was feeling extremely depressed by my pregnancy at the time". She added: "I feel the offer of an operation if I wished it was of great help, since I did not feel, after receiving the offer, that there was no way out of the situation. It also made me think more deeply about what I would do if I decided *not* to have the operation since being offered some alternative, or help, I felt able to consider the problem less frantically. Having had one abortion, I do not ever feel inclined to undergo another—not because I felt unpleasant mental or physical after-effects from the operation, but because the whole thing seemed to be the easy way out and the wrong decision morally."

CASE IV

Mrs. D., an unusually attractive 29-year-old cashier, separated from her husband, was referred when 26 weeks advanced in her fourth pregnancy. She had a moderately severe depressive illness of 4 months' duration characterized by depression, reduced working efficiency, suicidal ruminations, tension, anxiety, irritability, palpitations, tremors, insomnia, anorexia, and loss of weight. The pregnancy had resulted from intercourse with a 25-year-old labourer, coitus interruptus being the only contraceptive technique employed; the labourer would have nothing to do with the patient subsequently, and as she feared that her condition would interfere with her plans to divorce her husband on cruelty, she had repeatedly attempted to abort herself with douches, ergot, and other drugs. At the time of her referral she was living with her twin sister in the latter's house, together with the sister's 60-year-old paranoid schizophrenic husband, two of her own children, aged 5 and 1, and her second child, aged 4, who had been adopted by her sister. Mrs. D. had little contact with her parents, and described herself as normally being a sensitive, anxious, irritable, easily upset, emotional, and readily hurt individual; she had few friends or outside interests and had always been markedly moody; she smoked forty or more cigarettes daily but did not drink alcohol.

Mrs. D.'s father, a representative, though kind and affectionate, was away through much of her childhood. She was closer to her mother, from whom she had latterly become estranged following having her second child adopted. The patient and her twin sister, of whom she was jealous as a child, were born in Calcutta by Caesarean section, and they spent much of their childhood going to and fro between India and London, accompanied by their mother. Though neither of Mrs. D.'s parents had ever been ill, and though the father's side of her family was quite clear, there was a marked history of mental abnormality in the mother's family, for the patient's maternal grandmother had suffered from recurrent depression, had several times attempted suicide, and was in a mental hospital. The patient's maternal grandmother's sister was said to have been "as mad as a hatter", and the patient's maternal uncle had been in a general hospital following a suicidal attempt. In early life Mrs. D. had multiple neurotic traits—phobias of darkness and thunderstorms, fears of death, nightmares, somnambulism, stammering, nail biting, shyness, and excessive self-consciousness. She attended a private school in southern England between the ages of 5 and 9, and then spent a year in a convent in India. At the age of 10 she returned to England where she again attended a convent; she was naughty and played truant a great deal. Leaving at the age of 16 after an undistinguished career, Mrs. D. went on to technical school to learn at her mother's suggestion to become a nurse. She detested this and quickly gave it up, working between the ages of 18 and 23 in an office. Her menarche occurred at the age of 14 and she soon began to form friendships with boys. At 23, in defiance of her mother's wishes, Mrs. D. married a 26-year-old ex-public-school sales representative who was attractive initially but turned out to be badly in debt and helped himself to her savings. Unhappy with her husband, Mrs. D. took a lover by whom she became pregnant. Her husband then started to maltreat her, so after a year of marriage she left him. Later she became pregnant for the second time—again not by her husband— and though her mother supported her through this situation, she disapproved of the patient giving the child to her sister to bring up. Subsequently Mrs. D. rejoined her husband for 15 months, but they could not get on at all together; she then had a third child by another man. Mrs. D. attempted suicide with an overdose of aspirins 1 month after leaving her husband for the first time when she was in a very depressed state; she then received outpatient psychiatric treatment for a year. After rejoining her husband she again became depressed and an attempt was made, which fell through, to admit her to hospital for electro-shock therapy.

A diagnosis of a severe depressive illness provoked by an unwanted pregnancy in an intelligent but extremely unstable, separated married woman with a marked family history of mental illness was made. No relationship existed with the man responsible for her pregnancy—her fourth—and emotional support was limited to her twin sister, herself married to an elderly schizophrenic, and earlier much envied by the patient for her popularity with their parents. Termination of pregnancy was recommended on psychiatric grounds, but whilst sterilization was considered it was rejected in view of the patient's age.

Termination was carried out by hysterotomy through a low vertical incision under general anaesthesia; convalescence was uneventful. Seen psychiatrically 2 months later, Mrs. D. was more cheerful but said that she felt guilty and was suffering from the strain of keeping her condition from her mother and twin sister; she continued to complain of insomnia and tension for which she was given diazepam. Seen again 3 weeks later she was irritable and depressed; she said her twin sister was suffering from "intractable migraine" and was due shortly to enter a mental hospital, so that she [the patient] had had to stay away from work looking after the children. She was having an affair with a "rotter" who resided in an adjacent house—a divorced man who, impotent, had been deserted by the woman with whom he was living. Finally, the patient was angry with her 25-year-old girl friend for her stupidity in being in love with a married man whose wife would not divorce him. It seemed to the interviewer that the patient was well on the way to getting into further entanglements. Followed up by questionnaire 26 months after the operation, Mrs. D. said it had not helped her physically or had bad physical effects. However, it had helped mentally, she thought, by reducing her depression and relieving her of her fear of her family finding out about the pregnancy. It had had no adverse mental effects, she stated, and had helped her circumstances because it had prevented further demands on her crowded living space and had enabled her to get divorced and to continue to work full time to maintain her children (which her husband was failing to do). She said she was undecided regarding having had the treatment but "only so far as conscience is concerned". She reproached herself to a "slight" extent for having had the operation, and she wished that termination had been performed during the early stages of her pregnancy. To the question, What would you have done if you had not had the treatment? she responded: "I cannot imagine. With two children already—a complete failure of a marriage, bad financial problems, a 17–18 hour day, no house or security for my children and with a previous record of a breakdown, I expect I would have gone mental or something [electrical treatment had been recommended once before for depression]." She added: "I think this sort of treatment should be done early; I don't actually regret it, but I do have a bit of conscience and had a tremendous battle inwardly before the treatment. I had tried other things myself before the 3-month stage, and after that feared any damage I could have caused. The terrible part was feeling movement inside—knowing that one was responsible for destroying it. I would NOT have the treatment again if it were OVER the 3-month stage. ALSO if my private life had been secure and financial state secure I would not have had it done as I think the world of my children and would have liked a larger family."

CASE V

Mrs. E., a 32-year-old divorced West Indian housewife, was referred when 8 weeks advanced in her fifth pregnancy. She had a moderately severe depressive illness characterized by tearfulness, self-reproach, inability to work, social withdrawal, anxiety, irritability, suicidal ruminations, headaches, trembling attacks, insomnia, anorexia, and loss of weight. Her pregnancy had resulted from intercourse with an acquaintance, an anxious, unstable West Indian, who had himself had psychiatric treatment; she had not taken contraceptive precautions, she said, because she had been on oral contraceptives prior to the sexual liaison which led to her pregnancy and had just stopped taking the pill on her general practitioner's advice. At the time of her referral she was living in two rooms and a kitchen with her three children, aged 8, 7, and

6, and was working part-time as a cleaner. Prior to her illness she had evidently been a sensitive, rather dependent individual with few interests, friendships, or hobbies; she had always readily become upset and had been inclined to moodiness.

Mrs. E.'s father had left his native Barbados and had come to England, though the patient was not in touch with him and knew nothing of his whereabouts; her mother, who had run their small farm at home, had died in childbirth when the patient was 18, and had been greatly missed by her. As the second eldest of seven siblings and the eldest girl, Mrs. E. was early given the responsibility of looking after her younger brothers and sisters. She had a limited schooling, and after spending some years in her parents' home, came to England at the age of 22 to marry her husband, a West Indian bus conductor. Her first pregnancy, which occurred when she was 23, was difficult and she became depressed and fearful of dying like her mother in childbirth. Because of her depression, the marital disharmony which had started during her pregnancy became more severe after the birth of her child. She refused to go out or to interest herself in social activities and could not do her household tasks. Her second pregnancy was also difficult, and when this baby was 9 months old, Mrs. E. left her husband. The following year she had a third (illegitimate) child, and a year later, when Mrs. E. was aged 27, at her husband's suggestion she sent all three children back to Barbados to be cared for by his mother. She became very depressed at this time and was given antidepressant drugs by her general practitioner. Three years later, when aged 30, Mrs. E. again became depressed and was admitted to a psychiatric hospital whence she was transferred to a general hospital for a fourth (also illegitimate) pregnancy to be terminated. Despite her request, sterilization was refused at this time because of her age. Subsequently she arranged for her children to be sent back to England at her brother's expense, but she rapidly became disappointed and angry because, as a reaction to their long separation from her, they were hostile and difficult to control. Mrs. E.'s second child, who was considered to be backward, was referred to a children's psychiatric department 6 months before her referral for her (current) termination, and because of the patient's difficulties the psychiatric social worker (PSW) had continued to see her at regular intervals. The PSW regarded Mrs. E. as a dependent, insecure, anxious woman who functioned in a very limited way and was doing well to hold down a job; the PSW remarked: "Mrs. E. is anxious for termination and sterilization. She realizes that this is the doctor's decision, but I feel her request should be considered on the grounds that she is likely to break down, and she is unlikely to be able to care adequately for another child, and that the effect of this on the three children, who are already deprived to some extent, will be deleterious."

A diagnosis of a moderately severe depressive reaction produced by an unwanted fifth pregnancy in an insecure dependent woman with a personal history of a broken marriage and past psychiatric illness was made, and in view of the circumstances of the pregnancy, the existence of previous mental illness and the patient's strongly expressed wishes, termination of the pregnancy and sterilization on psychiatric grounds was recommended.

Termination was carried out under general anaesthesia, ovum forceps being introduced vaginally and soft curettage being performed. Sterilization was also carried out through a Pfannensteil incision, the ovarian tubes being crushed and ligated. Convalescence was uneventful. Seen by the PSW 3 weeks after the operation, Mrs. E. appeared brighter and less depressed. She had been somewhat alarmed by her discharge from hospital only 7 days after the operation, but she was relieved to have had it performed and she subsequently leaned on the PSW a good deal. Followed up by questionnaire 26 months after the operation, Mrs. E. said that treatment had not helped her physically and had had some mild adverse physical effects. She said: "I do get some pains in the lower part of my back after standing for a length of time, but the treatment is worth the pain." Asked if the treatment had helped her mentally she said: "Yes. I do not live in fear any longer; this is a very large fear; I do not have to live on drugs of any kind to calm me down or to make me sleep. I do not go to the doctor for my nerves any more. I am cured thanks to you all." Mrs. E. said the treatment had had no bad mental effects and she went on to explain that it had helped her circumstances. She said: "I am now planning to remarry again; without this treatment I do not think this would ever have happened, because I have already had three children, and there are very few men who really want to remarry a woman who is still making children after the first marriage had failed." She denied that the treatment had made her circumstances worse in any way whatsoever. In regard to having had the treatment she said: "I could not have been more pleased; to me this is half of the football pools jackpot. I am more than glad." She said that she never reproached herself for having had the treatment and stated that her attitudes had been altered by it. "Nothing gets me down, I can cope with the children better. Before the treatment if the children did anything wrong instead of talking to them I would cane them; not any more. And we all get on better together now than in the past. The children no longer want to run away from me." Had she not had the treatment she said: "If I had not had this treatment I might not have been alive, and if I did I might be in a mental home or hospital by now as I know I was heading for some kind of disaster." She added: "I only hope that many other women would not be made to suffer as long as I had to. Before this treatment I hated every doctor, I hated men because of what I thought they were doing to me, trying to make me have as many unwanted children as possible without trying to help me. Also, if anyone had done this for me in 1959–60 I would have saved my marriage then. Please try to help young wives in future suffering from the things I suffer from most, and I am sure you will also save lots of marriages; all of us cannot say what is worrying us but we all carry it inside of us, and sickness from the inside because of worry is hard to cure. I hope my answers do not worry you, also that you will be able to help someone else from what you have learnt through my report. Now I would like to say many, many thanks to all those who took part in my treatment."

CASE VI

Mrs. F., a 41-year-old housewife, was referred when approximately 10 weeks advanced in her fourth pregnancy. She had a moderately severe depressive illness characterized by anxiety, depression, concern regarding her husband and children, tearfulness, neglect of her housework, impoverished concentration, and feelings of tension. She was unable to enjoy things, reproached herself for her irritability and neglect of the house, and felt that were it not for her children she would rather have been dead. She was also troubled by sweating, trembling, restlessness, insomnia, lack of energy, anorexia, and loss of 14 lb in weight. The pregnancy had resulted from neglect of contraceptive precautions on a day when she had expected her period would start. Mrs. F.'s husband, 3 years her senior, had worked as a mail-van driver for the last few months, but was employed on night shift and had to do a great deal of overtime to make enough money to support the family. The patient and her husband were living in a two-bedroomed flat two flights above a shop, and their accommodation was unsatisfactory for it was damp and the floor-boards were rotten and there was no hot water. The eldest child, a daughter of 18, was working as a shorthand-typist, whilst two boys, aged 15 and 19, were at school; a third 4-year-old boy was also at school. When well, Mrs. F. pictured herself as being of a cheerful, happy disposition, interested in her home and her family. She was not, she said, normally apt to get swings of mood, and was a non-drinker and a very moderate smoker.

As the youngest of five children the patient was somewhat spoiled, and, it seems, may have been begotten to replace an elder sister who died of meningitis at the age of $3\frac{1}{2}$. There was no family or personal history of mental illness, and her background was uneventful. She was a shy little girl who blushed easily but did adequately at school which she left at 14. At this time the family were bombed out and were evacuated to Wales for 3 years where the patient learned hairdressing and spent some time as a nursing assistant. When she was 17 her mother died; after this, Mrs. F. looked after her father and her sister's children prior to her marriage at the age of 23. The marriage was happy but there were many financial vicissitudes, for her husband changed his original occupation as a cinema manager and tried a venture in hire purchase which left him heavily in debt. During the 9 or 10 years that he was in this firm, the worry provoked psoriasis in Mrs. F. but she later became free of the condition. Four years prior to her referral her husband left his business and joined a transport company as a bus driver, but after driving for 3 years transferred to another firm in order to make more money from overtime. Latterly he had been troubled by abdominal pains which had been attributed to gallstones and was awaiting surgical treatment in hospital for this, but he had been unable to spare time off work to enter hospital due to his heavy financial commitments.

A diagnosis of a moderately severe depressive reaction produced by an unwanted fifth pregnancy in an anxious, intelligent woman concerned regarding her sick husband, her three younger children, and her unsatisfactory housing conditions was made. The patient's husband at a separate interview confirmed her story, and added that he was extremely worried regarding his wife's condition and the adverse effect that he felt continuation of her pregnancy would have. In view of the situation, termination of pregnancy and sterilization on psychiatric grounds was recommended.

Vaginal termination was carried out under general anaesthesia, a first degree uterogenital prolapse with a deficient perineum and a retrocele being repaired. In addition, a small cervical polyp was removed. Sterilization was carried out abdominally, the tubes being cut and doubly ligated. Convalescence was uneventful. Followed up by questionnaire 18 months after her treatment, Mrs. F. said the treatment had not helped her physically or had had any adverse physical effects. She said it had helped her mentally by relieving her tension but had had no bad mental effects. She felt it had had no effect on her circumstances but had not made them worse. She stated that she was glad she had had the treatment and said she did not reproach herself for having had it. Her attitudes had been altered, she said, by relieving anxiety. Had she not had the treatment she felt she would "probably have had a nervous and mental breakdown". She added: "The treatment I had came as a Godsend to me, having already four children to bring up in bad housing conditions and on a limited income."

References

1. FERRIS, P., *The Nameless*, Harmondsworth, Penguin, 1967.
2. *Abortion in Britain*, Proceedings of a Conference held by the Family Planning Association at the University of London Union on 22 April, 1966, London, Pitman Medical, 1966.
3. DAVIS, A., 2,665 cases of abortion, a clinical survey, *Brit. Med. J.* 2 : 123–30 (1950).
4. BATEMAN, D., Cases of abortion treated at the Lambeth Hospital 1960–67, *J. Obstet. Gynaec. Brit. Commonw.* 75 : 1169–72 (1968).
5. TARNESBY, H. P., *Abortion Explained*, London, Sphere, 1969.
6. Methods and dangers of termination of pregnancy, *Proc. Roy. Soc. Med.* 62 : 827–34 (1969).
7. (Leading article), Maternal deaths, *Brit. Med. J.* 1 : 332 (1969).
8. Report by the Council of the Royal College of Obstetricians and Gynaecologists, Legalized abortion, *Brit. Med. J.* 1 : 850–4 (1966).
9. Report by BMA Special Committee, Therapeutic abortion, *Brit. Med. J.* 2 : 40-4 (1966).
10. RODGER, T. F., Attitudes toward abortion, *Amer. J. Psychiat.* 125 : 116–20 (1968).
11. Royal Medico-Psychological Association's Memorandum on Therapeutic Abortion, *Brit. J. Psychiat.* 112 : 1071–3 (1966).
12. ROBINSON, K., The law relating to abortion, *Proc. Roy. Soc. Med.* 55 : 373–4 (1962).
13. ZALBA, M., The Catholic Church's viewpoint on abortion, *World Med. J.* 13 : 88–92 (1966).
14. CHURCH ASSEMBLY BOARD, *Abortion: An Ethical Discussion*, London, Church Information Office, 1965.
15. WILLIAMS, G. L., The law relating to abortion, *Proc. Roy. Soc. Med.* 55 : 374–5 (1962).
16. SIMMS, M., (Letter) The abortion bill, *Lancet* 2 : 384 (1967).
17. SIMMS, M., (Letter) Sequels of unwanted pregnancy, *Lancet* 2 : 731 (1968).
18. EDELSTEIN, L., The Hippocratic oath, text, translation and interpretation, *Bull. Hist. Med.* 1 (sup.) (1943).
19. MORRIS, N., The law relating to abortion, *Proc. Roy. Soc. Med.* 55 : 375–6 (1962).
20. DAVIS, A., (Letter) 2,665 cases of abortion, *Brit. Med. J.* 2 : 1172–3 (1950).
21. CHESSER, E., (Letter) The case for abortion, *Brit. Med. J.* 2 : 626–7 (1950).
22. WHITE, R. B., Induced abortions—a survery of their psychiatric implications, complications and indications, *Texas. Rep. Biol. Med.* 24 : 531–58 (1966).
23. DE SOLDENHOFF, R., (Letter) Abortion law reform, *Brit. Med. J.* 1 : 1168 (1966).
24. SOCIETY FOR THE PROTECTION OF UNBORN CHILDREN, *Brit. Med. J.* 1 : 294 (1967).
25. MCLAREN, H. C., (Letter) The Abortion Bill, *Lancet* 1 : 565–6 (1967).
26. MCLAREN, H. C., (Letter) Sequels of unwanted pregnancy, *Lancet* 2 : 632 (1968).
27. MCLAREN, H. C., (Letter) Therapeutic abortion, *Lancet* 1 : 1032 (1968).

28. DEACON, A. L., (Letter) Sequels of unwanted pregnancy, *Lancet* **2** : 730 (1968).
29. THOMAS, J. M., (Letter) Termination of Pregnancy Bill, *Brit. Med. J.* **1** : 502 (1967).
30. BAIRD, D., Sterilisation and therapeutic abortion in Aberdeen, *Brit. J. Psychiat.* **113** : 703–9 (1967).
31. THOMPSON, B., and BAIRD, D., Follow-up of 186 sterilised women, *Lancet* **1** : 1023–7 (1968).
32. ACKNER, B., The law relating to abortion, *Proc. Roy. Soc. Med.* **55** : 376 (1962).
33. FRANKLIN, A. W., Leontine Young and *Tess of the d'Urbervilles*—some thoughts on illegitimacy, *Brit. Med. J.* **1** : 789–91 (1966).
34. SIM, M., Abortion and the psychiatrist, *Brit. Med. J.* **2** : 145–8 (1963).
35. ARKLE, J., Termination of pregnancy on psychiatric grounds, *Brit. Med. J.* **1** : 558–60 (1957).
36. STAFFORD-CLARKE, D., *Psychiatry for Students*, 3rd edn., London, Allen & Unwin, 1967.
37. HEMPHILL, R. E., The Abortion Bill, *Lancet* **1** : 324–6 (1967).
38. TYLDEN, E., Abortion law reform, *Brit. J. Psychiat.* **113** : 4–6 (supp.) (1967).
39. TREDGOLD, R. F., Psychiatric indications for termination of pregnancy, *Lancet* **2** : 1251–4 (1964).
40. ANDERSON, E. W., Psychiatric indications for the termination of pregnancy, *World Med. J.* **13** : 81–3 (1966).
41. HALDANE, F. P., (Letter) Sequels of unwanted pregnancy, *Lancet* **2** : 678–9 (1968).
42. HOWELLS, J. G., (Letter) Legalizing abortion, *Lancet* **1** : 728 (1967).
43. POND, D. A., No questions asked . . . ?, 1 *Lancet* **1** : 611–13 (1967).
44. JOYSTON-BECHAL, M. P., The problem of pregnancy termination on psychiatric grounds, *J. Coll. Gen. Practit.* **12** : 304–12 (1966).
45. CLARK, M., FORSTNER, I., POND, D. A., and TREDGOLD, R. F., Sequels of unwanted pregnancy, *Lancet* **2** : 501–7 (1968).
46. SIM, M., (Letter) Abortion and conscience, *Brit. Med. J.* **2** : 297 (1967).
47. SANDERSON, A., (Letter) Abortion and conscience, *Brit. Med. J.* **2** : 621 (1967).
48. (Leading article) Ethics and abortion, *Brit. Med. J.* **2** : 3 (1968).
49. SLATER, E., (Letter) Ethics and abortion, *Brit. Med. J.* **2** : 242–3 (1968).
50. ODLUM, D., (Letter) Ethics and abortion, *Brit. Med. J.* **2** : 243 (1968).
51. HOWELLS, J. G., The woman and extended birth control, *Brit. J. Psychiat.* **113** : 6–9 (supp.) (1967).
52. FISHER, E., (Letter) Legalizing abortion, *Lancet* **2** : 1077 (1966).
53. LEYS, D., (Letter) Legalizing abortion, *Lancet* **2** : 384–5 (1967).
54. Abortion law reform, *Brit. Med. J.* **2** : 1512–14 (1966).
55. Indications for termination of pregnancy, *Brit. Med. J.* **1** : 171–5 (1968).
56. (Leading article) Clinical indications for termination of pregnancy, *Brit. Med. J.* **1** : 133–4 (1968).
57. PRINCE, G. S., *Teenagers Today*, London, British Medical Association, 1968.
58. AYER, A. J., Rebels and morals. Part Four: The revolt of the young, *Evening Standard*, 26 September 1968.
59. GALDSTON, I., What troubles troubled youth?, *Lancet* **2** : 1179–82 (1969).
60. SCHOFIELD, M., *The Sexual Behaviour of Young People*, Harmondsworth, Penguin, 1968.
61. KIND, R. W., Young opinions, *Family Planning* **18** : 121–4 (1969).
62. SIMMS, M., Pregnancy advisory service, *Family Planning* **18** : 132–4 (1969).

63. (Leading article) Sexual promiscuity among students, *Brit. Med. J.* **1** : 711–12 (1967).
64. Kensington has highest illegitimacy, *Daily Telegraph*, 3 May 1969.
65. REGISTRAR-GENERAL, *Statistical Review of England and Wales for 1967, Part II, Population Tables*, London, HMSO, 1969.
66. BAIRD, D., Fertility control, *Brit. J. Hosp. Med.* **2** : 597–602 (1969).
67. RUSSELL, J. K., Pregnancy in the young teenager, *Lancet* **1** : 365–6 (1969).
68. (Leading article) Pregnancy in the young teenager, *Lancet* **1** : 353 (1969).
69. CHIEF MEDICAL OFFICER OF THE MINISTRY OF HEALTH, *On the State of the Public Health*, London, HMSO, 1968.
70. CATTERALL, R. D., The problem of gonorrhoea, *Brit. J. Hosp. Med.* **3** : 45–62 (1970).
71. BROGAN, D. J., Papal ban on contraception: "issue not settled", *Medical Tribune*, 3 October 1968.
72. "Rhythm" warning on birth control, *Evening Standard*, 8 April 1969.
73. Fox, T., The multiplication of man or Noah's new flood, *Lancet* **2** : 1238–44 (1966).
74. Family planning is basic human right, conference agrees, *International Planned Parenthood News*, No. 173, July 1968.
75. LOUDON, J., The importance of training for the family planning services, *Family Planning* **18** : 111–15 (1969).
76. PEEL, J., and POTTS, M., *Textbook of Contraceptive Practice*, Cambridge, Cambridge University Press, 1969.
77. Student contraceptive teaching inadequate, *Medical Tribune*, 14 March 1968.
78. DRAPER, E., *Birth Control in the Modern World*, London, Penguin, 1965.
79. (Annotation) The Family Planning Act, *Lancet* **2** : 34–5 (1968).
80. MACQUEEN, I. A. G., An integrated local authority family planning service, *Family Planning* **18** : 31–5 (1969).
81. PEBERDY, M., Family Planning as social medicine, *Lancet* **1** : 1363–5 (1968).
82. TOBERT, A., (Letter) Planned family planning, *Brit. Med. J.* **2** : 430 (1968).
83. STEELE, S. J., Family planning advice after abortion, *Lancet* **2** : 742–3 (1966).
84. PEEL, J., and BRUDENELL, J. M., *A Textbook of Gynaecology*, London, Heinemann, 1969.
85. (Leading article) Oral contraception and depression, *Brit. Med. J.* **2** : 380–1 (1969).
86. VESSEY, M. P., and DOLL, R., Investigation of relation between use of oral contraceptives and thromboembolic disease: a further report, *Brit. Med. J.* **2** : 651–8 (1969).
87. MELAMED, M. R., KOSS, L. G., FLEHINGER, B. J., KELISKY, R. P., and DUBROW, H., Prevalence rates of uterine carcinoma *in situ* for women using the diaphragm or contraceptive oral steroids, *Brit. Med. J.* **2** : 195–200 (1969).
88. SINGER, A., SHEARMAN, R. P., and SCOTT, G. C., (Letter) Contraceptives and cervical carcinoma, *Brit. Med. J.* **3** : 108 (1969).
89. FRAMPTON, J., and MATHEWS, D., Intrauterine contraceptive devices, *British Med. J.* **2** : 683–7 (1967).
90. WALTERS, D., (Letter) Complications with IUDs, *Brit. Med. J.* **2** : 692–3 (1969)
91. BLACKER, C. P., and JACKSON, L. N., Voluntary sterilisation for family welfare, *Lancet* **1** : 971–4 (1966).
92. £750 for women sterilised without consent, *Evening Standard*, 30 April 1969.

93. BLACKER, C. P., and PEEL, J. M., Sterilisation of women, *Brit. Med. J.* **1** : 566·7 (1969).
94. WILLIAMS, G. F. J., Tubo-ovarian implantation, *Lancet* **1** : 825–7 (1969).
95. (Leading article) Voluntary sterilisation in the male, *Brit. Med. J.* **3** : 508 (1968).
96. (Annotation) Vasectomy and after, *Lancet* **1** : 1300 (1968).
97. HANLEY, H. G., Vasectomy for voluntary male sterilisation, *Lancet* **2** : 207–9 (1968).
98. ALDERMAN, P., (Letter) Vasectomy for voluntary male sterilisation, *Lancet* **2** : 1137 (1968).
99. HICKINBOTHAM, P., (Letter) Vasectomy for voluntary male sterilisation, *Lancet* **2** : 1191 (1968).
100. The first his and hers contraceptive, *World Medicine*, 25 November 1969.
101. New style contraceptive: hormonal ring, *World Medicine*, 29 July 1969.
102. HELPER, M. M., COHEN, R. L., BEITENMAN, E. T., and EATON, L. F., Life-events and acceptance of pregnancy, *J. Psychosom. Res.* **12** : 183–8 (1968).
103. BURKE, M. F., (Letter) Suicide in pregnancy, *Brit. Med. J.* **2** : 49 (1968).
104. WHITLOCK, F. A., and EDWARDS, J. E., Pregnancy and attempted suicide, *Comprehen. Psychiat.* **9** : 1–13 (1968).
105. My abortion, *Hospital Medicine*, **2** : 70–3 (1967).
106. Information from National Council for the Unmarried Mother and her Child, May 1969.
107. SLAUGHTER, J., The plight of the single mother, *Observer*, 8 December 1968.
108. (Annotation) Fatherless families, *Lancet* **2** : 631–2 (1965).
109. (Annotation) Minding and fostering, *Lancet* **2** : 32–3 (1967).
110. AREN, P., and AMARK, C., The prognosis in cases in which legal abortion has been granted but not carried out, *Acta psychiat. neurol. scand.* **36** : 203–78 (1961).
111. HOOK, K., Refused abortion: a follow-up study of 249 women whose applications were refused by the National Board of Health in Sweden, *Acta. psychiat. neurol. scand.*, supp., **168** (1963).
112. PARE, C. M. B., A follow-up study of patients referred for termination of pregnancy on psychiatric grounds, *Brit. J. Psychiat.* **113** : 3–4 (supp.) (1967).
113. BOWLBY, J., *Child Care and the Growth of Love*, Harmondsworth, Penguin, 1965.
114. NORMAN, F., *Banana Boy*, London, Secker & Warburg, 1969.
115. MCGREGOR, W. R., Social aspects of family planning, *Family Planning* **18** : 118–21 (1969).
116. Children in care, *Lancet* **1** : 537 (1969).
117. PACKMAN, J., *Child Care: Needs and Number*, London, Allen & Unwin, 1969.
118. Adoption: social aspects that may concern the doctor, *Drug. Therap. Bull.* **7**: 29–31 (1969).
119. (Annotation) The need for more foster parents, *Lancet* **1** : 367 (1965).
120. FORSMANN, H., and THUWE, I., One hundred and twenty children born after application for therapeutic abortion was refused: their mental health, social adjustment and educational level up to the age of 21, *Acta. psychiat. neurol. scand.* **42** : 71–88 (1966).
121. (Annotation) Boys before the courts, *Lancet* **1** : 1085 (1969).
122. Instant crime and illegitimacy link, *Sunday Telegraph*, 26 January 1969.
123. SIMON, N. M., and SENTURIA, A. G., Psychiatric sequelae of abortion, *Arch. Gen. Psychiat.* **15** : 378–89 (1966).
124. KAY, D. W. K., and SCHAPIRA, K., (Letter) Psychiatric sequelae of termination of pregnancy, *Brit. Med. J.* **1** : 299 (1967).

125. ECKBLAD, M., Induced abortion on psychiatric grounds, *Acta psychiat. neurol. scand.*, supp., **99** (1955).
126. KUMMER, J. M., Post-abortion psychiatric illness—a myth?, *Amer. J. Psychiat.* **119** : 980–3 (1963).
127. PECK, A., and MARCUS, H., Psychiatric sequelae of therapeutic interruption of pregnancy, *J. Nerv. Ment. Dis.* **143** : 417–25 (1966).
128. NISWANDER, K. R., and PATTERSON, R. J., Psychologic reaction to therapeutic termination, *Obstet. Gynaecol.* **29** : 702–6 (1967).
129. SIMON, N. M., SENTURIA, A. G., and ROTHMAN, D., Psychiatric illness following therapeutic abortion, *Amer. J. Psychiat.* **124** : 97–103 (1967).
130. SORREL, W. E., Abortion—its psychodynamic effects, *Psychosomatics* **8** : 146–9 (1967).
131. PATT, S. L., RAPPAPORT, R. G., and BARGLOW, P., Follow-up of therapeutic abortion, *Arch. Gen. Psychiat.* **20** : 408–14 (1969).
132. McCOY, D. R., The emotional reaction of women to therapeutic abortion and sterilization, *J. Obstet. Gynaec. Brit. Commonw.* **75** : 1054–7 (1968).
133. MEHLAND, K. H., Combating illegal abortion in the socialist countries of Europe, *World Med. J.* **13** : 84–7 (1966).
134. Czech abortion laws cuts out back streets, *Medical Tribune*, 25 April 1968.
135. HULDT, L., Outcome of pregnancy when legal abortion is readily available, *Lancet* **1** : 467–8 (1968).
136. RUSHTON, D. I., (Letter) Effects of legalizing abortions, *Lancet* **1** : 692–3 (1968).
137. HARRISON, C. P., (Letter) Effects of legalizing abortions, *Lancet* **1** : 917–18 (1968).
138. FREDERIKSEN, H., and BRACKETT, J. W., (Letter) Effects of legalizing abortions, *Lancet* **2** : 167–8 (1968).
139. ROEMER, R., Abortion law: the approaches of different nations, *Amer. J. Pub. Health* **57** : 1906–22 (1967).
140. TIETZE, C., Abortion in Europe, *Amer. J. Pub. Health* **57** : 1923–47 (1967).
141. SCHWARTZ, R. A., Psychiatry and the abortion laws: an overview, *Comprehen. Psychiat.* **9** : 99–117 (1968).
142. The Abortion Act—Memorandum from the Medical Defence Union, *Brit. Med. J.* **1** : 759–62 (1968).
143. ROBB, D. F., The Abortion Act 1967, *Practitioner* **201** : 694–700 (1968).
144. MEDICAL PROTECTION SOCIETY, *The Abortion Act* 1967, London, Pitman, 1969.
145. SIMON, A., Psychiatric indications for therapeutic abortion and sterilisation, *Clin. Obstet. Gynaec.* **7** : 67–81 (1964).
146. AARONS, Z. A., Therapeutic abortion and the psychiatrist, *Amer. L. Psychiat.* **124** : 745–54 (1967).
147. KENYON, F. E., Termination of pregnancy on psychiatric grounds: a comparative study of 61 cases, *Brit. J. Med. Psychol.* **42** : 243–54 (1969).
148. (Annotation) Pregnancy diagnosis, *Lancet* **1** : 1084–5 (1969).
149. SHARMAN, A., (Letter) Pregnancy diagnosis, *Lancet* **2** : 599–600 (1969).
150. LUNAY, G. G., (Letter) Pregnancy tests over the counter, *Brit. Med. J.* **4** : 561 (1969).
151. WIDE, L., Early diagnosis of pregnancy, *Lancet* **2** : 863–4 (1969).
152. (Leading article) Therapeutic abortion, *Brit. Med. J.* **4** : 786–7 (1968).
153. KERSLAKE, D., and CASEY, D., Abortion induced by means of the uterine aspirator, *Obstet. Gynaec.* **30** : 35–45 (1967).
154. LACHELIN, C. G. L., and BURGESS, D. E., Therapeutic abortion using Utus paste, *J. Obstet. Gynaec. Brit. Commonw.* **75** : 1173–5 (1968).

155. SCHIFFER, M. A., Induction of labor by intra-amniotic installation of hypertonic solution for therapeutic abortion of intrauterine death, *Obstet. Gynaec.* **33** : 729–43 (1969).
156. WAGATSUMA, T., Intra-amniotic injection of saline for therapeutic abortion, *Amer. J. Obstet. Gynaec.* **93** : 743–5 (1965).
157. CAMERON, J. M., and DAYAN, A. D., Association of brain damage with therapeutic abortion induced by amniotic fluid replacement: report of two cases, *Brit. Med. J.* **1** : 1010–17 (1966).
158. MANABE, Y., Artificial abortion at midpregnancy by mechanical stimulation of the uterus, *Amer. J. Obstet. Gynaec.* **105** : 132–46 (1969).
159. (Leading article) Clinical use of prostaglandins, *Brit. Med. J.* **3** : 253–4 (1970).
160. KARIM, S. M. M., and FILSHIE, G. M., Use of prostaglandin E2 for therapeutic abortion, *Brit. Med. J.* **3** : 198–200 (1970).
161. MARKS, L., Rising abortion demand floods hospitals, *Observer*, 11 August 1968.
162. *Registrar General's Weekly Returns*, London, General Register Office, Nos. 2, 16, and 17, 1969.
163. (Leading article) Demand for abortion, *Brit. Med. J.* **1** : 199–200 (1969).
164. Abortions on foreigners, *Brit. Med. J.* **3** : 439 (1969).
165. DIGGORY, P., PEEL, J., and POTTS, M., Preliminary assessment of the 1967 Abortion Act in practice, *Lancet* **1** : 287–91 (1970).
166. GOODHART, C. B., (Letter) Abortion capital, *Lancet* **1** : 367 (1970).
167. Points from Parliament, *Brit. Med. J.* **2** : 832 (1969).
168. Operations for abortion, *Brit. Med. J.* **3** : 63 (1969).
169. *Registrar General's Quarterly Return for England and Wales*, No. 480, London, HMSO, 1969.
170. ABORTION LAW REFORM ASSOCIATION, *The First 18 Months of the Abortion Act*, Privately circulated in February 1970.
171. News and Notes, *Brit. Med. J.* **3** : **63**, 1969.
172. FERRIS, P., Abortionists looking for business, *Observer*, 3 November 1968.
173. FERRIS, P., Don't shoot the abortionist, *Observer*, 9 February 1969.
174. SIMMS, M., The Act affirmed, *Family Planning* **18** : 70–1 (1969).
175. DIGGORY, P. L. C., Some experiences of therapeutic abortion, *Lancet* **1** : 873–5 (1969).
176. (Annotation) Advice on abortion, *Lancet* **2** : 1025 (1968).
177. MCLAREN, H. C., (Letter) Ethics and abortion, *Brit. Med. J.* **2** : 622 (1968).
178. SIM, M., (Letter) Advice on abortion, *Lancet* **2** : 1138 (1968).
179. SIMMS, M., (Letter) Advice on abortion, *Lancet* **2** : 1240 (1968).
180. (Leading article) One year later, *Medical Tribune*, 24 April 1969.
181. Mother of 6 dies after £50 abortion, *Evening Standard*, 4 February 1969.
182. Private abortion hospitals face licence refusals, *Daily Telegraph*, 10 April 1969.
183. Crossman's men check nursing homes, *Evening Standard*, 16 April 1969.
184. (Leading article) Approval for abortion, *Brit. Med. J.* **13** (April 1969).
185. Abortion clinics, *Lancet* **1** : 948 (1969).
186. FERRIS, P., Abortion clinics hit back, *Observer*, 4 May 1969.
187. The pill ban: Catholic revolt grows in Britain, *Sunday Times*, 18 August 1969.
188. DOYLE, C., Help family planners to cut mounting abortion rate, *Observer*, 27 April 1969.
189. ABELS, S. R., (Letter) The first year of the Abortion Act, *Lancet* **1** : 1051–2 (1969).
190. (Leading article) The first year of the Abortion Act, *Lancet* **1** : 867–8 (1969).

191. RHODES, P., Reported in: Pregnancy termination: call for greater G.P. cooperation, *Medical Tribune*, 28 November 1968.
192. DENNY, F., (Letter) The Abortion Act, *Lancet* **1**: 377 (1969).
193. MACGILLIVRAY, I., Abortion, *Hospital Medicine* **2** : 1433–5 (1968).
194. LEWIS, T. L. T., The Abortion Act, *Brit. Med. J.* **1** : 241–2 (1969).
195. POTTS, M., (Letter) The Abortion Act, *Brit. Med. J.* **1** : 376–7 (1969).
196. DE SOLDENHOFF, R., (Letter) Abortion Act in practice, *Brit. Med. J.* **2** : 51 (1969).
197. HUGHES, J. H., (Letter) Abortion Act in practice, *Brit. Med. J.* **1** : 637–8 (1969).
198. NACHSHEN, D. S., (Letter) The first year of the Abortion Act, *Lancet* **1** : 940–1 (1969).
199. CONSULTANT PSYCHIATRIST, The nurse and termination of pregnancy on psychiatric grounds, *Nursing Mirror* **1** : 569–70 (1966).
200. Abortions "strike" by nurses, *Daily Telegraph*, 4 October 1969.
201. Reflections on the Act, *Medical Tribune*, 13 February 1969.
202. Abortion: the crazy pattern, *Daily Mail*, 18 February 1969.
203. MCLAREN, H. C., Abortion or modern obstetrics?, *Brit. J. Hosp. Med.* **2** : 607–12 (1969).
204. GROSS, W., Emotional involvement in therapeutic abortions, *Medical Tribune*, 6 March 1969.
205. LEE, N. C., (Letter) Abortion Act in practice, *Brit. Med. J.* **1** : 778 (1969).
206. TURK, D. C., (Letter) Abortion Act in practice, *Brit. Med. J.* **1** : 778 (1969).
207. RICHARD, E. F., (Letter) Abortion Act in practice, *Brit. Med. J.* **1** : 778 (1969).
208. HUNTINGFORD, P. J., Abortion—a matter for controversy, *Brit. J. Hosp. Med.* **2** : 555 (1969).
209. EDMUNDS, L., As the abortions queue grows, *Daily Telegraph*, 28 March 1969.
210. M.P. seeks change in Abortion Law, *The Times*, 17 February 1969.
211. SIMMS, M., The last-ditch assault in the Abortion Act battle, *Medical Tribune*, 27 February 1969.
212. Abortion capital of Western World, *Evening Standard*, 16 April 1969.
213. Working of Abortion Act, *Brit. Med. J.* **2** : 197 (1969).
214. Death of a baby: inquiry in Glasgow, *Brit. Med. J.* **2** : 704–5 (1969).
215. DOYLE, C., Girls told: don't lie to doctors, *Observer*, 25 May 1969.
216. U.S. wife, 18, dies on trip to London for abortion, *Daily Telegraph*, 23 May 1969.
217. U.S. church leader defends abortion aid service, *Daily Telegraph*, 27 May 1969.
218. More U.S. abortion seekers, *Daily Telegraph*, 5 July 1969.
219. M.P. wants abortion review, *Daily Telegraph*, 31 May 1969.
220. Greatest gain from Abortion Act could be relief from distress, says Sir George, *Medical Tribune*, 12 June 1969.
221. Taxpayers subsidising abortion clinics—M.P., *Daily Telegraph*, 22 June 1969.
222. Procuring abortion, *Brit. Med. J.* supp., **2** : 153 (1969).
223. Information supplied by the Registrar of the General Medical Council, 14 September 1970.
224. Advertising, *Brit. Med. J.*, supp., **2** : 153–4 (1969).
225. Danes organize £120 abortion trips to London, *Daily Telegraph*, 2 July 1969.
226. Abortion hotel. We've had 800 guests since September, *Daily Express*, 4 July 1969.
227. Abortion clinic fees cut to attract Danes, *Daily Telegraph*, 5 July 1969.
228. Crossman finds no "mass influx" for abortions, *Daily Telegraph*, 8 July 1969.
229. Surgeons to direct girls to clinics, *Daily Telegraph*, 11 July 1969.
230. Embassy report on abortions for Crossman, *Daily Telegraph*, 12 July 1969.

231. Abortion operations, *Brit. Med. J.* **3** : 185 (1969).
232. Seven taxi drivers are blamed, *Daily Telegraph*, 11 July 1969.
233. A doctor said "No" to abortion—without seeing the patient, *Evening Standard*, 3 July 1969.
234. Annual Representative Meeting, "Other motions", *Brit. Med. J.*, supp., **3** : 14–16 (1969).
235. COUPAR, S., and DAVIES, J., Abortion, *Daily Express*, 4 July 1969.
236. £300,000 for abortion doctors, *Daily Telegraph*, 5 July 1969.
237. "VAUX", (Letter) Good faith in abortion, *Medical Tribune*, 10 July 1969.
238. POTTS, D. M., (Letter) One brake on abortions, *Daily Telegraph*, 11 July 1969.
239. FERRIS, P., Abortion, *Observer*, 13 July 1969.
240. The sacred gadfly, *Sunday Times*, 20 July 1969.
241. ST. JOHN-STEVAS, N., (Letter) Growing demand for abortion, *Observer*, 20 July 1969.
242. Leave for Abortion Bill narrowly refused, *Brit. Med. J.* **3** : 245 (1969).
243. SIMMS, M., The Act affirmed, *Family Planning* **18** : 70–1 (1969).
244. Shock for backers of Abortion Act, *Daily Telegraph*, 16 July 1969.
245. (Leading article) Abortions: time to cool it, *Medical Tribune*, 24 July 1969.
246. (Leading article) Abortion: let the woman decide, *Observer*, 20 July 1969.
247. HANNAY, LADY FERGUSSON (DORIS LESLIE), (Letter) Living human being, *Daily Telegraph*, 21 July 1969.
248. ROBINSON, H., (Letter) Mental agony of abortion, *Daily Telegraph*, 21 July 1969.
249. Woman is best judge on abortion: liberal law needed, Sir Dugald tells U.S., *Medical Tribune*, 10 July 1969.
250. Therapeutic abortion in north-east Scotland, *Brit. Med. J.* **3** : 167–8 (1969).
251. Abortion: study problems of not terminating pregnancies, *Medical Tribune*, 17 July 1969.
252. Gynaecologists to hold inquiry on Abortion Act, *Daily Telegraph*, 17 July 1969.
253. Doctors abuse abortion rule, *Sunday Telegraph*, 20 July 1969.
254. HENRY, M. J., (Letter) Hypocrisy about abortion, *Medical Tribune*, 24 July 1969.
255. JONES, G., (Letter) Pregnancy termination, *Brit. Med. J.* **3** : 297 (1969).
256. Points from Parliament, *Brit. Med. J.* **2** : 246 (1969).
257. Advertising, *Brit. Med. J.*, supp., **3** : 96 (1969).
258. Action of Privy Council on appeals from GMC, *Brit. Med. J.* **3** : 292 (1969).
259. Deception of patients, *Brit. Med. J.*, supp., **3** : 101–2 (1969).
260. Abortion in New Zealand, *Brit. Med. J.*, supp., **3** : 100 (1969).
261. Advertising abortion service, *Brit. Med. J.*, supp., 100–1 (1969).
262. Doctor wins appeal to Privy Council, *Daily Telegraph*, 23 July 1970.
263. Held up by abortions, *Brit. Med. J.* **3** : 367 (1969).
264. GODBER, G. E., Safety of mother and child, *Lancet* **2** : 312–13 (1969).
265. (Annotation) A baseline for criminal abortion, *Lancet* **2** : 309 (1969).
266. GOODHART, C. B., Estimation of illegal abortions, *J. Biosoc. Sci.* **1** : 235–45 (1969).
267. WHITE, H., (Letter) Interpreting the Abortion Act, *Lancet* **2** : 590 (1969).
268. GODBER, G. E., (Letter) Interpreting the Abortion Act, *Lancet* **2** : 590 (1969).
269. SCOTT, J. S., (Letter) Interpreting the Abortion Act, *Lancet* **2** : 694 (1969).
270. Chemists start £2 pregnancy test business, *Daily Telegraph*, 16 September 1969.
271. (Leading article) Pregnancy tests over the counter, *Brit. Med. J.* **3** : 667 (1969).
272. Abortion fine for father, *Daily Telegraph*, 30 October 1969.
273. Abortion courts to name men, *Daily Telegraph*, 31 October 1969.

REFERENCES

274. GARDINER, J. S., (Letter) The first year of the Abortion Act, *Lancet* **1** : 1093 (1969).
275. GARDINER, J. S., (Letter) Scots "no" to clinics, *Medical Tribune*, 14 August 1969.
276. RUSSELL, C., and RUSSELL, W. M. S., Sociological factors, *J. Biosoc. Sci.* **1** : 289-96 (1969).
277. BROOKS, E., Political and economic factors, *J. Biosoc. Sci.* **1** : 297-305 (1969).
278. EMERSON, M. S., Personal factors, *J. Biosoc. Sci.* **1** : 307-13 (1969).
279. MOORE-ROBINSON, M., Future prospects, *J. Biosoc. Sci.* **1** : 315-20 (1969).
280. HILL, H., Educational factors, *J. Biosoc. Sci.* **1** : 321-5 (1969).
281. Sixpenn'orth of chips and a packet of pills, *Medical Tribunal*, 17 July 1969.
282. HILL, H., (Letter) F.P.A. doctors protest at attack, *Medical Tribune*, 14 August 1969.
283. RAMASWAMY, S., (Letter) F.P.A. doctors protest at attack, *Medical Tribune*, 14 August 1969.
284. ARTHURE, H., (Letter) Deaths from abortion, *Lancet* **2** : 547 (1965).
285. Questions in the Commons, *Brit. Med. J.* **3** : 244 (1969).
286. Doctors "should do more" to teach birth control, *Medical News-Tribune*, 7 November 1969.
287. BAIRD, D. (ed.), *Combined Textbook of Obstetrics and Gynaecology*, 7th edn., Edinburgh, Livingstone, 1962.
288. WOODROFFE, C., Laywork in hospital, *Family Planning* **18** : 50-4 (1969).
289. LAWS, B., Family Planning in hospital, *Family Planning* **18** : 93-5 (1969).
290. Family planning in hospitals, *Brit. Med. J.* **4** : 817 (1969).
291. F.P.A. headquarters are opened, *Medical News-Tribune*, 5 December 1969.
292. Family Planning Association training centre, *Brit. Med. J.* **4** : 631 (1969).
293. Opening of Margaret Pyke Centre, *Family Planning* **18** : 87-9.
294. (Leading article) Family planning services, *Brit. Med. J.* **4** : 760 (1969).
295. Call to educate school leavers on birth control, *Daily Telegraph* 12 January 1970.
296. Family Planning Advertisement on T.V., *Brit. Med. J.* **1** : 375 (1970).
297. Sequential oral contraceptives, *Brit. Med. J.* **2** : 583 (1969).
298. POLLER, L., and THOMSON, J. M., (Letter) Sequential oral contraceptives and clotting factors, *Brit. Med. J.* **2** : 822-3 (1969).
299. BUTLER, L., and HILL, H., Chlormadinone acetate as oral contraceptive, *Lancet* **1** : 1116-19 (1969).
300. CHRISTIE, G. A., (Letter) Chlormadinone acetate as oral contraceptive, *Lancet* **1** : 1262 (1969).
301. HOWARD, G., ELSTEIN, M., BLAIR, M., and MORRIS, N. F., Low-dose continuous chlormadinone acetate as an oral contraceptive, *Lancet* **2** : 24-6 (1969).
302. (Annotation) Continuous chlormadinone acetate: is it an effective oral contraceptive?, *Lancet* **2** : 197-8 (1969).
303. Women advised to take only low-dose brands of pill, *Daily Telegraph*, 12 December 1969.
304. U.S. company stops tests on pill, *Daily Telegraph*, 20 January 1970.
305. Sales curb unlikely, *Daily Telegraph*, 20 January 1970.
306. Mini-pill firm halts sales in New Zealand, *Daily Telegraph*, 23 January 1970.
307. Doubts on banned pill raised four years ago, *Sunday Times*, 25 January 1970.
308. A new warning on extensive use of oral contraceptives, *Medical News-Tribune*, 16 January 1970.
309. Women and the pill: "a grim race", *Evening Standard*, 15 January 1970.
310. Don't panic over the pill, *Evening Standard*, 22 January 1970.

311. Sterilisation for 7 ambulancemen afraid of pill, *Daily Telegraph*, 22 January 1970.
312. Mini-pill may be reissued if tests prove negative, *Daily Telegraph*, 26 January 1970.
313. (Leading article) Further doubts about oral contraceptives, *Brit. Med. J.* **1** : 252 (1970)
314. What do patients think of the Pill?, *World Medicine* **4** : 46–7 (1969).
315. VESSEY, M., Measuring the side effects of the pill, *World Medicine* **5** : 38–9 (1969).
316. KAY, C. R., SMITH, A., and RICHARDS, B., Smoking habits of oral contraceptive users, *Lancet* **2** : 1228–9 (1969).
317. SHULMAN, M., Telepanic and the pill, *Evening Standard*, 10 December 1969.
318. Pill women jam the phones, *Evening Standard*, 12 December 1969.
319. G.P.s kept in the dark on pill warning, *Daily Telegraph*, 15 December 1969.
320. Oral contraceptives, *Brit. Med. J.* **4** : 817 (1969).
321. (Leading article) Pill doubts, *Daily Telegraph*, 13 December 1969.
322. Pill makers act quickly on Dunlop report, *Financial Times*, 13 December 1969.
323. SCOWEN, E. F., (Letter) Oral contraceptives containing oestrogens, *Lancet* **2** : 1369 (1969).
324. (Leading article) Advising the profession, *Brit. Med. J.* **4** : 755–6 (1969).
325. (Leading article) Switching pills, *Brit. Med. J.* **4** : 759 (1969).
326. Changing oral contraceptives, *Brit. Med. J.* **4** : 789–91 (1969).
327. Publicity and the pill, *Brit. Med. J.* **4** : 803–5 (1969).
328. JACKSON, M. C. N., (Letter) The committee and the pill, *Lancet* **2** : 1427 (1969).
329. Couple sue birth pill firm for £417,000, *Evening Standard*, 30 January 1970.
330. POTTS, D. M., and SWYER, G. M., Effectiveness and risk of birth control methods, *Brit. Med. Bull.* **26** : 26–32 (1970).
331. Gynaecological Services, *Brit. Med. J.*, supp., **3** : 57–8 (1969).
332. Minister urged to set up national abortion clinics, *Daily Telegraph*, 23 July 1969.
333. Call for abortion clinics, *Daily Telegraph*, 29 September 1969.
334. Abortion Act, *Brit. J. Hosp. Med.* **2** : 2027 (1969).
335. Birth of the first all-abortion clinic, *Sunday Times*, 7 December 1969.
336. £24,000 offer to join abortion clinic, *Daily Telegraph*, 15 December 1969.
337. M.P.s query U.S. clinics plan, *Daily Telegraph*, 31 January 1970.
338. The Harley Street clinic—an apology, *Daily Telegraph*, 10 February 1970.
339. £500 abortion package deal, *Sunday Express*, 18 January 1970.
340. Summons for U.S. abortion man, *Sunday Express*, 1 February 1970.
341. Nabarro asks about "£500 package trips", *Daily Telegraph*, 10 February 1970.
342. £30 fare demand by abortion taxi touts, *Daily Telegraph*, 4 February 1970.
343. CHISHOLM, N., (Letter) Abortion Act amendment, *Brit. Med. J.* **3** : 783 (1969).
344. Few support abortion on demand, *Daily Telegraph*, 18 November 1969.
345. (Leading article) Abortion anxieties, *Daily Telegraph*, 18 November 1969.
346. (Leading article) Abortions by the N.H.S., *Medical News-Tribune*, 21 November 1969.
347. Motion for inquiry into Abortion Act, *Brit. Med. J.* **4** : 631 (1969).
348. All-party challenge on Abortion Act, *Hospital Times*, 5 December 1969.
349. Advertising, *Brit. Med. J.*, supp., **4** : 65–6 (1969).
350. Harley Street doctor cleared, *Daily Telegraph*, 28 November 1969.
351. Abortions for all, *Hospital Times*, 5 December 1969.
352. Government probing abortion law effects, *Hospital Times*, 5 December 1969.
353. Sterilization stories "much exaggerated", *Medical News-Tribune*, 5 December 1969.

354. Majority against changing law on abortion, *Daily Telegraph*, 24 January 1970.
355. Vested interests in conspiracy against the Abortion Act, *Medical News-Tribune*, 30 January 1970.
356. BIRD, R. G., Abortion-clinics, fee scale needed, *Medical News-Tribune*, 6 February 1970.
357. (Editorial) Abortion, *Sunday Times*, 8 February 1970.
358. (Editorial) Abortion reform?, *Evening Standard*, 12 February 1970.
359. (Editorial) Let the Act act, *Medical News-Tribune*, 13 February 1970.
360. G.P.s tend to support Abortion Act, *Medical News-Tribune*, 13 February 1970.
361. CUMIN, A., CLARKE, T. A. P., ESSEX, A., HODDES, S., SHERWIN, M., and FRANKLIN, O. W., (Letter) Abortion support, *Medical News-Tribune*, 13 February 1970.
362. Abortion girl's protest, *Daily Telegraph*, 9 February 1970.
363. Support for Bill, *Daily Telegraph*, 12 February 1970.
364. Newcastle heads the N.H.S. abortion "table", *Medical News-Tribune*, 13 February 1970.
365. Biggest abortion clinic not worried by "curb" Bill, *Daily Telegraph*, 12 February 1970.
366. Nurses' protest rally, *Evening Standard*, 13 February 1970.
367. Abortion reform bid talked out, *Evening Standard*, 13 February 1970.
368. Abortion Law (Reform) Bill talked out, *Brit. Med. J.* **1** : 508–9 (1970).
369. DIGGORY, P., PEEL, J., and POTTS, M., Preliminary assessment of the 1967 Abortion Act in practice, *Lancet* **1** : 287–91 (1970).
370. Population may double by 2009, *Daily Telegraph*, 11 March 1970.
371. Birth control on N.H.S. backed by Crossman, *Daily Telegraph*, 12 March 1970.
372. Birth control a duty, canon tells parents, *Daily Telegraph*, 6 February 1970.
373. TAYLOR, W., (Letter) Placing the responsibility, *Sunday Times*, 22 February 1970.
374. F.P.A. opens its first bureau for general sex problems, *Medical News-Tribune*, 13 March 1970.
375. The big secret of Mr. X's bulge, *Daily Mail*, 12 March 1970.
376. FRANKLIN, A. J., (Letter) Abortion, *Medical News-Tribune*, 13 March 1970.
377. ROBB, D., (Letter) Illegitimacy rate, *Daily Telegraph*, 9 March 1970.
378. Major step in abortions, *Daily Telegraph*, 10 March 1970.
379. (Letters to the Editor) Maternity and abortion, *Daily Telegraph*, 12 March 1970.
380. Tory M.P. calls on Wilson to sack Crossman, *Daily Telegraph*, 12 March 1970.
381. Warning on heart risk from pill, *Daily Telegraph*, 12 March 1970.
382. Surprising ignorance of pill effects, *Medical News-Tribune*, 11 March 1970.
383. DMPA is effective as contraceptive, *Medical News-Tribune*, 6 March 1970.
384. Birth control jabs may replace pill, *Daily Telegraph*, 11 March 1970.
385. Women are going back to the pill, *Daily Telegraph*, 23 March 1970.
386. Benefits from pill outweigh risks, says doctor, *Daily Telegraph*, 5 March 1970.
387. Women on pill "more sexually active", *Daily Telegraph*, 20 March 1970.
388. STEPTOE, P. C., and IMRAN, M., Combined procedure of aspiration termination and laparoscopic sterilization, *Brit. Med. J.* **3** : 751–2 (1969).
389. STEPTOE, P. C., Recent advances in surgical methods of control of fertility and infertility, *Brit. Med. Bull.* **26** : 60–4 (1970).
390. LISTON, W. A., BRADFORD, W., DOWNIE, J., and KERR, M. G., Female sterilisation by tubal electrocoagulation under laparoscopic control, *Lancet* **1** : 382–3 (1970).
391. WOOD, C., and LEETON, J., Sterilisation by ovariotexy, *Lancet* **2** : 1213–15 (1969).
392. Follow-up after vasectomy, *Lancet* **1** : 483 (1970).
393. (Leading article) Legality of sterilisation, *Brit. Med. J.* **1** : 704–5 (1970).

REFERENCES

394. Criminal convictions, *Brit. Med. J.,* supp., **1** : 77 (1970).
395. STALLWORTHY, J., Therapeutic abortion, *Practitioner* **204** : 393–400 (1970).
396. Abortion Bill M.P. wants rules to stop abuses, *Daily Telegraph,* 26 March 1970.
397. GOODHART, C. B., A decision that is too vital for one doctor, *Sunday Telegraph,* 5 April 1970.
398. PARE, C. M. B., and RAVEN, H., Follow-up of patients referred for termination of pregnancy, *Lancet* **1** : 635–8 (1970).
399. MCEWAN, J., The Abortion Act: a general practitioner's view, *Practitioner* **204** : 427–32 (1970).
400. The Abortion Act (1967): findings of an inquiry into the first year's working of the Act conducted by the Royal College of Obstetricians and Gynaecologists, *Brit. Med. J.* **2** : 529–35 (1970).
401. COMMITTEE ON SAFETY OF DRUGS, Combined oral contraceptives, *Brit. Med. J.* **2** : 231–2 (1970).
402. INMAN, W. H. W., VESSEY, M. P., WESTERHOLM, B., and ENGELUND, A., Thromboembolic disease and the steroidal content of oral contraceptives: a report to the Committee on Safety of Drugs, *Brit. Med. J.* **2** : 203–9 (1970).
403. Minister seeks assurances on abortions, *Daily Telegraph,* 4 April 1970.
404. London abortion fees jump to £100, *Evening Standard,* 9 April 1970.
405. Woman refused abortion has a mongol child, *Observer,* 5 April 1970.
406. (Leading article) Consultants' report on abortion, *Brit. Med. J.* **2** : 491–2 (1970).
407. ABORTION LAW REFORM ASSOCIATION, The first two years: a review of the working of the Abortion Act, 1967, Privately circulated in October 1970.
408. TIETZE, C., and LEWIT, S., Abortion, *Scientific American* **220** : 21–7 (1969).
409. Abortions on demand urged, *Daily Telegraph,* 20 October 1969.
410. Legal abortion mortality is far lower in eastern Europe, *Medical Tribune,* 5 June 1969.
411. Norway will not liberalise abortion law, *Daily Telegraph,* 21 August 1969.
412. Change urged in Swedish abortion law, *Daily Telegraph,* 16 March 1970.
413. "Immaturity" as ground for abortion, *Daily Telegraph,* 19 March 1970.
414. PECK, A., Therapeutic abortion: patients, doctors and society, *Amer. J. Psychiat.* **125** : 797–804 (1968).
415. POTTS, D. M., (Letter) Abortion in eastern Europe, *Medical Tribune,* 13 March 1969.
416. STEPHEN, J., (Letter) Abortion in eastern Europe, *Medical Tribune,* 27 March 1969.
417. Most Czech women polled resist abortion law repeal, *Medical Tribune,* 14 August 1969.
418. Abortion: where the N.H.S. has failed, *Sunday Times,* 6 July 1969.
419. GREENHILL, J. P., World trends of therapeutic abortion and sterilisation, *Clin. Obstet. Gynaec.* **7** : 37–42 (1964).
420. Abortion comes out of the shadows, *Life,* 16 March 1970.
421. BECK, M. B., NEWMAN, S. H., and LEWIT, S., Abortion—a national public and mental health problem—past, present and proposed research, *Amer. J. Pub. Hlth.* **59** : 2131–43 (1969).
422. GUTTMACHER, A. F., Newsletter number 38 from Planned Parenthood—World Population, New York, 26 February 1969.
423. INGRAM, J. M., Changing aspects of abortion law, *Amer. J. Obstet. Gynec.* **105** : 35–45 (1969).
424. HALL, R. E., Abortion in American hospitals, *Amer. J. Pub. Hlth.* **57** : 1933–6 (1967).

425. GOLDMAN, M. J., Abortion: Jewish law and the law of the land, *Ill. Med. J.* **135** : 93–5 (1969).
426. WESTOFF, C. F., MOORE, E. C., and RYDER, N. B., The structure of attitudes toward abortion, *Millbank Mem. Fund Quart.* **47** : 11–36 (1969).
427. HARTER, C. L., and BEASLEY, J. D., A survey concerning induced abortions in New Orleans, *Amer. J. Pub. Hlth.* **57** : 1937–47 (1967).
428. SHERWIN, L., and OVERSTREET, E. W., Therapeutic abortion: attitudes and practices of Californian physicians, *California Med.* **105** : 337–9 (1966).
429. PEYTON, F. W., STARRY, A. R., and LEIDY, T. R., Women's attitudes concerning abortion, *Obstet. Gynec.* **34** : 182–8 (1969).
430. LADER, L., Non-hospital abortions, *Look*, 21 January 1969.
431. Angel of Ashland, *Daily Telegraph*, 23 January 1970.
432. HALL, R. E., New York abortion law survey, *Amer. J. Obstet. Gynec.* **98** : 1182–3 (1965).
433. GOLD, E. M., Observation on abortion, *World Med. J.* **13** : 76–8 (1966).
434. WILLSON, J. R., Abortion—a medical responsibility?, *Obstet. Gynec.* **30** : 294–303 (1967).
435. Abortion: the doctor's dilemma, *Modern Medicine* **35** : 12–32 (1967).
436. CROWLEY, R. M., and LAIDLAW, R. W., Psychiatric opinion regarding abortion: preliminary report of a survey, *Amer. J. Psychiat.* **124** : 559–62 (1967).
437. SZASZ, T., The ethics of abortion, *Humanist* 147–8, September–October 1966.
438. Position statement on abortion, *Amer. J. Psychiat.* **124** : 450 (1967).
439. SLOANE, R. B., The unwanted pregnancy, *New Eng. J. Med.* **280** : 1206–13 (1969).
440. GROUP FOR THE ADVANCEMENT OF PSYCHIATRY, *The Right to Abortion: a psychiatric view*, New York, GAP Publications, October 1969.
441. A.M.A. policy on therapeutic abortion, *J. Amer. Med. Ass.* **201** : 544 (1967).
442. (Abortion) *Amer. J. Pub. Hlth.* **59** : 153 (1969).
443. WILLIAMS, R. H., Our role in the generation, modification and termination of life, *J. Amer. Med. Ass.* **209** : 914–17 (1969).
444. Amagrams, *J. Amer. Med. Ass.* **213** : 359–60 (1970).
445. Amagrams, *J. Amer. Med. Ass.* **213** : 1242 (1970).
446. OWEN, J. E., The American parent's worry, *Daily Telegraph*, 26 June 1969.
447. AYD, F. J., The teenager and contraception, *Pediat. Clins. N. Amer.* **16** : 355–61 (1969).
448. Abortion laws, "pill", Lolitas—all add to woes of today's physician, *J. Amer. Med. Ass.* **210** : 2176–81 (1969).
449. WEICHMANN, G., Move over, please, *J. Kansas Med. Soc.* **69** : 524–9 (1968).
450. MUDD, J. W., and SIEGEL, R. J., Sexuality—the experience and anxieties of medical students, *New Eng. J. Med.* **281** : 1397–1403 (1969).
451. The new doubts about the pill, *Life*, 16 March 1970.
452. "Pill" packets in U.S. must carry warning, *Daily Telegraph*, 8 April 1970.
453. £104,000 damages, *Daily Telegraph*, 17 April 1970.
454. One man's answer to overpopulation, *Life*, 30 March 1970.
455. GRUNEBAUM, H. V., and WEISS, J. L., (Letter) Maladjustment of unwanted children, *New Eng. J. Med.* **281** : 909 (1969).
456. PLAGENZ, L. States legislate abortion reform but hospitals are reluctant to comply, *Mod. Hosp.* **113** : 82–5 (1969).
457. Information from the American Bar Foundation, Chicago, Illinois, January 1970.

458. LAMM, R. D., DOWNING, S., and HELLER, A., The legislative process in changing therapeutic abortion laws, *Amer. J. Orthopsychiat.* **39** : 684–90 (1969).
459. DROEGEMUELLER, W., TAYLOR, E. S., and DROSE, V. E., The first year of experience in Colorado with the new abortion law, *Amer. J. Obstet. Gynec.* **103** : 694–702 (1969).
460. HELLER, A., and WHITTINGTON, H. G., The Colorado story: Denver general hospital experience with the change in the law on therapeutic abortion, *Amer. J. Psychiat.* **125** : 809–16 (1968).
461. STANFIELD, C., Colorado's abortion law, *Neb. State Med. J.* **54** : 745–7 (1969).
462. WHITTINGTON, H. G., Evaluation of therapeutic abortion as an element of preventive psychiatry, *Amer. J. Psychiat.* **126** : 1224–9 (1970).
463. *North Carolina Therapeutic Abortion Law with Guidelines for Implementing and Reporting*, Winsten-Salem, North Carolina, 1969.
464. RUSSEL, K. P., and JACKSON, E. W., Therapeutic abortions in California, *Amer. J. Obstet. Gynec.* **105**: 757–65 (1969).
465. MARDER, L., Psychiatric experience with a liberalized therapeutic abortion law, *Amer. J. Psychiat.* **126** : 1230–6 (1970).
466. THURSTONE, P. B., Therapeutic abortion, *J. Amer. Med. Ass.* **209** : 229–31 (1969).
467. (Leading article) Who may not have an abortion?, *J. Amer. Med. Ass.* **209** : 260–1 (1969).
468. KUMMER, J. M., New trends in therapeutic abortion in California, *Obstet. Gynec.* **34** : 883–6 (1969).
469. What your patients are reading, *Medical News-Tribune*, 17 April 1970.
470. What your patients are reading, *Medical News-Tribune*, 10 April 1970.
471. HALLEY, M. M., Law-medicine comment, *J. Kansas Med. Soc.* **69** : 530–3 (1968).
472. PERR, I. N., ROMAN, B. D., and SCHWAB, D. S., Position stand of the Ohio Psychiatric Association on suggested changes in the abortion laws of Ohio, *Ohio State Med. J.* **64** : 1343–4 (1968).
473. COPELAND, W. E., ULLERY, J. C., and ESSIG, G. F., Therapeutic abortion, *J. Amer. Med. Ass.* **207** : 713–15 (1969).
474. Delaware's abortion reforms, *Delaware Med. J.* **41** : 199 (1969).
475. CURRAN, W. J., Birth-control, judicial surgery and the wonderful one-hoss shay, *New Eng. J. Med.* **281** : 546–7 (1969).
476. Abortion—repeal of Alaska law?, *Alaska Med.* **11** : 105–7 (1969).
477. Abortion in New York, *Time*, 7 September 1970.
478. KINCH, R. A. H., WEARING, M. P., LOVE, E. J., and McMAHON, D., Some aspects of pediatric illegitimacy, *Amer. J. Obstet. Gynec.* **105** : 20–31 (1969).
479. HARRISON, C. P., Teenage pregnancy—is abortion the answer?, *Pediat. Clins. N. Amer.* **16** : 363–9 (1969).
480. Aequanimitas, *Canad. Med. Ass. J.* **101** : 176 (1969).
481. Catholics maintain a block on abortions despite amendment to criminal law, *Hospital Times*, 10 April 1970.
482. WARING, G., Parliament Hill, *Canad. Med. Ass. J.* **102** : 1234 (1970).
483. COFFEY, P. G. (Letter) Therapeutic abortion, *Canad. Med. Ass. J.* **102** : 90–1 (1970).
484. Correspondence, *Canad. Med. Ass. J.* **102** : 642–3 (1970).
485. Correspondence, *Canad. Med. Ass. J.* **102** : 1209–11 (1970).
486. High abortion rate but low mortality, *Medical News-Tribune*, 6 March 1970.

487. South Australia makes abortion legal at last, *Medical News-Tribune*, 2 January 1970.
488. Australia, *Lancet* **2** : 589 (1969).
489. London Newsletter, *Med. J. Australia* **2** : 32 (supp.) (1969).
490. Victorian Newsletter, *Med. J. Australia* **2** : 40 (supp.) (1969).
491. (Editorial) The abortion debate, *Med. J. Australia* **2** : 833–4 (1969).
492. BRETHERTON, R. C., The case for abortion law reform, *Med. J. Australia* **2** : 860–2 (1969).
493. SMITHURST, B. A., The Abortion Act, 1967, of the United Kingdom—an unsatisfactory law, *Med. J. Australia* **2** : 863–5 (1969).
494. Abortion racket alleged, *Hospital Times*, 6 February 1970.
495. Illegitimacy and ignorance, *Med. J. Australia* **1** : 515–16 (1970).
496. WURM, R. S., Abortion: condescension or prevention, *Med. J. Australia* **1** : 557–62 (1970).
497. DUNN, H. P., Therapeutic abortion in New Zealand, *N.Z. Med. J.* **68** : 253–6 (1968).
498. Legalized abortion in New Zealand, *Brit. Med. J.* **2** : 739 (1970).

Index

Aarons, Z. A. 82, 295
Abels, S. R. 112, 127, 296
Aberdeen 22, 23, 46, 66, 113, 122, 124, 147–51
Abortifacients 2–6, 240
Abortion 230
Abortion x, xi, 1, 2, 7–9, 14–19, 21, 22, 24–6, 28, 29, 31, 32, 37–9, 47, 58, 67, 68, 80–2, 87, 108, 111, 112, 122, 133–50, 152–60, 162–5, 167, 169, 170, 171, 179–99, 201, 204–8, 210, 211, 213–44, 247, 249–74
  after rape 8, 10, 11, 14, 18, 62, 81, 88, 141, 219, 222, 225, 227–30, 232, 233, 237, 238, 241, 242, 250, 253, 255, 257, 258, 261, 262, 264, 271
  backstreet 3, 4, 81, 141, 163, 192, 193, 195, 196, 201, 268
  complications of 5, 6, 19, 92, 94, 96, 214, 215, 221, 222, 231, 232, 235, 238, 243, 259, 270
  criminal 1, 2, 4, 14, 16, 19, 20, 28, 32, 38, 45, 57, 64, 67, 68, 88, 145, 153, 162, 191, 198, 219, 220, 224, 228, 234, 254, 256, 258, 260–3
  death following 5, 6, 7, 98, 104, 109, 128, 162, 190, 214, 215, 221, 222, 224, 232, 234, 243, 263, 264, 270
  fees for 4, 106, 136, 141, 153, 156–8, 182, 184, 185, 193, 195, 196, 205, 211, 231, 261, 263, 265
  foetal indications for 10, 33, 80, 147, 219, 222, 225–30, 232, 234–43, 250, 251, 253, 255–8, 260–2, 266, 271
  guilt after 6, 19, 56, 64–6, 81, 89, 90, 118, 119, 124, 147, 206, 231
  inquiry into 187, 211
  legal x, xi, xiv, 4, 5, 8, 9, 10, 19, 20, 44, 50, 59, 66–8, 79, 106, 110, 120, 131, 133, 198, 219, 220, 223, 230, 240
  medical indications for xiii, 26, 27, 80–4, 122, 149, 219, 225, 227–30, 232–5, 237, 238, 241–3, 250, 253, 255–7, 262, 264, 266, 267, 269, 271–3
  notification(s) 70, 73, 141, 199, 205, 206, 208
  on demand x, 9, 79, 82, 125, 127, 144, 146, 162, 181, 186, 187, 189, 190, 196, 205, 213, 215–17, 220, 221, 223, 227, 237, 238, 241, 244, 260–5
  private facilities for 136, 137, 139–43, 145, 146, 152–8, 160, 161, 181–7, 192, 193, 195–9, 211
  psychiatric indications for 18, 21, 23–30, 33, 59, 64–7, 81–90, 117, 120, 122, 123, 192, 193, 219, 220, 222, 225–30, 232, 233, 235, 237–43, 250–7, 259, 260, 262, 264, 266–9, 271–3
  psychiatric sequelae 32, 59, 64–6, 124, 147, 206, 207, 238–40
  "racket" x, 143, 144, 187, 194, 206, 272–3
  refused 59, 90
  regulations, 1968 72–5
  social grounds for 9, 21, 26, 27, 122, 147, 149, 198, 212, 219–21, 227–30, 233–5, 238–40, 243, 270
  spontaneous 2, 4, 149, 215, 222
  therapeutic ix, 6, 9, 18, 23, 26, 30, 32, 33, 45, 63–7, 80, 81, 83, 84, 90, 95, 98, 119, 140, 147, 149, 198, 219, 226, 227, 232–6, 238, 240–3, 251, 255–9, 262–74
Abortion Act, 1967 x, xiii, xiv, 1, 6, 14, 15, 17, 23–5, 28, 29, 31, 37, 41, 51, 69–80, 84, 102–13, 115–17, 119, 121–30, 132, 133, 137–47, 150, 152–6, 160–4, 168, 179–81, 183, 184–8, 190–9, 201–7, 211–18, 221, 267, 271

Abortion Act, 1967—*cont.*
 "conscience" clause 12, 29, 32, 71, 79, 105, 129, 142
 "social" clause 10–12, 69, 74, 79, 105, 129, 139, 186, 191, 192, 239
Abortion, attitudes towards xiii, 4, 40
 Church of England 14
 general practitioners 30–3, 147, 167, 207, 208, 234, 266
 general public 13, 16, 205, 215–17, 226, 265
 gynaecologists 17–23, 205, 206, 212–18, 232–6, 266
 Jewish law 226
 Methodist Church 14
 nurses 117–20, 196, 213, 215, 218, 259
 Protestant Church 226
 psychiatrists 23–30, 206, 207, 236–9
 registrars (residents) 213, 259
 Roman Catholic Church 13, 14, 226, 233, 234, 240
 Royal College of Obstetricians and Gynaecologists 11, 19, 21, 212–18
 Royal Medico-Psychological Association 26, 27
Abortion Bill 10–12, 20, 21, 28, 32, 132, 141, 145, 146, 193
 "conscience" clause 12
 government attitude towards 11
 "social" clause 12
Abortion Law Reform Association 7, 8, 10, 11, 14, 15, 107, 129, 144, 190, 192–4, 201, 211, 218, 302
Abortion Law (Reform) Bill 187, 190, 193–7
Abortion laws
 in America 68, 225–6, 229, 231–6, 239, 243, 249–65
  Alabama 250, 264
  Alaska 264
  Arkansas 250, 264
  California 231, 250, 257–61
  Colorado 231, 250–4, 265
  Connecticut 225
  Delaware 264
  District of Columbia 250
  Georgia 250, 261–2
  Hawaii 250, 264
  Kansas 250, 264
  Maryland 250, 262–3
  Massachusetts 250, 264
  New Jersey 250
  New Mexico 250, 264
  New York 225, 264–5, 268
  North Carolina 250, 254–6
  Ohio 264
  Oregon 250, 264
  Pennsylvania 250
  Puerto Rico 250
 in Australia 271–3
 in Bulgaria 67, 221
 in Canada 265–9
 in Czechoslovakia 19, 67, 221
 in Denmark 145, 219, 220
 in eastern Europe 10, 67, 220–3
 in eastern Germany 220
 in England and Wales 1, 7–9, 22, 24, 68–79, 243
 in Finland 145, 219
 in Hungary 54, 67, 220–1, 233
 in Iceland 219
 in Israel 269–70
 in Japan 9, 19, 50, 97, 223–4
 in New Zealand 273–4
 in Northern Europe 219, 220
 in Norway 145, 220
 in Poland 67, 220
 in Romania 21, 67, 205, 221
 in Russia 10, 67, 220, 221
 in Scotland 22, 68–79, 113, 147
 in Sweden 9, 19, 59, 63, 145, 219, 243
 in Yugoslavia 67, 221
Abortionists (criminal) 2, 4, 16, 31
Aburel, Professor E. 97
Ackner, Brian 24, 292
A. D. K. 267, 272
Adoption 61–2, 201, 218, 249
Aesculapius 16
Aghadiuno, Patrick Uwaezuoke 134
Aitken-Swan, Jean 148
Albutt, H. A. 43, 44
Alderman, Philip 53, 294
Alment, Anthony 124
Amark, Curt 59, 294
Ambulance drivers 174
American College of Obstetricians and Gynaecologists 50, 236
American Gynaecological Society 262
American Law Institute 240

INDEX

American Medical Association 236, 241–7
American Medical Enterprises Incorporated 183–4
American Medical Women's Association 225
American Population Council 50
American Psychiatric Association 29, 236, 238, 253, 258
  position statement on abortion 237
American Public Health Association 236, 242
Amniocentesis *see* Termination of pregnancy
Amulree, Lord 10
Anderson, Professor E. W. 26, 81, 292
"Angel of Ashland" 231
Anglican Church Assembly 200
Anglo-Danish Social Service Agreement 137
Apollo 16
Aren, Per 59, 294
Aristotle 13, 17
Arkle, James 24, 25, 292
Arnwine, Don 254
Arthure, Humphrey 168, 299
Ashe, J. R. 256
Association for the Study of Abortion (U.S.) 236
Association of American Physicians 243
Australia
  abortion laws in 271–2
  abortion "protection racket" in 272–3
  abortions performed in 271
  education in sex and contraception in 273
  medical grounds for terminating pregnancy 271, 272
  Melbourne 272
  physicians' attitudes to induced abortion 271, 272
  population of 271
  psychiatric grounds for termination 272
  public attitudes to legal abortion 271
  South Australia Abortion Reform Bill 272
  Victoria, induced abortion situation in 271
  Victorian Branch of the Australian Medical Association 271
  Victorian police and abortion 271–2
  Australian Medical Association 271
Ayd, F. J. 245, 246, 303
Ayer, Professor A. J. 11, 35, 292
Ayrshire 20, 113, 114

Baird, Professor Sir Dugald 11, 20, 22, 31, 38, 43, 48, 52, 66, 123, 124, 147, 169, 292, 293, 299
Balfour-Lynn, Stanley 183, 184
Banana Boy 60
Barnes, A. C. 263
Bateman, David 2
Beard, R. W. xv
Beasley, J. D. 228, 303
Beck, M. B. 224, 236, 302
Bell, Arthur George 159
Belous, Leon 260, 261
Bergman, M. 265
Bergmann, E. 9
Bird, Reginald Geoffrey 188–9, 192–3, 201, 301
Birkett, (Lord) Norman 7
Birmingham 21, 107–8, 122, 145, 148, 152, 162, 181–2, 195, 198, 218, 247
Birth control *see* Contraception
Birth Control Investigation Committee 45
Birth rate x, xiii, 21, 67, 68
Blacker, C. P. 52, 294
Borsch, R. N. 268, 269
Boston 132, 184, 252
Bourne, Aleck 8, 9
  case 4, 8, 9, 11, 25–6, 28, 115, 205, 219, 260, 272
  decision 9, 25, 27, 115, 205, 219, 219, 260, 272
Bowlby, John 60, 294
Brackett, J. W. 68, 295
Bradlaugh–Besant trial 43, 247
Braun, Carl 99
Brayer, F. T. 41
Breckenridge, Alistair 202
Bretherton, R. C. 272, 305
Bridges, P. K. xv
Brighton Symposium on Personal and Community Factors in Fertility Control 165
British Departmental Committee on Sterilization 51

310 INDEX

British Medical Association 12, 29, 32–3, 78, 83, 128, 138–41, 144, 147, 152–3, 179–81, 186–7, 193, 196–7
Brooklyn 247, 248
Brooks, Caspar 176
Brooks, Edwin 46, 112, 132, 165, 166, 190, 299
Brown, D. B. 139
Brudenell, Michael ix–xi, xv, 293
Bulgaria
  abortion laws in 67, 221–2
  complications after induced abortion in 222
  restriction of liberalized abortion laws in 222
Burgess, D. E. 96, 97, 295
Burke, M. F. 57, 294
Burstoft, Mrs. Leila 161
Butler, L. 173, 299
Bygdman, M. 100

Caesarean section 51, 52, 95
California
  abortion laws in 231, 250, 257
  abortions performed in 261, 263
  beagle dogs, research in 174
  Board of Medical Examiners 257–8
  "Community Service Center and Women's Abortion Clinic" 261
  gynaecologists' attitudes to abortion 233
  Los Angeles 261
  Los Angeles County—University of Southern California Medical Center's Therapeutic Abortion and Sterilization Committee 258–9
  Los Angeles Metropolitan Area 258–9
  male opinions on abortion 230
  Medical Association 225, 240
  physicians' attitudes to abortion 240
  public attitudes to abortion 229
  rubella epidemic 229, 240, 257
  San Francisco 132, 229
  San Francisco Bay Statistical Area 257–8
  San Francisco Nine 229, 257, 260
  San Mateo County General Hospital 259

Stanford University School of Medicine 259
Superior Court 260
Supreme Court 260–1
Therapeutic Abortion Act 257–8, 261, 263
Calthorpe Nursing Home 181, 182, 211
Cameron, J. M. 98, 296
Canada
  abortion laws in 265, 267–9
  back-street abortions in 268
  Criminal Code of 265
  "free abortion" activists 268
  gynaecologists' attitudes to legal abortion 266
  hospital termination committees in 267
  Lutheran Theological Seminary in 269
  Montreal 265
  physicians' attitudes to therapeutic abortion 265, 269
  pregnant teenagers in 266
  psychiatric grounds for termination 265
  psychiatrist's role in recommending termination 265–6, 267
  public attitudes to therapeutic abortion 265, 268, 269
  therapeutic abortion in 265, 268
  unmarried mothers in 266
  Western Ontario study 266
Carne, Stuart 31, 84
Casey, Donn 93, 295
Catchment area(s) 105, 109, 115
Catholic Doctors' Guild 11
Cavendish Biomedical Centre Limited 135–6
Central Criminal Court (Old Bailey) 8, 204
Chesser, Eustace 18, 24, 291
Chest and Heart Association of London 202
Chicago 65, 248
Child Welfare Act 58
Children in care 60–1
Chisholm, Norman 185, 300
Chlormadinone acetate 48, 166, 173–4, 178
Christie, G. A. 173, 299

Church of England see Abortion, attitudes towards
Cicero 13
Citizens' Advice Bureau 108
Clark, M. 60, 66, 292
Clayton, S. G. xv
Cleveland Clergy Consultation Service 131–2
Coffey, P. G. 268, 304
Cohen, Lord, of Birkenhead 133
Cole, Martin 3, 107, 182
Colorado
  abortion laws in 132, 250–4
  abortions performed in 251
  Denver 243, 246, 250, 251, 254
  grounds for legal abortion in 250–4, 265
  hospitals performing legal abortions in 251
  House of Representatives 250
  Medical Society 252
  methods of termination employed in 252
  problems following liberalized abortion law in 251–4, 265
  psychiatric reactions to liberalized abortion law in 252–4
  psychiatric sequelae of legal abortion in 252–3
  Psychiatric Society 252
  residency requirement for legal abortions performed in 251–2
  teenage terminations in 252
  University Department of Obstetrics and Gynaecology 251
  University Medical Center 251
Committee on the Safety of Drugs (the Dunlop, later the Scowen Committee) 173–4, 176–8, 202, 208–9
Comstock Act (1873) 247
Conduct of Nursing Homes Regulations, 1963 110
Connecticut 225, 248
Conservation Society 172
Contraception x, xi, xiii, 14, 16, 20, 25, 28–9, 34, 37, 39, 40, 43–7, 50–4, 56, 67–8, 88, 102, 111–12, 123, 129, 140, 150, 165–80, 200, 203, 205, 207, 218, 222, 227, 233, 235, 237, 244–8, 258, 269, 273
Contraceptive(s) 43, 46–8, 199, 230, 234, 240, 242, 255
  advice 53, 90, 166, 168–9, 235
  failure 84, 88, 138, 207, 235, 242
  methods
    abstinence 43, 246
    C-film 54
    cervical cap 47
    chemical 47
    coitus interruptus 47, 221
    condom (male sheath) 47, 221
    Dutch cap (diaphragm) 47, 167, 170, 207
    Grafenberg Ring 50
    intra-uterine devices (IUDs) 47, 49–51, 54, 67, 138, 167, 240, 245
    oral 37, 39–41, 44, 47–9, 67, 166, 167, 173–80, 202, 207–9, 221, 245, 248, 255, 257
      composition 48, 208, 209
      effectiveness of 48–9
      mode of action 48
      risks 49, 208, 209, 248
      sequential 173, 209
      side-effects 49, 175, 248
        adverse
          depression 49
          hypertension 49
          jaundice 49
          thrombo-embolic 49, 175, 202, 208–9, 245, 248
        useful 49
    pessaries 49
    post-coital pills 54
    rhythm ("safe" period) 41, 47, 170, 246
    spermicides 47, 54
    vaginal rings 54
  use-effectiveness 47
Cooper, Struan 141
Copeland, W. E. 264, 304
Crossman, Richard 110, 112, 130, 137, 143–4, 153–4, 168, 170, 172, 181, 184–6, 190, 195–6, 200–2, 205, 210–11, 215
Crowley, R. M. 237, 303
Cunningham, George 261
Curran, W. J. 304
Czechoslovakia
  abortion laws in 67, 221

Czechoslovakia—*cont.*
  abortion rate in 223
  abortion substituting for contraception in 67, 222
  abortions performed in 67
  deaths after induced abortion 67
  illegal abortions 67
  legal abortions 67, 222
  live births in 67
  recurring demands for abortion after liberalized law 19

Dame Juliet Rhys-Williams Memorial Lecture 132, 162–3
Danish Association for the Individual and Society 136–7
Davies, James 141
Davis, Albert 2, 4, 18, 291
Davis, Hugh 174
Dawson of Penn, Lord 247
Day nurseries 58
Dayan, A. D. 98, 296
Deacon, A. L. 21–2, 292
Declaration of Oslo 218
Declaration on Population Growth and Human Dignity and Welfare 42
Delinquency 26, 62–3, 245
Denmark
  abortion laws in 219
  abortion rate in 145, 223
  abortion seekers coming to London from 137–8
  Anglo-Danish Social Services Agreement 137
  complications of oral contraceptives in 209
  death after induced abortion in 220
  Parliament 220
  social grounds for legal abortion 220
Dennis, K. J. 149
Denny, Frank 113, 181, 297
Depression 25, 49, 56, 60, 65, 80–1, 83–4, 87, 118–19, 124, 207, 252, 259
de Ribes, Champetier 99
de Soldenhoff, Richard 20, 114, 291, 297
de Watteville, H. 6
Diggory, Peter 2, 80, 103, 107, 112, 114, 124, 198–9, 296, 301
Doll, Richard 49, 202, 293

Donald, Professor Ian 21, 122, 123
Doyle, Christine 131, 296, 297
Draper, Elizabeth 45, 293
Droegemueller, William 251, 254–6, 304
Drugs (Prevention of Misuse) Act, 1964 204
Drysdale, G. 43
Dudley-Brown, Margaret 125
Duke of Edinburgh 170–1
Dunlop, Sir Derrick 173
Dunlop Committee *see* Committee on the Safety of Drugs
Dunn, H. P. 273, 274, 305
Dunwoody, John 170, 197

Eckblad, Martin 63–4, 295
Edelstein, Ludwig 17, 291
Edinburgh 43, 204
Edmunds, Lynn 127, 297
Edwards, J. E. 57, 294
Embrey, M. P. 100
Embryo 11, 155–7, 259
Emerson, M. S. 166, 299
Endometriosis 95, 98
Ennals, D. H. 176
Enovid 48, 248
Episcopal Diocese of New York 225
Ergometrine 92, 93, 95, 100
Ethinyloestradiol 178, 209
Eugenic Protection Law (Japan) 9, 223–4

Fallopio, G. 47
Family Law Reform Act 78
Family planning x, 42, 44–7, 111–12, 165, 171–2, 200–4, 218, 229, 233
Family Planning Act, 1967 *see* National Health Service
Family Planning Association (FPA) 43, 46, 48, 111–12, 138, 167–72, 176–7, 200
Family planning clinics 16, 32, 46, 48, 50, 120, 167–72, 176, 178
Faridian, Parviz 160–1
Farmer, C. 150
Federation of Protestant Welfare Agencies (U.S.) 225
Ferguson, M. B. 9

INDEX

Feroze, R. M. xv
Ferris, Paul 1, 10, 12, 109, 111, 135, 143–4, 291, 296, 298
Fertility 49, 51
Field Research Corporation (U.S.) 229
Filshie, G. M. 100, 121, 296
Finland
  abortion laws in 145, 219
  abortion rate in 145
Finlay, S. E. 37
Fisher, Evelyn 30–1, 292
Foetus(es) ix, 1–3, 10, 13–14, 18, 29, 30–1, 33, 71, 80–1, 98–101, 118–22, 130–1, 194, 225, 230, 233, 235, 237, 241, 259, 262, 269
Food and Drug Administration (FDA) 248
Foote, Edward Bliss 247
Foote, Edward Bond 247
Foreign women, terminations performed on 103, 108, 128–9, 131–2, 136–8, 141, 145, 153, 155–6, 160–1, 183–6, 188–90, 192, 197, 206
Forsmann, Hans 62, 249, 294
Fox, (Sir) Theodore 41, 43, 246, 293
Frangenheim, H. 52
Franklin, A. S. 201, 301
Franklin, A. W. 24, 56, 292
Frederiksen, H. 68, 295
Freud, Sigmund 239
Frith, Kathleen 139, 181
Frost, David 175
Fruits of Philosophy, The 247
Fullerton, W. T. 150

Galdston, Iago 36, 292
Galen 13
Gardiner, J. S. 165, 299
General Medical Council 145
  composition of 133
  disciplinary committee hearings 128, 133–6, 152, 154–61, 188–9, 204–5
Georgia
  abortion laws in 250, 261–2
  Board of Health 262
  Department of Health 262
  House of Representatives 261
  Medical Association of 261
  Senate 261
  Solicitor-General 262

Supreme Court 262
Germany
  advertising abortion services in West 155–6, 160, 188–9
  Grafenberg ring 50
  legal abortions performed on German women 103
  methods of terminating pregnancy
    abortifacient paste 96
    mechanical stimulation of the uterus 99
Gibson, Ronald 141
Gilliatt, (Sir) William 8
Glasgow 21, 123, 130, 148, 267
Godber, Sir George 132, 142, 152, 161–3, 195, 298
Gold, E. M. 232–3, 303
Golding, Alan 181
Goldman, Rabbi M. J. 226, 303
Goldzieher, J. W. 48
Gonadotropins 48, 54
Goodhart, C. B. 103, 162, 206, 296, 298, 302
Gordon, H. 180
Grafenberg, E. 50
Greater World Church 158
Greenhill, J. P. 223, 226, 302
Gross, William 124, 297
Group for the Advancement of Psychiatry, *The Right to Abortion: a psychiatric view*. New York: GAP Publications, October 1969 239–40, 303
Grunebaum, H. V. 249, 303
Guild of Catholic Doctors 11
Gustafson, Carl 250
Guttmacher, A. F. 225, 246, 254, 260–1, 302
Gwynne, John 261

Haire, Norman 50
Haldane, F. P. 28, 292
Hall, R. E. 232, 236, 250, 302
Halley, M. M. 264, 304
Hamburg 154, 188
Hanley, H. G. 53, 294
Hannay, Lady Fergusson (Doris Leslie) 146, 298
Happel, J. S. 139
Harlow, T. xv

Harrison, C. P. 266, 269, 304
Harter, C. L. 228, 303
Havranek, F. 67
Hawaii 250, 264
Haward, John 186
Hay, David 182
Health Education Council 172
Health Services and Public Health Act, 1968 165
Heath, D. F. 139
Heenan, Cardinal 155, 189
Hegar dilator(s) 91–2, 203
Heine, Cezar 269
Heinemann, Dr. 156
Heller, A. 252, 304
Helper, M. M. 229, 294
Hemphill, R. E. 25, 292
Henry, M. J. 153, 298
Hertz, Roy 174
Hickinbotham, Paul 53, 294
Hill, Hilary 166–7, 171, 173, 299
Hippocrates 16, 17
Hippocratic Oath 16–17
Holloway Prison 4
Hook, Kerstin 59, 89, 294
Horder, Lord 8
Hospitals
  Charity Hospital of New Orleans 228
  Grosvenor Hospital, London 62
  Hammersmith Hospital, London 202
  Johns Hopkins Hospital, Baltimore 262–3
  King's College Hospital, London 100, 118–21
  National Women's Hospital, New Zealand 273
  Ohio State University Hospital 264
  Scarborough Hospital, Yorkshire 119
  Sinai Hospital, Baltimore 262
  St. Bartholomew's Hospital, London 206
  Tel Hashoner Maternity Government Hospital, Israel 270
  University College Hospital, London 29, 66, 169
  Walker Park Hospital, Newcastle upon Tyne 195
  Whittington Hospital, London 170
Houghton, Mrs. Vera 11
Houghton, Rt. Hon. A. L. N. D. 197

House of Commons 10, 12, 140, 144–5, 176, 184, 186–7, 194, 196, 200
House of Lords 10, 12, 140, 145, 164
Howard, Geraldine 173, 299
Howe, (Sir) Geoffrey 125, 129
Howells, J. G. 29, 292
Hughes, J. H. 116, 125, 297
Huldt, Lars 67–8, 295
Human chorionic gonadotropin (HCG) 85–6
Human Rights Day 42
Humanae Vitae 41, 166
Hungary 205, 221–3
Huntingford, Professor P. J. xv, 127, 168, 297

Illegitimacy 28, 58, 132, 201, 241
  rate 38, 61, 63, 194, 198, 201, 263
Illegitimate births 37–8, 58, 63, 148, 166, 198, 201
Illegitimate children 58, 60–1, 77, 171, 202, 215, 239
Imran, N. 203, 301
Infant Life (Preservation) Act 7, 8, 13, 71
Infant mortality 58, 60
Infertility ix, 49, 105, 120, 164, 175, 200
Ingram, J. M. 225, 250, 254, 256, 261–2, 302
Inman, W. H. W. 208–9, 302
Institutionalization 60–1
Interdepartmental Committee on Abortion 7
International Medical Group 247
International Planned Parenthood Federation (IPPF) 93, 167, 168, 221, 247
International Union for the Scientific Study of Population 247
Interpretation Act 72
Irvine, B. G. 187, 190, 193–7
Israel
  abortion laws in 269–70
  abortions performed in 270
  Committee for the Study of Maternal Mortality in 270
  complications following termination of pregnancy 270
  death after termination of pregnancy 270

INDEX 315

Israel—*cont.*
  Kaput Holim (sick fund) institutions in 270
  medical grounds for terminating pregnancy 270
  physicians' attitudes to termination 270
  population of 270
  psychiatric grounds for termination 270
  punishments for illegal abortion 270
  social grounds for termination 270
  Tel Hashoner Maternity Government Hospital 270

Jack, E. M. 140
Jackson, E. W. 257–8, 304
Jackson, M. C. N. 178, 300
Jacobi, Abraham 247
Japan
  abortion laws (Eugenic Protection Law) in 9, 223–4, 238, 243
  abortion on demand in 223
  abortion substituting for contraception in 235
  complications after induced abortion in 98
  deaths after induced abortion in 98, 223
  illegal abortions in 19, 223
  increase in contraception following Eugenic Protection Law 223–4
  Jikei University, Tokyo 223
  legal abortions in 223
  live births in 223
  methods of inducing abortion used in 98–100
  net reproduction rate in 224
  population growth in 223
  recurring demand for abortion after liberalized law 19
Jenkins, Roy 11
Jersey (Channel Islands) 157–9
Jewish law 226
Joint Commission on Accreditation of Hospitals (U.S.) 236, 241, 257
Jones, Garth 153–4, 298
Jones, O. H. 256
Joyston-Bechal, M. P. 28, 81, 292
Jurukovski, J. N. 92, 94

Kansas
  abortion laws in 250, 264
  Judicial Council 264
  Medical Society 264
Karim, Professor S. M. M. 100–1, 121, 296
Kay, C. R. 175, 300
Kay, D. W. K. 63, 66, 294
Kempis, Thomas à 246
Kenyon, F. E. 83, 295
Kerby, Captain H. B. 195
Kerslake, Dorothea 93, 124
Kinch, R. A. H. 266, 304
Kind, R. W. 37, 292
Kinsey, Alfred 248
Klopper, A. I. 151
Knaus, H. 40
Knight, Mrs. Jill 129, 137, 144, 146, 195, 201
Knowlton, Charles 247
Krause, A. 99
Kross, Judge Anna 225
Kummer, J. M. 64, 260–1, 295, 304

Lachelin, C. G. L. 96–7, 295
Lader, Lawrence 230–1, 303
Laidlaw, R. W. 237, 303
Lamm, R. D. 250, 254, 304
Langham Pregnancy Advisory Bureau 210
Latin America 233
Laurie, Jean 139
Laws, Barbara 170, 299
Lederberg, J. 243
Lee, N. C. 126, 297
Leeds 21, 123
Leeton, J. 204, 301
Lewin, W. 180
Lewis, T. L. L. 114, 123, 126, 297
Lewit, S. 223, 226, 302
Leys, Duncan 31, 292
Liberalized Abortion Law 240
Liley, Professor A. W. 274
Liston, W. A. 203, 301
Liverpool 123, 132, 148, 198
Local authorities 46, 61, 111–12, 166, 173, 201, 206
London Agency Incorporated (U.S.) 184

London Emergency Bed Service 106, 218
London Society of Family Planning Doctors 46
Loudon, John 43, 44, 293
Lyall, A. 139
Lysergic acid diethylamide (LSD) 253
Lyster, W. R. 63

McCance, C. 150
McCoy, D. R. 66, 67, 295
McEwan, John 207, 302
MacFarlane, K. T. 265
MacGillivray, Professor Ian 114, 122, 124, 147-8, 151, 297
McGregor, W. R. 61, 62, 294
McLaren, Professor Hugh 15, 20, 21, 22, 122-3, 291, 297
Macnaghten, Judge 8-9, 11, 25
Macnaughton, M. C. 2
MacQueen, I. A. G. 46, 165, 293
Maddox, Governor 261
Malleson, Joan 8
Malone, A. E. 180-1
Malthus, Reverend Thomas 43
Malthusian League 43
Manabe, Yukio 99, 296
Mant, A. K. 5
Maramatsu, M. 223
Marcus, Harold 64, 295
Marder, Leon 258-9, 304
Margaret Pyke Centre 170-1
Margaret Sanger Research Bureau 249
Marker, Russel 48
Marks, J. H. 140
Martha May Eliot Award (1969) 147
Martin, G. R. 135
Martin-Manautau, J. 48
Maryland
 abortion laws in 250, 262-3, 264
 Baltimore 262, 263
 criminal abortions in 263
 first abortion bill in 262
 Johns Hopkins Hospital 262-3
 Joint Commission on Accreditation 262
 Maternal Welfare Committee of 263
 Medical Society 262
 Sinai Hospital 262
 State Board of Health 262
 teenage illegitimacy rate in 263
Massachusetts
 abortion laws in 250, 264
 American Psychiatric Association Meeting, Boston, 1968 252
 population density in 239
Mauriceau, A. M. 247
Medical Act, 1956 134, 159
Medical Defence Union 76, 143-4, 193
Medical journals
 British Medical Bulletin 179
 British Medical Journal 25, 29, 110, 125, 147, 160, 174, 177, 185, 217
 Canadian Medical Association Journal 266
 Journal of the American Medical Association 260
 Journal of the Kansas Medical Society 246
 Lancet, The 50, 162-3, 178
 Medical and Surgical Reporter 247
 Medical Journal of Australia 272
 (International) Medical (News-) Tribune 109, 142, 153, 187, 194
 Michigan Medical News 247
 Modern Medicine 236-7, 241
 New England Journal of Medicine 239, 249
 Nursing Mirror 117
Medical Protection Society 76, 116, 125, 129, 193
Medical Research Council 177
Medical Women's Federation 32, 45
Mehland, Professor K. H. 67, 295
Meinert, Mrs. Roberta 248-9
Menhennitt, Mr. Justice 271
Menninger, Karl 239
Mental defect 83, 86, 88
Menuhin, Yehudi 172
Mestranol 48, 178, 209
Methodist Church 14
Milne, G. P. 148
Mini-pill *see* Chlormadinone acetate
Minister of Health 12, 20, 27, 46, 70, 107, 163, 176-7, 180-1
Model Penal Code of the American Law Institute (ALI) 225, 232-3, 236, 240, 250, 264

Montefiore, Canon Hugh 200
Moonman, Eric 183–4
Moore, Gerald Ernest 134–6
Moore-Robinson, Miriam 166, 298
Moral Physiology 247
Morris, Professor Norman 18, 123
Mother love 62, 86
Mott, Elizabeth 196
Mudd, J. W. 247–8, 303
Munday, Diane 16, 190, 192, 201, 212

Nabarro, Sir Gerald 184–5
Nachshen, D. S. 117, 297,
National Association for the Repeal of Abortion Laws (U.S.) 230
National Centre for Health Statistics (U.S.) 224
National Council for the Unmarried Mother and her Child 58
National Fertility Study (U.S.) 227, 230
National Health Service 3, 5, 21, 164
  abortion units 106, 115, 179–82, 213
  consultants 12, 20, 105, 123, 125, 133, 140, 145, 154, 185–8, 191, 193–6, 198, 213–16
  facilities for legal abortion xiv, 20, 70–3, 102–9, 115, 130, 133, 137–43, 145–6, 148, 154, 162–3, 168, 186–7, 195–9, 201, 213–18
  Family Planning Act 46, 113, 132, 165–6, 168
National Institute of Child Health and Development (U.S.) 224
National Institute of Mental Health (U.S.) 224
Nebraska State Medical Association Meeting (1969) 252
Neurosis 26, 60, 62, 64, 81, 84, 123
Neustatter, W. L. 26
New Jersey
  abortion laws in 250
  population density in 239
New Mexico abortion laws in 250, 264
New York
  Abortion Law Reform Bill 264
  abortion laws in 225, 250, 264–5, 268
  abortions performed in 265
  Academy of Medicine 224–5

Buffalo, effect of terminations in 64
Chamber of Commerce 225
City 264
Civil Liberties Union 225
Council of Churches 225
deaths after Abortion Law Reform Bill passed 264
"freestanding" abortion clinics 265
gynaecologists in 232–3, 265
Margaret Sanger Research Bureau 249
Martha May Eliot Award 147
oral contraceptive complications in 49
pregnancy consultation service 132
State 264
New Zealand
  abortion laws in 273
  grounds for terminating pregnancy in 273
  hospital therapeutic abortion committees in 274
  Medical Council 159
  Medical Register 159
  notification of therapeutic abortions in 274
  Perinatal Mortality Conferences in 273–4
  physicians' attitudes to legalized abortion in 274
  physicians' attitudes to therapeutic abortions in 273
  population of 273
  Society for the Protection of Unborn Children 273, 274
  Supreme Court of 159
  therapeutic abortion in 273
  Waipukurau 159
Newcastle upon Tyne 124, 145, 163, 180, 218
Newspapers and periodicals
  Catholic Herald 11
  Daily Express 136, 141, 176
  Daily Mail 202
  Daily Telegraph 142, 184, 187, 201
  Evening Standard 194, 196
  Life 254
  Marriage Guidance 181
  New Statesman 11
  Observer 11, 135, 146
  Stern 154–6, 188–9

Newspapers and periodicals—*cont.*
  Sun 160-1
  Sunday Mirror 135
  Sunday Telegraph 11
  Sunday Times 153, 193-4
  The Times 11, 178
Newton, L. A. 9
Niswander, K. R. 64, 295
Nixon, Professor 169
Norethisterone (norethindrone) 48
Norethynodrel 48, 209
Norman, Frank 60, 294
North Carolina
  abortion law in 250, 254-6
  Duke (University) Medical Center 256
  General Assembly of 255
  Medical Care Commission 255
  Medical Society, Committee on Maternal Health 255
  Obstetrical and Gynaecological Society 256
Norway
  abortion laws in 220
  abortion rate in 145
Nurses Night and Day Ltd. 160-1
Nursing homes and clinics
  Harley Street Nursing Home, London 183-4
  Lady Margaret Nursing Home, Ealing 131, 135
  Langham Street Clinic 160-1, 185, 195-6, 210
  New Cross Clinic 109, 133, 135

Obsessional states 81, 83
Oestriol sulphate 151
Oestrogen 48-9, 176, 178-9, 202, 208-9
Offences Against the Person Act 7, 8, 69, 72
Ogino, K. 40
Ohio
  abortion laws in 264
  abortion: live birth ratio in 264
  attitudes of psychiatrists to abortion in 264
  pregnancy consultation service in 131
  Psychiatric Association 264
  State University Hospital 264

Olley, P. C. 149-50
Onyesoh, Felix 161
Oregon abortion laws in 250, 264
Outwin, G. R. 181
Overpopulation 14, 41, 82, 200, 239
Overstreet, E. W. 229, 233, 261, 303
Ovulation 48, 50, 86
Ovulen 179
Owen, Professor J. E. 244
Owen, Robert Dale 247
Oxytocin 95, 96, 98-9

Packman, Jean 61
Pare, C. M. B. 59, 66, 90, 206-7, 294, 302
Palmer, R. 52
Parker, R. T. 256
Parliament x, xiii, 7, 10, 29, 70, 72, 102, 110, 126-30, 132, 142, 153, 181, 187, 196, 215
Parviz Holdings Ltd. 1690-1
Patt, S. L. 65, 295
Patterson, R. J. 64, 295
Paul, David 138
Peberdy, Mary 46, 293
Peck, Arthur 64, 220, 238, 295, 302
Peel, John 16, 43, 48-9, 53-4, 247, 293
Peel, Sir John 52, 143, 294
Pennsylvania
  abortion laws in 250
  therapeutic abortion prosecution in 236
  University of, study of sexuality in 248
Permissive society 36, 38-9, 111, 123
Perr, I. N. 264, 304
Peyton, F. W. 229-30, 245, 303
Piatrow, Mrs. Phyllis 202
Pill, the *see* Contraceptive(s), oral
Plagenz, Lorry 250, 303
Planned Parenthood Federation (U.S.) 224-5, 265
Planned Parenthood—World Population 246
Plato 13
Platt, Sir Robert (Lord) 11, 172
Poland 67, 223
Poller, L. 173, 299

INDEX

Pond, Professor D. A. 28, 82, 292
Pope John XXIII 40
Pope Paul VI 41
Pope Pius IX 13, 40
Pope Pius XI 13
Pope Pius XII 40
Population control 10, 45, 165, 216
Population explosion 43, 50, 257
Potts, Malcolm 43, 48–9, 53–4, 114, 142, 167, 175, 179, 202, 221, 247, 293, 297, 298, 300, 301
Power, Michael 62
Pregnancy Advisory Service (PAS) 126, 127, 181
  in Birmingham 106–7, 112, 182
  in London 106–7, 112, 126, 142
Pregnancy testing 85, 163–4, 171
Prime Minister 172, 187, 202
Prince, G. S. 34, 292
Privy Council, Judicial Committee of the 157, 159, 161
Progesterone 48, 202
Progestogen 48, 166, 173, 178–9, 208
Promiscuity, sexual 38–9, 266
Prostaglandin 91, 100–1, 120–1
Protestant Church 14, 40, 226
Psychopathy 81, 88–90
Psychosis 24, 65, 80–1, 88–9, 123
Public Health Act, 1936 110
Puerperal psychosis 24
Puerto Rico, abortion laws in 250
Pyridoxine 49
Pythagoras 17

Quickening 7, 225, 243
Quinn, Robert 184

Raban, Erwin 270
Ramaswamy, Saroja 168, 299
Raven, H. 206–7, 302
Reagan, Governor Ronald 257, 260
Rees, J. R. 8
Reeves, Joseph 9
Reiss, H. E. 98
"Repeat" pregnancies, problem of 90, 205
Rhode Island, density of population in 239

Rhodes, Professor Philip 4, 5, 18, 113, 123, 297
Richard, E. F. 126, 297
Robb, Mrs. D. 201, 301
Robb, D. F. 76, 295
Robinson, Hugh 146, 298
Robinson, Kenneth 10
Rodger, Professor T. F. 27–8, 291
Roemer, Ruth 68, 226, 295
Roman Catholic Church 11, 13–14, 40–1, 172, 221, 226, 240, 246
Romania
  abortion laws in 67, 205, 221
  complications of induced abortion in 222
  effect of liberalized abortion laws in 21
  restriction of liberalized abortion laws in 222
Ross, R. A. 255–6
Royal College of General Practitioners 76, 116, 174, 177
Royal College of Obstetricians and Gynaecologists xiii, 6, 11, 12, 19, 44, 52, 78–9, 124, 144, 152–3, 183, 186–7, 193, 196–7, 212, 216
Royal College of Physicians 43, 132
Royal Medical Board (Sweden) 220
Royal Medico-Psychological Association 26–7, 29, 45
Rushton, D. I. 68, 295
Russel, K. P. 257–8, 264, 304
Russell, Claire 165, 299
Russell, Professor J. K. 39, 293
Russell, W. M. S. 165, 299
Russia
  abortion laws in 10, 67, 220
  methods of termination
    abortifacient paste 96–7
    vacuum aspiration 93

Saltman, Jack 160
Sanderson, A. 29, 292
Sanger, Margaret 247–8
Sargant, William 26
Schapira, Kurt 63, 66, 295
Schiffer, M. A. 97, 295
Schizophrenia 81, 204
Schofield, Michael 36–7, 292

INDEX

Schwartz, R. A. 68, 224, 226–7, 295
Scotland
 Abortion Act 69–79
 Ayrshire 20
 law of corroboration in 165
  abortion rate in 148
  birth rate in 148
  complications of induced abortion in 151
  factors determining legal abortion in 150
  indications for termination in 149
  methods of terminating pregnancy in 150–1
  personality factors 149–50
  social characteristics 148–9
 north-eastern
  therapeutic abortion in 147
 specialist gynaecologists in 196
 sterilizations performed in 190
Scott, Professor J. S. 21, 163, 298
Scowen, Professor, E. F. 173, 176–7, 300
Scowen Committee *see* Committee on the Safety of Drugs
Searle, G. D., & Co. 48, 179, 248
Second World War 46, 50–1, 63
Seldel, Bjoern 136–7
Senate Small Business Monopoly Subcommittee 248
Senturia, A. G. 63, 294
Sexual education 36, 233, 235–6, 248, 273
Sheffield 148, 198
Sheridan, M. R. 180
Sherwin, L. 229, 233, 303
Short, Mrs. Renee 10, 130, 190, 196–7
Shulman, Milton 175
Siegel, R. J. 247–8, 303
Silkin, Lord 10, 12, 140
Sim, Myre 21, 24–5, 29, 57, 292
Simms, Madeleine 15, 37, 107, 129, 291, 292, 296, 297
Simon, Alexander 80, 226, 295
Simon, N. M. 63, 294
Simon Population Trust 53, 204
Slaughter, Joanna 58–9, 294
Sloan, Henry James 157–8
Sloane, Professor R. B. 239, 303
Smithurst, B. A. 272, 305

Society for the Protection of Unborn Children 21, 122, 186, 195, 206, 274, 291
Society for the Provision of Birth Control Clinics 45
Sorrel, W. E. 65, 295
Spencer, A. M. 141
Spencer, Robert 231–2
St. John-Stevas, Norman 128–9, 139–41, 143–6, 153, 161, 185–8, 197, 201, 298
St. Louis 65, 225
Stafford-Clarke, D. 25, 292
Stallworthy, Professor J. A. 106, 163, 205, 302
Stanfield, Clyde 252–3, 304
Stanley, P. 196
State Board of Medical Examiners (California) 229
Steel, David 10, 11, 16, 32, 140, 145, 186, 192, 197, 205
Stephen, John 221, 302
Steptoe, P. C. 52, 203, 301
Sterility 6, 52, 67, 245
Sterilization
 female x, xi, 20, 51, 54, 81, 85, 90, 190, 203–4, 226, 255–60
  after Caesarean section 51–2
  after hysterotomy 22, 52, 203
  diathermy (electrocoagulation) 203
  grounds for 52
  hysterectomy 52
  irradiation 52
  laparoscopic 203, 204
  ovariotexy 204
  "package deal" 19, 190
  post-partum 23, 54
  post termination 22, 66
  reversal of 53
  salpingectomy 52
  tubal excision 52
  tubal ligation 22–3, 52
   Madelener technique 52–3, 203
   Pomeroy technique 52–3, 203
  post vaginal hysterotomy 95
 male, vasectomy 47, 51, 53, 90, 203–4, 248–9
Stockton, Alice B. 247
Stopes, Marie 45
Stothert, J. C. 184

Student American Medical Association 225
Stungo, Ellis 9
Suicide 30, 57, 60, 64–7, 80–1, 83–4, 87, 159–233, 235, 239, 259–60
Summerskill, Baroness 152
Summerskill, Shirley 176, 178
Swan, Christopher Michael 204–5
Sweden
 abortion laws in 9, 243
 abortion on demand proposed in 220
 abortion rate in 223
 complications of oral contraceptives in 209
 legal abortions performed in 220
 methods of termination, prostaglandin therapy in 100
 recurring demands for abortion after liberalized law in 19
 refused abortion, effect on child 62
 Royal Medical Board 220
 sequelae after legal abortion 59
 sterilization after legal abortion 59
Switzerland 219
Swyer, G. M. 177–9, 300
Symes, M. H. xv
Syntex Corporation 48, 173–4
Szasz, Thomas 237–8, 303

Tacchi, Derek 180
Tarnesby, H. P. 3, 154–7, 291
Taussig, F. 225
Taxi-drivers 136, 138, 185, 197, 210–11
Taylor, J. L. xv
Taylor, Mrs. Winifred 200, 301
Television
 British Broadcasting Corporation (BBC) 160, 184, 208
 Panorama 160–1
 24 Hours 176
 Independent Television Authority (ITA) 172, 175–6, 208
Temple University School of Medicine, Philadelphia 233
Termination of pregnancy, methods
 abdominal hysterotomy 6, 22–3, 52, 66, 94–7, 101, 106, 115, 119, 130, 138, 150–1, 251

abortifacient paste 6, 96–7, 101, 120
aspiration *see below*, suction evacuation
curettage 23, 92–4, 96, 98, 101, 115, 150
dilatation 91–4
 and curettage 4, 6, 91, 97, 118–19, 251, 261
hysterectomy 251
intra-amniotic injections
 glucose 4, 99, 101, 259
 saline 4, 6, 66, 97–9, 101, 120–1, 150–1
laminaria tents 91
mechanical stimulation of the uterus 99
prostaglandin 91, 100–1, 120–1
rivanol installation 99–100
suction evacuation 93–4, 96, 119, 150, 203, 265
vaginal 6, 65, 151
vaginal hysterotomy 95
Thalidomide 147, 257
Thomson, J. M. 173, 299
Thurstone, P. B. 259–60, 304
Thuwe, Inge 62, 249, 294
Tietze, Christopher 68, 223, 226, 295, 302
Timanus, G. L. 234
Tobert, Alexandra 47, 293
Tooley, P. H. 116
Toulson, Leslie 160
Toynbee, Arnold 171
Trall, R. T. 247
Tredgold, R. F. 26, 81, 116, 292
Tryptophan metabolism 49
Turk, D. C. 126, 297
Tylden, Elizabeth 25, 292

United Nations 41, 171
United States 43, 48, 51, 54, 103, 132, 224–66
Universal Declaration of Human Rights 41–2, 246
Unmarried mother(s) 37, 50, 58, 62, 266
Unwanted child(ren) 15, 26–7, 29, 30, 51, 62, 111, 192, 198, 200–2, 249
Unwanted pregnancy ix, xi, xiv, 2, 4, 5, 21–3, 26, 30, 32, 34, 47, 55–63, 68,

Unwanted pregnancy—*cont.*
 80, 84, 86–90, 103, 107, 111–13, 117,
 127, 146, 160, 163, 166, 168, 199,
 201, 204, 222, 235, 238–9, 243–4,
 249, 250, 253, 256, 259, 266, 268–9
"Unwed mother's syndrome" 249
Utus paste 96–7

"Vaux". 142
Venereal disease 39, 44, 47, 200, 245
Vessey, M. P. 49, 175, 293, 300
"Vindictive husband" 262
von Euler, U. S. 100

Wagatsuma, Takashi 97, 296
Wainer, Bertram 272
Walker, A. H. C. 96–7
Walsh, P. B. 269
Waring, Gerald 268, 304
Washington, D.C. 132, 179
Watanabe, Professor Y. 223
Weichmann, Gerry 246, 303
Weir, James 38
Weir, J. G. 4
Weiss, J. L. 249, 303
Westoff, C. F. 227, 303
Wheelwright, Reverend Fairley 132
White, Howard 162, 298
White, R. B. 18, 63–4, 81, 291
Whitlock, F. A. 57, 294

Whittington, H. G. 252, 253, 254, 304
Wide, Leit 86, 295
Wife's Handbook, The 44
Williams, Professor Glanville 11, 15
Williams, G. F. J. 53, 294
Williams, R. H. 243, 303
Willson, J. R. 233–6, 303
Wilson, Lord 165
Wiqvist, M. 100
Wiseman, Aviva 175
Wolff, Heinz 30
Women's Liberation Movement (and Workshop) 189
Wood, C. 204, 301
Woodroffe, Caroline 169
Woodside, Moya 4, 16
Woolf, Rowena 31
Woolwich, Bishop of 11
World Health Organization 260
World Medical Association 218
World Population Conference (1927), first 247
"Worn-out" mothers 56, 81, 89
Wu, H. C. 93
Wu, Y. T. 93
Wurm, R. S. 273, 305
Wynn, Victor 175

Young, H. N. 160
Young, Leontine 56, 57
Yugoslavia 92, 94

Kirtley Library
Columbia College
8th and Rogers
Columbia, MO. 65201